M. David Litwa
We Are Being Transformed

Beihefte zur Zeitschrift für die neutestamentliche Wissenschaft

und die Kunde der älteren Kirche

Herausgegeben von

James D. G. Dunn · Carl R. Holladay
Hermann Lichtenberger · Jens Schröter
Gregory E. Sterling · Michael Wolter

Band 187

De Gruyter

M. David Litwa

We Are Being Transformed

Deification in Paul's Soteriology

De Gruyter

ISBN 978-3-11-028331-0
e-ISBN 978-3-11-028341-9
ISSN 0171-6441

Library of Congress Cataloging-in-Publication Data

A CIP catalog record for this book has been applied for at the Library of Congress.

Bibliographic information published by the Deutsche Nationalbibliothek

The Deutsche Nationalbibliothek lists this publication in the Deutsche Nationalbibliografie; detailed bibliographic data are available in the Internetat http://dnb.d-nb.de.

Printing: Hubert & Co. GmbH & Co. KG, Göttingen
∞ Printed on acid-free paper

Printed in Germany

www.degruyter.com

For my mother
Oct 25, 1950–Aug 4, 2011
You left so soon

"The purpose and goal of the Greeks is to deify man,
not to humanize deity.
This is not anthropomorphism but theomorphism."

—Goethe, Myrons Kuh (1812)

Preface

This monograph is the product of several years of reflection on the topic of deification in the Greco-Roman world and in early Christianity. My intent is to be historical throughout, although the nature of the project involves me in some theological judgments. Nevertheless, my honest desire is not to do (modern) theology, but to understand ancient theology and soteriology in its first-century Greco-Roman context. My aspiration has been to hear the larger symphony of deification playing in the Greco-Roman world as I listen to the individual melody of deification in its Jewish and Christian subcultures.

Today, biblical scholarship on deification is more or less dominated by theological discourse and presuppositions. In this climate, it is tempting to simply focus on Christian forms of deification when treating Paul. I am convinced, however, that scholars will never understand Paul and deification until they open themselves up to honest historical inquiry about other, larger discourses of deification in the Greco-Roman world.

This opening up is important because most biblical scholars and theologians tend to see non-Christian forms of deification through the lens of polemical Jewish and Christian sources (e. g., Wisdom, Philo, later Greek and Latin patristic writers). Such Jewish and Christian sources tend to use hackneyed forms of Euhemerism and later theological distinctions to neutralize and eliminate forms of deification they perceive as "pagan" and "idolatrous." Unfortunately, some biblical scholars and theologians have adopted the viewpoint of these authors when speaking of non-Christian forms of deification (such as in Greek philosophy and the ruler cult). Leaving largely unexplored the vast amount of epigraphical and literary evidence witnessing to non-Christian forms of deification, Christians scholars continue to quickly (and sometimes smugly) dismiss these "pagan" forms of deification as in no way related to purified and Christianized versions.

If we are going to achieve a truly historical understanding of deification in the Greco-Roman world (including Christian deification), it seems to me that scholars need to be more sympathetic to ancient forms of thought. In modern theology, the very way we think about humans and God(s) tends to preclude deification. This is not, I contend, how ancient people (including ancient Jews and Christians) thought. We need new eyes for this topic, and supple minds to understand ancient conceptions. In this study I try—as best I can—to peer behind centuries of Christian theological discourse about deification. But the road is hard. Some of the texts are scattered and unfamiliar. My argument requires deep and sympathetic listening to Greco-Roman sources and the careful reconstruction of ancient modes of thought. I fear that the one who reads only one or two chapters that focus merely on Paul will fail to grasp my argument as a whole. The best reader of this study is the one who will bracket later theological distinctions (e.g., the essence/energies distinction, synergy vs. *sola gratia*, "natural" vs. adoptive sonship) in an effort to look at the evidence afresh and with an open mind. Every author desires such readers, but the controversial nature of this study requires that I must ask for them.

The specific theological objections to deification are well known to me (exclusivist monotheism and *creatio ex nihilo*). I wait to address these topics in the final chapters (8–9). I would ask that the reader carefully read my approach (in the introduction) and my arguments (chs. 1–7) before tackling these later essays.

In this study, my practice is to cite the Old Testament using the Septuagint (LXX) version. Even though our modern critical reconstructions of the LXX cannot be equated with the text of Paul's Bible, the LXX is still closer to its wording and sense than modern English versions that try to represent the Masoretic Text. Even though I believe that Paul could read Hebrew, it seems that the Bible he used and most often cited in his letters was a form of the LXX. Therefore, as part of the discipline of reading Paul in his larger context, I quote from this version. Accordingly, verse numbers are given according to the LXX. Where the versification differs, the English versification is given alongside in parentheses or brackets. The translations of the LXX are my own.

I owe many debts of gratitude to those who throughout the years have aided or challenged me on this project. The intellectual environment at the University of Virginia is very free and rich thanks to open-minded professors like Harry Gamble, Judith Kovacs, and Martien Halvorson-Taylor. I have deep appreciation for Michael Gorman who has been open-minded toward my project (though it differs in approach from his own). His comments on an earlier draft of this book were thoughtful and decisive on several issues. Stephan Finlan took time out of his busy schedule to raise a couple red flags. I especially thank my friends Andrew Guffey and Blaire French for reading and thoughtfully commenting on select chapters of this work. Professor Engberg-Pedersen provided time at the 2011 SBL to meet with me and discuss ideas related to the book. Ben Blackwell was kind enough to send me the manuscript of his monograph before it was published. Although I cannot agree with Blackwell on many points, for me this only deepens and adds color to our continued intellectual friendship. As I have told him, I think that in the end our approaches are complimentary. My deepest thanks go to my wife who through our nearly six years of marriage has kindly supported my studies. She is the breath in my nostrils, and the peace in my heart.

This book is dedicated to my mother, whose early passing prevented her from seeing it through to publication. May you rest in peace, mom.

Contents

Part II Sharing the Divine Identity

Abbreviations

Note: Almost all of the abbreviations I use for biblical and classical materials can be found in *The SBL Handbook of Style* (Peabody: Hendrickson, 1999) supplemented where necessary by *The Oxford Classical Dictionary* (3rd edition). Other abbreviations are as follows:

Ab urbe cond.:	*Ab urbe condita*, by Livy
ap.:	*apud*
ET:	English translation
NTA:	*New Testament Apocrypha*, 2d ed., edited by W. Schneemelcher
OG:	*The Old Greek*
Vit. Philosoph.	*Vitae Philosophorum*, by Diogenes Laertius

Introduction:
The Logic and History of
Deification in Pauline Research

> "A soul in this state makes its way
> to the invisible, which is like itself, the
> divine and immortal and wise, and
> arriving there it can be happy, having
> rid itself of confusion, ignorance, fear,
> violent desires and the other human ills
> and, as is said of the initiates, truly
> spend the rest of time with the Gods."
>
> —Plato, *Phaedo* 81a,
> trans. G. M. A. Grube

Transcendence and Deification in Hellenistic Religion

Historically, religions of every sort have tended to posit a dualism between two types of being: the mortal, weak beings who dwell on earth, and the powerful immortal beings who dwell in a super-terrestrial sphere. Such is the divine/human duality. Sometimes the two types of being are pictured as fundamentally similar, and at other times as drastically different. At any rate, many religions tend to generate meaning out of the distance posited between these two types of being. "God is in heaven, you are on earth, therefore let your words be few" (Eccl 5:2). More broadly than moral injunctions, however, the dualism between Gods[1] and human beings deeply affects one's understanding of the world and one's understanding of the human condition. If God is strong, infinite, and perfect, then humans are weak, sinful, mortal, etc. As Calvin so colorfully put it: "Thus, from the feeling of our own ignorance, vanity, poverty, infirmity, and—what is more—deprav-

---

1   Here and throughout the book I have capitalized the plural "Gods" and "God" even when it does not refer to the Jewish and Christian God. Although keeping a lower-case "g" for non-biblical "gods" is still customary in scholarship, it promotes a division between the true "God" and false "gods" which is not always conducive to historical inquiry.

ity and corruption, we recognize that the true light of wisdom, sound virtue, full abundance of every good, and purity of righteousness rest in the Lord alone."[2] Knowledge of God shapes knowledge of the self and vice versa.

The divine/human duality can be put in a larger framework for understanding religion. Pauline religion is, like the philosophy of the *Phaedo* sampled in the epigraph, in many respects a "utopian" form of religion.[3] Unlike "locative" religion, wherein the actors seek to maintain boundaries to put all reality in its "place," utopian religionists find themselves somehow out of place and thus restlessly try to break boundaries and escape structures perceived as limiting or even oppressive. Smith's comments on utopian religion in the Hellenistic period will illustrate this idea:

> To ascend to another world of freedom and openness becomes the aim of Hellenistic man and the chief concern of his religion. Hellenistic man discovered himself to be an exile from his true home, a home beyond the borders. He strives to return to the world-beyond-this-world which is his true place; to the god-beyond-the-god-of-this-world who is the true god; to awaken the part of himself which is from the beyond and strip off his body which belongs to his present constricted realm.[4]

In accordance with this utopian line of thought, Paul's gospel presents a mode of transcending this world often called "salvation" (σωτηρία). Religions of salvation, understood in a broad sense, perceive some "lack" in human existence, and present a remedy for that lack. In theistic models, the lack is often some form of alienation from the divine, and the remedy consists in somehow overcoming the separation between the divine and the human. In ancient Judaism, this attempt to overcome alienation aimed at proximity to the God Yahweh. In this case, it was a covenantal proximity, which can be viewed as a kind of moral and relational approximation to God (i.e., conformation to Yahweh's righteous character and holiness).

---

2   *Institutes of the Christian Religion* (ed. John T. McNeill; trans. Ford Lewis Battles; 2 vols.; Library of Christian Classics 20; Philadelphia: Westminster, 1960), 1:36, 38.

3   For "utopian" vs. "locative," see Jonathan Z. Smith, *Map is Not Territory: Studies in the History of Religion* (Chicago: University of Chicago Press, 1978), xii, 100–103, 130–42, 147–51, 160–66, 169–71, 185–89, 291–94, 308–309.

4   *Ibid.*, 140. See also Smith's comments on Diaspora religions in "Native cults in the Hellenistic period," *History of Religions* 11 (1971): 237–238.

Following the dominant intellectual trends of its time, Diaspora Judaism in the late Hellenistic and early Roman periods (ca. 100 B.C.E.–125 C.E.) adopted—and adapted—a generalized Platonic scheme of salvation.[5] Generally speaking, Platonism added (or accentuated) three elements to Jewish (and later, Christian) models of salvation. First, it retrojected human proximity to God far back into the past. Platonism tended to think of this world as a fall from that original proximity, and salvation as a return to origins (e. g., *Phaedr.* 248a-249c). Second, Platonism conceived of proximity to God in realistic (i. e., ontological) terms (e. g., *Resp.* 472b6-c2; 509b). Likeness to the divine was likeness to God's immortal and supersensuous nature. Third, this realistic likeness to God was viewed as something already possessed, if only dormantly, in one's own most inward self (the soul, or the spirit) (e. g., *Tim.* 90a-c).[6] The goal of salvation was thus to "become what you are," often by stripping away the aspects of the self which do not express— and even undermine—one's true nature. Chiefly in view here is the body or flesh (*Gorgias* 493a; cf. Ps.-Sen, *Herc. Ot.* 1966–68).

These three basic Platonic trends had practical instantiations in Jewish soteriology. First, Jews began reading Gen 1–3 as a fall narrative, i. e., a story of primitive likeness to God lost (see, e. g., *L.A.E.* 12– 17). Second, they began seeing human godlikeness in realistic terms. Humans made in God's image are humans who share the divine (i. e., immortal) nature (e. g. Wisd 2:23). Third, this divine image was viewed as the essential self of human beings. Hellenistic Jews like Philo and Josephus, for instance, readily accepted the doctrine of the immortal soul (*Leg.* 1.108; *B.J.* 3.372). Conversely, the body was seen as basically distant from the divine, and ascetic practices were engineered (or accentuated) to mortify it. Essential likeness to God, it was concluded, could

---

5   I say "generalized" since Jews were not, for the most part, directly borrowing from Plato's writings, but responding to the Platonic notions distilled in Hellenistic culture. By using the phrase "scheme of *salvation*" I am admittedly giving Platonic teachings a bit of a Christian color. It could just as easily be called a "scheme of transcendence." To construct his vision of transcendence, Plato himself may have been adapting Pythagorean and Orphic teachings which preceded him.

6   In the *Phaedo*, Plato even sets out to prove that *every* soul is immortal (80d-84b; cf. *Phaedr.* 245c-249c; *Tim.* 41a-d). Although Plato did not here draw out the religious implications of his teaching, the doctrine could be taken to imply the essential divinity of the soul, at least in its highest (intellectual) manifestation. For the soul as a daimon, see *Tim.* 90a.

only be achieved when the body was somehow transformed into glory (Dan 12:2–3; 2 Bar 51:3–10) or fully sloughed off (Philo, *QG* 2.69; *Mos.* 2.288).

What I have described in the last paragraph outlines a general utopian trend to which there were many exceptions and shades of difference. Still, the general tendency shows a Hellenistic Jewish adaptation of a Platonic soteriology of transcendence. This Platonic model of salvation, pervasive in Greek (and later Roman) thought, posits an overlap between the human and divine natures. This overlap can be accentuated by assimilation to the divine or to divine qualities (e.g., immortality, strength, stability). This assimilation results in ontological proximity between humans and God. It can be conceived of as a process of addition (i.e., humans receive or cultivate something which makes them divine), subtraction (i.e., humans lose something which makes them all-too-human and not divine), or both. Whether innately or as something bestowed, humans foster a divine principle in their true self (the immortal soul, the divine image, the divine spirit, etc.). To become fully divine, they need to strip away or transform what makes them "un-divine" (i.e., the mortal, earthly body with its passions and evil deeds) and ascend to the upper reaches of the universe.

In this (very generalized) model, salvation involves some sort of transcendence of human nature as it is normally conceived. To become "what one is" requires one to become "what one is not" (at least currently). At the present time, the human is perceived as a weak, fleshly body controlled by passions and subject to external powers (human or daimonic). In the transcendent state, the human becomes an immortal, free entity unburdened by internal passions and external powers.

In Paul's day, there were various strategies of attaining transcendence: through the study of holy texts, the life of philosophy, a system of ethics, personal asceticism—or any combination of these. For Paul, the way to become transcendent was through participation in the divine Christ and specifically the immortality, power, and virtue that constituted Christ's divinity.[7]

---

7   For a recent and readable historical treatment of Jesus' divinity in early Christianity (notably Paul), see Larry W. Hurtado, *How on Earth did Jesus Become a God? Historical Questions about Earliest Devotion to Jesus* (Grand Rapids: Eerdmans, 2005). For a theological defense of Christ's divinity, see Gordon D. Fee, *Pauline Christology : An Exegetical-Theological Study* (Peabody, Mass.: Hendrickson Publishers, 2007). Richard Bauckham argues strongly for Christ's di-

For Paul, Jesus Christ mediates human transcendence as one who is himself "born of woman" (Gal 2:4) and then "appointed son of God," and "Lord" (Rom 1:4; Phil 2:9–11; cf. Acts 2:36).[8] In his resurrection, Christ already exhibited a universal power and immortal corporeality that proleptically united heaven and earth, the human and the divine.[9] Paul envisions a "glorification" of those who, due to the sin of the first Adam, fell short of the glory of God (Rom 8:29; 3:23). He preaches that the divine spirit or pneuma of Christ has been unleashed into the flesh of those "in Christ," a down payment of their own new corporeality (Rom 8:1–11; 2 Cor 4:16–17). Through Christ's pneuma, humans have the promise of attaining the transcendence of the immortal, incorruptible (and thus superhuman) state of Christ. As those assimilated to the power and immortality of the divine Christ, such human beings gain the power to be called "children of God" (Rom 8:15–16) and owners of all things (Rom 8:32; 1 Cor 3:21–23). One way to understand this complex of ideas is through the category of deification—a native category pervasive in Paul's culture.

vinity in the Pauline literature in *Jesus and the God of Israel: God Crucified and Other Studies on the New Testament's Christology of Divine Identity* (Grand Rapids: Eerdmans, 2008), 182–232. Worth noting also is the monograph of D. B. Capes, *Old Testament Yahweh Texts in Paul's Christology* (WUNT 47; Tübingen: Mohr Siebeck, 1992).

8   Although "son of God" is often thought to be a vague category, Suzanne Nicholson rightly points out that for Christ it is connected with "sending language" (Gal 4:4) that "implies Christ's preexistence," and thus a very close relationship between God and Christ. Christ as "son of God" is the divine Christ (*Dynamic Oneness: The Significance and Flexibility of Paul's One-God Language* [Eugene, OR: Pickwick, 2010], 246–47).

9   In speaking of Christ's divinity, then, there is no claim that he is equal to or "*homoousios*" with the high God, or "the Father." This maximalist understanding of divinity based on later trinitarian theology is not required for my argument. In this study I need only assert that for Paul, Christ is divine in the same way as other Greco-Roman deities were perceived of as divine: he is a preexistent (Phil 2:6), immortal being with tremendous power who produces benefaction (i.e., salvation) for those who worship him. In the words of 2 Clem, "Brothers, we must think about Jesus Christ as we think about God" (1:1). See further ch. 1: "What is a God?"

The "Otherness" of Deification

Deification, which etymologically means something like "God-making," must always sound alien and unnatural to post-Enlightenment, empirically-minded thinkers as well as to Christians and post-Christians working with modern schemas of theology and anthropology. Modern religious sensibilities add an additional layer of complication. Especially for Protestant theologians, deification has the air of hubristic, "pagan" (and thus prohibited) religion.[10] In the modern climate, deification at best can be counted as an over-audacious metaphor.

Nonetheless, the literal language of God-making in the ancient world should chasten the tendency to too quickly metaphorize ancient thinking. According to the imperial historian Velleius Paterculus, the emperor Tiberius not only *called* Augustus a God, but *made* him one (*non appellavit eum, sed fecit deum*) (*Res ges. divi Aug.* 2.126.1). Ovid, writing in the same era, says that Venus *made* Aeneas a God (*fecitque deum*) (*Met.* 14.605–08). Likewise an inscription of Mytilene between 27 and 11 B.C.E. promises to fulfill any further honors which will further make Augustus a God (θεοποιεῖν) (*OGIS* 456.44–50).[11] This idea is

---

10   So Benjamin Drewery: "I must put it on record that deification is, in my view, the most serious aberration to be found not only in Origen but in the whole tradition to which he contributed, and nothing that modern defenders of ἀπο-θέωσις … have urged has shaken in the slightest my conviction that here lies the disastrous flaw in Greek Christian thought" (quoted in Norman Russell, *The Doctrine of Deification in the Greek Patristic Tradition* [Oxford: Oxford University Press, 2004], 3). Cf. C.E.B. Cranfield, a prominent Pauline exegete of the previous generation: "The idea of apotheosis was acceptable to pagans of the centuries before and after Christ, but to one who has lived in the light of the OT can it be anything but nonsense?" ("Some Comments on Professor J.D.G. Dunn's *Christology in the Making* with Special Reference to the Evidence of the Epistle to the Romans," in *The Glory of Christ in the New Testament: Studies in Christology in Memory of G.B. Caird* [eds. L.D. Hurst and N.T. Wright; Oxford: Clarendon, 1987], 271). See J.D.G. Dunn's response to this comment in *Christology in the Making: A New Testament Inquiry into the Origins of the Doctrine of Incarnation* (2nd ed.; Grand Rapids: Eerdmans, 1996), 'Foreword to Second Edition,' xxi-xxii.

11   Cf. Seneca, who writes that "We believe him [Augustus] to be a God—not as if we were ordered to do so (*deum esse non tamquam iussi credimus*)" (*Clem.* 1.10.3). Similarly, Pliny the Younger declares to Trajan, "You introduced your father [Nerva] to the stars not to put fear into your subjects, not as an insult to the Gods, not for your own honor, but because you believe that he is a God

alien to the dominant Christian mentality where God-making is impossible, and even blasphemous. This ancient way of speaking (and thinking) thus serves as a reminder that when one hears and speaks of deification, one is (conceptually speaking) treading on foreign territory. Deification is a concept which was born and nourished in another culture with its own values and frameworks. Like ethnologists who step off the boat onto unexplored territory, one must take the time to learn the native language, culture, and context of the term in order to translate and appropriately interpret it.

Since the second century C.E., there have been many attempts to translate the idea of deification in a way that makes sense to Christians. One thinks here of the long history of deification operative in Eastern Orthodox branches of Christianity.[12] Particularly interesting are the recent attempts to translate the idea to modern Western (mostly Protestant) Christians.[13]

One of the dangers of translation when dealing with an alien concept is *over*-translation. By this I mean making a concept so amenable to one's own native constructs that the peculiar features of the concept are lost. Most modern Western theologians normally suspect, or even excoriate deification as something frightful (humans as Gods?!). The mi-

---

(quia deum credis)" (*Pan.* 11.2). See further Ittai Gradel, *Emperor Worship and Roman Religion* (Oxford: Oxford University Press, 2002), 298–99.

12   For an introduction to the Eastern Orthodox perspective with further bibliography, see Petro B. T. Bilaniuk, "The Mystery of Theosis or Divinization," in *The Heritage of the Early Church: Essays in Honor of Georges Vasilievich Florovsky* (ed. David Neiman and Margaret Schatkin; Rome: Pontifical Institute of Oriental Studies, 1973), 337–59; or more recently, George A. Maloney, *The Undreamed has Happened: God Lives Within Us* (Scranton: University of Scranton Press, 2003), esp. 65–66. A fuller bibliography has been compiled by Jeffery A. Wittung in Michael J. Christensen & Jeffery A. Wittung, eds., *Partakers of the Divine Nature: The History and Development of Deification in the Christian Traditions* (Grand Rapids: Baker Academic, 2007), 294–310.

13   Stephen Finlan and Vladimir Kharlamov, eds., *Theōsis: Deification in Christian Theology* (Eugene, OR: Pickwick, 2006); Frederick W. Norris, "Deification: Consensual and Cogent," *Scottish Journal of Theology* 49 (1996): 411–28; Roger E. Olson, "Deification in Contemporary Theology," *Theology Today* 64 (2007): 186–200; Ron Kangas, "Becoming God," *Affirmation & Critique* 7 (2002): 3–30. See the other articles in this issue of *Affirmation & Critique*. For recent Evangelical and Mormon interest in deification, see the articles cited in Carl Mosser, "The Earliest Patristic Interpretations of Psalm 82, Jewish Antecedents, and the Origin of Christian Deification," *Journal of Theological Studies* 56 (2005): 33–34, n. 11; 42, n. 27.

nority who defend it sometimes try to make it applicable to modern theology or religious experience by distinguishing it from elements perceived as "other" or "pagan."[14] It is the role of the historian neither to scorn deification, nor attempt to defend it as (1) the most meaningful path to spiritual grandeur or (2) the key to ecumenical unity.[15] Historically speaking, our first task is to recognize it as something "other."

Those who recognize the "otherness" of deification might be tempted to view it as a mythological way of thinking. What this amounts to is the realization that deification does not fit the categories of Western empirical worldviews. It is difficult enough conceiving what a God is in a scientific age, let alone what it means to become one. Yet even though a historian recognizes that deification is mythical, this does not mean "primitive" or "unreal." Calling Pauline deification part of Paul's myth or mythic imagination (as I will) is not an attempt to falsify it but an attempt to defamiliarize it. It helps one to view what one *thought* was one's own tradition as something "other." This is because myths are stories of "those who are not us" (and thus often confused with simply false stories).

---

14   This is the thrust of Otto Faller, "Griechische Vergottung und christliche Vergöttlichung," *Gregorianum* 6 (1925): 404–35. Martin George ("Vergöttlichung des Menschen. Von der platonischen Philosophie zur Soteriologie der griechischen Kirchenväter," in *Die Weltlichkeit des Glaubens in der alten Kirche: Festschrift für Ulrich Wickert zum siebzigsten Geburtstag* [ed. Dietmar Wyrwa; Berlin & New York: Walter de Gruyter, 1997], 115–56) updates Faller in a more nuanced article, but still essentially aims to divorce Greek from Christian (specifically patristic) forms of deification.

15   Paul Collins, for instance, studies deification "to assess how the Church today can receive the witness of this common patristic heritage in order to understand and live out the divine purpose in creating and redeeming the cosmos" (*Partaking in Divine Nature: Deification and Communion* [London & New York: T&T Clark, 2010], 49, cf. 11). Present here is not only modern spirituality, but the modern ecumenical interest in uniting Eastern and Western branches of Christianity. Paul L. Gavrilyuk is absolutely correct when he says that the "present retrieval of the deification theme in an impressive number of western theological authorities cannot be attributed simply to diligent historical excavation work. It is probably more accurate to describe the retrieval of deification as a *theological achievement* thinly disguised as historical theology" ("The Retrieval of Deification: How a Once-despised Archaism Became an Ecumenical Desideratum," *Modern Theology* 25 [2009]: 655, italics his). Many recent studies on the topic, he points out, are "historical-expositions-turned ecumenical-overtures" (*ibid.*).

Another way to explain (and explain away) the "otherness" of deification is to see it as essentially metaphorical. This seems to be the approach of Norman Russell, who introduces the whole topic of patristic deification under the subheading, "The Metaphor of Deification."[16] To be sure, Russell then makes "realistic" deification (by which he means likeness to God and participation) a *subcategory* of metaphorical deification. But by "realistic," Russell simply means a kind of deification that "in some sense" involves transformation.[17] In none of the three ways of deification that he outlines (nominal, analogical, and metaphorical) does Russell think that the deified Christian is *actually* made a God. One would think that deification by participatory union would involve ontological change. Yet Russell (following Bigger), reduces participation to a mere "relation" of two beings "of diverse ontological type." This reduces participation to likeness (in which two fundamentally dissimilar beings have secondary similarities).[18] What this amounts to is the idea that—even in the most "realistic" mode of deification—deified humans always remain ontologically other than God (or deity); that is, they always remain *human*. But how, I might ask, is this "realistic" deification?[19] This framework, from my perspective, requires revision.[20]

---

16 *Doctrine of Deification*, 1. Russell's influence has been pivotal. He is followed by Paul Collins, who continues the practice of calling deification a metaphor (*Partaking in Divine Nature*, 4, 9, 48, and throughout). He is also followed by Ben C. Blackwell, whose "attributive" understanding of deification "corresponds to Russell's 'metaphorical' category" (*Christosis: Pauline Soteriology in Light of Deification in Irenaeus and Cyril of Alexandria* (Tübingen: Mohr Siebeck, forthcoming), 105).

17 *Ibid.*, 2.

18 Blackwell, who uses the language of "relational participation" (*Christosis*, 106) follows Russell. It is clear that both Russell and Blackwell are thinking in terms of later patristic theology. But later patristic theology is not determinative for Paul.

19 Russell is willing to use the term "ontological" to refer to deification. But by it he means "transformation in principle" (*ibid.*), not that deified humans ontologically (realistically!) become divine or God(s).

20 It seems to me that Russell (as mentioned in n. 18) is thinking in categories internal to patristic theology, and not in distinctly historical categories. What I want to remain open to in this study is the idea that Christian deification may not have been (at least at first) so different from deification in the larger Greco-Roman world. I want to remain open to the idea, in other words, that Christian deification was not simply metaphorical (or nominal or analogical), but that it involved a realistic transformation into deity such that humans truly transcended their (human) nature and became Gods or divine.

Metaphor, it seems to me, is not the appropriate overarching historical category through which to view deification (and here I include
Christian deification). Metaphorizing is often a strategy of one culture
trying to understand a concept of an alien culture ("surely they don't
mean that literally"). Metaphorizing deification, or making it into a
kind of simile, is often the price of fitting deification into a modern
"monotheistic" framework, which assumes that there can only be numerically one God. A historian, however, cannot take for granted the
meaning of monotheism in the ancient world. He or she certainly cannot impose modern conceptions of monotheism onto ancient thinkers
(see chapter 8). It is sufficient to point out at this juncture that at least
some ancient sources do not speak of deification as a metaphor or figure
of speech. It seems advisable, then, not to take for granted (at least at the
outset) that it is fundamentally metaphorical.

Paul and Deification

It is often assumed (and sometimes argued) that Greco-Roman deification ultimately presupposes a world picture that does not jibe with the
Pauline conception of the divine and the human. In Greco-Roman
worldviews, nothing prevents people from changing into Gods. In
some cases, such a promotion is even a natural process, the true destiny
of the soul. No allowance for this, it is thought, is ever made in Paul's
thought. Paul believed that Christ, being "in the form of God" (Phil
2:6), took on human form. In adopting this form, Christ transformed
it in his resurrection. In Christ, the human becomes a "new [but
human] creation." Salvation, in this line of thought, is an assimilation
purely to the *humanness* of Christ, which involves the impartation of a
new righteousness before God. In this view, humans are never thought
to actually be or become divine.

Nevertheless—even though Paul avoids the specific vocabulary of
deification—the language of his soteriology has long suggested a form
of deification at work in his thought. As noted above, in Eastern Orthodox theology this tradition of interpretation stretches from the second
century C.E. up to our own time. The Eastern doctrine of deification

is complex, and I will not be treating it in this study.[21] For the moment, it is sufficient to point out some of the things in Paul's letters which have suggested (to ancient and modern readers) the inner logic of deification.

First, Paul expects himself and his communities to attain a state of deathlessness and incorruption (1 Cor 15:35–53). This state is achieved by receiving a sort of bodily immortality. Since mortality is one of the basic (if not *the* basic) conditions of human existence, Paul evidently promises a kind of life beyond normal human conditions. The body he anticipates is not only immortal, but freed from the laws of generation and decay. This new, pneumatic body, that is, will not grow old or waste away. In addition, Paul thinks that he will be "glorified" or marked with the same brilliance which characteristically appears in theophanies (Rom 8:29; cf. Phil 3:21; 2 Cor 3:18; Ex 24:17; Ezek 1:28). He tells his converts—as if it were common knowledge—that they will someday judge higher, superhuman beings ("angels," 1 Cor 6:3). In promising this, he seems to assume that he and his community will one day have an existence—or at least a status—above those angelic beings (cf. Rom 16:20). Such a cosmic role seems to be part and parcel of transformed Christians judging the whole "cosmos" (1 Cor 6:2). They are those who will be given "all things" by God (Rom 8:32), and who will come into possession of grandiose cosmic realities—including life, death, things present, things to come, and even the world itself (1 Cor 3:21–23).

Paul also repeatedly emphasizes his assimilation to Christ, particularly in the two fundamental acts of death and resurrection. For Paul, participation in Christ's death manifests itself in his repeated sufferings during his mission (best illustrated in 2 Cor 4:8–12; 11:16–12:10). In turn, Paul experienced Christ's resurrection life as a power which surged in the moments of his confessed weakness. This participation in the two "acts" of the (Pauline) Christ myth is not a haphazard or *ad hoc* element of Paul's theology. He constantly urges a rigorous homology between Christ and believers as both a reality and an ideal for his converts. They are expected to recapitulate or live out Christ's paradigmatic acts of death and resurrection in their own lives (Rom 6:1–11; 1 Cor 15:22, 49).

---

21 See Russell, *Doctrine of Deification*, as well as his *Fellow Workers with God: Orthodox Thinking on Theosis* (Crestwood, N.Y.: St. Vladimir's Seminary Press, 2009).

This communion—or union?—of destiny between Christ and believer is well demonstrated by Paul's striking use of "co-" compounds.
Pauline converts are said to be "co-heirs" (συγκληρονόμοι) with Christ
(Rom 8:17; cf. Eph 3:6) if they "co-suffer" with him (συμπάσχομεν)
(Rom 8:17; cf. 2 Cor 1:5; Col 1:24). Paul calls himself "co-crucified"
(συνεσταύρωμαι) with Christ (Gal 2:19; cf. Rom 6:6). He apparently
expects a similar destiny for his followers, insofar as they are "co-
grown" (σύμφυτοι) to the likeness of Christ's death (Rom 6:5;
cf. 6:8; 2 Cor 4:10; Phil 3:10; Col 2:20), and "co-buried" with Christ
(συνετάφημεν) (Rom 6:4; Col 2:12). Subsequently they "co-live"
(συζήσομεν) with Christ (Rom 6:8; 2 Tim 2:11) by being "co-glori-
fied" with him (συνδοξασθῶμεν) (Rom 8:17; cf. 2 Thess 2:14).[22] Perhaps the strongest statement of homology is in 2 Cor 3:18, where Christians become the "same image" (τὴν αὐτὴν εἰκόνα) of (or as) Christ—
who is later identified as the image of God (4:4).

This union Paul himself professes to have with Christ is a kind of
kinship. Pauline Christians become "sons" of God (Rom 8:14; 9:26;
Gal 3:26; 4:6) just as Christ was declared "son of God" (Rom 1:4).
Christ and Christians are thus siblings (ἀδελφοί) (Rom 8:29), or images
of the same divine Father (cf. Gen 5:1–3). These kinship metaphors
seem to express a kind of relatedness which is rightly called "genetic";
i. e., having to do with the γένος—the race or class into which two entities belong. In short, Christ and believers as kin belong to the same
class of beings, namely divine "sons of God." Christians as divine children of the Father are certainly pictured as subordinate to Christ their
elder brother. The fact, however, that believers are pictured as Christ's
siblings, made in the same image, and heirs of the same world, indicates
a relative parity between believer and Christ.

Paul's relation to Christ even borders on identification. He confesses
that "I have been crucified with Christ. I no longer live; Christ lives in
me" (Gal 2:19–20). His statement that the Galatians have seen "before
their very eyes" Christ crucified may be a reference to them seeing Paul
himself (Gal 3:1; cf. 4:14). In addition, Paul talks about his converts

---

22 According to Deutero-Pauline literature, Christians are "co-raised" (συνεγείρω)
with Christ (Eph 2:6; Col 2:12; 3:1), and are "co-enlivened" (συζωοποιέω)
with him (Col 2:13; Eph 2:5). Subsequently, they "co-reign" with Christ
(συμβασιλεύω) (2 Tim 2:12), sitting "co-enthroned" with him in the heavenly
realms (συγκαθίζω) (Eph 2:6). Though not in genuine Pauline letters, these are
(I believe) genuinely Pauline thoughts.

being the corporate body of Christ (1 Cor 3:6; 6:3; 12:1) and individually "one spirit" with Christ (1 Cor 6:17).

It is thus primarily three factors, all closely intertwined, that suggest a form of deification in Paul, namely: (1) ruling over "all things" (including superhuman beings), together with (2) the expectation of existing in a superhuman, immortal and incorruptible corporeality. Both of these factors are viewed as functions of (3) assimilation to Christ, a divine being.[23] Whether or not the combined presence of these three elements allows us to call Paul's soteriology a soteriology of "deification" is the focus of this study. Keen attention to prior research will help orient our discussion.

History of Research[24]

That Paul's soteriology included a form of deification was (and is) highly controversial in scholarship. The trend was set by Adolf von Harnack, who believed that deification—a confessedly popular Greco-Roman idea—was foreign to the early Christian gospel.[25] After several generations of "Hellenization," the early church's "glowing hope of the 'Kingdom of heaven'" (*die brennende Hoffnung auf das 'Reich der Himmel'*) eventually turned into "a doctrine of immortality and deification" (*Unsterblichkeits- und Vergottungslehre*) at the hands of the church fathers.[26] This separation between Jewish ("kingdom of heaven") and Hellenistic ("immortality and deification") streams in Christian thought was to define New Testament studies for the next century (hints of it still coloring contemporary research).[27] It strongly characterized the work of one of the pioneers of the History of Religions school, Richard Reitzenstein.

For Reitzenstein, unlike for Harnack, "Hellenization" was not tainted with thoughts of impurity. Reitzenstein more or less assumed

---

23 Homology by itself does not indicate deification. It is when the homology involves an assimilation to a divine being (such as Christ) that we can speak of deification.

24 Blackwell provides a briefer history of research on *Christosis*, 5–13.

25 *Lehrbuch der Dogmengeschichte* (5th ed.; 3 vols.; Tübingen: J. C. B. Mohr, 1931), 1:136–37.

26 *Ibid.*, 52–53. For the theme of Hellenization in Harnack, see William Rowe, "Adolf von Harnack and the Concept of Hellenization" in *Hellenization Revisited: Shaping a Christian Response within the Greco-Roman World* (ed. Wendy E. Helleman; Lanham: University Press of America, 1994), 69–98.

27 See further Martin George, "Vergöttlichung des Menschen," 117–119.

that Paul was thoroughly Hellenized. In accord with this assumption, Reitzenstein proposed that Paul taught a version of deification like that found in the Greek mystery religions.[28] The mysteries, as Reitzenstein presented them, used language for deification that did not properly distinguish a particular deity from the person deified. For instance, a common idea in the mysteries was that the one who sees the vision of a God becomes this God through a substantial transformation.[29] According to Reitzenstein, this is essentially what Paul taught in 2 Cor 3:18 ("beholding the glory of the Lord we are being metamorphosed into the same image"). "[T]he soul itself," he interprets, "must assume the μορφὴ θεοῦ [form of God], and God brings this about, by entering into the soul ... Hence it is immediately understandable that an abiding vision of God produces in us a μεταμόρφωσις, a transformation in nature in an ever increasing glory to one and the same image."[30] According to Reitzenstein, the mysteries conceived of union with God as "a sexual union whereby the man receives the inner-most essence and power of a god, his seed."[31]

When Reitzenstein propounded the view that deification was a "Hellenistic" category whose main feature was a substantial (even sexual) fusion with the Godhead, it was little wonder that scholars who recognized Paul's heavy debts to Jewish forms of thought—such as Gustav Adolf Deissmann,[32] Wilhelm Bousset,[33] H. A. A. Kennedy,[34] and Albert Schweitzer[35]—denied that Paul had any notion of deification. And yet these scholars maintained a keen sense of what might be called Paul's "mystical piety."

Deissmann, for instance, underscored that Paul was a devotee of "Christ-mysticism."[36] This scholar understood mysticism in a broad

---

28 *Hellenistic Mystery-Religions: Their Basic Ideas and Significance* (trans. John E. Steely; Pittsburgh: Pickwick Press, 1978). The German was originally published in 1910.

29 For the significance of the vision of God, see *ibid.*, 370.

30 *Ibid.*, 455, cf. 458.

31 *Ibid.*, 34.

32 *Paul: A Study in Social and Religious History* (trans. William Wilson; 2nd ed.; New York: George H. Doran Co., 1926), 147, 150–53. The German original (*Paulus: Eine kultur- und religionsgeschichtliche Skizze*) appeared in 1911.

33 *Kyrios Christos; a History of the Belief in Christ from the Beginnings of Christianity to Irenaeus* (trans. John E. Steely; Nashville: Abingdon Press, 1970), 164–76.

34 *St Paul and the Mystery-Religions* (London: Hodder and Stoughton, 1913), 292.

35 *Die Mystik des Apostels Paulus* (Tübingen: Mohr Siebeck, 1930), 15–18.

36 Deissmann, *Paul: A Study in Social and Religious History*, 147.

sense. It denoted "every religious tendency that discovers the way to God direct through inner experience without the mediation of reasoning. The constitutive element in mysticism is immediacy of contact with the deity."[37] Deissmann distinguished four types of mysticism by two criteria: origin and aim. Classified by *origin*, there are two types: "acting" and "reacting." Deissmann called these two types the "mysticism of performance" and "the mysticism of grace."[38] Classified by *aim*, there are again two types: that which strives for *unio* (union), and that which strives for *communio* (communion). Deissmann thought of *unio* as "transformation into the deity" with a consequent "loss of the human personality in God." By contrast, *communio* was a "sanctification of the personality through the presence of God," and a "conformation of the human towards the divine."[39] Deissmann classified Paul, somewhat predictably, as a "reacting" and "*communio*-mystic."[40] He concluded that Paul "was not deified, nor was he transformed into spirit by this communion, nor did he become Christ."[41]

Deissmann rejected a Pauline form of deification because of how he understood the term. For him, deification meant the same thing as *unio*, a construct of late medieval (Catholic) piety which later disturbed Protestants because it hinted at fusion with deity and subsequent loss of individuality.[42] Understood in this way, Deissmann was right to deny that Paul taught *unio*.[43] At the same time, however, his understanding of deification was too narrow and unhistorical—with an eye more toward

---

37   *Ibid.*, 149.

38   *Ibid.*, 150.

39   *Ibid.*, 150–51.

40   *Ibid.*, 152.

41   *Ibid.*, 152–53.

42   Evelyn Underhill, in her study *Mysticism: A Study in the Nature and Development of Man's Spiritual Consciousness* (12th ed.; New York: Meridian, 1955)—originally published the same year as Deissmann's study (1911) and often reprinted—defines mysticism this way: "the science of union with the Absolute," which "passes over into that boundless life where Subject and Object, desirous and desired, are *one*" (72, emphasis original). She goes on to define deification as the state "in which the mystic holds his transfigured self to be identical with the Indwelling God" (99, cf. 102) and "the utter transmutation of the self in God" (415).

43   The "secret of Paul's spiritual life," according to Deissmann, is "Christ in Paul (Gal. 2:20), Paul in Christ" (*ibid.*, 135). Paul's experience of Christ is deep and realistic. It is participation (κοινωνία) in Christ (1 Cor 1:9; 10:6; Phil 3:10). Deissmann calls it "Christ-intimacy" (*Christ-Innigkeit*) or "Christ-mysticism" (*Christusmystik*)—not deification.

modern understandings of mysticism than reliable and representative ancient sources for deification.

In 1913, H.A.A. Kennedy wrote *St. Paul and the Mystery-Religions* in response to Reitzenstein. Kennedy understood that faith, for Paul, was the means of the "unspeakably intimate relation of the soul to Christ." He insisted, however, that the relation to Christ is "a personal relationship established by adoring trust in and devotion to Him in whom Paul has reached the possibility of a life which shall be 'right' with God."[44] Kennedy does not directly attack the doctrine of deification, only the "rash inferences" drawn from it that threatens the integrity of human personality.[45] Like Deissmann, he was utterly opposed to a union with Christ that meant fusion with the deity and the loss of human identity. His definition of life in Christ is "the triumphant continuance of personality beyond the barriers of earth and time, in *conformity with the nature of the glorified Lord.*"[46]

Wilhelm Bousset understood that the goal of Greek piety in Paul's milieu was deification. His two main sources were Hermeticism and the mystery religions.[47] Speaking of Hermeticism, he defines deification as a person's "exaltation into the world of the divine element."[48] In the mystery religions, this exaltation involved a mystical identification with the deity, so that the adept died and rose with a God.[49] Equipped with this understanding of deification, Bousset denied that Paul had any such notion:

> There is no doubt that Paul with his formula ἐν Χριστῷ εἶναι [to be "in Christ"] takes a distinctive position as contrasted with these views [Hermeticism and the mystery religions]. In him the plain and bare formula that the

---

44 *St. Paul and the Mystery-Religions*, 223.

45 *Ibid.*, 292.

46 *Ibid.*, 298, emphasis his.

47 Indeed most of Bousset's case rests on the foundation of the *Corpus Hermeticum* (*Corp. herm.*), as it was digested and interpreted by Reitzenstein in his book *Poimandres: Studien zur griechisch-ägyptischen und frühchristlichen Literatur*. In *Corp. herm.*, deification has a notably pantheistic and theosophical cast.

48 *Kyrios Christos*, 186.

49 *Ibid.*, 164., citing Apul., *Met.* 11.24. Later he turns to what are perhaps earlier witnesses which describe the initiation ceremony in the Attis cult: "When in the Attis initiation the initiate, following the example of his cult-hero, performs on himself the fearful act of emasculation, he himself thereby becomes Attis and experiences with him his death and his return from death." Bousset goes on to claim that in the Attis and the Isis mystery cults, "... the initiate serves as the incarnate deity of the mystery" (*ibid.*, 165).

believer becomes the Christos himself is never uttered. Paul rather instinc-
tively shrinks back from this formula ... Christ remains the surpassing element, the spirit being who takes the believers into himself. The piety of the
mystery system is absolutely individualistic, eudaemonistic, egoistic; the individual mystic achieves for himself the blessed state of deification. The divine is completely absorbed into the human. These perils are avoided in
Paul. Christos remains the Kyrios. The believer is taken up into his
being, but this is not inverted.[50]

At the same time, however, Bousset suggested that several of Paul's
phrases and ideas suggest a close union with the divine (and specifically,
the divine Christ). For Paul, denials of his truthfulness "are a blasphemy
against his Lord and *his* truthfulness (2 Cor 1:19; 11:10)." Since he believes that Christ speaks in and through him (2 Cor 13:3), an attack on
his "fitness and probity" is an attack against Christ himself.[51] Furthermore, Bousset called Paul "in part" a "religious superman, a θεῖος
ἄνθρωπος" or "divine man," which meant, for Bousset, a "pneumatic".[52] Ritually, as well, Bousset recognized "a certain affinity between
the Pauline Christ mysticism" and the mystery piety of the Greek milieu. For instance, Bousset says that for Paul "baptism serves as an act
of initiation in which the mystic is merged with the deity, or is clothed
with the deity. Thus in baptism the Christians have become one with
the Son, and hence themselves have become sons."[53]

And yet for Bousset, Paul could not have understood salvation in
Christ in terms of deification for two reasons. First, the basic feature
of Paul's "mysticism" is its distinction between Christ and the believer.
As tantalizing as some of Paul's statements are, he never outright identified himself with Christ. Second, Paul's mysticism is fundamentally
communal. It is a mysticism of the body of Christ. In contrast to the
ontological absorption featured in the mystery religions, Paul's "in
Christ" means only the "absorption of the individual *will* into one
great surpassing, world-embracing will which is expressed in the totality
of a comprehensive fellowship."[54] Again, it was the substantial "fusion"
model of deification in which the person ceases to have an independent
personality that proved the bugbear to be avoided.

---

50 *Ibid.*, 166.
51 *Ibid.*, 169, emphasis his.
52 *Ibid.*, 170.
53 *Ibid.*, 158.
54 *Ibid.*, 168–69, emphasis added.

A great popularizer of Pauline mysticism was Albert Schweitzer. As much as he emphasized Paul's sense of union with Christ, Schweitzer still denied that Paul had a doctrine of deification. Agreeing with Reitzenstein and Bousset, Schweitzer believed that Hellenistic mysticism was rooted in the idea of deification (which he understood as transformation into the substance of the divine). Yet since, according to Schweitzer, Paul chiefly thought in Jewish (apocalyptic) terms and not in Hellenistic categories, "deification" in this sense was excluded. Paul had what Schweitzer called a "Christ mysticism," in which he experienced a certain fellowship with the risen Christ.[55] Christ, in Paul's system, was not considered to be (a) God, but only a heavenly being. Thus fellowship with Christ was not a deification "but only a transference into a state of supersensuous corporeity."[56] Although Schweitzer announced that such a transference made the Christian into a "supernatural being" (*übernatürliche Wesen*),[57] to call this a "deification" seemed far too Greek.[58] The opposition is again between Hellenism and Judaism, which goes hand in hand with the reconstructed model of "fusion" with God in the mystery religions versus "Jewish" eschatological "fellowship."

Among the chorus of those who denied a Pauline form of deification, Hans Windisch stood out with the opposite view (even if the only true recipient of deification, Windisch believed, was Paul himself). In Windisch's understanding, deification meant "a becoming 'Christ'" (*ein "Christ"-werden*), "a fusing with Christ" (*ein Zusammenschmelzen mit Christus*), "a becoming like him (*ein gleichwerden mit ihm*), which is both a conscious following after (*ein bewußtes nachfolgen*) and at the same time a mystically and ethically (*mystisch-ethisch*) grounded *imitatio Christi*."[59] This mystically grounded *imitatio* was rooted in baptism, which produced a "symbiosis" of the believer and Christ. They die together, are buried together, and are raised together (Rom 6:3–11; Col

---

55 *Mystik*, 4–6, 15–18.
56 *Paul and His Interpreters: A Critical History* (London: Adam and Charles Black, 1912), 223.
57 *Mystik*, 111.
58 Schweitzer comments: "Going along together with ... the un-Hellenistic character of Paul's mysticism is that to him the concept of deification is alien (*ihm die Vorstellung der Vergottung fremd ist*)" (*Mystik*, 15). If Paul is not "Hellenistic," he could not have envisioned a form of deification.
59 Hans Windisch, *Paulus und Christus* (Leipzig: J.C. Hinrichs'sche, 1934), 230.

2:11–15).[60] Windisch roots Paul's own deification in his personal experience of being sanctified and created anew by Christ (which Paul generalizes to all believers in Rom 6 and 2 Cor 5:17).[61] Especially significant is 2 Cor 3:18, where Paul transfers his experience of "the transformation of his inner person into the Christ-nature" (*die Verwandlung seines inneren menschen in die Christusnatur*) to all believers.[62] Though Paul is absolutely dependent on Christ, Christ and Paul stand in a single trajectory, different in degree but not in kind.[63] They are both "prophetic pneumatics," pneumatics teachers and scholars, eschatological-messianic heralds, and miracle workers. In short, both represent the type of the ancient "man of God" (*Gottesmann*).[64]

In 1938, Jules Gross published his *La divinisation du chrétien d'après les pères grecs*, a survey of the doctrine of deification in the Greek Fathers. When discussing biblical antecedents, Gross claimed that Paul presented "a mysticism of the divinization of Christians,"[65] by which he meant a moral and ontological union with Christ.[66] Here he was careful to distinguish Paul's view from the view that the human personality was "absorbed" into God, with a back glance at the understanding of deification among the representatives of the History of Religions School.[67]

Until the early 1970s, both the proponents and opponents of a Pauline form of deification were agreed on at least one point: that there was a divide between Judaism and Hellenism, and that deification fell on the Hellenistic side of that divide. Scholars who emphasized the Jewish or Hellenistic side of Paul thus derived different conclusions. Some who accepted Paul's deep debts to Hellenism were prepared to acknowledge a Pauline doctrine of deification. The votaries of Paul's Jewish heritage, on the other hand, rejected such a teaching. Such a rejection was predictable because Schweitzer and others had allowed figures like Reitzenstein to define deification according to artificially constructed "Hellenistic" categories, derived in large part from a defective understanding

---

60 *Ibid.*, 231.
61 *Ibid.*, 231–32.
62 *Ibid.*, 234.
63 *Ibid.*, 6. Windisch especially sees a homology, or an "*Analogiehaftigkeit*" between the earthly Jesus and the charismatic Paul (*ibid.*, 7), and criticizes Deissmann for only emphasizing the superiority of Jesus to Paul (*ibid.*, 8).
64 *Ibid.*, 10.
65 *Divinisation du chrétien d'après les pères grecs* (Paris: J. Gabalda et Cie, 1938), 102.
66 *Ibid.*, 101.
67 *Ibid.*, 102.

of the Greek mystery cults. When in the 1960s the speculative reconstruction of mystery piety in the History of Religions School was debunked and fell out of favor,[68] discussion of a Pauline form of deification fell off the map.[69]

The general loss of interest in the mystery cults for enlightening Pauline soteriology was a necessary step, however, in coming to a proper understanding of deification. The meaning of deification was not wed to Hermeticism and the mystery religions. These religious systems may have presented a form of deification, and this form may even have presented a theory of fusion with (a particular) deity. Yet even if these two points are granted (and generally they are not at all granted by current scholars of the mystery religions)—*the fusion model is not a representative understanding of deification in the ancient world.* In fact, it is safe to say that the fusion model is a scholarly construct which may have more to do with Protestant disgust for *unio* (read Catholic) mysticism than with the ancient mysteries.[70] Consequently, though it can be granted that Pauline soteriology does not involve a fusion with divine substance that involves a loss of personality, *this is not what deification is.* All the previous rejections of deification were, then, based on a fundamentally false premise.

---

68 The death-knell was sounded more or less by Günther Wagner, *Pauline Baptism and the Pagan Mysteries: The Problem of the Pauline Doctrine of Baptism in Romans VI.1–11, in the Light of its Religio-Historical "Parallels"* (Trans; J. P. Smith; Edinburgh & London: Oliver & Boyd, 1967). The German original *Das religionsgeschichtliche Problem von Römer 6,1–11* appeared in 1962.

69 Instead, deification was commonly attributed to Paul's enemies who supposedly upheld a "theology of glory" as opposed to Paul's *theologia crucis.* See Blackwell's brief discussion of Ernst Käsemann in *Christosis*, 5. This idea can also be found in a more recent interpreter like Calvin Roetzel—and to a certain extent Blackwell himself seems to subscribe to this view (see *ibid.*, 237, where Roetzel is quoted).

70 Since *unio* mysticism was sometimes associated with the Roman Catholic mystical tradition, it tended to be viewed with suspicion in Protestant scholarship. For Protestant scholarship's anti-Catholic construction of the mystery religions (with a helpful corrective), see J. Z. Smith, *Drudgery Divine* (Chicago: Chicago University Press, 1990), esp. 31–33, 43–45, 55–84, 101–15, 120–21, 125–43.

Recent Research on Paul and Deification

A new era of Pauline studies was made possible in the 1970s by two broad movements: (1) the increasing criticism of the methods of the old History of Religions school,[71] and (2) later studies which began to break down the Hellenism-Judaism divide.[72] Nonetheless, what best served to reopen the discussion of deification (though only indirectly) was the work of E. P. Sanders, *Paul and Palestinian Judaism*. Sanders was successful in translating Schweitzer's language of "mysticism" into a language more enlightening and useable for scholars studying Pauline soteriology, namely "participation." Participation—in fact an ancient category—was a way for modern scholars to talk about the more realistic and transformative aspects of Pauline soteriology which had become incomprehensible to the modern mind. Paul's realistic soteriology includes ideas such as becoming the righteousness of God (2 Cor 5:21), living in the power of Christ's death and resurrection (Rom 6; 2 Cor 4:8–12), and experiencing final "glorification" (Rom 8:29). The language of participation took seriously Paul's realistic language because it resisted the Bultmannian tendency to demythologize Paul. Unfortunately, however, the idea of participation was itself vague and even somewhat vacuous because it did not explain how scholars should *interpret* Paul's realistic language.[73] How, after all, does one "become" the righteousness of God, or become "one spirit" with Christ (1 Cor 6:17), or pass from "glory to glory" (2 Cor 3:18)? Even the basic meaning of these terms—righteousness, spirit, glory—seems to slip through the hands like water. Sanders himself admitted that he could offer no "new category of perception" with which to un-

---

71 See, e.g., Carsten Colpe, *Die religionsgeschichtliche Schule: Darstellung und Kritik ihres Bildes vom gnostischen Erlösermythus* (Göttingen: Vandenhoeck & Ruprecht, 1961).

72 Most notably, Martin Hengel, *Judaism and Hellenism: Studies in their Encounter in Palestine during the Early Hellenistic Period* (Philadelphia: Fortress Press, 1974). See more recently Erich S. Gruen, *Heritage and Hellenism: The Reinvention of Jewish Tradition* (Berkeley: University of California Press, 1998), 335; John J. Collins and Gregory Sterling, *Hellenism in the Land of Israel* (Notre Dame, Ind.: University of Notre Dame Press, 2001), 343; and especially the essays in Troels Engberg-Pedersen, ed. *Paul Beyond the Judaism/Hellenism Divide* (Louisville: Westminster/John Knox Press, 2001).

73 "As central as the notion of participation is for understanding deification, greater precision in using the term is in order" (Gavrilyuk "The Retrieval of Deification," 651).

derstand these terms.[74] But Sanders' success at highlighting the concept of participation—even if not perfectly lucid—was a great stride forward in understanding the meaning of deification. Since the second century, "participation" (μέθεξις) had been a way for early Christians to talk about the reality of deification. The revival and popularization of this concept in (Western) scholarship paved the way for students of Paul to make the same connections as early Christians: participation in the life and qualities of Christ meant participation in the life and qualities of a divine being. But this was (and is) a way of speaking about deification. Importantly, it is a way of speaking about deification that does not indicate fusion with (Christ's) deity.

During the next twenty years, however, few if any scholars traced the thread of participation to deification. Those who did express an opinion on deification in Paul were not very clear on what they meant by it. James Tabor, for instance, argued that Paul's notion of "many sons of God" was a version of "mass apotheosis."[75] He related it to the new religious sense prominent in the Hellenistic age, namely that the true home of the human race is not the lowly realm of earth, but the highest heaven.[76] Nevertheless "mass apotheosis," it must be admitted, is rather undefined. What is it and how does it come about?

A decade later, Willem F. Smelik claimed that intertestamental Judaism posited an eschatological and "mystical transformation [of the righteous] into light." He asserted that this "mystical transformation" could be called "apotheosis," and he believed that this tradition of apotheosis was found in Paul. As his main evidence, Smelik cited 1 Cor. 15:35–55 (Paul's account of the resurrection body) and 2 Cor. 3:18 with little development.[77]

The turn of the millennium saw more interest in biblical versions of deification as a topic. James Starr's *Sharers in Divine Nature: 2 Peter 1:4 in its Hellenistic Context*—even though it does not focus on Paul—is important because it directly examines the idea of participation in the divine

---

74 *Paul and Palestinian Judaism: A Comparison of Patterns of Religion* (Philadelphia: Fortress Press, 1977), 522–23.

75 "Paul's Notion of Many 'Sons of God' and its Hellenistic Contexts," *Helios* 13 (1986): 87, 95.

76 *Ibid.*, 94–96.

77 "On Mystical Transformation of the Righteous into Light in Judaism"," *Journal for the Study of Judaism* 26 (1995): 122. See also Christopher Morray-Jones, "Transformational Mysticism in the Apocalyptic-Merkabah Tradition," *Journal of Jewish Studies* 43 (1992): 1–31.

nature. Starr divided the divine nature into a list of ontological and moral attributes. Ontological attributes included immortality and incorruptibility. The moral attributes (or qualities) included a host of virtues, especially justice, but also faithfulness, love, etc. Both sets of attributes were in principle able to be shared by both God and human beings. The former (ontological) attributes, however, were (according to Starr) unshareable in the present life. Starr thus pushed ontological participation into the (post-parousia) future.[78] This is an important move for Starr, since it allowed him to focus solely on the moral side of sharing divinity.[79]

Starr also avoided defining "divine nature" (θεῖα φύσις) as divine substance or essence.[80] To be sure, Starr initially defined "divine nature" as in part the divine "constitution,"[81] a word which can designate the physical make-up of a being. But Starr was much more keen to emphasize the "qualities ... or condition adherent to God" as a definition of "divine nature," at least for the author of 2 Peter.[82] Why he tends in this direction becomes clear later. If "divine nature" designated essence, then sharing divine nature would suggest a Hellenistic form of deifica-

---

78 *Sharers in Divine Nature: 2 Peter 1:4 in its Hellenistic Context* (Stockholm: Almquist & Wiksell, 2000), 48.

79 Starr continues to push a moralistic interpretation in a later essay "Does 2 Peter 1:4 Speak of Deification?" (in *Partakers of the Divine Nature: The History and Development of Deification in the Christian Traditions* [eds. Michael J. Christensen and Jeffery A. Wittung; Grand Rapids: Baker Academic, 2007]). Yet here he has to admit that "2 Peter tends to minimize the moral side of sharing in divine nature to such an extent that it has not generally been observed in the twentieth century" (88). This point is related to his general emphasis in this essay that Christian deification must occur by grace, and not through innate reason (putatively seen in 2 Macc and Philo) or moral perfection (an idea that Starr dubiously attaches to Plutarch) (87–88). Yet there is little evidence that the knowledge which begins (according to Starr) the moral and physical transformation in 2 Pet requires no human effort. Note, for instance, 2 Pet 1:5: "For this very reason, *you must make every effort* (σπουδὴν πᾶσαν παρεισενέγκαντες) to support your faith with virtue, and virtue with knowledge" (NRSV, modified). Knowledge comes with and after effort as a supplement to faith.

80 In a "Hellenistic context," Starr admits in a later essay, divine nature "appears to mean an impersonal, objectifiable essence of God" ("Does 2 Peter 1:4 Speak of Deification?" 81).

81 *Sharers in Divine Nature*, 1.

82 *Ibid*. He says later, "The 'divine nature' then in which Christ believers are to share will be a taking on of *qualities* associated with Christ's nature" (45, emphasis added).

tion (sharing in the essence of God). However, if divine nature designated a list of moral attributes, then humans could share divine nature and
still remain human. So, in order to separate Christian thought from
"pagan" deification, Starr consistently forged a highly dubious distinction between sharing the divine nature and being deified.[83]

In 2004, the survey of deification by Gross was updated by Norman
Russell in *The Doctrine of Deification in the Greek Patristic Tradition*. Unlike Gross, however, Russell denied that Paul presented an idea of deification. In this judgment Russell followed Schweitzer who believed
that Paul never spoke of "being one with God."[84] But Russell marshaled
further arguments to support Schweitzer's view: (1) since "Christ is not
called 'God' unequivocally before the second century," "union with
Christ is not the same as union with God," (2) Paul "did not have a
fixed technical term for participatory union with Christ," and (3)
Paul's expressions for participatory union are "metaphorical images,"[85]
whereas the terminology of deification only arises "when the Pauline
metaphors are re-expressed in metaphysical language."[86] In sum, for
Russell, Paul presents a theology of participatory union with Christ
which approaches but is not yet a doctrine of deification.

In contrast to Russell, a survey of deification in Christian theology
edited by Stephan Finlan and Vladimir Kharlamov claims that "*Theōsis* is
central to the theology of Paul throughout."[87] According to Paul, they
affirm, Christians are "being transformed into the likeness of Christ,
who is the embodiment of God. Believers are 'conformed to' and
'transformed into' the image of Christ (Rom. 8.29; 2 Cor. 3.18;
Phil. 3.21), even having the 'mind of Christ' (Phil. 2.5; 1 Cor. 2.16).
One may, perhaps, suppress the divinizing implications of these passages, but not of those that say that believers will become the righteousness

---

83 *Ibid.*, 45–6. What believers share in, Starr says, is not "Deity, as in the apoth-
    eosis of human beings, but in some specific attributes belonging to Christ"
    (*ibid.*, 47; cf. 109, 189, 232). "Apotheosis" is here used as a pejorative term re-
    ferring to a Hellenistic form of deification (which for Starr means sharing in
    God's essence). Starr will later allow that 2 Peter speaks of deification in the
    sense of "the participation in and enjoyment of specific divine attributes and
    qualities" ("Does 2 Peter 1:4 Speak of Deification?" 85, 90).
84 *Doctrine of Deification*, 84.
85 *Ibid.*, 81–82.
86 *Ibid.*, 85. The logic of Russell's argument is maintained by Paul Collins (*Partak-
    ing in Divine Nature*, 46).
87 *Theōsis*, 4. The authors ask the reader to examine the "deification concepts" in
    Col 1:9; 27; 2:10; 3:10; Eph 3:19; 4:23–24; 5:1.

of God' (2 Cor. 5.21), and after death 'will also bear the image of the man of heaven' (1 Cor. 15.49)." When put in this form, the notion of deification in Paul is enticing, but has not yet reached the level of argument. What we have is still sketchy—mere quotations of unexplained proof texts which can only whet the appetite.

The real exegetical labor of arguing for a notion of deification in Paul is performed by Finlan in a later essay.[88] Here, Finlan examines several of Paul's soteriological ideas which, he believes, cumulatively constitute a Pauline version of deification. The first idea is that of the spiritual (or pneumatic) body.[89] *Pace* N. T. Wright, Paul's spiritual body is—so Finlan—not just a body animated by Spirit. The spiritual body is a body which differs in *kind* from a physical body because of a difference of "*life force, nativity, and substance.*"[90] Emphasizing the category of substance, Finlan says that the change from the psychic to the pneumatic body is an "ontological" change.[91] This ontological change is expressed in Paul's terms as a transformation, which Finlin closely associates with resurrection.[92] Resurrection life, Finlan notes, begins with faith. Its moral outcome is an "ability to discern God's will" (1 Cor 2:16; Rom 12:2), and "a willingness to manifest God's love," which exemplifies the "unselfish character of Christ" (Phil 2:5).[93] Coupled with the moral transformation in this life is the metaphysical transformation in the next. After being fully resurrected with Christ, believers will reflect God's glory. Reflecting God's 'glory,' for Finlan, includes both the outward shining and the inward growth in spiritual knowledge and character.[94] Finlan concludes that "gaining an ability to discern the will of God [the moral element], and being transformed into Christ-likeness [the metaphysical element][95]... can truly be called theosis [or deification]."[96]

Michael Gorman's recent book, *Inhabiting the Cruciform God*, carries on the work of Sanders and Finlan with a view toward deification. For Gorman, "participation" is the key term used to define "theosis," a term

---

88 "Can we Speak of *Theosis* in Paul?" in *Partakers of the Divine Nature*, 68–80.
89 *Ibid.*, 68.
90 *Ibid.*, 69, italics his.
91 *Ibid.*, 70.
92 *Ibid.*, 72–73.
93 *Ibid*, 74.
94 *Ibid.*, 75.
95 Finlan says that being "Christified" does not mean becoming Christ, but rather "Christ-like in substance and character" (*Ibid.*, 79).
96 *Ibid.*, 78.

which he explains with a rich array of Pauline theological concepts: transformation, kenosis, cruciformity, and Spirit-empowered conformity to God in Christ.[97] In chapter 2 (the "soul of the book"[98]), Gorman reads justification as participation in God, meaning "co-crucifixion with Christ." Co-crucifixion is a particularly Pauline mode of becoming "like God."[99] This likeness to God is conceptualized as holiness (chapter 3), which Gorman understands mainly in terms of the character of God and Christ.[100] Here Gorman shows his tendency to emphasize the social, moral, and (especially in chapter 4) the political dimensions of Pauline deification.[101]

My own contribution, "2 Corinthians 3:18 and Its Implications for Theosis,"[102] was developed from an insight of Cuthbert Lattey,[103] who saw Paul's theology of becoming God's image in terms of deification. In this article, there were two basic observations. First, becoming "the same image" as Christ does not mean (as some argue) *only* becoming like Christ in his humanness. For Paul, Christ as image of God (2 Cor 4:4) is the divine image, representing the power and nature of God. Becoming that image, therefore, carries implications for deification. Second, deification in Paul does not mean fusion with the Godhead. This is a lingering misconception commonly used to discount the idea of Pauline deification, and is rightly discarded.

The recent book by Ben Blackwell (*Christosis: Pauline Soteriology in Light of Deification in Irenaeus and Cyril of Alexandria*) shows how two Christian authors in late antiquity (Irenaeus and Cyril) read Pauline soteriology in terms of deification. The interpretations of these two authors is important, because it shows how Paul was read by those closer to his world and to his horizon of understanding. In this respect, Blackwell's study brings us closer to a historical reading of Paul (i.e., a reading conversant with the concepts and interpretive possibilities of Paul's

97 *Inhabiting the Cruciform God: Kenosis, Justification, and Theosis in Paul's Narrative Soteriology* (Grand Rapids: Eerdmans, 2009), 7.
98 *Ibid.*, 2.
99 *Ibid.*, 90.
100 *Ibid.*, 112.
101 See further Gorman's article on "Romans: The First Christian Treatise on Theosis," *JTI* 5 (2011): 13–34.
102 *JTI* 2 (2008): 117–133.
103 See his short article "The Deification of Man in Clement of Alexandria: Some Further Notes," *Journal of Theological Studies* 17 (1916): 257–62.

own world), even if the historical dimension is limited to the categories of later Christian theology.

Results

A few brief evaluative comments are in order. In the first half of the twentieth century, the rejection of a Pauline version of deification was, I believe, largely based on a misunderstanding of what Pauline deification is. *Pauline deification does not involve fusion with the Godhead or loss of personality*. This is to misunderstand Paul and (I might add) the Greek mysteries. Pauline deification cannot be rejected based on this misconception.

Russell's more recent reasons for rejecting deification in Paul are different but still problematic. His view that Christ was not called "God" unequivocally before the second century (although technically wrong, if John 1:1 was composed in the late first century) does not mean that Paul and other first-century thinkers did not think of and worship Christ as a divine being.[104] That Paul, moreover, did not have "a fixed technical term for participatory union with Christ" is beside the point, since a variety of terms—whether technical or not—can still amount to a notion of deification. Finally, that Paul expressed his ideas about participatory union in metaphors is no argument that these metaphors cannot express the idea of deification. Here Russell assumes that metaphors are not "conceptual language."[105] To the contrary! Metaphors can be nicely engineered to express the concept of deification. The Greek fathers indicate this by using metaphors that they explicitly intend to connote deification realistically understood.[106] (This is not to say, *pace* Russell, that Christian deification was universally viewed as a metaphor.) The model of deification is thus a real possibility through which to understand Paul's soteriology.

---

104 See on this score Larry Hurtado, *Lord Jesus Christ: Devotion to Jesus in Earliest Christianity* (Grand Rapids: Eerdmans, 2003), 134–54.

105 *Doctrine of Deification*, 11.

106 Russell's arguments also depend on the idea that Paul has a "*doctrine*" of deification. This term calls up images of a systematic and consistent teaching. In this sense, Paul does not have a doctrine of almost anything. Although I am not entirely opposed to the idea that Paul has a "doctrine" of deification in the sense of a simple *teaching*, I will prefer to speak of a "vision," "idea," or "form" of deification.

Finlan and Gorman have greatly advanced the study of Paul and deification by allowing Paul, as best as possible, to define the notion himself. Here we are far from the language of fusion and loss of personality supposedly present in the mystery religions. These scholars recognize that we cannot fit Paul's soteriology to the mold of reconstructed motifs drawn from obscure sources. If Paul presents a notion of deification, it must be understandable in terms of Paul's own thought world and horizon.

Where Finlan and Gorman fall short, however, is a lack of historical discussion of deification in light of the Greco-Roman sources.[107] Reading these two scholars, one gets the impression that Paul's understanding of deification was untouched by outside influence, or uniformly hostile to other Greco-Roman forms of deification. Indeed, Gorman suggests that Pauline deification can have nothing to do with other versions of deification in the Mediterranean world (he especially notes ruler cult), since these are "unChristian."[108] But it seems here that the pendulum has swung too far away from a religio-historical understanding of Paul. If we cut off Paul from other discourses of deification in his time—and yet claim that he taught (or that his teaching amounted to) deification—we do not possess real historical criteria for assessing that claim.

Blackwell's study of Paul in light of deification in Irenaeus and Cyril is an interesting alternative approach to the topic. Even though it does not use a strictly historical method, a *Wirkungsgeschichte* approach has a valid place in deification research. Nevertheless, to let Irenaeus and Cyril alone provide the categories of interpretation for Paul is to me a tragic decision.[109] These two heresiologists are prone to make totaliz-

---

107 Gross offered, in *La divinisation*, about 50 pages of "Hellenic Analogs" to deification. Russell's *Doctrine of Deification* devotes about the same space to deification in the Greco Roman world. Both are somewhat general and perfunctory.

108 Gorman, *Inhabiting*, 4. Cf. Paul Collins: "Christian understandings of deification may easily be confused with pagan notions such as 'apotheōsis'" (*Partaking in Divine Nature*, 3). For a critique of this persistent bias in Christian scholarship, see Christoph Auffarth, "Herrscherkult und Christuskult," in *Die Praxis der Herrscherverehrung in Rom und seinen Provinzen* (eds. Hubert Cancik and Konrad Hitzl; Tübingen: Mohr Siebeck, 2003), 283–318.

109 Blackwell provides four basic principles of patristic theology culled from Irenaeus and Cyril: "1) the Creator-created distinction, 2) a Trinitarian God, 3) likeness through participation (which entails distinction; otherwise, it would identification [*sic*]),and 4) new creation as re-creation (namely, somatic immor-

ing, metaphysical distinctions between God and creation as well as Christ and believer that are simply not present in Paul's letters. These distinctions were specifically designed to create an orthodoxy that protected the church from so-called "pagan" and "Gnostic" ideas. Based on the nature of his study and his own predilections, Blackwell has the tendency to read exactly these orthodox distinctions back into Paul—distinctions which were generated in late second and fifth century (proto-)orthodox polemics.[110] Would it not have been better to give some voice to a Clement of Alexandria or an Origen who do not construct their doctrines of deification in such open polemical opposition to a perceived non-Christian "other"? Clement is particularly apropos because he identifies deification as the appropriate destiny for the Christian "gnostic" (thus calling into question any final opposition between Christianity and "gnostic" thought.) These Christian fathers also speak of deification based on Pauline theology, but tend to think outside the box Blackwell constructs around his argument—which is essentially the box created by later Christian orthodoxy.

There is perhaps a more fundamental problem with Blackwell's study which takes us back to the question of history. Although I think that his study (at least potentially) takes us a step closer to a historical reading of Paul, it would be problematic to *solely* define Pauline deification in terms of patristic interpretation because of the dangers of reading too much of later patristic doctrines of deification into Paul. The fathers of the church, though many were comfortable with the language of deification, did not create that language *ex nihilo* as they interpreted Paul. Although later patristic writers may have succeeded in creating a distinctly Christian form of deification, what Paul could and did understand about deification was grounded chiefly in his (Greco-Roman) culture. (Christian theology in Paul's time was still being invented.)[111] Thus if the claim that Paul's soteriology can be categorized

---

tality)" (*Christosis*, 108). All these patristic principles show up later in Blackwell's interpretation of Pauline soteriology.

110 Blackwell's language of "triune divine relationship" in Paul (*ibid.*, 254, 257–59), his neat distinction between divine attributes and divine essence (267), and his intense emphasis on the creator-creature divide for Paul (*passim*) seem to me to be colored by later theology. His apparent assumption that the idea of *creatio ex nihilo* exists in Paul (259) is simply unjustified (see ch. 9).

111 Blackwell is open to what he calls a "history of religions" approach to deification (*ibid.*, 14, 271). Ultimately, he chooses the path of reception history or

as a form of deification is in any way going to represent a historical judgment (and not merely a "theological construct"[112]), we must understand the meaning of deification in Paul's own time and culture. The diverse world of the ancient Mediterranean had forged, shaped, and refined the language of deification. This language continued to be used in various contexts as Paul wrote his letters. The historical measure, then, by which to judge whether Paul's language amounts to deification is the contemporaneous discourse of deification in the Greco-Roman world.

The Method of this Study

Simon Price, in his influential study of deification, argued that while we are obliged to redescribe the meaning of the ancients in our own terms, "still we must start by looking at the subject, as far as possible, *through their eyes*."[113] This study attempts to do just that. Paul, as already noted, did not invent the language of deification. In terms of strict vocabulary, he did not even use it. Thus in comparing Pauline soteriology and the discourse of deification, one cannot point to verbal parallels. One can only point to *conceptual* parallels, and specifically conceptual parallels that have to do with the structure of thought in a particular culture.[114] In Paul's culture, there is a reservoir of shared concepts about the divine and the human relation to the divine, as well as about the human potential to become divine that Paul employs.

The assumption here is the not-so-radical idea that Paul was influenced by his culture. The influence was not genetic, in the sense that Paul consciously borrowed a specific phrase or idea that can be traced in the existing literature. Rather, the influence was cultural, having to do with the integration of general notions and patterns of thought which are part of human socialization. We only get an inkling of

---

"history of interpretation" rather than a strictly historical investigation (15–25). The two approaches, as he notes on 23, are not opposed.

112 Blackwell, *Christosis*, 20.

113 *Rituals and Power: The Roman Imperial Cult in Asia Minor* (Cambridge: Cambridge University Press, 1984), 19, emphasis added.

114 L. Michael White and John T. Fitzgerald, "Quod est Comparandum: The Problem of Parallels" in *Early Christianity and Classical Culture: Comparative Studies in Honor of Abraham J. Malherbe*, eds. L. Michael White, John T. Fitzgerald and Thomas H. Olbricht (Leiden: Brill, 2003), 31.

these largely presupposed patterns of thought by reading a broad range of ancient sources.

Going along with this view is the basic conviction that Paul, though emically opposed to (religiously "other") features of his environment,[115] shared many of the assumptions and conceptual schemes of his milieu. Paul did not "Hellenize" Judaism (or Christianity). He was born into a Judaism already conversant with Greek and Roman culture for centuries. Deification in the Roman ruler cult is an idea which Paul most certainly would have rejected as something "other" and false. This does not mean that he did not share some of the logic of deification assumed in the ruler cult. That logic can only be unpacked through careful attention to the dominant cultural patterns of discourse around Paul.

In short, then, my method is to see how Paul was influenced on the cultural, "deep-structure" level of basic assumptions and conceptual frameworks. Thus I will not be drawing specific genetic links between Paul and Greco-Roman philosophy and ruler cult. Rather, I will be drawing out limited structural similarities (or analogies) between patterns of ideas in Paul's culture and specific aspects of Paul's soteriological thought. Based on these analogies, I will argue that it is appropriate to redescribe and categorize aspects of Paul's soteriology as constituting a form of deification.

Conclusion: A Working Definition of Deification, and Issues of Clarification

I cannot end this introduction without giving a working definition of deification. Such a definition must of necessity be general. This does not annul the fact that deification in the ancient world came in many types.[116] Such types can be described in terms of chronology (post-mortem? pre-mortem?), mode (through ritual? moral practice?), motivating power (divine benefaction? or through human action?), result (union with a greater deity or independent Godhood?), etc. All these

---

115   John M. G. Barclay, *Jews in the Mediterranean Diaspora: From Alexander to Trajan (323 BCE-177CE)* (Edinburgh: T&T Clark, 1996), 390–93.

116   For a taste of the variety of deification in the ancient world, see the charts in Hans Hauben, "Aspects du culte des souverains à l'epoque des Lagides," in *Egitto e Storia Antica dall'Ellenismo all'Eta Araba* (eds. Lucia Criscuolo and Giovanni Geraci; Bologna: Clueb, 1989), 441–467.

features, I believe, are more or less secondary characteristics—out-
growths of more fundamental conceptions. The basis of deification—
as I understand it—is sharing in *a* or *the* divine identity—that is, sharing
in those distinctive qualities which make (a) God (a) God. It is not
enough, in other words, to define deification in terms of "likeness"
to God.[117] For likeness is too vague in terms of content (*how* are two
beings alike?) and degree (*to what extent* are two beings alike?). Anything, strictly speaking, can be "like" anything else with respect to
some more basic element: a chair is like a mosquito in that both are
made of atoms. For "like" language to work, the likeness has to be defined with reference to specifically divine qualities. But not just any
qualities will do. The qualities must be constitutive of the divine identity. (I will discuss what these qualities are in chapters 1 and 7.) In this
way, participation in divine qualities results in a participation in the divine identity. Likeness language, in contrast, tends to distinguish the
identities of God and the deified. This is because likeness never
means identity. Participation means more than likeness. Likeness says
that "x is like y with respect to z." Participation, as I use the term,
says that "x and y share part of the identity of z without being fused
with z." Participation language, in other words, allows us to speak
about sharing identity. Two beings can participate in a single identity
while remaining distinct.[118] In short, then, deification is the participation in the divine identity of (a particular) God. This particular God
for Paul is the one he and his communities worshiped as "the Lord
Jesus Christ."

Two other points of clarification remain before we close. The first
regards my terminology for deification. I would like to avoid the term
"theosis." Even though the Neo-Platonist Damascius was comfortable

---

117 This is fairly standard practice among theological interpreters (Gorman, *Inhabiting*, 4–5; Finlin and Kharlamov, *Theōsis*, 1). This does not mean that they do
not specify in what *ways* believers are like God and/or Christ. This is not the
real issue. Ultimately I want to probe the appropriateness and sufficiency of
"like" language *per se*.

118 Blackwell does not want to transcend "likeness" language because he is worried
(I think wrongly) that going beyond "likeness" will lead to fusion models of
deification (i. e., the loss of distinction between humans and God) (*Christosis*,
106). Sharing the divine identity, however, does not involve a loss of distinction
between humans and God. Later theology recognizes this. Christ sharing the
divine identity of God the Father does not involve a fusion of the Father
and Christ or a loss of distinction.

using the term after it was coined by Gregory of Nazianzus, it is not the best term for a historical analysis.[119] In its modern manifestation, "theosis" is often preferred by Christian theological writers and exegetes to refer to the distinctly Christian version of deification.[120] Though this is sometimes not explicit, using the term "theosis" allows Christian readers to think of Christian forms deification as *essentially different* from non-Christian forms, which usually go under the name of "apotheosis."[121] Theosis is thus a term which Christian scholars feel much more able to control and shape as they see fit. The problem is that it subtly perpetuates the myth of the uniqueness of Christian deification. "Christian" deification (and here I would like to limit myself to its Pauline instantiation) may be distinctive, but in order to mean anything historically, it cannot be cut off from the meaning(s) of deification in Paul's culture.[122]

Second, as was indicated above, some interpreters have associated a Pauline version of deification with a Pauline "mysticism."[123] I want also

---

119 The term was used by the late Christian writers Ps-Dionysus, Maximus the Confessor and John Damascene (Russell, *Doctrine of Deification*, 341).

120 Frederick Norris has this to say about the term theosis: "It was not first a Christian word nor always employed by only Christians after they made it central. From within his deep contemplative life and from previous Church Tradition the Theologian [Gregory of Nazianzus] picked it up, cleaned it up [!] and filled it with Christian sense [!]. He and his fellow theologians took it captive and used it to speak about Christian realities" ("Deification: Consensual and Cogent," 415). Blackwell feels the need to admit that theosis is a "later," and thus "anachronistic" term when used of Paul (*Christosis*, 263). Here he implicitly acknowledges that "theosis" only means "*Christian* deification." The idea (and terminology) of deification *in the Greco-Roman world*, however, precedes Paul by several centuries.

121 In the words of the theologian Paul Gavrilyuk: "To their credit, most present-day critics of deification recognize that pagan *apotheosis* and Christian *theosis* are not quite the same thing" ("The Retrieval of Deification," 649).

122 I say this in partial condemnation of myself, since I have used the language of "theosis." My point is not that the term is wrong, but that it better fits the trajectory of theological interpretation. The term "Christosis," preferred by Blackwell (*Christosis*, 264–267), presents little problem provided that we understand it as designating a Pauline form of *deification* (since Christ is a Pauline God) and not something somehow "less" than deification. The term is serviceable because it highlights the fact that the Pauline version of deification is assimilation to the God Christ, and thus only indirect assimilation to Paul's high God (or "the Father").

123 The connection is present in two essays by Martin Dibelius, "Glaube und Mystik bei Paulus," and "Paulus und die Mystik" both in *Botschaft und Geschichte:*

to avoid this term—not because I am uninterested in Pauline religious experience, but because "mysticism" is usually associated with experiences that are exclusive, individual (or subjective), non-conceptual, and which sometimes involve fusion with a particular God. In my reading, Pauline deification is (1) not an experience limited to a few, (2) is mostly worked out in community, (3) can be explained using concepts, and (4) does not involve a confused mixing with divinity.

We now turn to the task ahead—asking the most basic question that we can about deification, namely, "what is a God?"

Gesammelte Aufsätze (ed. Günther Bornkamm; 2 vols.; Tübingen: Mohr Siebeck 1956), 1.94–116; 134–59. For more recent research on Paul and mysticism, see Josef Blank, "Gnosis und Agape: Zur christologischen Struktur paulinischer Mystik," in *Grundfragen christlicher Mystik: Wissenschaftliche Studientagung Theologia Mystica in Weingarten vom 7.–10. November 1985* (ed. Margot Schmidt; Stuttgart-Bad Cannstatt: Friedrich Frommann, 1987), 1–13; Daniel Marguerat "La Mystique de l'Apôtre Paul," in *Paul De Tarse: Congrès de l'ACFEB* (ed. Jacques Schlosser; Paris: Les Éditions du Cerf, 1996), 307–29.

Part I:
The Context of Deification in Paul

Chapter 1:
What is a God?
Defining Divinity in the Greco-Roman World

> "What is a God (τί θεός)? Ruling
> power (τὸ κρατοῦν).
>
> —Menander *ap.* Stob.,
> *Anth.* 3.32.11

Introduction

"At all times," writes James Tabor, "the historian must consider the various indigenous categories and points of reference which form the context in which discussions and debates about 'divine' status make sense."[1] This procedure is surely correct, and appropriate for historical scholarship of the Bible. Strangely, however, when contemporary biblical scholars turn to study deification, they rarely attempt to excavate those "indigenous categories" which shape the content of divinity in the ancient Mediterranean. Consequently, scholars who study deification in Paul have not yet even laid the groundwork for what deification means.[2] To put it simply: if one is to understand deification in its most basic sense as becoming (a) God, one cannot get very far without first asking τί θεός;—"*What is a God?*" (that is, in Paul's culture). This question assumes that "God" in Paul's culture is not necessarily defined in the same way that it is today. It also assumes that in Paul's world θεός is not a proper name, but a predicate with definite semantic content.[3]

---

1   *Things Unutterable: Paul's Ascent to Paradise in its Greco-Roman, Judaic, and Early Christian Contexts* (Lanham: University Press of America, 1986), 78.

2   Blackwell provides "a brief excursus" on immortality and the Gods on *Christosis*, 46–47. His discussion is cursory, and dependent on some rather outdated sources like Kleinknecht's article on "θεός" in *TDNT*, and a 1959 article by Werner Jaeger.

3   Marianne Meye Thompson, *The God of the Gospel of John* (Grand Rapids: Eerdmans, 2001), 20–22, 28. For this point, Thompson is dependent on Simon Price, "Gods and Emperors: The Greek Language of the Roman Imperial Cult," *JHS* 104 (1984): 79.

In the previous chapter I defined deification more precisely as sharing in (a) God's identity. Our task, then, is to study Paul's culture to uncover the *content* of that divine identity. Accordingly, the chapter falls into two parts: (1) the meaning of "God" (θεός) in the larger Greco-Roman culture, and (2) the meaning of "God" (אלהים, θεός) in the smaller Jewish subculture. First, however, some basic objections to the question must be addressed.

Formulating the Right Question

For those in Christian theology, "What is a God?" might sound like an odd question. Indeed, if divinity is anything like the "Wholly Other" described by Rudolf Otto, God cannot be conceptualized at all.[4] In the language of Anselm, God is "that than which nothing greater can be conceived." Thus it seems that a kind of impiousness—or downright stupidity—attaches to the question "what is a God?" Greek philosophy (specifically Middle Platonism) made the essence of God ineffable!

To the historian of religion, however, "What is a God?" is a perfectly legitimate question to ask. Otto himself realized that religion necessarily traded in concepts, and that such conceptual discourse about God (θεολογία) was a legitimate enterprise. Furthermore, although Middle Platonic philosophers emphasized the unknowability of God's essence, they were referring to the primal or high God beyond the universe and beyond being.[5] Generally speaking, the peoples of the first-century Mediterranean world did not envision their Gods as totally beyond space and time, beyond the world, and beyond being itself. Gods were real beings who lived within time and in the upper stories of the cosmos. In the words of Cicero, "This world is as a common house (*communis ... domus*) of Gods and human beings" (*Nat. d.* 2.62 §154). Readers who suppose that the Jewish and Christian God(s) were on a totally different plane should be reminded how active and this-worldly the biblical God really is. With the exception of Philo and some others, Greek philosophy had not pushed the Jewish God beyond this world and beyond being. The Platonic picture of God would not enter Christianity until the work of Apologists such as Justin Martyr. Even then, the

---

4   *The Idea of the Holy* (London: Oxford University Press, 1950).
5   John M. Dillon, *The Middle Platonists: A Study of Platonism, 80 B.C. to A.D. 220* (2d ed.; London : Duckworth, 1996), 46.

philosophical picture of an extracosmic, metaphysically transcendent God would not have a great effect on the Christian masses. Paul, although his concept of God is by no means simplistic, is certainly not thinking in terms of technical Greek philosophical theology. Paul's God is not ineffable—beyond human speech and reason. Just as his contemporaries, Paul regularly speaks of God without qualm or qualification. It is from these statements that the perceived nature of divinity (as it could be known to human beings) becomes clear to us. In sum, for ancient Mediterranean peoples (including Paul) divinity was not only the *mysterium tremendum* (shutting out whatever is human and earthly), but also the *mysterium fascinans*—involving the human, and drawing it within.

The correctness of the question, "what is a God?" however, has also been impugned as *overly* philosophical. This is the charge of Ittai Gradel in his book *Emperor Worship and Roman Religion*. Such a question, he says, removes us from the realm of *practiced* religion, where "what is a God?" was never asked. It was never asked because all divinity in (Greco-)Roman religion was, according to Gradel, "relative" (classed with humanity on a sliding-scale) not "absolute" (in a class of its own). The scholar who focuses on belief about the Gods and their nature is thus already "Christianizing" the material.[6]

Although Gradel's points help to balance out the biases of scholarship before his time, one wonders whether he has not swung too far to the other side. First of all, on the issue of philosophy, it is not really possible to make a sharp division between philosophical and non-philosophical ideas. David Levene points out that "philosophy, no less than other genres of ancient writing, was necessarily developed in the context of the conceptual frameworks familiar to the wider society. The very least that can be said is that philosophical arguments have to be so framed as to make sense to their contemporaries, and in fact the influ-

---

6   *Emperor Worship*, 28. Gradel repeatedly emphasizes the difference between "absolute" (Christian) divinity and "relative divinity" (see, e.g., 330). It is odd, then, that he makes Seneca argue against Claudius' "absolute" divinity in *Apocolocyntosis* (327). At death—when no emperor had power—the only thing maintaining their divine status, says Gradel, was belief in their "absolute" divinity (335). How then, according to Gradel, can there be no such thing as "absolute divinity" for Romans? Gradel also rightly notes that in the sacrificial ritual, the distinction between people and Gods was "clear and unequivocal" (30).

ences are often far closer even than that."[7] Philosophers like Aristotle
intentionally used and adapted ideas from traditional theology as ana-
logues for philosophical considerations.[8] Philosophers are often those
who thought explicitly about the question, "what is a God?" and it
would be unwise to eliminate their testimony due to *a priori* definitions
of religion as essentially practice. Though we must use philosophical
texts with caution (carefully balancing them with ideas from other sources and genres), I believe that they can be used, and will be used in what
follows.

Secondly, religious practice (or ritual), I think, assumes some mod-
icum of belief. "[W]hile 'belief,'" writes Levene, "was not the primary
criterion by which the Romans assessed the correctness or otherwise of
religious behaviour, Roman writings on religion, as on other topics,
constantly present, explicitly or implicitly, accounts of the conceptual
assumptions underlying religious practices and religious narratives, and
indeed it is often hard to make sense of those practices and narratives
without taking into account the underlying assumptions."[9]

Focusing on beliefs cannot be called "Christianizing" given that the
beliefs of early Christians—like those of the other ancient Mediterranean peoples—tended to grow out of practices as well. Paul, although
he might have adapted the meaning of baptism (Rom 6:1–6), did
not invent the practice. It is false to assume that, for Christians, all practice derives from belief. It is also false to assume that, for Christians, beliefs are always valued more highly than rituals (an assertion which has
somewhat of a Protestant ring). The assumption, furthermore, that
Christianity (as a religion of belief) is something fundamentally different
than other religions "could itself be the product of a Christianizing bias
in favor of Christian uniqueness," notes Charles King. "One cannot
simply assume a priori that the presence of ideas within Christianity

---

7   "What is a God? Defining the Divine in Rome," *Transactions of the American Philological Association*, 142, forthcoming spring, 2012.
8   For this argument, see Richard Bodéüs, *Aristotle and the Theology of the Living Immortals* (trans. Jan Edward Garrett; Albany: State University of New York, 2000), 15–16, 27, 41, 53.
9   "What is a God?" forthcoming, n.1. See further M. Linder and John Scheid, "Quand croire c'est faire. Le problème de la croyance dans la Rome ancienne," *Archives de Sciences Sociales des Religions* 38 (1993): 47–61.

constitutes evidence of the absence of those ideas in another tradition."[10]

As for the notion of "absolute" divinity, Levene has shown that there is little doubt that in Greco-Roman religion deity was something "absolute" in the sense of being different from humans in kind and not merely in degree. This point is absolutely central, though it contradicts much of what biblical scholars have claimed about Greco-Roman views of deity. I will return to this point in chapter 3.

Divinity in the Greco-Roman World

We are now ready to tackle our question: "What is a God?" in the Greco-Roman world.[11] Simon Price argues that "there were no institutional controls and no uncontroversial criteria for the use of 'is a *theos* [God]'" in the Greek world.[12] There were, in fact, various kinds of Gods. In the first century C.E., Aëtius distinguishes seven kinds: (1) Manifest and Aerial Gods (e.g., Heaven and Earth), (2) Harmful Gods (e.g., the Erinyes, Ares), (3) Benefactor Gods (e.g., Zeus, Hera, Demeter), (4) Abstract entities (e.g., Hope, Justice), (5) Deified Passions (e.g., Eros, Aphrodite, Desire), (6) the Gods of poetic mythology (e.g., Hyperion and Iapetos), and (7) Gods who were once men but honored for their benefactions (e.g., Heracles, Dionysus, and the Dioscuri) (*SVF* 2.1009 = *Plac.* 1.6). What was it about all these particular beings that allowed them to be called "Gods"?

The place to get a foothold for our inquiry is the corpus of the first Greek theologian, Homer. Homer (or the Homeric poets) quite frequently uses the epithet "godlike" (θεοείκελος, ἰσόθεος, ἀντίθεος, etc.) to describe his heroes. To be sure, sometimes this epithet may have simply been metrically convenient. But we cannot assume that the poet therefore employs the term haphazardly, or has a blurred conception of what it means. As we examine the uses of "godlike" for various figures, a relatively coherent picture of the adjective's meaning emerges.

---

10 "The Organization of Roman Religious Beliefs," *Classical Antiquity* 22 (2003): 276.
11 For the similarity of Greek and Roman Gods, note Fritz Graf, "Les dieux des Grecs et le dieu des Romains: Plus ça change …" *Archiv für Religionsgeschichte* 5 (2003): 131–45.
12 "Gods and Emperors," 81.

Among well-known figures, Achilles takes first place. Odysseus calls Achilles "godlike" (θεοείκελος) and a "good fighter" in the same breath (*Il.* 1.131; 19.155). When Achilles goes out for battle, dressed in the armor made for him by Hephaestus, he terrifies the Trojans by his resemblance to "the murderous war God [Ares]" (*Il.* 20.46). As Achilles charges Hector in a surge of rage and passion, he is described as "equal to a God" (δαίμονι ἶσος) (*Il.* 20.447; cf. 19.279, 297; 23.80). Priam, in book 24 of the *Iliad*, wonders at the "size and beauty" of Achilles, "for he is like the Gods" (θεοῖσι γὰρ ἄντα ἐῴκει) (630–31). Similarly, in the war council Agamemnon is "powerful ... with eyes and head like Zeus ... like Ares for girth, and with the chest of Poseidon; like some ox of the herd pre-eminent among others, a bull, who stands conspicuous in the huddling cattle" (*Il.* 2.477–81, trans. Richard Lattimore). Diomedes son of Tydeus is taken to be a God after a successful slaughtering of Trojans (*Il.* 5.177, 183). Hector, greatest warrior of Troy, was "a God among men" (θεὸς ἔσκε μετ'ἀνδράσιν), according to his father Priam, "for he did not seem like one who was a child of a mortal man, but of a God" (*Il.* 24.258–59); he is "a man like the murderous war God" (*Il.* 11.295). He is even prayed to as a God (*Il.* 22.394). Menelaus of Sparta, when he slings his sword around himself and puts on "fair sandals" appears "like a God in presence" (θεῷ ἐναλίγκιος ἄντην) (*Od.* 4.310). Nestor appears "as an immortal" to Telemachus. This is apparently because "the righteousness and thought in his mind outstrip others, and they say he has been lord over three generations of men" (*Od* 3.244–46). Patroclus, son of Menoetius, a "man like a God" (ἰσόθεος φώς) (*Il.* 9.211) comes out "like the war God" at the call of Achilles (*Il.* 11.602–03). "[W]ith the force of the running war God" Patroclus charges the Trojans, "screaming a terrible cry, and three times he cut down nine men; but as for the fourth time he swept in, like something greater than human" (δαίμονι ἶσος) (*Il.* 16.783–87; cf. 16.705). He is also "a counselor equal to the Gods" (θεόφιν μήστωρ ἀτάλαντος) (*Il.* 17.477, *Od.* 3.110). Polyphemus (the Cyclops) is "like a God" (ἀντίθεον) because his "power is greatest over all the Cyclopes" (*Od.* 1.70–71). Theseus, a man "in the likeness of the immortals" (ἐπιείκελον ἀθανάτοισιν) (*Il.* 1.265–67) calls Odysseus "godlike" (θεῖος) because he is "beyond all other men in mind" (*Od.* 1.65–66). Mentor calls Odysseus "godlike" (θεῖος) because "he was kind, like a father" (*Od.* 2.233–34). Calypso, "shining among divinities" had hopes to make Odysseus immortal (*Od.* 5.136, 209). Athena herself proclaims, in the form of a herald, that Odysseus, with refer-

ence to his shape, "is like the immortals" (δέμας ἀθανάτοισιν ὁμοῖος)
(*Od.* 8.14). Telemachus, when the true form of his father Odysseus
had been revealed to him, "was astonished and turned his eyes in the
other direction, fearing this must be a God, and spoke aloud: '...Surely
you are one of the Gods who hold the high heaven (μάλα τις θεός ἐσσι,
τοὶ οὐρανὸν εὐρὺν ἔχουσιν) ...'" (*Od.* 16.178, 183).[13]

After this barrage of examples, one is prepared to answer what
makes the Homeric human godlike. Godlikeness can, as should be evident, be the result of many things. Nevertheless, the touchstone of divinity for Homer is in some way to exceed normal mortal limitations
and expectations. To be godlike is to be extraordinary in mind—but
more often in body. The characteristics of divinity are often in the superlative: it is to be the biggest, the fastest, the strongest, the cleverest,
the most beautiful, the most glorious. It is to have more power, whatever its manifestation. "The Gods," as Homer says, "have power to do
all things" (θεοὶ δέ τε πάντα δύνανται) (*Od.* 10.306).

Later writings agree that there was a wide array of qualities that
qualified one to be divine: stability,[14] beatitude,[15] self-sufficiency,[16] im-

---

13 Other not so well-known figures include (1) Arete, wife of Alcinous the Phaiacian, who is viewed as a Goddess among her people, since (according to the
testimony of her daughter Nausicaa) "there is no good intelligence that she herself lacks. She dissolves quarrels, even among men, when she favors them"
(*Od.* 7.71–74); (2) Eurymachus son of Polybus "whom," says Telemachus,
"now the people of Ithaca look on as on divinity, since he is their best man
by far" (*Od.* 15.520–21); (3) Euryalus son of Naubolus, the Phaiacian, "a
man like murderous Ares" since "he was best of all the Phaiacians in build
and beauty" except for Laodamas (8.116–17); (4) Hecamede, with lovely
hair, is called "the woman like the immortals" after mixing a healing potion
for wounded Machaon (*Il.* 11.637); (5) Nausicaa, daughter of Alkinoös the
Phaiacian, "like the immortal goddesses for stature and beauty" (*Od.* 6.16).
Odysseus likens here to Artemis, "the daughter of great Zeus, for beauty, figure, and stature," and asks if she is a "mortal or a Goddess?" (6.150–52).

14 In the *Statesman,* Plato puts into the mouth of his Visitor the statement that:
"Remaining permanently in the same state and condition (τὸ κατὰ ταὐτὰ καὶ
ὡσαύτως ἔχειν ἀεί), and being permanently the same (καὶ ταὐτὸν εἶναι), belongs
only to the most divine things of all (τοῖς πάντων θειοτάτοις), and by its nature
body is not of this order" (269d5–7, trans. C. J. Rowe). Cf. Arist. *Cael.* 1.9,
279a31–35.

15 Epicurus, for instance, wrote that it was a "common conception" (κοινὴ νόησις)
of humankind that God is an "incorruptible and blissful living creature" (ζῷον
ἄφθαρτον καὶ μακάριον) (*Letter to Menoeceus ap.* Diog. Laert., *Vita Philosoph.* 10.123). The two criteria of divinity given by the Epicureans, according
to Cotta, are "blessedness" and "eternity" (Cic., *Nat. d.*, 1.68).

perturbability,[17] goodness,[18] beauty,[19] etc. Nevertheless, a review of Greek literature indicates that the two fundamental qualities of divinity were immortality and power.[20]

Immortality

The primary divine attribute is, according to the classic study of W. K. C. Guthrie, immortality.[21] "*Athanatos* (immortal) is an adjective, and may therefore be used in conjunction with *theos* [God]. But it may equally well stand alone, and its meaning then is unambiguous: it means *god* and nothing else, just as *theos* does."[22] This judgment still holds today. In the words of the poet: "Celebrate the sacred race of immortals, always existing, who were born from Earth and starry Heaven" (Hes., *Theog.* 105–106).

For the importance of immortality to the basic structure of divinity, consider the following primary evidence. "What is the divine?" the philosopher Thales once asked. "What has neither beginning (ἀρχήν) nor end (τέλος)" (*ap.* Clem., *Strom.* 5.96.4). In a fragment of Stobaeus we read that Socrates was once asked: "What is God?" He replied,

---

16   Aristotle, *Pol.* 1253a.

17   Cic., *Nat. d*, 1.85.

18   Philostrat., *Vita Apoll.* 8.5.7.

19   Charax, *FGH* 103 Frag 13, end.

20   Cf. Walter Pötscher, "ΘΕΟΣ: Studien zur älteren griechischen Gottesvorstellung" (Diss. Wien, 1953), 12, 82. This is not to say that these qualities make up the immutable essence of divinity. The diversity of conceptions shows that there is no pure "essence" of divinity in Greco-Roman culture. There is simply a cluster of qualities which shared a family resemblance. In other words, divinity is a polythetic category (for this term, see King, "Organization of Roman Religious Beliefs," 285–86). That is, there are a variety of traits that constitute the set called "divinity"; no one member of the class has all the traits, but each member has some. Thus one member in the class will have traits 1, 2, and 3; another 2, 3, and 4, another 3, 4, and 5. Rarely is there a complete overlap. Nevertheless, even in a polythetic set, some criteria are more prominent and held by all members of the set (*ibid.*, 288). Power and divinity, I am arguing, are these more prominent criteria. If we keep the metaphor of family resemblances, divine power and immortality serve as roots in the great family tree of divine characteristics.

21   *The Greeks and their Gods* (London: Methuen, 1950).

22   *Ibid.*, 115. He goes so far as to say that, "To believe in the immortality of the soul was the same as saying: 'Man is a kind of god'" (*ibid.*, 116).

"What is immortal and everlasting" (ἀθάνατον καὶ ἀίδιον) (*Anth.* 1.29a). Sophocles wrote that "to the Gods alone old age does not come, nor ever the doom of death; all other things all-powerful time obliterates" (*Oed. col.* 607–09). These quotes can only be counted as representative, not exhaustive.

Aristotle gives us a fuller theory of divine immortality. "The activity of a God," he writes, "is immortality" (θεοῦ δ'ἐνέργεια ἀθανασία) (*Cael.* 2.3, 286a9; cf. *Top.* 4.2, 122b13–14).[23] The Philosopher, however, makes a distinction between immortality—the extension of the current kind of life—and eternal life, which he views as a different *kind* of life.[24] Immortality is simply a modification of life (*Top.* 4.5, 126b36–37). The Gods are immortal, for Aristotle, because they have *eternal* life, which involves agelessness and blessedness. So Aristotle defines a God as "an eternal living being" (*Metaph.* 12.7.9, 1072b29–30). Gods must be eternal, for what comes to be is necessarily mortal and corruptible (*An. pr.* 2.22, 68a9–10; *Top.* 5.7, 137a36–37; 6.6, 145b22–23).

Immortality as central to the identity of divine beings is not simply a notion of the most ancient poets and philosophers. In the first century C.E., Seneca writes, "In truth, a good man differs from (a) God in the element of time only (*quidem bonus tempore tantum a deo differt*)" (*Prov.* 1.5). A generation later, Plutarch writes that "Deity is held to be distinguished by three characteristics: imperishability, power, and virtue" (*Arist.* 6.2–4). Likewise, Sextus Empiricus holds it to be a common conception that God is "blessed and imperishable (ἄφθαρτος) … exhibiting very great power (πλεῖστη δύναμις) in the universe" (*Math.* 9.44). The mention of power brings us to the second basic identifying feature of deity.

---

23 Cf. *Metaphysics* 12.7.9, 1072b: "We hold then that God is a living being, eternal, most good; and therefore life and a continuous eternal existence belongs to God; for that is what God is."

24 Bodéüs, *Living Immortals*, 115.

Power

In the ancient world, "Power was the essence of divinity."[25] This summary judgment of Robin Lane Fox nicely sums up the matter (though "essence" is not to be taken in a philosophical sense). Besides immortality, no one single quality better represented Godhead to the common person in the Hellenistic world. To prove this thesis, I again turn to survey the most influential and representative primary evidence I can gather.

"No man," says the wise Nestor, "not even the strongest, can resist the purpose of Zeus, since his power is far greater than ours" (*Il.* 8.143–44). All the Immortals are much "stronger" or "better" (φέρτεροι) than the boldest of heroes (*Il.* 20.367–68). Hesiod says: "For He of the immortals all is King and Lord / With God none else in might may strive (αὐτὸς γὰρ πάντων βασιλεὺς καὶ κοίρανός ἐστιν ἀθανάτων· σέο δ' οὔτις ἐρήρισται κράτος ἄλλος)" (frg. 308 West & Merkelbach, *ap.* Clem. Alex., *Protr.* 7. 73. 3).[26] "For it is light expenditure," we read in the *Bacchae* of Euripides, "to consider that *this* has power (ἰσχύν): whatever is divine (ὃ τι ποτ' ἄρα τὸ δαιμόνιον)" (893–894). This is a presupposition virtually universal in Greek poetry.

Later philosophy agrees with the poets. "For this is God and divine power (τοῦτο γὰρ θεὸν καὶ θεοῦ δύναμιν εἶναι): to rule, but not to be ruled (κρατεῖν, ἀλλὰ μὴ κρατεῖσθαι); and God is the strongest of all (πάντων κράτιστον εἶναι). Consequently, insofar as a being does not have power, it is not God (καθὸ μὴ κρείττων, κατὰ τοσοῦτον οὐκ εἶναι θεόν)" (Ps. Arist., *De Melisso, de Xenophane, de Gorgia* 3, 977a 27–29 = DK 21 A 28). Xenophon (ca. 430–354 B.C.E.) has Socrates affirm that "the divine is the strongest (τὸ μὲν θεῖον κράτιστον), and that which approaches most closely to the divine (τὸ δ' ἐγγυτάτω τοῦ θείου) is that which most closely approaches supreme strength (ἐγγυτάτω τοῦ κρατίστου)" (*Mem.* 1.6.10).

---

25 *Pagans and Christians* (London: Viking, 1986), 98. For power in Late Antiquity, see Arthur Darby Nock, *Essays on Religion in the Ancient World* (ed. Z. Stewart; 2 vols. Oxford: Clarendon, 1972), 1.34–45. Speaking of "power" is admittedly abstract (since power was experienced in particular ways through particular deities); yet this kind of abstraction is necessary to say anything theologically coherent in the sea of diversity called "Greek religion."

26 Frg. 308 in R. Merkelbach and M.L. West, eds., *Fragmenta Hesiodea* (Oxford: Clarendon Press, 1967).

Power is most often conceived of as the ability to rule. Accordingly, Plato has his Socrates assert that "the divine (τὸ μὲν θεῖον) is what by nature can rule and lead" (ἄρχειν τε καὶ ἡγεμονεύειν) (*Phaed.* 80a). Pyrrhus is praised by Timon for "alone among human beings showing hegemony (ἡγεμονεύων) in the manner of a God (θεοῦ τρόπον)" (Diog. Laert., *Vit. Philosoph.* 9.65). Menander in one of his plays has the line, "for what is strongest (τὸ κρατοῦν) is now thought to be God (θεός)" (*ap.* Stob., *Anth.* 3.32.11). Cicero, in his famous "Dream of Scipio" states that God "is that which lives, feels, remembers, and foresees, and which rules, governs, and moves (*regit et moderatur et movet*) the body over which it is set—as God rules this world (*quam hunc mundum ille princeps deus*)" (*Rep.* 6.24.26). In the late first century c.e., Aëtius takes as axiomatic that "of all things the divine is the most authoritative" (τῶν μὲν ἁπάντων τὸ θεῖον κυριώτατον) (*SVF* 1.1009 = *Plac.* 1.6; cf. Ps. Plut. *Plac. philos.* 880d). In Plutarch's *Life of Alexander*, Alexander accepts the teaching of the Egyptian philosopher Psammon who says that "all human beings are ruled by God, for what rules in each case and holds power is divine" (τὸ γὰρ ἄρχον ἐν ἑκάστῳ καὶ κρατοῦν θεῖόν ἐστιν) (27.8).[27] In the fourteenth tractate of the *Corpus Hermeticum*, we learn that God is God because of his power (διὰ τὴν δύναμιν) and maker "because of his activity" (διὰ τὴν ἐνέργειαν) (§4). This pervasive understanding of divinity is perhaps best summed up in the fragment from a papyrus of the second century b.c.e.: "What is a God (τί θεός)? Controlling power (τὸ κρατοῦν)."[28] Accordingly, οἱ κρείττονες ("the Strong Ones") came to be a common designation for the Gods.

Power, Divinity, and Kings

Since, as we have seen, divinity was conceived of as ruling power, it was often assumed that rulers who controlled states or empires drew nearest to the divine. Ariphron of Sicyon (fourth century b.c.e.) wrote that kingly rule for human beings is equality to divinity (ἰσοδαίμονος) (*ap.*

---

27 Cf. *Numa* 9.1, where Plutarch writes that an important college of priests are called "pontiffs" because they "serve the Gods, who are powerful and supreme over all the world" (ὅτι τοὺς θεούς ... δυνατοὺς καὶ κυρίους ἁπάντων ὄντας).

28 Heidelberg Papyrus Collection Inventory Number 1716, verso. For the full fragment, see Fr. Bilabel, "Fragmente aus der Heidelberger Papyrussammlung," *Philologus, Zeitschrift fur das klassische Alterum* 80 (1925): 339–40. The statement is attributed to Menander *ap.* Stob., *Anth.* 3.32.11.

Plut., *Virt. mor.* 10 [*Mor.* 450b]). Herodotus has Alexander (a Macedonian) tell the Athenians that that "the king's [Xerxes'] power is superhuman (ὑπὲρ ἄνθρωπον)" (*Hist.* 8.140). For Aristotle, kingship—like divinity—is granted by euergetic acts of power (*Pol.* 1285b 7–8). The connection between kingship and divinity is best expressed, however, in Hellenistic treatises on kingship (fragments of which are preserved in Stobaeus).[29] One such treatise attributed to Diotogenes draws this analogy:

> So just as God is the best of those things which are most honorable by nature, likewise the king is best in the earthly and human realm. Now the king bears the same relation to the state as God to the world; and the state is in the same ratio to the world as the king is to God. For the state, made as it is by a harmonizing together of many different elements, is an imitation of the order and harmony of the world, while the king who has an absolute rulership, and is himself Animate Law, has been metamorphosed into a deity among men (θεὸς ἐν ἀνθρώποις παρεσχαμάτισται). (Stob., *Anth.* 4.7.61)

According to another treatise on kingship (ascribed to Sthenidas of Locri):

> The king must be a wise man, for so he will be a copy and imitator of the first God. For God is the first king and ruler by nature, while the other is so only by birth and imitation. The one rules in the entire universe, the other upon earth ... And he would best imitate God by keeping himself greatminded, merciful, and lacking in few things, and by evincing a fatherly disposition to those beneath him. For it is in this way that the first God is recognized as father of Gods and men, by the fact that he is merciful to everything which is subject to him, and never relinquishes his hold of the leadership; nor is he satisfied at being the maker of all things alone, but he is the supporter and teacher of all that is beautiful, and the lawgiver equally to all. Such a leader upon earth and among men ought he also to be who aspires to be king ... Indeed he who is both king and wise will be a lawful imitator and servant of God. (Stob., *Anth.* 4.7.63)

A group of anonymous fragments (attributed to Ecphantus the Pythagorean) teach that the king is the image of God, by which he shares in divinity.

> He [the king] claims the lion's share of the better elements in our common nature. He is like the rest [of humankind] indeed in his earthly tabernacle, inasmuch as he is formed out of the same material; but he is fashioned by

---

29 The treatises are best dated to the third or second century B.C.E. See the discussion in Glenn F. Chesnut, "The Ruler and the Logos in Neopythagorean, Middle Platonic, and Late Stoic Political Philosophy," *ANRW* 16.2:1313–1315.

the supreme Artificer, who in making the king used himself as an Archetype. Accordingly the king, as a copy (τύπος) of the higher king, is a single and unique creation … [T]o his subjects he appears as though he were in a light, the light of royalty … Thus royalty is explained in the fact that by its divine character and excessive brilliance it is hard to behold … Royalty is then a sure and incorruptible thing, very hard for a human being to achieve by reason of its exceeding divinity … And the one who thus lives in royalty ought to share in its immaculate nature, and to understand how much more divine he is than the rest, and how much more divine than he is are those others [the Gods]—to whom by likening himself he would do the best for himself and his subjects. (Stob., *Anth.* 4.7.64)[30]

The function of a king, for these authors, is the same function as that of the high God who rules the universe (often conceived of as Zeus). Kings who share the attributes of this God (such as power and mercy) also share in the God's appearance (the "brilliance" of kinship). As image (τύπος) of the high God, the king is not greater than all the other Gods, but is in a subordinate place of vice-regency.[31]

The basic point, however, is that kingship and deity ran together in the minds of many Mediterranean peoples. This confluence seems to have been rooted in the fact that both kingship and divinity are based on the same principle: ruling power. "[F]rom Zeus come kings; for nothing is diviner (θειότερον) than the kings of Zeus" (Callimachus, *Hymn. Jov.*, lines 78–79).

This link between rule and divinity continues strong in literature postdating Paul. Plutarch wrote that "The ruler is the image of God who orders all things (εἰκὼν τοῦ θεοῦ τοῦ πάντα κοσμοῦντος)." Such a ruler, says Plutarch, needs no Phidias or Polyclitus or Myron (all great sculptors) to model him, but by his virtue he forms himself to the likeness of God (ἀλλ' αὐτὸς αὑτὸν εἰς ὁμοιότητα θεῷ δι' ἀρετῆς καθιστάς) (*Princ. iner.* 3 [*Mor.* 780e-f]; cf. Stob., *Anth.* 4.5.99; 3.32.7). Therefore Athenagoras, a Christian apologist, is only slightly exaggerating when he cries, "what wonder if some should be called Gods (κληθῆναι θεούς) … on the ground of their rule and sovereignty (ἐπὶ ἀρχῇ καὶ τυραννίδι)?" (*Pro Christianis* 30.1–2).[32] In the *Acta Sanctorum*, Africanus,

---

30 The translations of these fragments on kingship are taken in a modified form from E. R. Goodenough, "The Political Philosophy of Hellenistic Kingship," *Yale Classical Studies* 1 (1928): 68–77.

31 For the ruler as the embodiment of the Logos in Plutarch, Seneca, Cicero, and Philo, see Chestnut, "The Ruler and the Logos," 1321–1329.

32 Cf. Irenaeus, who, while criticizing Marcion and the Valentinians, defines God in terms of ruling power: "whatever is greater and stronger and more domi-

the putative second century governor of Pontus, chides St. Phocas, who
refuses to call the emperor Trajan a God: "Come now, has not every
bellicose race been destroyed by his hands? Who then can he be but
God?"[33] The fundamental idea is perhaps best summed up in the second
statement of the papyrus fragment quoted above ("What is a God? Controlling power"): "What is a king? Like [or equal to] (a) God
(ἰσόθεος)."[34] The king as a wielder of power participated in divinity.

Ancient Jewish Conceptions of Divinity

If we can ask "What is a God?" to Greeks and Romans, can we do the
same for Jews in the Hellenistic and Roman periods? On this score Richard Bauckham has raised the point that "for Jewish monotheistic belief" we do better to ask *who* God is rather than *what* God is.[35] Bauckham is right insofar as the central Jewish deity (Yahweh) is almost always
conceived of anthropomorphically as a person. (This is generally true for
Greeks as well.) Nevertheless, Bauckham's distinctions are too theologically subtle. The *identity* of God (the "who") cannot be separated from
the *nature* of God (the "what"). If we can talk about the Hebrew God as
a person we can also ask what makes God God. (The same is true, I
might add, for human beings.) In his insistence on "who," one gets
the impression that because Bauckham believes that the God of ancient
Judaism is a person, this God is not part of a class (hence Bauckham's
oft-repeated adjective "unique"). For the historian of religion, however,
even God falls into a class.[36] (Just as humans, though unique as persons,

---

nant, this will be God (*quod maius est et firmius et magis dominus, hoc erit deus*)"
(*Haer.* 2.1.2). Cf. 5.3.1: "For how has a person learned that he is weak and mortal by nature, but God immortal and powerful (*deus autem immortalis et potens*),
unless he had learned both by personal experience?"

33 Cited by Price, *Rituals and Power*, 125.

34 Cf. Isoc., *Nic.* 5; Hom., *Il.* 2.565; *Od.* 1.324; Aesch., *Per.* 80, 856. For further
commentary on the connection assumed in this period between royalty and divinity, see Manfred Clauss, "Deus Praesens: Der römische Kaiser als Gott," *Klio*
78 (1996): 427.

35 *Jesus and the God of Israel*, ix, 183.

36 Yahweh admits as much when he includes himself in the "us" of Gen 3:22:
"See, the man has become like one of us." The "us" apparently refers to the
divine council, made up of beings in the divine class (David Penchansky, *Twilight of the Gods: Polytheism in the Hebrew Bible* [Louisville: Westminster John
Knox, 2005], 30).

fall into the class "human being.") This is true whether one thinks that *one* person makes up the "God class" or (as most Christians do) three persons—or for that matter 3,000. Even if many separate identities are in the class, this does not change the fact that there are basic features and characteristics which go into making up the class called "divinity." Bauckham admits as much when he talks about the "unique, defining characteristics by which Jewish monotheism identified God as unique."[37] A central argument in his essay "God Crucified" is that at least two beings shared these central divine characteristics, namely God and Christ. Thus God "the Father" and Christ are both in the class of "God." Nevertheless, the characteristics which make up the divine identity (which Bauckham calls "unique") cannot, it seems to me, be unique to the person (note the formula "God in *three* persons"), but unique (or rather distinctive) to the *class* of beings called "divine" or "God." Thus when we ask, "What is an ancient Jewish God?" we are inquiring about the characteristics that constitute the class of divinity as it was conceived by Jews in the Greco-Roman world.

"What is a God?" is, then, a question about taxonomy. Ancient Jews are not essentially different from their Hellenistic contemporaries in their classification of divine beings (even if not all Greek divinities are personal beings).[38] Classification largely proceeds by identifying characteristics distinctive to a particular class.[39] Unlike my practice with Greek literature, I cannot list these key characteristics in representative pithy quotes. Jewish religion is revealed in story, so Jewish conceptions of divinity are inferred from the stories Jews tell about God (and in some instances, Gods).

---

37 *Jesus and the God of Israel*, ix.

38 Philosophical Gods are often accused of being impersonal. But note on this point Michael Frede: "There is nothing impersonal about Aristotle's God, or the God of the Stoics, or the God of Numenius or Plotinus" (Polymnia Athanassiadi and Frede, eds., *Pagan Monotheism in Late Antiquity* [Oxford: Clarendon, 1999], 48).

39 Charles Gieschen has proposed five criteria for identifying a divine being: (1) divine position, (2) divine appearance, (3) divine functions, (4) divine name, and (5) divine veneration (*Angelomorphic Christology: Antecedents and Early Evidence* [Leiden: Brill, 1998], 30–33). Although helpful to some extent for classification, none of these criteria, I think, get to the heart of what divinity is. For this we need characteristics constitutive of the divine identity (i.e., qualities characteristic of the divine class).

We can begin our search for divine characteristics using the Septuagint version of Genesis 2–3.[40] This story, as many have observed, indicates that ancient Jews conceived of divinity as consisting of at least two
characteristics: (1) knowledge (of good and evil) and (2) immortality.[41]
The humans who attain knowledge are, we come to find out, only
quasi-divine. They are, in biblical language, "like/as Gods" (כאלהים/
ὡς θεοί) (Gen 3:5; cf. Ezek 28:2–5), but not fully Gods. Full divinity
comes only with immortality.[42] This is what worries Yahweh in the
final scene of this episode: "See, Adam has become like one of us,
knowing good and evil; and now, lest he reach out his hand and take
also from the tree of life, and eat, and live forever …" (Gen 3:22,
LXX). The statement appears broken off, possibly indicating Yahweh's
distress. Evidently, if Adam and Eve taste the fruit, they will become
members of the divine *genus*. Yahweh God realizes this, and takes meas-
ures to prevent it. Knowledge alone, it seems, is not constitutive of the
divine identity—but knowledge combined with eternal life is.

The immortality of God himself is taken for granted by the Jewish
scriptures. He exists "in the beginning" (ἐν ἀρχῇ) (Gen 1:1) and "from
of old" (ἀπ ἀρχῆς) (Hab 1:12). He is the "God who lives" (θεὸς ζῶν)
(e.g., Deut 5:26; Josh 3:10; 2 Kgs 19:16; cf. 2 Cor 3:3; Rom 1:23;
9:26). He not only lives, he is Being itself (Ὁ ὤν) (Ex 3:14), a refuge
"from generation to generation" (Ps 89[90]:1). Paul continues this tradition. For the Apostle, God is he who gives life to the dead and calls
"the things which are not as though they were" (Rom 4:17; cf. *Jos.
As*. 8:2–3).

If God's immortality is assumed in the Jewish scriptures, his sovereignty (or ultimate power) is loudly celebrated.[43] In fact, the great Israeli
scholar Yeḥezkel Kaufmann argued that the idea of God's supremacy is

---

40   All translations which follow, unless otherwise noted, are made from the LXX.
     For background on this particular story in Gen, see James Barr, *The Garden of
     Eden and the Hope of Immortality* (Minneapolis: Fortress, 1992), esp. chs. 1 and 3.

41   On this point, see esp. Tryggve N. D. Mettinger, *The Eden Narrative: A Literary
     and Religio-historical Study of Genesis 2–3* (Winona Lake: Eisenbrauns, 2007),
     chs. 5–7.

42   So those deprived of immortality in Ps 82:6 are also deprived of divinity. Death
     proves that one is not a God (Ezek 28:9).

43   For God's ruling power, Bauckham lists the following passages: Dan 4:34–35;
     Bel 5; Add. Esth 13:9–11; 16:18, 21; 3 Macc 2:2–3; 6:2; Wisd 12:13; Sir
     18:1–3; Sib. Or. 3:10, 19; Sib. Or. frag. 1:7, 15, 17, 35; 1 En 9:5; 84:3; 2
     En 33:7; 2 Bar 54:13; Jos. *Ant*. 1.155–56 (*Jesus and the God of Israel*, 9, n. 9).

the "basic idea of Israelite religion."[44] More recently, Bauckham makes universal rule one of the two primary factors which make up Yahweh's identity.[45] Mark Smith (whose approach widely differs from that of Bauckham) also suggests that divinity "in biblical and ancient Near Eastern terms was thought, metaphysically speaking, to be constituted by power."[46] Closer to Paul's time, the writer of Judith calls God "the God of all power and might" (9:14), and Philo calls God "the highest and greatest power" (θεὸς δ' ἡ ἀνωτάτω καὶ μεγίστη δύναμις ὤν) (*Mos*. 1.111; cf. *Mut*. 29; Mark 14:62).[47]

Sometimes the power of Yahweh is the dangerous, raw power of a whirlwind (Job 38–41). The Jews, however, primarily experienced the power of their God as a salvific force. At the key moments in Israel's history, Yahweh reveals himself as "a righteous God and a Savior (ἐγὼ ὁ θεός ... δίκαιος καὶ σωτήρ)" (Isa 45:21d). He vindicates his people in the eyes of their enemies, and makes the entire world recognize his power to save and to choose a people for himself.[48]

The supreme power of the Jewish God is played out in a master narrative of salvation: the exodus. For Israel as a nation, the exodus is the ultimate act of salvific power. Celebrated in the annual rite of Passover, arguably no other story had more influence in the mythic imagination

---

44 *Religion of Israel*, 60.

45 *God Crucified: Monotheism and Christology in the New Testament* (Grand Rapids, Mich.: W.B. Eerdmans, 1999), 10–11. The other factor, creative power, is, I would argue, a function of Yahweh's absolute sovereignty. That is, the fact that Yahweh has created the world makes him absolutely sovereign over the cosmos. For more on this point see chapter 9.

46 *God in Translation: Deities in Cross-Cultural Discourse in the Biblical World* (Tübingen: Mohr Siebeck, 2008), 14. See further his *The Memoirs of God: History, Memory, and the Experience of the Divine in Ancient Israel* (Minneapolis: Fortress Press, 2004), 161–62. Compare also Jean-Pierre Vernant: "A god is a power that represents a type of action, a kind of force" (quoted in H. S. Versnel, "Three Greek Experiments in Oneness" in *One God Or Many Concepts of Divinity in the Ancient World* [ed. Barbara Nevling Porter; Casco Bay: Casco Bay Assyriological Institute, 2000], 83).

47 Note also the less familiar *L.A.E.* 28: "You [God] are the true light shining above all light, living life, Power of incomprehensible greatness (*incomprehensibilis magnitudinis virtus*)."

48 Cf. Bauckham: "... it is because of YHWH's exercise of power on their [Israel's] behalf that Israel is to recognize him as *hāᵃlōhîm* [God] ... What makes YHWH, by comparison with the gods of the nations, 'the God' (or 'god of gods and lord of lords, the great god' as [Deut] 10:17 puts it) is his unrivalled power" (*Jesus and the God of Israel*, 69).

of ancient Jews. When Yahweh identifies himself at Sinai, he identifies himself in terms of this basic narrative of powerful deliverance: "I am the God of your fathers, who brought you up from the land of Egypt, out of the house of slavery" (Ex 20:2). When Jews celebrate and ritually remember the exodus, they come to know, in the favorite phrase of Ezekiel, that "I am [the] Lord" (ἐγὼ κύριος). They come to know, in other words, who Yahweh is. In short, they recognize his deity: "As a helper and defender, he became my salvation; this is my God (זֶה אֵלִי; οὗτός μου θεός), and I will glorify him" (Ex 15:2, LXX). In other words, when Jews experience Yahweh's saving power, they know what for them deity is. For them, their deity—"the Lord"—is salvific power.[49]

In the Exodus, Yahweh's display of awesome power means that he becomes king over his people. Images of kingship are often depicted as rule over the primeval waters. Thus Yahweh shattered the heads of Leviathan or Rahab (Ps 73[74]:12–15; 88:10–15 [ET 89:9–14]); he tamed the primeval rivers (Ps 92[93]:1, 4–5); he is king over the roaring sea (Ps 97[98]:6–8); he sits enthroned over the flood (Ps 28[29]:10); he is master over the deep (Ps 103[104]:6–9). All these images can be read, interestingly, as echoes of the Exodus tradition which involved a conquering of the Re(e)d Sea.

In the exodus, Yahweh defeats the forces of chaos. He judges opposing kings. He shows his mastery over human affairs. He is Lord over Israel's history. It is by meditating on and recasting the exodus traditions that the author of Second Isaiah proclaims Yahweh's absolute sovereignty even while in exile (e.g., Isa 43:1–2). But this prophet takes it one step further. Yahweh's power is not just power to save a particular people at a particular time, now it is absolute power over the entire world.

> It is he who holds the circle of the earth,
> and its inhabitants are like grasshoppers;
> who establishes the heavens like a vault,
> and spreads them like a tent to live in;
> who gives rulers to rule for nothing, and made the earth as nothing.
> (Isa 40:22–23; cf. Ps 2:4–5)

---

49 Cf. the scene in 1 Kings 18 when Yahweh sends down fire on his drenched altar (thus showing more power than Baal). The people respond: "Yahweh, he is God! Yahweh, he is God!" (v. 39).

It is Yahweh's universal kingship that, at least in part, makes the Jewish God God. This it seems is the factor that led ancient (and modern) Jews to perceive Yahweh's divinity as unique. No other God, it was thought, had the power that Yahweh had. Baal and Chemosh may have had the power to save their people temporarily (e.g., 2 Kings 3:27)—but no other God had the universal power to save like Yahweh. He was unique in Jewish eyes not for any philosophical reason, but because no other God had displayed such power before their eyes (ἐνώπιόν σου βλέποντος) (Deut 4:36). For Jews, therefore, divinity was something seen and shown through immortality and unmatched power.

The Pauline Understanding of Divinity

Paul's writings disclose a Jew who generally thought about God along the lines sketched out above. The sole time that Paul uses the word "divinity" (θειότης), he puts it in parallel with God's "eternal power": "Ever since the creation of the world, his [God's] eternal power and divinity (ἥ τε ἀΐδιος αὐτοῦ δύναμις καὶ θειότης), invisible though they are, have been understood and seen through the things he [God] has made" (Rom 1:20; cf. Jos., *Ap.* 2.167). The close association of divinity and power indicates that, like so many in the Greco-Roman world, Paul saw divinity in terms of might. Divine beings other than God Paul calls "Powers" (δυνάμεις) (Rom 8:38; 1 Cor 15:24).[50] And God's Spirit is an agent of power (Rom 15:13; cf. v. 19; 1 Cor 2:4; 1 Thess 1:5).

Christ especially is the manifestation of God's power. In fact, he is at one point simply called "God's Power" (1 Cor 1:30). The resurrection, effected by divine power (ἐν δυνάμει), is a manifestation of Christ's divinity in that he is appointed "son of God" (Rom 1:4). The κύριος title, the standard (oral, if not written) substitute for the divine name Yahweh, was at this time granted to Christ, and signified his absolute authority over human and superhuman beings (Phil 2:9–11).[51] When

---

50 For God as associated with power (often power in weakness) elsewhere in Paul, see 1 Cor 2:5; 2 Cor 4:7; 6:7; 13:4.

51 Universal rule, whether viewed as "functional" or "ontological" divinity, is still one of the basic features making up the divine identity. (For the distinction, see Adela Yarbro Collins, "'How on Earth did Jesus Become a God?': A Reply" in *Israel's God and Rebecca's Children: Christology and Community in Early Judaism and Christianity: Essays in Honor of Larry W. Hurtado and Alan F. Segal* [eds. David B. Capes, Larry W. Hurtado and Alan F. Segal; Waco, Tex.: Baylor Uni-

seen in the light of Greco-Roman culture, there is thus strong evidence that Paul viewed Christ as a God.[52]

For Pauline Christians, Christ was quickly assimilated to the divine (Jewishly understood) because he fit into the collective representation of divinity as redeeming power. On the cross he even came to represent the redemptive activity of God in a new exodus. He is called "our paschal lamb" (τὸ πάσχα) (1 Cor 5:7, NRSV). He defeats Death which reigned as king from Adam to Moses (Rom 5:14). In the resurrection, he was given God's universal power as viceregent. God subjects "all things" (πάντα) to him (1 Cor 15:27). In the minds of early Christians, the universal power of Christ gave him a share in God's distinctive "divine identity" (to use Bauckham's term). In the Pauline churches, the worship of Christ thus became an assumption.

Christ is also immortal. This is true by virtue of the resurrection. Though it is God who alone is properly immortal and incorruptible (Rom 1:23; cf. 1 Tim 6:16), God granted immortality to the resurrected Christ. As a "life-making pneuma" (πνεῦμα ζῳοποιοῦν) (1 Cor 15:45), Christ attained a kind of corporeality according to which he cannot die. "Death no longer has dominion over him." The life he lives, he lives to (or in) God (ζῇ τῷ θεῷ) (Rom 6:9–10). The pneuma that Christ gives is the "pneuma of life (τῆς ζωῆς)" (Rom 8:2). For believers, Christ's pneuma is their life (Rom 8:10; cf. Col. 3:4). For Paul, it is evident that Christ shares the life of God to such an extent that he shares the divine identity. Paul and his converts, then, were moved to see Christ as (a) God because of his universal power and indestructible life. The worship of Christ as a God made good sense in the Greco-Roman world, and was not in any way opposed to the notions of the divine in first-century Judaism.

---

versity Press, 2007], 57). If divinity is power, then those who have superhuman power (i.e., who *function* as divine beings) *are* divine beings. Doing implies being. If Christ does what God does (i.e., if he is universal ruler), he is what God is. Note the functional definition of divinity in Pliny the Elder, *Nat.* 2.18: "To a mortal, God is the act of helping a mortal (*deus est mortali iuvare mortalem*)." For an additional argument against the dichotomy of "functional" and "ontological" divinity, see Bauckham, *God Crucified*, 41.

52 Some, in arguing for Christ's deity, have put a good deal of weight on individual verses such as Rom 9:5 (which is, unfortunately, grammatically unclear) (James D. G. Dunn, *Did the First Christians Worship Jesus? The New Testament Evidence* [Louisville: Westminster John Knox, 2010], 132–33). It is better to see Christ's deity as an outcome of the structure of Paul's thought as a whole, which is of a piece with how his culture conceived of the divine.

Conclusion

Admittedly, I cannot claim that in every way Paul's concept of divinity (and the divine Christ) conformed to the way of conceptualizing divinity in ancient Judaism or the Greco-Roman world. The Greek and Roman texts in particular are very different from Paul's letters in both genre and content. Frankly, Paul never cares to define divinity explicitly. His understanding must therefore be carefully culled out by close reading. After we perform this close reading, however, what we find is that Paul's conception of divinity was not out of step with his Greco-Roman and Hellenistic Jewish culture. That is—regardless of some differences—Paul showed himself in broad agreement with ancient Mediterranean culture that power and immortality are central (if not *the* central traits) of the divine. These are not traits which exhaust the nature of God (this was never claimed).[53] They are traits, however, which at least in part constitute the divine identity for the Apostle. This is shown most decisively in Christ, who was declared to be "son of God" (and "Lord" in Phil 2:9–11) "in power" (i.e., in a clear manifestation of divinity) ... "by resurrection from the dead" (i.e., when he received God's immortal life) (Rom 1:4). By sharing in the immortality and power of the son of God, Pauline converts (who become "children of God," Rom 8:16–17) share in Christ's divine identity. This basic pattern of participation plays itself out in a specific way in Paul, which we will treat in chs. 4–6. For now, we turn to a general survey of deification—paying keen attention to a concept which later appears in Paul, namely, assimilation to a specific deity.

---

53 For Paul and other Hellenistic Jews, wisdom especially was an important quality which defined the identity of God. Other qualities like permanence or justice could also be mentioned. The work of H. S. Versnel, *Coping with the Gods: Wayward Readings in Greek Theology* (Leiden: Brill, 2011), came into my hands only after typesetting. He emphasizes the fuzziness of the category "God"/Θεός and advises care when "devising universal markers of divinity" (391). Nevertheless, he admits that "Many Greek authors agree on a fixed set of 'deificators,'" which include immortality (plus agelessness), blessedness, knowledge, and power (391–92). The qualities emphasized tend to shift with context, but polythetic classification ably copes with this variation. My point is that immortality and power—even if not universal markers of divine identity (some Gods die)—were the most widely recognized markers of deity in Greco-Roman culture.

Chapter 2:
Survey of Deification:
Assimilation to Specific Deities

> "[D]ivinity and mortality are
> irreconcilable, but for the Greeks they
> are inseparable."
>
> —Cedric Hubbell Whitman[1]

Introduction

To understand the logic and content of deification in the Greco-Roman world, I turn to key examples. Throughout I will be concerned with some basic questions. Who participated in the superhuman power and immortality of the Gods? How did the participation come about? Why was divine power and immortality shared at all? I hope to approach an answer to these questions by sketching patterns of deification in three different fields: mythology, Greek ruler cult, and Roman ruler cult. A representative sampling of deification is the goal here; I have no pretensions of being comprehensive. In discussing ruler cult, I will attempt to describe how rulers assimilated to specific deities which (I hope to show) is a pattern that appears also in Paul. As a preliminary to this discussion, however, it is necessary to briefly treat the Greek terminology of deification.

The Greek Vocabulary of Deification

The archaic poets did not have a term for deification. Nevertheless, Dietrich Roloff has listed three ways for the most ancient poets to designate the idea:

---

1   *The Heroic Paradox: Essays on Homer, Sophocles, and Aristophanes* (ed. Charles Segal; Ithaca: Cornell University Press, 1982), 25.

1. to "set/make immortal/ageless (ἀθάνατον καὶ ἀγήραον τιθέναι/ ποιεῖν),"
2. to "make (τιθέναι/ποιεῖν) a God (θεός/δαίμων)"
3. to "seize (ἀνερείπεσθαι/ἁρπάζειν) so as to be with the immortals, (ἵν' ἀθανάτοισι μετείη)."[2]

The actual vocabulary of deification began to be invented in the 3rd century B.C.E. Norman Russell has gathered most of the evidence here, and we need only present a condensation of his work.[3]

The language of ἀποθεόω/ἀποθέωσις originally belonged to Hellenistic mythology and the ruler cult.[4] The comic poet Nicolaus, probably writing in the second century B.C.E., refers to the apotheosis of Ganymede, the Trojan prince (Γανυμήδης οὗτος ἀποθεούμενος).[5] Polybius (ca. 200–118 B.C.E.) states that Callisthenes, Alexander the Great's court historian "wished to deify (ἀποθεοῦν) Alexander" (Hist. 12.23.4). The Jewish author Ps.-Aristeas (second century B.C.E.) uses ἀποθεόω to criticize the cult of benefactors (Ep. Arist. 136–37). In 118 B.C.E., Ptolemy VIII (Physcon) refers to his previously deified royal ancestors as the ἀποτεθεωμένοι.[6] Also in the second century B.C.E., a decree for a gymnasiarch at Pergamum speaks of the "apotheosis of the royal couple" (τὴν τῶν β|ασιλέων ἀποθέωσιν). Diodorus of Sicily (fl. 60–30 B.C.E.) writes that Titaea, the mother of the Titans was deified (ἀποθεωθῆναι) after her death because of her benefactions (Bibl. 3.57.2).[7] An Egyptian inscription (first century B.C.E.) uses the verb ἀποθειόω to refer to the deification of "sacred animals." Similarly, two Egyptian papyri (second century C.E.) refer to the ἀποθέωσις of the sacred bulls Apis and Mnevis.[8] Plutarch (ca. 46–120 C.E.) refers to the apotheosis of Romulus (Num 6.3). Moreover, in his Life of Demetrius, "apotheoses" are the highest honors given by cities to Hellenistic rulers (30.4–5, cf. Apophth.

---

2   Dietrich Roloff, Gottähnlichkeit, Vergöttlichung, und Erhöhung zu seligem Leben: Untersuchungen zur Herkunft der platonischen Angleichung an Gott (Berlin: Walter de Gruyter, 1970), 83.
3   For the references below, see Appendix 2 in his Doctrine of Deification, 333–344.
4   Ibid., 333–35. Russell also reports that the deification of animals in Egypt was expressed by the verb ἀποθειόω.
5   Cited in ibid., 333.
6   Ibid.
7   According to the same historian, the Egyptians deified (ἀπεθέωσαν) the goat and the crocodile (Bibl. 1.88–89).
8   Doctrine of Deification, 335.

Lac. 25 [*Mor.* 210c-d]). Demosthenes, says Plutarch, had "apotheosized" the soldiers of Marathon in his swearing oaths by them (*Glor. ath.* 8 [*Mor.* 350c]; cf. Longinus, *Subl.* 16.2). According to a Hermetic tractate, all people who reject the corporeal in preference to the spiritual experience apotheosis (*Corp. herm.* 4.7).

Another term for deification, θεοποιέω, seems to have begun its semantic life in the context of the ruler cult. The citizens of Mytilene sometime between 27 and 11 B.C.E. promise to seek out honors that can deify (θεοποιεῖν) Augustus (*OGIS* 456.44–50). Dionysus of Halicarnassus (ca. 60–7 B.C.E.) notes that the phenomena surrounding Romulus' death lent credence to those 'who deify mortal things' (τοῖς θεοποιοῦσι τὰ θνητά) (*Ant. Rom.* 2.56.6). In the second century C.E., Lucian jokes that the Athenians deify (θεοποιέω) a Scythian in Greece (*Scyth.* 1). At the turn of the third century, Sextus Empiricus writes that the Pythagoreans used to deify (θεοποιέω) Pythagoras (*Math.* 7.94). He adds that the Stoic sage who never opines is made divine (ἐθεοποιεῖτο) (7.423), and that men of power, according to Euhemerus, became Gods (θεοποιηθέντας) (9.51).

The verb ἐκθειόω refers to the deification of the goddess *Fides* in Rome by Numa (Dion. Hal., *Ant. Rom.* 2.75.2). Later it is pejoratively used by Philo of Alexandria to refer to the deification of animals, men, and heavenly bodies (*Dec.* 8, 53, 70, 79; *Spec. Leg.* 1.10, 344; *Conf.* 173). In the early second century C.E., Plutarch writes that the barbarians deified (ἐκθειόω) the mortal Io (*Her. mal.* [*Mor.* 856e]).

The noun ἐκθέωσις refers to the deification of Arsinoë I (the Egyptian queen) in the title of a poem by Callimachus (305–240 B.C.E.). It is a synonym of ἀποθέωσις in the Canopus Decree of 238 B.C.E (*OGIS* 56.53). Philo uses this term to refer to setting up false Gods and for the self-deification of Caligula (*Legat.* 77, 201, 332, 338, 368; *Dec.* 81). The term is not attested again until the Neoplatonist Proclus.

The verb θεόω first appears in the Hellenistic poet Callimachus, who writes that the flesh of Heracles had been deified (θεωθείς) (*Hymn. 3 Cer.* 159–60). The author of the *Letter of Aristeas* uses θεόω pejoratively to criticize the cult of benefactors (§136).[9] A Cynic of the second century C.E. also uses θεόω to scorn a version of deification

---

9   Here I follow the reading printed in the critical edition of André Pelletier, *Lettre d'Aristée a Philocrate* (SC 89; Paris: Éditions du Cerf, 1962), 170. For other options (which do not significantly change the meaning of the text), see his apparatus on 170.

he considers naïve (*ap.* Eus., *Praep. ev.* 5.34). In the Hermetic tractate *Poimandres*, θεόω is used to describe the state of the soul stripped of the passions and assimilated to the celestial Powers (*Corp. herm.* 1.26; cf. 13.10; Clem. Alex., *Strom.* 4.23.152.1).

Evaluation

In his survey, Russell is eager to emphasize that the Christian fathers evolved "their own distinctive terminology for deification."[10] This conclusion is somewhat surprising because his investigation shows that in fact there was, strictly speaking, little distinctive about the Christian language of deification.[11] Christians did not invent any of the terminology for deification with the exception of the nouns θεοποίησις and θέωσις (which derive from the already invented verbs θεοποιέω and θεόω). Θέωσις was later employed by the Neoplatonist Damascius. Admittedly, there were some terms for deification that Christians generally avoided—namely ἐκθειόω and ἐκθειάζω[12]—but this does not make their terminology distinctive. The only thing distinctive Russell can show about the terminology is the Christian *preference* for the verbs θεοποιέω and θεόω with their nouns θεοποίησις and θέωσις. Yet the use of this terminology (with the exception of θεοποίησις) is not distinctively Christian. Christians may have later semantically adapted the language of deification, but they did not invent it. The sense of most of the terms was set long before Christians adopted the language, or even came onto the scene.

As Russell's survey shows, the terminology of deification was used by Greek speakers to refer to deifications which occurred in Greek mythology. Later, it could be used philosophically to refer to the purification and immortalization of the soul. Its original semantic home, however, seems to have been the ruler cult. In what follows, then, I will focus on deification in mythology and the ruler cult to gain a general sense of what deification meant in Paul's culture. In chapters 4, 5

---

10 *Doctrine of Deification*, 344.
11 Cf. Martin George: "It is misleading and against the consistent Greek linguistic usage of pagan and Christian literature to distinguish in German [and English] between the 'Greek deification' of Gentiles and 'Christian deification'" ("Vergöttlichung des Menschen," 121).
12 The terms ἀποθεόω and ἀποθέωσις only began to be avoided by Christians in the fifth century C.E. (Russell, *Doctrine of Deification*, 344).

and 7, I will have opportunity to treat deification in philosophical sources.

Deification in Homer

As we saw in chapter 1, Homer's various adjectives translated by "godlike" or "divine"—far from signifying permanent attributes—indicate some momentary brilliance. Odysseus is nothing special when he is dirty and covered with seaweed early in the *Odyssey* book 6. Yet after he gets himself cleaned up, Nausicaa says that he "resembles one of the gods, who hold high heaven (θεοῖσιν ἔοικε, τοὶ οὐρανὸν εὐρὺν ἔχουσιν)" (243). A change in circumstances, however, deprives the heroes of divine brilliance—especially death. This was the case of Castor, son of Hylacus. He, according to the invented report of Odysseus, was "honored among the Cretans in the countryside as a God is … for wealth and power and glorious children. But then, you see, the death spirits caught and carried him from us to the house of Hades" (*Od.* 14.204–08). When Calypso offered Odysseus deification, he turned her down (*Od.* 5.135–36, cf. 7.251–59; 23.333–37). If he became a God, Odysseus would cease to be a hero. Thus Odysseus (in many ways, the archetypal Greek) chooses the way of κλέος, or "fame," even though it involves great suffering.[13] "It is a condition of heroism in the Homeric poems," Helen Bacon observes, "that the transition from mortality to divinity is not made."[14] For Homer, though heroes can become "godlike," they do not thereby become Gods.

This is not to say that Homer completely excludes the notion of deification. In the margins of the Homeric epics there are, on my count, three persons who receive deification.[15] The first is Ganymede, "the loveliest born of the race of mortals, and therefore the Gods caught him away to themselves, to be Zeus' wine-pourer, for the sake of his

---

13 For Odysseus' refusal of deification, see especially Martha Nussbaum, *Love's Knowledge: Essays on Philosophy and Literature* (New York: Oxford University Press, 1990), 365–92.

14 Helen H. Bacon, "The Aeneid as a Drama of Election," *Transactions of the American Philological Association* 116 (1986): 315. See further Whitman, *Heroic Paradox*, 19–43.

15 In the *Odyssey*, Heracles is part ghost, part God (*Od.* 11.601–16); and the Dioscuri are admitted to be semi-divine (*Od.* 11.300–304), but the poet does not describe their actual deifications.

beauty, so he might be among the immortals" (*Il.* 20.232–35). The second is Ino, daughter of Cadmus, who "had once been one who spoke as a mortal, but now in the gulfs of the sea she holds degree as a Goddess [Leucothea]" (*Od.* 5.334–35). The third is Cleitus son of Mantius, who was carried away by the Dawn of the golden throne "because of his beauty, so that he might dwell among the immortals" (*Od.* 15.250–51). But in works as large as the Homeric epics, the general lack of interest in deification is noteworthy. Gods and human beings, for Homer, remain as essentially different sorts of beings.

Deification in Hesiod, Pindar, and the Homeric Poets

Even more than Homer, the poets of the late archaic and early classical ages (600–400 B.C.E.) tended to emphasize the differences between Gods and human beings. It was believed, to be sure, that in very ancient days Gods and human beings were kin. Hesiod writes that "from the same race [came] the Gods and mortal humans (ὡς ὁμόθεν γεγάασι θεοὶ θνητοί τ' ἄνθρωποι)" (*Op.* 108).[16] The word "same" (the adverb ὁμόθεν) usually suggests blood kinship.[17] Likewise, Pindar, though he recognizes that Gods and human beings now come from a different race (or family [γένος]), says that "from a single mother [Earth] we both draw our breath" (*Nem.* 6.1–3).

Nevertheless—although in the distant past there was a close family relation between humans and Gods—the two groups have at the present time branched off and become very different species. Hesiod attributes this separation to the primal sin of Prometheus (*Theog.* 535–557). Yet there were other explanations. The point of agreement was, at least in the current state of affairs (Hesiod's "Iron Age"), that people and Gods were very different kinds of being. In the same Nemean Ode quoted above, Pindar states the content of this difference:

---

16   The line is disputed by one critic, but rightly attested in the old scholia and the commentary of Proclus on Hesiod and others. See the apparatus in Merkelbach and West, eds., *Hesiodi Theogonia; Opera Et Dies; Scutum* (3d ed.; Oxford: Clarendon, 1990), 53.

17   M. L. West, *Works & Days* (Oxford: Clarendon, 1978), *ad loc.* For an introduction to Hesiod, with a focus on divine-human relations, see Jenny Strauss Clay, *Hesiod's Cosmos* (Cambridge: Cambridge University Press, 2003).

There is one race of men, another of gods (ἒν ἀνδρῶν, ἒν Ͽεῶν γένος);
but from one mother [Earth] (cf. Hes. *Op.* 108)
we both draw our breath. Yet the allotment of a wholly
different power (δύναμις) separates us, for the one race is nothing,
whereas the bronze heaven remains a secure abode forever [for Gods].
(lines 1–5; trans. William H. Race, LCL)[18]

The difference is a difference not in genealogical roots, but in power.
That power differential had always to be respected. Pindar twice advises
human beings not to seek to become a God as a warning not to obtain
too much power (*Ol.* 5.24; *Isth.* 5.16).

But Pindar (and, we might add, Homer) was technically censuring
not the *fact* that a human could become a God—this was admitted as
a rare possibility—but the *hubris* of a man who made himself like (a)
God. Bellerophon, who tried to soar above Olympus, was rightfully
thrown down (Pind., *Isth.* 7.43–48).[19] Others, however, who did not
try to break divine-human boundaries, achieved the end unsought. Ganymede, as we saw above, was swept up to Olympus, because of his
beauty (διὰ κάλλος), to become "deathless and unageing, even as the
Gods" (ὡς ἔοι ἀθάνατος καὶ ἀγήρως ἴσα θεοῖσιν) (*Hom. Hymn
Aphr.* 203, 214).[20] Phaethon was made a "bright divinity" (δαίμονα δῖον)
by Aphrodite (Hes., *Theog.* 987–92). Ariadne was made "deathless and
ageless" (ἀθάνατον καὶ ἀγήρων) by Zeus (947–49). Diomedes was
made a God (ἔθηκε θεόν) by Athena (Pind., *Nem.* 10.7).

We might also add the attempted deifications of Demophoön (*Hom.
Hymn Dem.* 2.231–63), and Tithonus (*Hom. Hymn Aphr.* 5.218–25). In
the *Homeric Hymns*, Tithonus was a Trojan warrior loved by Eos, or
Dawn. She asked Zeus to make him immortal. Zeus agreed, but cun-
ningly did not grant eternal youth (5.237–38). The great goddess Demeter, disguised as an old woman, took care of the noble infant Demophoön. Nightly she rubbed him with ambrosia, breathed upon him, and

18 But even Pindar admits, "Nevertheless, we do somewhat resemble the immor-
    tals, either in greatness of mind or bodily nature." In this text, what really dis-
    tinguishes humans from the Gods is that humans are ignorant of their destiny
    (lines 6–7).

19 A similar tradition is found in Roman sources. According to a legend handed
    down by Cato (*ap.* Macrobius 3.5.10), the Tuscan king Mezentius demanded
    divine honors by claiming the first fruits which the Rutulians offered to the
    Gods. This *contemptor divum* died in the war against Aeneas.

20 Cf. Theog., *Elegies* 2.1344–47; Apoll. Rhod., *Argon.* 3.115–17; Virg.,
    Aen. 5.244–57; Ovid, *Met.* 10.155–61.

set him within the blazing fire. The boy would have been immortalized had not his mother panicked at the sight of the boy in the blaze (*Hom. Hymn Dem.* 2.231–69).[21]

These deifications are not mere honors given by a community; they are physical transformations which can be effected through physical means. They can occur, for instance, through anointing with a special oil, or through a special diet. K. Sara Myers notes that "Nectar and ambrosia, the food of the gods, often figure in scenes of apotheosis. In Theocr. [= Theocritus, *Idylls*] 15.106–108 Aphrodite deifies Queen Berenice by anointing her with ambrosia. In Pindar *Pythian Ode* 9.62–65, Aristaeus is made immortal by the dropping of nectar and ambrosia on his lips. In Apollonius Rhodius' *Argonautica* 4.870–2, Thetis anoints Achilles with ambrosia to make him immortal."[22] In the Jewish romance *Joseph and Asenath* (ca. 100 B.C.E.–100 C.E.), we find reference to similar transformative substances, such as the bread of life, a cup of immortality, oil of incorruption, and a honeycomb full of the "spirit of life" (8:5; 15:4; 16:8–16, cf. 19:5; 21:21). When Asenath eats this honeycomb, an angel says to her: "Behold, you have eaten bread of life, and drunk a cup of immortality, and been anointed with ointment of incorruptibility. Behold, from today your flesh (will) flourish like flowers of life from the ground of the Most High, and your bones will grow strong like the cedars of the paradise of delight of God, and untiring powers will embrace you, and your youth will not see old age, and your beauty will not fail for ever" (16:16) (trans. C. Burchard). If this were not a Jewish text, scholars would view this as an obvious instance of deification. As in other Hellenistic deifications, it occurs through very physical means. I will return to the physical and bodily nature of deification in chapters 4–5.

The reason behind these (attempted) deifications is sometimes unclear. We can observe that many of those deified already had a quality that set them apart from the common lot of human beings. Ganymede and Ariadne had beauty. Diomedes had strength and bold deeds. But other ancient heroes had the same sort of beauty and strength, and were not made divine. Roloff points out that many of these heroes had a special (sometimes erotic) relationship with the Gods. Ariadne be-

---

21 Cf. the case of Achilles in Apollonius, *Argon.*, 4.869–72; Apollodorus, *Bibl.* 3.13.6; cf. also Plut., *Is. Os.* 16 (*Mor.* 357c).
22 K. Sara Myers, ed., *Ovid Metamorphoses Book XIV* (Cambridge: Cambridge University Press, 2009), 158. For Roman evidence, see Apul., *Met.* 6.23.4–5.

came the wife of a God (Dionysus), and Ganymede fired the heart of Zeus.[23] But the generalization works less well for Ino, Diomedes, and Demophoön. Still Roloff's larger point stands: "In none of these cases does deification have its ground in a personal achievement of a hero … Rather, it is always a gift, something which is not to be striven for, and is in part contrary to expectation." In short, deification in this period "derives from the benevolence of the gods."[24] The possible exception, admits Roloff, is Heracles with his twelve labors. But in archaic sources (Hes., *Theog.* 950–55; Pind., *Nem.* 1.69–74), Heracles does not anticipate and actively work for deification; rather, it is given to him as a reward.

What is clear in this period, at least, is that only Gods can make mortals into Gods. It is not a decision of a human community. Further, we can say that deification in these ancient poems was viewed as a real change in the nature of the one deified. The individual actually becomes immortal, and lives the blissful life of a God in the divine sphere. This involves a change in race (γένος), so that one is literally made akin to the Gods (deathless and ageless). The real transformation of these figures might not seem surprising, because these ancient deifications are all said to be "mythological." But mythology to the ancient Greeks was widely viewed—even by Greek intellectuals—as ancient history.[25] Thus there is no *prima facie* reason to exclude such deifications as precursors for political deifications in time to come.

Historical Precursors to Ruler Cult

As we come further into the classical period (500–323 B.C.E.), we discover historical personages who are deified (or claim to be). A strange fragment from Empedocles (ca. 490–430 B.C.E.) (DK 31 B 112 = Diog. Laert., *Vit. Philosoph.* 8.62) has the philosopher declare himself to be an "immortal God, no longer mortal" (θεὸς ἄμβροτος, οὐκέτι θνητός), actually worshiped (σεβίζομαι) by men and women. Empedocles appears to have viewed himself as a fallen God come down to earth as a guide to human beings. There are various death legends which

---

23   *Gottähnlichkeit*, 91.
24   *Ibid.*, 91.
25   This tendency is well exemplified in Book 1 of Diodorus' *Library of History*, but many other sources could be cited in support.

make him into a God as well. One has Empedocles, after he had brought a woman back to life, called back to heaven in the middle of the night amidst a heavenly light and a "glitter of lamps." After a search for his body, his friend Pausanias thought it necessary that he receive sacrifices as one who had become a God (καὶ Θύειν αὐτῷ δεῖν καθαπερεὶ γεγονότι Θεῷ) (Diog. Laert., *Vit. Philosoph.* 8.68). In another account, Empedocles saves a city from plague by cleansing the waters of a river. When Empedocles suddenly appears along its banks, the citizens rise, worship, and pray to him as to a God (ἐξαναστάντας προσκυνεῖν καὶ προσεύχεσθαι καθαπερεὶ Θεῷ) (8.70). Empedocles confirmed this belief by jumping into a fire.

In the early fifth century, Theagenes of Thasos was reputed to have won 1400 crowns as a boxer, pancratist, and runner (Paus., *Descr.* 6.11.5; Suidas, *s.v.* Νίκων). There is also evidence for his activity as a successful politician and religious reformer.[26] The story of his deification, repeated in several places (Paus., *Descr.* 6.11.6–9; Oenomaus *ap.* Eus., *Praep. ev.* 5.34.6–9 and Dio Chrys., *Or.* 31.95–97), does not begin in his lifetime, however, but after his death (ca. 430 B.C.E.). When a former enemy whipped the statue of Theagenes at night, it crashed down on him and killed him. According to Draconian law, the statue was arraigned, convicted, and flung into the sea. Harvests failed, and after the reason had been elicited from Delphi, the statue, wondrously recovered by fishermen in their nets, was set up where it had stood before. Accordingly, sacrifices were made customary to Theagenes "just as to a God" (ἅτε Θεῷ). Pausanias in the second century C.E. adds that he knows that Theagenes had many other statues both in Greece and in "barbarian" parts, and that he healed sicknesses and received honors from the natives (*Descr.* 6.11.9). In his satire *Parliament of the Gods* (§12), Lucian confirms that the statue of Theagenes in Thasos healed diseases. A. D. Nock wrote that Theagenes had "an active cult in his own home centuries later, in which anyone who wished (i. e., not citizens only) was invited to make offerings for the good of himself and of his family."[27]

In general, what these figures show us is that those who shared the power of Gods could become Gods. This could happen during life (as in

---

26 Jean Pouilloux, *Recherches sur l'histoire et les cultes de Thasos: De la fondation de la cité à 196 avant J.-C.* (Paris: E. de Boccard, 1954), 62–105, esp. 105.

27 Arthur Darby Nock, "Deification and Julian" in *Essays on Religion and the Ancient World*, 2.842. See further Pouilloux, *Recherches*, 104.

the case of Empedocles) or after death (as with Theagenes). Both of these figures were also considered to possess a life which transcended death. There is little indication that the deification of these men was not understood in a realistic sense. Theagenes possessed a kind of life after death, and Empedocles (apparently) a life before birth *and* after death. Empedocles displayed divine power in his earthly life, and Theagenes displayed such power after death. The honors they received were a response to the powers they manifested.

Deification in the Ruler Cult

At the end of the classical period, deification became a formal, political act. These political deifications now come under the heading of "ruler cult." Ruler cult is a massive topic, and I cannot hope to cover it in any depth here. Instead, I will attempt to give a thick description of ruler cult for key figures in critical periods of Greek and Roman history: (1) Philip II and Demetrius Poliorcetes in the fourth and early third century B.C.E. Greece, (2) the Ptolemies (notably Ptolemy IV and IX) in third to first century B.C.E. Egypt, and (3) Marc Antony in the eastern half of the Roman empire in the mid to late first century B.C.E. My focus will not be ruler cult in general, but specific rulers conformed to specific Gods. Although kinship with the Gods was sometimes claimed by rulers, a more important factor (for my purposes) was their assimilation to a particular God who served as a sort of paradigm.

Philip II

The historian Diodorus tells us that on the last day of Philip II's life, he held an early morning procession in a theater packed with representatives from all over the Greek world. In the procession, the statues of the twelve Olympian Gods were solemnly paraded among the guests. Each statue was produced with extraordinary workmanship, and adorned wonderfully with the brilliance of wealth (*Bibl.* 16.92.5). Philip then sent in his own statue, fit for a God (θεοπρεπές). The idea that in this ceremony Philip presented himself as the thirteenth Olympian is probably a later interpretation. Diodorus says that Philip "demonstrat-

ed" (ἀποδεικνύντος) himself as συνθρόνος with the Gods (16.92.5).[28]
The word συνθρόνος, according to Ernst Fredricksmeyer, appears here
first in Greek literature.[29] Since the throne symbolizes the rule of the
king, Philip may have indicated that by the supremacy and magnitude
of his rule he shared in divine power. This is in accord with what Diodorus later remarks about the king: "So Philip, having become greatest
(μέγιστος) of those kings in Europe of his time, numbered himself as
viceregent (συνθρόνος) with the twelve Gods on account of the greatness of his rule (διὰ τὸ μέγεθος τῆς ἀρχῆς)" (16.95.1). Fredricksmeyer
thinks that "This interpretation probably derives from Diodorus' source
who was an eyewitness (Theopompus?)."[30] Although this may be special pleading, it is right for Fredricksmeyer to point to Aristotle as a
background for Philip's logic:

> But if there is any one man so greatly superior in outstanding valor
> (τις ἔστιν εἷς τοσοῦτον διαφέρων κατ' ἀρετῆς ὑπερβολήν) ... so that the
> valor of all the rest and their political ability is not comparable ... it is
> no longer proper to count these men a part of the state; for they will be
> treated unjustly if deemed worthy of equal status, being so widely unequal
> in valor and in their political power (ἄνισοι τοσοῦτον κατ' ἀρετὴν ὄντες καὶ
> τὴν πολιτικὴν δύναμιν): since such a man will naturally be like a God
> among   men   (ὥσπερ γὰρ θεὸν   ἐν ἀνθρώποις εἰκὸς εἶναι τὸν τοιοῦτον).
> (Arist., Pol. 3.13, 1284a3−14; cf. 1284b30−34)

Aristotle had joined Philip in Pella in 342 B.C.E as tutor for his son
(Alexander the Great). Thus these ideas, though published after Philip's
death, may have been known to the king (and likely were known to
Alexander). Later, Philip was indeed undisputed master of Europe, hav-
ing stunned Athens and Thebes in the battle of Chaeronea (338 B.C.E.).
As head of the Corinthian League, Philip was poised to invade Asia to
take vengeance on the Persians. That others in the Greek world viewed
Philip as "superior in outstanding valor" is not far-fetched.

The Athenian orator Isocrates made the deification of Philip explicit
by encouraging his assimilation to the God Heracles. Heracles had attained the rank of a God because of his victorious campaign against

---

28 E. Fredricksmeyer, "Divine Honors for Philip II," *Transactions of the American
    Philological Association* 109 (1979): 56−57.
29 *Ibid.*, 57.
30 *Ibid.*

the "barbarians" of the east (*Phil.* 137).[31] That same path to deification, urged Isocrates, was now open to Philip:

> Now, while all who are blessed with understanding ought to set before themselves the most powerful (τὸν κράτιστον), and strive to become like them, it behooves you [Philip] above all to do so. For since you have no need to follow alien examples (παραδείγμασιν) but have before you one from your own house [Heracles], have we not then the right to expect that you will be spurred on by this and inspired by the ambition to make yourself like the ancestor of your race? I do not mean that you will be able to imitate Heracles in all his exploits; for even among the Gods there are some who could not do that; but in the qualities of the spirit, in devotion to humanity (φιλανθρωπίαν), and in the good will (εὔνοιαν) which he cherished toward the Hellenes, you can come close to his purposes. (*Phil.* 113–114; trans. George Norlin, LCL, modified; cf. 109–15)

For Isocrates, Heracles showed liberality and goodwill to the Greeks because he conquered the barbarians. By the same victory, Philip would prove to be a kindly benefactor to the Greek cities. Participation in these particular Herculean qualities would be Philip's mode of deification. If Philip conquered and enslaved the Persians, Isocrates prophesied, "then will nothing be left for you except to become a God (οὐδὲν γὰρ ἔσται λοιπὸν ἔτι πλὴν θεὸν γενέσθαι)" (*Ep. 2 ad Phil.* 5). This statement cannot be tossed aside as mere rhetoric. It expresses the deep sensibility of the Greek spirit developing in this period. The myth of the deified Heracles had become, for this fourth-century Athenian, a political promise. Twelve years later, in 324 B.C.E., Philip's son Alexander cashed in on that promise when he was deified by the Greek states Athens and Sparta (Plut., *Apoph. lac.* [*Mor.* 219e]; Ael. *Var. Hist.* 2.19; 5.12). No one in the Greek world could have expected the tremendous success of Alexander's Persian campaigns. In ten years, Alexander conquered a region stretching from the Danube in modern Bulgaria to the Indus river in India. Suddenly Isocrates' promise of Heraclean godhood had become reality.

---

31 For Heracles as prototype of world-ruler, see, Homer, *Il.* 19.103; Dio Chrysos., *Orat.* 1.84; Eur., *Heracl.* 1309; 1252; Hesiod, *Scut.* 27–29.

Demetrius Poliorcetes

The deification of Alexander in 324 B.C.E. "marks an epoch" in the history of deification in the Greek world.[32] Before him, the deification of living men was rare.[33] After him, cases of deification dramatically increase.[34] For Greece, I have space only to discuss the example of Demetrius Poliorcetes, perhaps the most (in)famous of Alexander's successors. In 307, after he delivered Athens from the "tyrant" Demetrius of Phalerum, Demetrius Poliorcetes and his father Antigonus (the "One-eyed") were cultically honored as "Saviors" (Σωτῆρες) with a priest, an altar, and sacrifices (Plut., *Dem.* 10.4; 46.1). Two new Athenian tribes were named after them (10.6; Diod., *Bibl.* 20.46.2), and their images were woven into the *peplos* (the body-length gown) of Athena (Plut., *Dem.* 10.5; 12.3; Diod., *Bibl.* 20.46.2). Later in 304/3 the Athenians established a cult of Demetrius the "Descender," an epithet usually reserved for Zeus (Plut., *Dem.* 10.5 [*Mor.* 338a]; Clem Al., *Prot.* 4.54.6).[35] In 294–295, when Demetrius drove off the tyrant Lachares after a long siege, the Athenians voted to call their month Munychion "Demetrion" and called one day per month "Demetrias."

---

32 E. Badian, *Protocol of the Colloquy of the Center for Hermeneutical Studies in Hellenistic and Modern Culture: The Deification of Alexander the Great* (Berkeley: Center for Hermeneutical Studies, 1976), 3.

33 For precedents, see E. A. Fredricksmeyer, "On the Background of the Ruler-Cult" in *Ancient Macedonian Studies in Honor of Charles F. Edson* (ed. H. Dell; Thessaloniki: Institute for Balkan Studies, 1981), 145–56; N. G. L. Hammond, "Heroic and Divine Honors in Macedonia before the Successors," *Ancient World* 30 (1999): 109–110.

34 Badian rightly points out that the deification of living men is poorly attested between Lysander and Alexander the Great ("The Deification of Alexander the Great" in *Ancient Macedonian Studies*, 43). He wrongly denies, however, the Samians' deification of Lysander during his lifetime based on (1) his dubious assumption that an inscription dated to the fourth century must refer "to a time well into that century," (2) his argument *e silentio* that Duris did not mention that Lysander was alive when he received the honors, and (3) his rejection of Plutarch's clear statement that Lysander once presided over the Lysandreia in person (*ibid.*, 33–36).

35 On the other honors given to Demetrius, some not considered divine, see Kenneth Scott, "The Deification of Demetrius Poliorcetes: Part II," *American Journal of Philology* 49 (1928): 238–39; Christian Habicht, *Gottmenschentum und griechische Städte* (2d ed.; München: C.H. Beck'sche Verlagsbuchhandlung, 1970), 45; and Jon D. Mikalson, *Religion in Hellenistic Athens* (Berkeley: University of California Press, 1998), 79–81.

Since Demetrius entered the city during the celebration of the Dionysia (an important Athenian festival in the spring) the festival was renamed the "Dionysia and Demetreia."[36]

In the celebration of the Mysteries of Demeter in 291, an ithyphallic hymn was composed in Demetrius' honor for public and private performance.[37] At the time, the Aetolians, in alliance with Thebes, held Delphi and threatened to remove an important Athenian dedication of shields originally hung in honor of their victory over the Persians. The Athenian hymn asks Demetrius to attack Aetolia to ensure the preservation of the shields as well as access to the oracle. The text of the hymn preserves some interesting details on why some Athenians considered Demetrius worthy of deification. I quote the relevant section:

> The greatest and dearest of the Gods
> are present for the city,
> for good fortune brought together here Demeter
> and Demetrius.
> She comes to perform the sacred mysteries of Kore.
> He is present handsome, laughing, and cheerful,
> as a God ought to be.
> It is a revered sight—his friends all in a circle,
> himself in the middle,
> as if his friends were stars, he the sun.
> Hail, son of Poseidon, most powerful God, and of Aphrodite!
> The other Gods are either far distant,
> or do not have ears,
> or do not exist
> or pay no attention to us,
> But we see you present (σὲ δὲ παρόνϑ' ὁρῶμεν),
> not made of stone or wood,
> but real (ἀληϑινόν).
> We pray to you:
> First, dearest one, create peace, for you are Lord (κύριος γὰρ εἶ σύ).
> And especially punish the Sphinx that tramples over
> not Thebes but all Greece,

---

36   Habicht, *Gottmenschentum*, 51–52, citing Jacoby's commentary to *FGH* 328 F 166.

37   For the relationship of Athens to Demetrius during the twenty year period spanning 307–287 B.C.E., see Mikalson, *Hellenistic Athens*, 75–104; Christian Habicht, *Athens from Alexander to Antony* (Cambridge, Mass.: Harvard University Press, 1997), 67–97.

the Aetolian who sits on a rock, like the old Sphinx,
and snatches up and carries off all of us.[38]

Most striking for our purposes is the emphasis on Demetrius' physical
presence in the hymn, in contrast to the absence of the other Gods.[39]
Demetrius is portrayed as the living God. (Indeed, there is a superficial
similarity of the hymn to the invective of Hebrew prophets against
Gods of wood and stone.) Demetrius' appearance in Athens is an epiphany. This epiphanic immanence is at least one of the factors that made
Demetrius worthy of divine honors, for "the greatest ... of the Gods are
present." Demetrius is the son of specific deities (Poseidon and Aphrodite) and bears the divine quality of joviality.

Equally important to note is Demetrius' power. "First, dearest one,"
the Athenians ask, "create peace, for *you are Lord* (κύριος)." The power
expected here is power to do good: to defeat the Aetolian-Theban alliance and restore the honor of Athens at Delphi. Demetrius is already a
God in Athens, so the Athenians ask for a manifestation of his divinity
through benefaction—topple the Aetolians and retake Delphi.[40] The
God who will triumph over his enemies is the rightful "Lord" (religiously and politically) of Greece.

Besides obvious associations of an *ithyphallic* hymn with Dionysus,
Angelos Chaniotis has pointed out further associations of Demetrius
with Dionysus. As mentioned above, Demetrius had freed the city of
Athens from the tyrant Lachares in 295, and had entered the city during
the festival of Dionysus. In this act, Demetrius conformed himself to

---

38 Duris of Samos (*FGH* 76 F 13) *ap.* Athen., *Deipn.* 6.253b–f; paraphrased in
Demochares *FGH* 75 F2. The translation, slightly modified, is taken from Mikalson, *Hellenistic Athens*, 94–95. Mikalson warns against taking the hymn as a
serious representation of Athenian religion, citing its playfulness and probable
composition by a foreigner (*ibid.*, 96). The playfulness is better attributed to
the hymn's association with Dionysus and the theater, and the hymn's author-
ship is in doubt (Angelos Chaniotis, "The Ithyphallic Hymn for Demetrios Poliorcetes and Hellenistic Religious Mentality" in *More than Men, Less than Gods:
Studies in Royal Cult and Imperial Worship. Proceedings of the International Colloquium Organized by the Belgian School at Athens (1–2 November 2007)* [eds. P.P. Iossif, A.S. Chankowski, and C.C. Lorber; Leuven: Peeters 2011], 97, n. 5). It is
best, with Chaniotis and others, to take the hymn as a serious expression of religion.

39 For divine presence in the hymn, as well as divine efficacy and affability, see
Chaniotis, "Ithyphallic Hymn," 106–109.

40 Cf. Chaniotis, "The Divinity of Hellenistic Rulers" in *A Companion to the Hellenistic World* (ed. Andrew Erskine; Malden: Blackwell, 2003), 432–33.

Dionysus *Eleuthereus*, an epithet taken to mean "Dionysus *of freedom*."[41]
When Demetrius returned to Athens in 291, he was, like Dionysus,
coming from the sea.[42] As he entered the city, he not only received
the ithyphallic hymn, but also an official *xenismos*, or *adventus* ritual cus-
tomarily performed for the Gods Dionysus and Demeter. The ritual included the burning of incense, the crowning of altars, and the pouring
of libations. The privilege of such a divine reception had been officially
decreed for Demetrius four years earlier (Plut., *Dem.* 34). During the
Dionysia every spring, Demetrius had rights to these rites, because he
was arriving at his *own festival* (the "Dionysia *and Demetria*").

Chaniotis also notes that Herodian (*Ab excessu divi Marci* 1.3.3) mentions that Demetrius imitated Dionysus, exchanging the royal diadem,
the Macedonian felt hat and the scepter for the ivy garland and the thyrsus. "Although there were a number of occasions on which Demetrios
could have exchanged the symbols of royal power for the Dionysiac
costume, his reception in Athens during an evidently Dionysiac ritual
provided him with the ideal opportunity to perform his *imitatio Diony-
si*."[43] Chaniotis thus suspects that the God in the hymnic phrase "He is
present handsome, laughing, and cheerful, *as a God ought to be*" is "no
other than Dionysos."[44]

Ruler Cult in Ptolemaic Egypt

In Egypt, ruler cult centered less on the acts of an individual king than
on an institution of divine kingship: the dynastic cult. For the native
Egyptian, the dynastic cult had a 3,000 year history. In his coronation,
the Egyptian Pharaoh was proclaimed "son of Re" the sun God, and
was divine by nature of his office. No further action was required for
him to remain in the divine sphere, although proof of his divinity
was often expected through military achievements and monumental
building projects.[45] For the Egyptians, Alexander the Great had dutifully

---

41 "Ithyphallic Hymn," 101.
42 *Ibid.*, 104.
43 *Ibid.*, 105. The text in Herodian actually refers to Antigonus. "It is, however,
    obvious," says Chaniotis, "that Herodian means Demetrios" (*ibid.*, n. 47)
44 *Ibid.*, 109, see also n. 85 on the same page.
45 Erik Hornung, "The Pharaoh" in *The Egyptians* (ed. Sergio Donadoni; trans.
    Robert Bianchi et al.; Chicago: University of Chicago, 1997), 288, 301–
    308. Interestingly, Ptolemy IV and his wife are only integrated into the dynastic

fulfilled this office. He had travelled to the oracle of Ammon in Siwah
to confirm that he was the son of Ammon-Re (identified with Zeus),[46]
and was officially coronated as son of this God in Memphis. Already,
then, Alexander conformed to the Egyptian understanding of the divine
king. His later conquering of Persia established for all time the reality of
his divinity, such that the legitimacy of Alexander as Pharaoh was (apparently) never questioned. In fact, a later myth arose—perhaps from
Egyptian priestly circles—that Alexander was the physical son of the
last native Egyptian Pharaoh, Nectanebo (*Alexander Romance* 1.1–7).

The Ptolemies, when they sought to found their own divine cult,
grafted it onto the pre-existing cult of Alexander. In the reign of Ptolemy I, Alexander had become an official state God.[47] This occurred
sometime before 285/4, when we find Menelaus, Ptolemy I's brother,
named as priest of Alexander on a papyrus document.[48] The Ptolemies
themselves were only included in this cult after Ptolemy I's death in
281. The next year, Ptolemy II proclaimed his father Ptolemy I a
God with a special cult, games (the *Ptolemaia*), and a cult title, "Savior"
(Σωτήρ).[49] Ptolemy I's deification then became part of Ptolemaic state
mythology. Writing in the style of Hesiod and Pindar, the court poet
Theocritus declared that Zeus made Ptolemy Soter

> equal in honor even to the blessed immortals, and a golden throne is built
> for him in the house of Zeus; beside him, kindly disposed, sits Alexander,
> the God of the dancing diadem, who brought destruction to the Persians.
> Facing them is established the seat of centaur-slaying Heracles, fashioned

---

cult *after* their victory in the battle of Raphia (Gunther Hölbl, *A History of the Ptolemaic Empire* [London: Routledge, 2001], 169). See further Eric Turner, "Ptolemaic Egypt" in *Cambridge Ancient History* (eds. F. W. Walbank and A. E. Astin; 2d ed.; 14 vols.; Cambridge: Cambridge University Press, 1984), 7.1.168.

46 The cult of the Libyan Ammon had already been established in Macedonia from the late fifth century (Hölbl, *History*, 10).

47 Turner "Ptolemaic Egypt," 168.

48 P.M. Fraser, *Ptolemaic Alexandria I-II* (Oxford: Clarendon, 1972), 1.215–16.

49 The cult title may have come from a pre-existing cult of Ptolemy in the Greek world. Ptolemy I was first recognized as a God by the Rhodians for his bene-factions while they fought for survival against Demetrius Poliorcetes (304 B.C.E.). They erected a sanctuary in his honor called the *Ptolemaion*. An embassy sent to the oracle of Ammon at Siwah confirmed that Ptolemy could be wor-shiped as a God (Diod., *Bibl.* 20.100.3–4; Paus., *Descr.* 1.8.6). About eighteen years later, the Island League thanked Ptolemy for helping to expel Demetrius and restore the old constitution. They gave him divine honors, erecting an altar for him at Delos.

from solid adamant; there he joins in feasting with the heavenly ones and rejoices exceedingly in the grandsons of his grandsons, for the son of Kronos has removed old age from their limbs, and his very own descendents are called immortal (ἀθάνατοι). (*Idyll.* 17.16–25, trans. Richard Hunter)

In this scene, Ptolemy I has obtained post-mortem immortality and incorruption among other deified conquerors.[50]

When Ptolemy I's wife Berenice died in 279, she was included in Soter's cult, with king and queen being referred to as "Savior Gods" (Θεοὶ Σωτῆρες). The official dynastic cult, however, only began in 272, the fourteenth year of Ptolemy II (Philadelphus), when he added a cult of himself and his wife/sister Arsinoë (both still living) to that of Alexander under the name of "Sibling Gods" (Θεοὶ Ἀδελφοί). The deification of a married couple—between full brother and sister—seems to have been influenced by native Egyptian customs. Nonetheless, ingratiating Greeks immediately turned to the model of Zeus and Hera (married divine siblings).

In time, more deified royal couples were added to the dynastic cult. Additional priesthoods were added for notable queens, starting with Arsinoë Philadelphus (who died in 270), and greatly expanded by Cleopatra III (died ca. 102).[51] In the dynastic cult, Godhood became linked to blood and was thus something inherited. The source of divinity was linked back to the throne of Pharaoh Alexander. Initially there was a break in the link because Ptolemy I and Berenice I were not part of the dynastic cult. This gap was later bridged by Ptolemy IV Philopator, who inserted the Savior Gods into their rightful place after Alexander.

---

50 Blackwell's idea that "Greco-Roman apotheosis of heroes and emperors" is primarily conceptualized as a form of "immortality through remembrance"—not an actual immortality—is simply wrong (*Christosis*, 47, 103). He erroneously reads Werner Jaeger's discussion of archaic and classical texts as applicable to the Hellenistic and Roman periods (Werner Jaeger "The Greek Ideas of Immortality: The Ingersoll Lecture for 1958," *HTR* 52 [1959]: 135–147, cited in Blackwell, *Christosis*, 47, n. 56). Cf. the Roman tradition, where Romulus is regarded as a God because his soul survives "to enjoy eternal life" (Cic., *Nat. d.* 2.62).

51 F. W. Walbank, "Monarchies and Monarchic Ideas" in *Cambridge Ancient History*, 7.1.97; Fraser, *Ptolemaic Alexandria*, 1.221.

Ptolemaic Assimilation to Dionysus[52]

On his father's side, Ptolemy I was thought to be descended from Philip II and ultimately from Heracles (Theocr., *Idyll.* 17.26–27). On his mother's side, he was thought to be descended from Dionysus.[53] We have two artistic depictions of Ptolemy I with the traits of Dionysus. One, a metal relief in Hildesheim, shows Ptolemy with a Dionysian headband. The other, a bronze bust in Baltimore shows Ptolemy draped in an ivy crown.[54] As the history of the Ptolemaic kings went on, the importance of Dionysus as a state God became ever more pronounced.

Background on Dionysus-Osiris

Diodorus of Sicily presents three accounts of the "anthropomorphic" Dionysus supplied by the writers of his day (3.63.1). The third account has Dionysus born from Semele and, after his mother's demise, brought to Nysa in Arabia. This account seems to have been widely taken for granted in Ptolemaic royal ideology, and is worth reproducing here:

> There [in Nysa] the boy [Dionysus] was reared by nymphs and was given the name Dionysus after his father (*Dios*) and after the place (*Nysa*); and since he grew to be of unusual beauty he at first spent his time at dances and with bands of women and in every kind of luxury and amusement, and after that, forming the women into an army and arming them with thyrsi, he made a campaign over all the inhabited world.[55] He also instructed all men who were pious and cultivated a life of justice in the knowledge of his rites and initiated them into his mysteries, and, furthermore, in every

---

52 For the assimilation of Alexander to Dionysus, see Nock, *Essays on Religion*, 1.136–44. The evidence postdates Alexander, but gives insight into how later thinkers conceptualized Alexander's deification as an assimilation to a particular God.

53 *Ibid.*, 1.139, esp. n. 22.

54 For the figures, see Günther Grimm, "Die Vergöttlichung Alexanders des Grossen in Ägypten und ihre Bedeutung für den ptolemäischen Königskult" in *Das Ptolemäische Ägypten: Akten des internationalen Symposions 27.–29. September 1976 in Berlin* (eds. Herwig Maehler and Volker Michael Strocka; Mainz: Philipp von Zabern, 1978), 109, figs. 85–86. For further examples, see J. Tondriau, "La dynastie ptolemaique et la religion dionysiaque," *Chronique d'Égypte* 49–50 (1950): 283.

55 For a similar campaign attributed to Osiris, see Diod., *Bibl.* 1.17.1.

place he held great festive assemblages and celebrated musical contests.[56] (3.64.5–7; trans. C. H. Oldfather, LCL; cf. 4.4.2–4)

Here we learn of three significant events in Dionysius' life that became paradigmatic for the Ptolemies. First, he spent his early life in dances with bands of women "in every kind of luxury" (παντοδαπῇ τρυφῇ). Second, we learn that Dionysus formed an army and conquered the inhabited world (in particular, the East). Third, the account relates that after his war, Dionysus collected a great mass of spoils and returned to his native country in triumph, complete with festivities and games.

The imitation of all three aspects is best illustrated by the Grand Procession of Ptolemy II Philadelphus, performed sometime in the 270s. The procession depicted various scenes from the life of Dionysus in the form of gigantic and richly decorated floats. The scenes climaxed with depictions of Dionysus' eastern triumph. A snippet from the description of Callixeinus (preserved in Athen., *Deipn.* 5.196a-203b) will give some taste of the national importance of Dionysus, and the extravagant attempt of the Ptolemies to conform themselves to his myth.

After a rich display of elaborate floats portraying scenes from Dionysus' life, there was rolled in:

> another four-wheeled cart, which contained the 'Return of Dionysus from India', an eighteen foot statue of Dionysus, having a purple cloak and a golden crown of ivy and vine, lay upon an elephant. He held in his hands a golden thyrsus-lance, and his feet were shod with felt slippers embroidered with gold. In front of him on the neck of the elephant there sat a young Satyr seven feet tall, wreathed with a golden crown of pine, signaling with a golden goat-horn in his right hand. The elephant had gold trappings and a golden ivy crown about its neck.
>
> Five hundred little girls followed him, dressed in purple chitons and golden girdles. The first 120 girls were wreathed with golden pine crowns. One hundred and twenty Satyrs followed them, some wearing silver armour, others bronze. After them marched five troops of asses on which rode crowned Silenoi and Satyrs [all companions of Dionysus]. Some of the asses had frontless and harnesses of gold, others of silver. After them marched twenty-four elephant quadrigae, sixty bigae of goats, twelve of saiga antelopes, seven of oryxes, fifteen of hartebeest, eight bigae of ostriches, seven of onelaphoi, four bigae of onagers, and four quadrigae of horses.[57]

---

56 For Osiris as patron of the arts, see *ibid.*, 1.18.4–6.

57 Translation from E. E. Rice, *The Grand Procession of Ptolemy Philadelphus* (London: Oxford University Press, 1983), 17–19. See his commentary on *ibid.*, 83–86.

The text proceeds with lavish lists of exotic "eastern" animals (with equally exotic names) which convey cartfuls of spoils (including pretended prisoners of war) from Dionysus' Indian campaigns. The opulence of the display showed the vast wealth gained from the spoils of Dionysus' (and Ptolemy's) campaigns. Clearly this was a decisive event in the history of Dionysus, as well as in the history of Ptolemaic state mythology. By reenacting this scene from the life of the God, Ptolemy II conformed himself to the myth and character of the conquering Dionysus. This point was made evident as the procession went on.

After the procession of Dionysus came a parade of Alexander "whose golden statue was borne upon a quadriga of real elephants with Nike [Victory] and Athena on either side."[58] Alexander's connection to Dionysus through his eastern campaigns was here vividly portrayed. He was the Dionysian victor *par excellence*. Following Alexander were the thrones of Ptolemy I Soter made of 10,000 gold pieces. The Ptolemies were here portrayed as the Dionysian successors of Alexander. Their conquering armies, in full panoply, closed the great procession in a show of Ptolemaic military might. To be like the God Dionysius was not only to be exotic, to be full of cheer, and to display luxury—but to conquer.

After his victory in the east, it was said that Dionysus became patron of the arts by holding processions and offering musical competitions. By this means, Dionysius established peace in his domain, and freedom from disorder. It was this third aspect of Dionysius that Ptolemy II (and his heirs) attempted to imitate through the creation of the Alexandrian Library and Museum, and in general through their generous subsidizing of the arts—tragic, musical, and poetic.

In later periods of Ptolemaic rule, the open assimilation of rulers to Dionysus continued apace. A marble bust from Tmuis, preserved in the Cairo Museum presents Ptolemy III with the traits of a young Dionysus—two small horns and a Dionysiac headband.[59] There are many more iconographic examples of Ptolemy IV's assimilation to the God, conveniently catalogued by François Dunand: "a terracotta head in the Benaki collection, a plaster medallion in a private collection of Am-

---

58   *Ibid.*, 21.
59   Dietrich Wildung and Günter Grimm, eds., *Götter und Pharaonen:[Ausstellung] Römer- und Pelizaeus-Museum, Hildesheim, 29. Mai-16. September, 1979* (Mainz/Rhein: P. von Zabern, 1979), no. 91.

sterdam, a silver alabaster of Palaiokastro on which the infant Dionysus perhaps bears the traits of Philopator."[60]

Ptolemy IV Philopator, Dunand shows, had a particularly close relationship with Dionysus. He founded festivals involving sacrifices of all sorts in honor of the God, for instance the "Wine Flask-Carrying Festival" (Λαγυνοφόρια).[61] The king himself took an active role, according to Plutarch, in these religious rites. In his palace he would go about gathering devotees [or begging like a priest of Cybele] while holding a timbrel (τελετὰς τελεῖν καὶ τύμπανον ἔχων ἐν τοῖς βασιλείοις ἀγείρειν), and he "devoted himself to women and Dionysiac routs and revels" (ἐν γυναιξὶ καὶ θιάσοις καὶ κώμοις συνέχοντος ἑαυτόν) (Plut., Cleom. 33.2, 34.2; cf. Justin, 1 Apol. 30.1). The king was tattooed with ivy leaves (φύλλοις κισσοῦ κατεστίχθαι), the plant sacred to Dionysus (Etymologicum magnum s.v. Γάλλος, 220.19–20; cf. 3 Macc 2:29). Ptolemy IV also undertook a reform of the administrative organization of Alexandria, giving to the "Berenice" tribe the name "Dionysia" and replacing the ancient names of the demes of this tribe by the new names borrowed from the Dionysiac cycle (Thoantis, Staphylis, Euantheus, Maroneus, Deianeireus, Althaeus, Ariadnis) (Satyrus ap. Theophilus of Antioch, Autol. 2.7).[62] This reform showed the spread of Dionysiac mythology in the Alexandrian milieu and the desire of the king to place his capital under the patronage of his ancestor Dionysus.[63]

According to Clement of Alexandria, Ptolemy IV also received the nickname Neos Dionysus ("New [or Young] Dionysus)" (Protrep. 4.54.2).[64] This title (θεὸς νεὸς Διονύσος) was also borne by Ptolemy XII Auletes, Cleopatra VII's father (OGIS 186.9–10, 191.1, 741.1; SEG 8.408; Porphyry ap. Eus Chron. = FGH 260.2 [12] and [15]).[65]

---

60 Francoise Dunand, "Les associations dionysiaques au service du pouvoir Lagide (III S. Av. J.-C.)" in L'Association dionysiaque dans les sociétés Anciennes: Actes de la table rond organisée par l'École française de Rome (Palais Farnèse: L'École française de Rome, 1986), 87.

61 This report comes from Eratosthenes of Cyrene (ap. Athen., Deipn. 7.276a-c), who lived in the court of Ptolemy IV.

62 For discussion, see Fraser, Ptolemaic Alexandria 2.120, n. 48.

63 Dunand, "Les associations dionysiaques," 87–88.

64 For Ptolemy IV as Dionysus in epigraphy, see Paulus Riewald, "De imperatorum romanorum cum certis dis et comparatione et aequatione" (Diss. Halle, 1912), 318.

65 For other references on inscriptions and papyri to Ptolemy XII as Neos Dionysus, see J. Tondriau, "Rois Lagides comparés ou identifiés à des divinités," Chron. d'Egypte 45–46 (1948): 137–38.

"The real significance of such a title," F. W. Walbank comments, "is not easy to discover. Nock has suggested that Ptolemy XII may have been influenced by the Pharaonic concept of his reincarnation of Osiris."[66] Others see the designation as "little more than a cult title."[67] At the very least, the title suggests some kind of assimilation to the God.

Auletes was also depicted as Dionysus in art.[68] In addition, two cities in the Fayyum were renamed "Bacchias" and "Dionysias" in his honor.[69] Lucian of Samosata also tells this colorful tale which probably refers to Auletes:

> At the court of Ptolemy surnamed Dionysus (Πτολεμαίῳ τῷ Διονύσῳ ἐπι-
> κληθέντι), a man accused Demetrius, a Platonic philosopher, of drinking
> water and of being the only one who did not assume the feminine habits
> in the Dionysia. Now if Demetrius, called in the next morning had not
> drunk wine under the eyes of all the court, or clothed himself in a robe
> of Tarentum, striking cymbals and dancing—he would have perished as
> one displeased with the life of the king, as one who tried to refute and op-
> pose the opulence of Ptolemy (τῆς Πτολεμαίου τρυφῆς). (Cal. 16; cf. Strab.,
> Geog. 17 795.6 and 796; Dio Chrys., Or. 32 383, 22; Athen., Deipn. 4
> 176e–)

The Beginnings of Roman Ruler Cult:
Marc Antony's Assimilation to Dionysus

At the end of the Hellenistic period, Dionysiac royal ideology was transferred to the person of Marc Antony, the Roman triumvir.[70] Two of the charges, according to the historian Dio Cassius, leveled against Antony were that he gave himself the title of "Osiris" or "Dionysus" (ἑαυ-τὸν Ὄσιριν καὶ Διόνυσον ἐπικεκληκότα) (50.25.2–4), and posed for portraits and statues as Osiris/Dionysus (50.5.3). There are some doubts about whether Antony ever called himself "Osiris."[71] It is historically re-

---

66 Walbank "Monarchies and Monarchic Ideas," 86. Nock himself only allowed
    for the idea of incarnation in Egypt (for Auletes), where Dionysus was identi-
    fied with Osiris (Essays on Religion, 1.147, 151–52).
67 Fraser, Ptolemaic Alexandria, 1.244. But compare his comments on 1.237.
68 See the bust in Robert S. Bianchi, Cleopatra's Egypt: Age of the Ptolemies, 1988),
    155, cat. 58.
69 Ibid., 156.
70 Hölbl, History, 291.
71 Since Dionysus was widely identified with Osiris, Antony as Osiris may have
    been the interpretatio aegyptiaca current during Antony's time.

liable, however, that he desired to be known officially as the "New [or Young] Dionysus" (Νέος Διονύσος) (Plut., *Ant.* 60.3; *IG²* §1043, line 23).[72] When Antony was in Athens after defeating Brutus and Cassius, he called himself "Dionysus" (*Liberum Patrem*), had himself addressed by this title and asked to have it inscribed on his statues (Sen., *Suas.* 1.6). According to the elder Seneca, Antony "imitated Bacchus [= Dionysus] in dress and retinue (*habitu quoque et comitatu Liberum imitaretur*). The Athenians with their wives and children met him on his arrival, and greeted him as 'Dionysus.'" The Athenians then "proceeded to offer him in marriage [to] their Goddess Minerva [= Athena], and to entreat him to wed her. Antony said he would marry her, but exacted 1000 talents as dowry: whereupon one of the Greeks said: 'Sire, Zeus had your mother, Semele, to wife without a dowry.' This jest passed unpunished, but the betrothal cost the Athenians 1000 talents" (*Suas.* 1.6). The "betrothal" sum was probably closer to four million sesterces—one sixth the amount given by Seneca (Dio Cass., *Rom. Hist.* 48.39.2)—but still a blow to the Athenians. Socrates of Rhodes reveals more about Antony's stay in Athens:

> when Antonius himself spent some time in Athens after this, he had a roughly framed hut built in a conspicuous spot above the theater and covered with green brushwood, as they do with Bacchic 'caves'; and he hung drums, fawn skins, and other Dionysiac paraphernalia of all sorts in it. He lay inside with his friends, beginning at dawn, and got drunk; musicians summoned from Italy entertained him, and the whole Greek world gathered to watch. Sometimes, he says, Antonius moved up onto the Acropolis, and the entire city of Athens was illuminated by the lamps that hung from the ceilings. He also gave order that from then on he was to be proclaimed as Dionysus throughout all the cities. (*ap.* Athen., *Deipn.* 148b-c = *FGH* 192 F2)

Crossing over to Ephesus in 41, Antony was again hailed as Dionysus, this time with the epithets "Bringer of Joy" (Χαριδότης) and "Mild" (Μειλίχιος) (Plut., *Ant.* 24.3). Thus Antony assumed not only the *habitus* of the God—his condition and deportment—but also his character. Joy and festivity surrounded Antony's "epiphany" in the cities. These festivities were apparently designed to give participants the joy and transport

---

72 Iohannes Kirchner, ed., *Inscriptiones Graecae: Inscriptiones Atticae Euclidis anno posteriores* (Preussische Akademie der Wissenschaften; 2d ed. Minor Pars Prima; Berlin: G. Reimer, 1916), 479, no. 1043, line 23. The Athenian inscription, part of a monument for ephebes, mentions ΑΝΤΩ]ΝΙΟΥ ΘΕΟΥ ΝΕΟΥ ΔΙΟΝΥΣΟ[Υ. It can be dated to 39–38 B.C.E.

experienced in the cult of Dionysus. Nonetheless, Plutarch points out that if Antony was mild with his friends, he was terrible to his enemies. But here we must remember that ferocity too, as we learn from Euripides' *Bacchae*, has much to do with Dionysus.

Antony did more than assume the disposition of the God—he intentionally sought to recapitulate the God's actions in his life. This was, I suggest, at least a partial motivation for his Parthian invasion: like Dionysus, he would march forth into the East and bring back spoils.[73] During his "triumph" over Armenia in 34, Antony ordered that he be called "Dionysus" (*se Liberum Patrem appellari iussisset*). He crowned himself with ivy and dressed in the gold-embroidered gown of Dionysus (*redimitus hederis crocotaque velatus aurea*). In this way, he made his way through Alexandria, holding the thyrsus stick in his hand and wearing tragic high boots on his feet—just as Dionysus (*et thyrsum tenens cothurnisque succinctus curru velut Liber Pater vectus esset Alexandriae*) (Velleius Paterculus, *Res gest. divi Aug.* 2.82.4). Plutarch refers to the well-known "luxuries, excesses, and parades of Antony" (Ἀντωνίου τρυφὰς καὶ ἀκολασίας καὶ πανηγυρισμούς) while in Alexandria. Antony took these to be "cheerful and beneficent actions" (ἱλαρὰ πράγματα καὶ φιλάνθρωπα) (*Adul. am.* 12 [*Mor.* 56e]; cf. Strabo, *Geog.* 17.11). In this way Antony, in the words of Plutarch, "completely assimilated and exactly adapted himself" (συνεξομοιῶν καὶ συνοικειῶν) to Dionysus (Plut., *Ant.* 75.4; cf. 60.3).

Although the ancient sources are full of jokes and hostility toward Antony, one cannot simply brush aside this evidence of assimilation as imaginative propaganda. Antony's enemies did not make up the fact that he assimilated to Dionysus—they exposed it with relish. It is thus appropriate to ask "What did Antony's assimilation to Dionysus mean?"

Duncan Fishwick discusses and interprets several forms of assimilation.[74] First, there is the ruler portrayed with the God's attributes (which occurs mostly on coins).[75] Next there is the attachment of a

---

73   The campaign itself was a disaster.
74   Duncan Fishwick, *The Imperial Cult in the Latin West: Studies in the Ruler Cult of the Western Provinces of the Roman Empire* (Leiden: E.J. Brill, 1987), 29–31.
75   I briefly note that in 39 B.C.E., Antony minted a series of "cistophoric" silver tetradrachms for distribution in the province of Asia. Here he is assimilated Dionysus—but only in terms of the ivy crown and not in terms of any other feature (J. Pollini, "Man Or God: Divine Assimilation and Imitation in the Late Republic and Early Principate" in *Between Republic and Empire: Interpretations of Augustus and His Principate* [eds. Kurt A. Raaflaub, Mark Toher and G. W. Bo-

cult title to a ruler's name such as *Basileios* ("Kingly") or *Kataibates* ("Descender"). A third, "higher degree of assimilation" occurs when the ruler is represented as a God in coins or in epigraphy with the addition of a God's name (e.g., "Arsinoë Aphrodite"). Sometimes the ruler may be addressed by the name of the God alone. "What this amounts to," says Fishwick, "is formal recognition of the ruler as the god in another shape and, as such, the practice is commonly called identification." It does not signify incarnation, for Fishwick, but only that the ruler "is conceived as exercising some of the functions or qualities of a god." Fourth, a ruler might impersonate (i.e., dress up as) a deity. Lastly he may take on the title of a "New" God, such as "*Neos Dionysus.*" In Egypt, this might have signified that the ruler was an avatar of the God. Fishwick is inclined, however, to see in it only that "the personality of some ruler gives the powerful impression that he reproduces here and now the qualities and achievements of Dionysus and in so doing appears as a new, fresh edition of that god."

Scholars have traditionally been skeptical and dismissive of any real religious meaning present in Antony's deification, or in ruler cult in general. Partly this is because Antony himself appears as an unsavory brute in historical documents. Nevertheless, it should be granted that, given the power of religious mythology over time, Antony's assimilation to Dionysus cannot simply be passed off as *only* as a piece of political propaganda. Nor was it, given the presuppositions of his culture, simply an empty mask. It is not far-fetched, I think, to assert that Antony was widely believed to manifest the power of Dionysus—in cheer, in luxury, and in military might. In this way it is not unreasonable to think that many of his devotees believed that Antony embodied the essential qualities of the God. Antony's attempt to make himself akin to the God was thus not—or rather not *just*—an attempt to secure legitimacy; it was the real assumption of the God's power and persona. The assimilation of Antony to Dionysus was so marked that some (as we have seen) have thought that Antony considered himself a real incarnation of the God.[76] Although I dare not say so much, it is fair to say that Antony's participation in the distinctive powers of Dionysus allowed him to share that God's identity.

---

wersock; Berkeley: University of California Press, 1990], 345). For the image, see *ibid.*, 359, no. 12.

76   Hölbl, *History*, 292.

Conclusion

Assimilation to a specific God was once thought to be part and parcel of the Greek mysteries. A far better place to look for such assimilation, however, is the ruler cult. Although not every ruler assimilated himself or herself to a specific God, such assimilation was often a way for rulers to manifest their specific powers to their subjects. Isocrates urged Philip II, descendent of the God Heracles, to conform himself to the qualities of that God. The Ptolemies had a long history of assimilation to Dionysus (also thought to be a distant ancestor). The Roman triumvir Marc Antony, before and after his stint with Cleopatra VII, assimilated himself to the same God. Cleopatra herself was the "New Isis" in Egypt. Later Roman emperors periodically continued the practice of assimilation to various deities up until Late Antiquity.[77] By such assimilation, rulers participated in the specific powers of the various Gods, and (after death) shared their immortality. Such assimilations constituted, I propose, a form of deification analogous to Paul's concept of moral and corporeal assimilation to the God Christ (1 Cor 11:1; 2 Cor 3:18; Rom 8:29; 15:1–3; Phil 3:21). That Christ is a very different kind of God (with different powers and virtues) is readily admitted. But this does not undermine the attempt to construct a historical analogy (which sees similarity *in* difference). Each God will have his or her own fundamental qualities which makes up his or her own identity. The bottom-line is that in both Paul and the ruler cult human beings could share the identity of specific Gods, and thus gain a share of their power and immortality. These points will be more fully fleshed out in chapters 5 and 7. For now, we turn to the Jewish roots of deification.

---

77 For a survey, see the still significant study of Riewald, "De imperatorum romanorum cum certis dis."

Chapter 3:
The Jewish Roots of Deification

> [F]or we hope that the remains of
> the departed will soon come to the light
> (again)
> out of the earth; and afterward they
> will become Gods (θεοί τελέθονται).
>
> —Ps. Phocylides,
> *Sentences* 103–104

Introduction: Jews and Greeks on the Boundaries Between the Human and the Divine

It is sometimes asserted that ancient Jews were essentially different from other Mediterranean peoples in their view of the relation between the human and the divine. Whereas ancient Romans, Greeks, and Hellenized peoples saw no sharp dividing line between divinity and humanity, it is thought that ancient Jews imagined an impermeable boundary separating God and human beings. In this way, many scholars have sought to underscore Jewish (and later Christian) uniqueness, and deny any Jewish notion of deification.[1]

On the face of it, such scholars have a great deal of biblical support, for a number of passages present humans and God as apparent binaries.

> God is not as a human (οὐχ ὡς ἄνθρωπος ὁ θεός) to be deceived, nor as a son of a human to be terrified by threats. (Num 23:19, LXX)
> The Egyptian is a human and not a God (ἄνθρωπον καὶ οὐ θεόν), fleshly bodies of horses. (Isa 31:3)
> No, I will not do according to the rage of my anger. I will simply not abandon Ephraim that he be wiped out, because I am (a) God and not a human (διότι θεὸς ἐγώ εἰμι καὶ οὐκ ἄνθρωπος), holy among you. (Hos 11:9)

---

1   Cf. the statement of the Jewish scholar Yeḥezkel Kaufmann: "The continuity of the divine and human realm is the basis of the pagan belief in apotheosis, in the possibility of man's attaining godhood" (*History of the Religion of Israel: From the Babylonian Captivity to the End of Prophecy* [New York: Ktav Pub. House, 1976], 36). Jews, it is assumed, never affirmed this divine-human continuity.

Yet in all these cases, it should be noted that God does not oppose himself to human beings absolutely, but always with respect to a particular quality. He is not (a) human *with respect to* his intrepidness, *with respect* to his transcendence of the flesh, and *with respect* to his holiness. Thus, although there are aspects of God which humans will never share, humans and God are not depicted in the Bible as absolute binaries. If they were, any anthropomorphic features of God (such as personhood) would be impossible.

It cannot be denied, however, that Jews (especially Jewish apologists) around Paul's time enjoyed emphasizing the differences between humans and God. Josephus, for instance, in his retelling of the Exodus story, relates that Pharaoh was unimpressed with Moses' staff-turned-snake, because Egyptian magicians could produce the same miracle. In response, Moses cries out: "Indeed, O king, I too disdain not the cunning of the Egyptians, but I assert that the deeds wrought by me so far surpass their magic and their art as things divine are remote from what is human (ὅσῳ τὰ θεῖα τῶν ἀνθρωπίνων διαφέρει)" (*Ant.* 2.286).[2] Likewise, Moses orders Korah—who refuses to leave judgment to God—not to make himself better (or stronger) than God (μὴ σαυτὸν ποίοι τοῦ θεοῦ κρείττονα) (*Ant.* 4.33). Philo, the quintessential Hellenistic Jew, often excoriates the man who wishes to be a God (*Mut.* 181). "The arrogant man is always filled with the spirit of unreason, holding himself, as [note well!] Pindar says, to be neither man nor demigod, but wholly divine, and claiming to overstep the limits of human nature" (*Virt.* 172; cf. *Post.* 114–15). In another passage, Philo writes that the unchastised grow sleek, fat, and impious. Due to this prosperity, "they fancy themselves to be Gods," forgetting God, who alone truly exists (*Cong.* 159).[3]

As for the language of deification, Philo and the author of the *Epistle to Aristeas* (§§136–37) employed the terminology pejoratively. The reason is fairly clear. The terminology was perceived to be far too "other" and dangerous, rooted as it was in the Hellenistic and (later Roman) cult

---

2   Seneca actually says something similar. Speaking to his friend Lucilius, he says that "between the two branches of philosophy [that dealing with humans and that dealing with Gods] there is as much difference as there is between man and God (*inter duas interest quantum inter deum et hominem*)" (*Nat. Q.* 1.2; cf. Arist., *Nic. eth.* 7.7.5; 1159a5–7).

3   Philo's fulminations against the divine pretensions of Gaius Caligula are well-known (*Legat.* 75–76, 93, 114–15, 118, 143, 162), and conform to Greco-Roman sources (see below).

of benefactors, culture heroes, and rulers.[4] All this is taken as evidence that the relation between the human and the divine was fundamentally different for Jews and Greeks.

For Greeks and Hellenized Romans, the divine and human realms (it is claimed) overlapped, forming a single spectrum of divine and human contiguity and consanguinity. In the writings of the poets, Gods appear as large, powerful, and beautiful superhuman beings. They wield superhuman power and are, generally speaking, immortal, but they are not transcendent in any philosophical sense. Gods also resemble human beings in their (sometimes wild and uncontrolled) passions and demand for honor. Such observations have led modern scholars to conclude that for the Greeks the "barrier between human nature at its highest and divine nature at its lowest is thus sometimes practically obliterated, and it may even be suggested that in this way the human sometimes encroaches upon and overlaps the sphere of the divine."[5] In the words of one classicist, "The boundary between gods and men was narrower in Graeco-Roman belief than in ours and more fluid."[6] A recent German monograph on the imperial cult emphasizes that "The dividing line between divinity and humanity was blurred."[7] A prominent New Testament scholar puts it this way: the "membrane separating the human and the divine [in Greco-Roman thought] was permeable, with traffic moving in both directions."[8] In such a worldview, for humans to become Gods was no surprise, and no offence either. This theory sometimes seems to assume that for Greeks and Romans Gods and humans—though separated in status and rank—were part of the same kind or "species" of being. Gods—in the adage of Heraclitus—were immortal humans, and humans mortal Gods (*ap.* Lucian, *Vit. auct.* 14).

---

4   Significantly, later Christian thinkers like Clement of Alexandria could use the same terminology for deification pejoratively (in reference to a religious other) and approvingly (with reference to their own conception of deification). See Russell, *Doctrine of Deification*, 122–23.
5   Erland Ehnmark, *The Idea of God in Homer* (Uppsala: Almquist Wiksells, 1935), 3.
6   Fishwick, *The Imperial Cult in the Latin West*, 41.
7   Manfred Clauss, *Kaiser und Gott: Herrscherkult im römischen Reich* (Stuttgart: Teubner, 1999), 30.
8   Luke Timothy Johnson, *Among the Gentiles: Greco-Roman Religion and Christianity* (New Haven: Yale University Press, 2009), 36. The view is ubiquitous.

Unfortunately, this viewpoint has been seriously overdrawn and over-generalized. It seems to involve an implicit contrast with Judaism that—even if true in many cases—blocks a nuanced understanding of ancient Greek and other Hellenistic religions. As we have seen, many Greeks, from Homer onwards, were critical of humans who strove, at least by their own accord, to enter the divine sphere. Apollo himself shouts to Diomedes in the *Iliad*: "Think, son of Tydeus, and shrink back! Never think yourself the Gods' equal—since there can be no likeness ever (οὔ ποτε φῦλον ὁμοῖον) between the race of immortal Gods and men who walk on the ground" (5.440–42). Xenophanes of Colophon says something similar, though in a monotheistic vein: "There is one God, greatest among Gods and humans, like to mortals in neither form nor thought (οὔτι δέμας θνητοῖσιν ὁμοίιος οὐδὲ νόημα)" (DK 21 B 23). Bacchylides wrote that the Gods "resemble human beings in no respect (οὐδὲν ἀνθρώποις ἴκελοι)" (*ap.* Clem. Alex., *Strom.* 5.14.110.1). The moral engraved on the temple of Delphi read: "Know thyself," meaning "Know that you are a mortal and not a God." Pindar bids his reader "Seek not to become Zeus. For mortals a mortal lot is right." And again: "Mortal minds must seek what is fitting at the hands of the Gods, knowing what lies at our feet, and to what portion we are born. Strive not, my soul, for an immortal life, but use to the full the resources that are at thy command" (*Isth.* 5.14; *Pyth.* 3.59). "The divine and the human constitute the poles of Hesiod's cosmos," writes Jenny Strauss Clay.[9] The birth of heroes temporarily destabilizes the cosmos because heroes bridge the boundary between the human and the divine. Zeus eventually does away with mortal and immortal unions, a fact which Calypso bitterly complains against in the *Odyssey* (5.118–29). Her complaint, however, shows that "the possibility of such intimacies belongs to a bygone era."[10] After the deceit of Prometheus at Mekone, according to Hesiod, "the inequality of status between immortal gods and mortal men cannot be bridged and remains eternally fixed."[11]

We should not underestimate the value of poets like Homer, Hesiod, and Pindar. Up until Late Antiquity they were read by every educated person and continued to mold the ethos of Greco-Roman society. Unsurprisingly, then, later sources can be cited that affirm the same

---

9   *Hesiod's Cosmos*, 150.
10 *Ibid.*, 164.
11 *Ibid.*, 171. See Hes., *Theog.*, 535–616.

point. Take this example from Apuleius of Madaura, who says that the Gods

> differ profoundly from humans in the loftiness of their position, the perpetuity of their existence, and the perfection of their nature. The two have no close intercommunication, since such an interval of height separates the highest habitations from the lowest; since for the one realm life is everlasting and unwearying, while for the other it is fragile and a mere remnant; and since divine natures are raised up to bliss, while human natures are sent below to misery ... For, as that same Plato of ours says [cf. *Symp.* 203a], no God mixes with human beings (*nullus deus miscetur hominibus*), and this indeed is a particular token of their sublimity that they are not polluted through any contact with us." (*De Deo Socr.* 127–28)

What such texts generally assume, it seems to me, is that humans and Gods—far from blurring into each other—were fundamentally different sorts of beings. Humans were not mortal Gods, and Gods were not immortal humans. Rather, they were members of a different class or "species." Some, by the grace of the Gods, were able to cross this species gap. But the cases of deification treated in chapter 2 should not obscure a more basic point: deification in all periods of the ancient world (Classical, Hellenistic, and Roman) was rare and—until Christians devised their own forms of deification—limited to a few extraordinary individuals. For the vast majority of people, a real and widely recognized boundary separated human beings and Gods. The attempt to cross this boundary on one's own was generally viewed as hubristic for humans (even for great heroes and kings), and morally reprehensible.

In Greek sources, the punishment for self-deifying promotion was severe. In Book 7 of his *Histories*, Herodotus depicts Xerxes as one who exercised godlike pretensions (such as whipping the waters of the Hellespont). Yet all this culminates at Salamis with the experience of a devastating fall and retreat. Greek tragedy, too, offers plenty of admonitions warning mortals not to imagine themselves to be—or be able to be—immortals. For instance, the chorus in Euripides' *Bacchae* sings: "unwise are those who aspire, who outrange the limits of man. Briefly, we live. Briefly, then die. Wherefore, I say, he who hunts a glory, he who tracks some boundless, superhuman dream, may lose his harvest here and now and garner death. Such men are mad, their counsels evil" (395–401, trans. William Arrowsmith). In a powerful scene at the end of this play, the God Dionysus—standing above the human characters—executes judgment on them. When Cadmus complains that his sentence is too harsh (he is to become a snake), Dionysus responds bluntly: "I am a God. I was blasphemed by you (καὶ γὰρ πρὸς ὑμῶν Θεὸς γεγὼς ὑβριζόμην)" (1347). The judgment and power is absolute; the humans can do nothing but abjectly accept their fate. The difference between humanity and divinity could not be depicted more starkly. In the words of Apollodorus, Dionysus "showed the Thebans that he was a God (δείξας ... ὅτι Θεός ἐστιν)" (*Bibl.* 3.5.2).

The polemic against self-deifying humans (especially kings) was real—but hardly limited to Jews. If ancient Jews could ridicule self-deifying rulers, they learned to crack these jokes from the Greeks themselves. "And is not almost any king called Apollo if he hums a tune, Dionysus if he gets drunk, and Heracles if he wrestles?" asks Plutarch (*Adul. am.* 12 [*Mor.* 56 f]). When the Thasians wanted to deify Agesilaus (the Spartan king), he asked if their country had the power to deify (ἀποθεόω) people. When they answered in the affirmative, he said, 'Go; make Gods of yourselves first, and if you can accomplish this, then will I believe that you will be able to make a God (Θεὸν ποιέω) of me also" (Plut., *Apoph. lac.* [*Mor.* 210d]). This is a story of Plutarch. This philosopher also tells the story of Antigonus Monophthalmus, one of Alexander's successors. When a certain Hermodotus in a poem proclaimed him to be "the offspring of the Sun and a God," he burst out, "the slave who attends to my chamber pot is not conscious of any such thing!" (*Is. Os.* 24 [*Mor.* 360c-d]). In yet another story, Lysimachus, ruler of Thrace ("the mere outskirts of the kingdom of Alexander"), "reached such a pitch of arrogance and boldness as to say, 'The Byzantines now come to me when I am touching heaven with my spear.' But Pasiades of Byzantium, who was present, said, 'Let us be off, lest he make a hole in the sky with his spear-point!'" (*Alex. fort.* 5 [*Mor.* 338a-b]). Vespasian's dying words are well-known: "Oh no! I think I'm becoming a God! (*Vae, puto deum fio*)" (Suet., *Vesp.* 23.4).[12]

Deification could also be deprecated as something ignorant and menial. Cicero (106–43 B.C.E.) puts into the mouth of Cotta (his representative of the New Academy):

> Why, even in Greece, among the Gods they worship are many who were earlier human beings—Alabandus at Alabanda, Tenes at Tenedos, and throughout Greece Leucothea who was formerly Ino, and her son Palaemon. Then too we have our Hercules, Aesculapius, the sons of Tyndareus,

---

12 Scholars who desire to *reduce* deification to a joke often support their case on Seneca's *Apocolocyntosis*—a satire of Claudius' deification fulfilling a personal vendetta.

and Romulus, who together with many others the common folk believe
have been admitted into heaven as newly enrolled citizens.

"Such" Cotta says, "are the beliefs of the ignorant" (*Nat. d.* 3.39–40).

In the mid-second century C.E., the traveler Pausanias was ready to
admit that in olden days "certain human beings were turned into Gods
and even today are still honored," (e.g., Aristaeus, Heracles, Polydeuces). "But in my time, when wickedness has increased to the last degree
and has spread over the entire earth and all its cities, no human being
ever becomes a God, except in name only and to flatter authority,
and the wrath of the Gods is a long time falling on the wicked and is
stored away for those who have departed from the world"
(*Descr.* 8.2.4–5)

Plutarch—although he had deep connections with Roman power—
displayed significant ideological disagreements with rulers claiming to be
Gods. For instance, he complains against those rulers who take on the
titles "God" or "son of God" (*De laude* 12 [*Mor.* 543e]). He denies
that souls become Gods by civic law (*Rom.* 28.10).[13] In one passage
he speaks against the self-deifying pretensions of rulers with all the
fire of Philo Judaeus:

> But if some, 'elated by a great self conceit,' as Plato says, 'with souls enkin-
> dled with the fire of youth and folly accompanied by arrogance,' have as-
> sumed to be called Gods and to have temples dedicated in their honor, yet
> has their repute flourished but a brief time, and then, convicted of vain-
> glory and imposture, 'Swift in their fate, like to smoke in the air, rising up-
> ward they flitted,' and now, like fugitive slaves without claim to protection,
> they have been dragged from their shrines and altars, and have nothing left
> to them save only their monuments and their tombs. (*Is. Os.* 24 [=
> *Mor.* 360c-d])[14]

Such authors show that not all Greeks accepted the "permeable membrane" between Gods and humans. The very idea of a community deifying a ruler or—what's far worse—a self-deified *living* ruler was the
height of impiety and impossibility.

But if some Greeks rejected the premises of deification, it cannot be
said that all Jews did. Even Philo, the great enemy of Gaius Caligula's

---

13 Cf. Dio Cassius, who puts in the mouth of Maecenas, the advisor of Augustus:
    "no one ever became a God by a vote (χειροτονητὸς δ' οὐδεὶς πώποτε θεὸς
    ἐγένετο)" (*Rom. Hist.* 52.35.5).

14 Similarly, Sextus Empiricus remarks that "those who openly proclaimed them-
    selves Gods in their own right were, instead, despised" (*Math.* 9.38).

self-deifying pretensions, showed himself open to other legitimate forms of deification.

> Heracles purged the earth and the sea, undergoing trials of endurance most necessary and profitable for all humankind in order to destroy things which are mischievous and baneful to either form of life … Again, the Dioscuri are said to have shared the immortality between them, for since one of them was mortal and the other immortal he who had been judged worthy of the higher destiny did not think it fit to gratify his selfish instinct instead of showing affection to his brother … he achieved a great and marvelous reciprocation in that he mingled mortality with his own lot and indestructibility with his brother's … All these, Gaius, received and still receive admiration for the benefits for which we are beholden to them and were judged worthy of worship and the highest honors (καὶ σεβασμοῦ τε καὶ τῶν ἀνωτάτω τιμῶν ἠξιώθησαν). (*Legat.* 81–86, trans. F. H. Colson, LCL, modified)

Here Philo talks about the deification of Heracles and the Dioscuri without a hint of condemnation. They are examples of those who performed acts of justice and benefaction, and thus were rightfully deified (i.e., made immortal). They did not deify themselves, but received highest honors through their virtuous acts and benefactions. Likewise Augustus, on account of "the vastness of his imperial sovereignty as well as the nobility of character" gained the title "*Sebastos*," or "Augustus" (i.e., the "Venerated One") and so became "the source of veneration" (ἀρχὴ σεβασμοῦ). In all the virtues, says Philo, Augustus "transcended human nature (ὁ τὴν ἀνθρωπίνην φύσιν ὑπερβαλὼν)" (*Legat.* 143). Power and virtue were traditional reasons for deification, and Philo again shows little hint of disapproval. Even if these are simply illustrations for his non-Jewish audience, Philo cannot use them without in some measure acceding to the logic of divine honors. He is ready to see Augustus as a super-human being, and worship him in any way permissible with Jewish law (*Legat.* 356; *Flacc.* 49). When Philo honored Augustus, he recognized that there was no authority except that which was instituted by God. A good king could be appointed as God's viceregent, a minister for the good (cf. Rom 13:1–7). The subordination of Augustus to higher divine power was a basis for Augustus' authority even among Romans. Horace's great line, addressed to the Romans in general, fits the logic of Augustan rule exactly: *dis te minorem quod geris, imperas* ("You rule because you hold yourself less than the Gods") (*Odes* 3.6.5; cf. Dio Chrys., *Or.* 3.51–52, 55).[15] It would be

---

15 Cf. Auffarth, "Herrscherkult und Christuskult," 287–292.

wrong, then, to let the rhetoric against self-deifying kings (who are not the norm) override attempts to construct a balanced picture of Philo's political theology.[16]

When we examine other Jewish sources, some seem surprisingly open to the idea of deification. In Ezekiel's *Exagoge*, for instance, Moses dreams that he is crowned and enthroned on Sinai. Viewing the world below, he sees "a host of stars" (τι πλῆθος ἀστέρων) fall prostrate at his feet "like a squadron of mortals" (ὡς παρεμβολὴ βροτῶν) (lines 86–88). The "stars" which prostrate themselves before Moses are a common poetic designation for angels (Job 38:7; 1 *En.* 104:2–6). These angels are in battle formation as they are depicted in Judg 5:20. Moses' ability to count them assimilates him to God (Ps 147:4; cf. Isa 40:26), and signifies his rulership over them. Indeed Moses, it is not a stretch to say, is here depicted as the "Lord of (angelic) hosts." "The implication," says David Runia, "is that Moses is actually deified."[17]

In the Prayer of Joseph fragment A (first c. C.E.?), we read this self-testimony:

> I, Jacob, who is speaking to you am also Israel, an angel of God and a ruling spirit. Abraham and Isaac were created before any work. But, I, Jacob, whom men call Jacob but whose name is Israel and he who God called Israel which means, a man seeing God, because I am the firstborn of every living thing (πρωτόγονος παντὸς ζῴου) to whom God gives life. (trans. J.Z. Smith)

Just as the deified Christ (Col 1:15, "firstborn of all creation [πρωτότο-κος πάσης κτίσεως]), Jacob is πρωτόγονος παντὸς ζῴου. The phrase in Colossians is clearly meant to indicate the divine nature of Christ. We might assume no less for Jacob in the *Prayer of Joseph*.

---

16 Note the comments of Stanley K. Stowers, *A Rereading of Romans: Justice, Jews, and Gentiles* (New Haven: Yale University Press, 1994), 58. Auffarth states that "Philo's Jewish critique of Caesar's demand for divine honors makes clear that even within Judaism the faith in the one God of Israel does not exclude a Mediator and other Gods" ("Herrscherkult und Christuskult," 311).

17 "God and Man in Philo of Alexandria," 51. Cf. K. J. Ruffatto: "In the *Exagoge*, Moses does not merely ascend and have a vision of God's throne: God bids Moses to *sit on* his divine throne. Moses is given God's own scepter and crown, God's insignia. Moses *shares* God's throne: he is divinized. Moses thus not only sees God's throne as did Enoch: he rules from God's own throne" ("Polemics with Enochic Traditions in the *Exagoge* of Ezekiel the Tragedian," *Journal for the Study of Pseudepigrapha* 15:3 [2006]: 204, emphasis his).

In Daniel 2:46, the Theodotion text reads that king Nebuchadnezzar "fell on his face and worshiped (προσεκύνησεν) Daniel and [ordered his servants] to offer offerings and fragrances to him." The Old Greek Version has the king likewise falling on his face to the ground and worshiping Daniel (προσκυνέω). But instead of vague offerings and incense, the king orders full sacrifices (θυσίας) and libations (σπονδάς) to be made to Daniel. Josephus, reformulating this tradition, explains that falling with one's face to the ground is a gesture of worship meant for a God (ᾧ τρόπῳ τὸν θεὸν προσκυνοῦσι). He also agrees with the Old Greek that Nebuchadnezzar offered sacrifices to Daniel "as to a God" (ὡς θεῷ) (*Ant.* 10.211–212). Even though Nebuchadnezzar is a foreign king, neither the book of Daniel nor Josephus offer any word of disapproval for their hero receiving divine honors. Coated with irony and humor, the worship was in all likelihood accepted with relish.[18]

We see something similar in the Jewish writer Artapanus (probably late third c. B.C.E.). He depicts Moses in the typical guise of a Greek benefactor with the typical result: deification through receiving honors equal to (a) God (ἰσόθεος τιμή). Moses is even assimilated to a particular God, Hermes, for his interpretation (ἑρμηνεία) of Egyptian sacred letters. Moses as Hermes/Thoth is superior to Egyptian theriomorphic Gods, whose cult Moses establishes (*ap.* Eus., *Praep. ev.* 9.27.4–6)!

Moreover, the Jewish writer Ps-Phocylides has little difficulty in declaring that (apparently all?) the resurrected dead "become Gods." "It is not good," he advises, "to dissolve the human frame,

> for we hope that the remains of the departed will soon come to the light (again)
> out of the earth; and afterward they will become Gods (θεοὶ τελέθονται).
> For the souls remain unharmed among the deceased.
> For the spirit (pneuma) is a loan of God to mortals, and (his) image.
> For we have a body out of earth,
> and when afterward we are resolved again into earth
> we are but dust; and then the air has received our spirit …
> We humans live not a long time but for a season.
> But (our) soul is immortal and lives ageless forever.
> (lines 102–115, trans. P. W. van der Horst)

The logic of deification, according to Ps.-Phocylides, is that the pneuma given to humans as a loan is the image (εἰκών) of God which is received into the air at death (106, 108). This true, immortal self is evidently

---

18   See further B. A. Mastin, "Daniel 2.46 and the Hellenistic World," *ZAW* 85 (1973): 80–93.

what the author calls a "God." This is the true self of human beings. The phrase "to become Gods" (Θεοὶ τελέθονται) is unmistakably the language of deification.[19]

We can turn, finally, to the New Testament—written for the most part by (self-perceived) faithful Jews. Here also there are places where the boundary between humans and God seems relatively permeable. Besides Christological statements which state or imply that Jesus (a human being) was a God (e.g., John 1:1 Tit 3:4–6), we have the testimony of the Johannine Jesus himself that those "to whom the word of God came" were rightfully called "Gods" (John 10:34–36). In Acts, we find on Paul's lips a famous line from Aratus of Soloi (ca. 315–240 B.C.E.): Τοῦ [Διὸs] γὰρ καὶ γένος ἐιμέν: "For we are of the race (or family) [of Zeus]" (*Phaen.* 5; Acts 17:28). Here a God—and we are apparently to take "Zeus" as referring to the Jewish God (cf. *Ep. Arist.* 16)—and humans appear to be part of the same "race" or "family" (γένος). This reading is supported by Luke 3:38, where Adam is apparently depicted as the natural ("genetic") "son of God" in a great family tree.

Such observations go to show that one cannot make hard and fast distinctions about the boundaries Jews and Greeks perceived between the human and the divine. In Paul's time, Greeks thought differently from other Greeks, and Jews thought differently than other Jews. If Jews were generally united in their opposition to self-deifying rulers, Hellenistic Jews at least were not necessarily opposed to the deification of their own mythic heroes and ancestors. Although statements about the separation of humans from God are frequent among Jews, we must not forget that such statements are sometimes rhetorical or polemical, and are often made about divine qualities which even the Greeks would agree were totally unshareable (e.g., eternality, the ability to create worlds, omnipresence, etc.). Such qualities—as many Greeks would admit—belong to the high God alone, whom Philo, following Ex 3:14, calls the "Existent" (ὁ ὤν). Human beings cannot assimilate to this being (who—for Philo and other Middle Platonists—is Being itself). They

---

19 John Collins views the deification expressed here as "a variant of a common Jewish belief that the righteous are elevated to heaven after death to shine like stars or become companions of the angels (who are often called *elohim*, gods, in contemporary Hebrew texts, such as the Dead Sea Scrolls)" ("Life after Death in Pseudo-Phocylides," in *Jewish Cult and Hellenistic Culture: Essays on the Jewish Encounter with Hellenism and Roman Rule* [Leiden: Brill, 2005], 133). Yet if the righteous truly do "become Gods," this cannot be reduced to a species of mere angelification.

can, however, assimilate to mediate divinities (such as Philo's Logos, 1
Enoch's "Son of Man," Paul's Christ).[20] It is dangerous, then, to make
blanket statements about divine-human permeability for Greeks and divine-human impermeability for Jews. Though many Jews were hostile
to forms of deification associated with cult,[21] the idea of deification
was in many ways creatively adapted to and integrated into their own
system(s) of thought.[22] In what follows, I will discuss some of the biblical
resources Jews had to develop their own notions of deification in the
Hellenistic and Roman periods.[23]

The Biblical Roots of Deification

A necessary part of the context of Paul's thought world is the Hebrew
Bible, chiefly in its Greek recensions stemming from Alexandria (which
for convenience we will call "the LXX").[24] It is generally thought that
deification is inherently foreign to the these scriptures. Nevertheless if
we see deification as the Jewish God's attempt to let his divine identity
partially overlap with human beings, deification is in fact intrinsic to
biblical thought. For though by no means on every page, the Jewish
scriptures provide key images and stories depicting the overlap of
God's distinctive qualities with human beings. Sometimes this involves
people in sharing God's luminous, fiery body. At other times, it involves
sharing in the more functional aspects of God's selfhood, such as the divine sovereignty.

---

20 For a discussion of mediate divinities, see ch. 9.
21 It should be carefully noted that not every deified person receives cult.
22 See further William Horbury, *Jewish Messianism and the Cult of Christ* (London:
     SCM Press, 1998), 68–77, esp. his conclusion on 77.
23 In the end, my purpose is not so much to deny the generalization that ancient
     Jews tended to view deity as more transcendent than other peoples of the
     Greco-Roman world. My purpose is to question the apologetic presupposition
     that often lurks beneath this claim—that there is, namely, an essential difference
     between Jewish and Greek (or "pagan") thought. Throughout this book I am
     testing the possibility that Jews in the ancient Mediterranean were not so differ-
     ent in their thinking about the divine and the human. This notion arises out of
     the (now commonly accepted) thesis that Jews in Paul's time had long been
     Hellenized (i. e., adapted to the larger culture) both in Palestine and in the Di-
     aspora.
24 Accordingly, all translations which follow, unless otherwise noted, are made
     from the LXX.

Perhaps the most famous text in which we see the close homology between God and human beings comes at the beginning of the canon, where God declares: "Let us make a human according to our image" (Gen 1:26). The author of Wisdom (late first century B.C.E.?) interprets this text as follows: "God created us [humans] for incorruption, and made us in the image of his own peculiar nature (ἰδιότητος)."[25] In the words of one recent study of Gen 1:26, here "Human beings reflect and embody divinity … human beings will represent divine presence and participation on earth."[26] In other words, Genesis 1:26 indicates that humans begin life already as theomorphic beings, iconically related to their maker. Humans are God's icons. This is a declaration never made of plants or animals. Even though the human is similar to animals in mode of reproduction and need for food (v.29), the human is specifically marked out by God as something above the animal because the human is created in (or as) the image of God.

The notion of humans as mediating between animals and God underlies a host of texts in the Hebrew Bible. In retellings of the creation myth, for instance, the animal is associated with the primevally chaotic. "You crushed the heads of the dragon (τὰς κεφαλὰς τοῦ δράκοντος); you gave him as food to the people of Ethiopia" (Ps 73[74]:14). Important to recognize here is how easily a great serpent can come to represent a human or human group perceived as foreign or dangerous:

> Thus says the Lord:
> Lo, I am against Pharaoh,
> the great dragon (τὸν δράκοντα τὸν μέγαν)…
> I will fling you down in all speed, …
> To the animals of the earth and to the birds of the air
> I have given you as food. (Ezek 29:3–5)

This habit of presenting undesirable humans theriomorphically is pervasive in the Hebrew Bible. The enemies of the psalmist are the "fat bulls of Bashan," (21[22]:13); the wicked ruler is a "hungry lion" or "thirsting wolf" (Prov 28:15; cf. Job 10:16; Ps 7:2); Mephibosheth is a "dead dog" (2 Sam 9:8; cf. 16:9; 2 Kings 8:13); corrupt judges are "Arabian wolves" (Zeph 3:3; Ezek 22:27). Perhaps the most famous example is

---

25 The Rahlfs-Hanhart handbook edition of the LXX prints ἀΐδιότητος (eternity) in 2:23, but it is best to read ἰδιότητος, following Vaticanus, Sinaiticus, and Alexandrinus

26 W. Randall Garr, *In His Own Image and Likeness: Humanity, Divinity, and Monotheism* (Leiden: Brill, 2003), 88.

the four beasts of Daniel 7 who represent great and oppressive empires. Specifically, these beasts represent human groups in their violent and prideful aspects.[27]

Thus the human, in the Hebrew mind, can be reduced to the animal—a reality we see quite literally in the case of Nebuchadnezzar (who is changed into something between a bird and a cow) (Dan 4:33, Theodotion). Conversely, the divine often manifests itself in human form: God walks in a garden (Gen 3:8); he stretches out his arm (Jer 21:5; et al.); he sits on a throne (Dan 7:9). At one point, he is revealed in explicitly human terms: "and seated above the likeness of a throne was something that seemed like a human form" (ὁμοίωμα ὡς εἶδος ἀνθρώπου) (Ezek 1:26b). What is important to recognize is not just that human chaos is beastly and that the divine is anthropomorphic; but that in the imagination of ancient Jews, the human *can bridge both the divine and the animalic.*

The fact that the basic structure of Hebrew thought about God is anthropomorphic has important consequences for later developments in Judaism. When the Jews thought of God in anthropomorphic terms, they already assumed a fundamental analogy between the human and the divine. Conceptually speaking, this basic divine-human analogy paved the way for the theomorphic character of human beings. We have already seen that human beings when originally created were theomorphic (Gen 1:26–27; cf. 9:6) Although unique to Genesis, the fact that this statement stands at the beginning of the canon allows it to have a greater shaping effect than it would otherwise.

In contrast, it is never said that an animal is made in the image of humankind. There is no programmatic statement, like we have in Gen 1:26–27, declaring that animals are anthropomorphic. This is important, because though it is hard in Hebrew thinking both for a human to become God and an animal to become human, it is harder for an animal to be conceived of as human than for a human to share the form of God. Stated structurally: when there is approximation between God, humans, and animals, the approximation will tend more strongly toward God and human beings. In Genesis 1, humans stand between animals and God. Yet, according to Gen 1:26–27 (part of the "P" source), humans stand far closer to God.

---

27 Here very explicitly we see "the human-like one" (v. 13) mediating between the beasts and the Ancient of Days as a divine figure coming with the clouds.

The likeness between Gods and humans is so basic to the primeval history (Gen 1–11) that there is even the possibility of blurring the categories. In Genesis 6, the divine "sons of God" are anthropomorphic (more precisely, andromorphic) enough to have intercourse with human women. There is no talk of their transformation to *become* men. "Sons of God" and men are already of the same species, as evidenced by the ability of both to fertilize human females. A similar point can be made about those who build the Tower of Babel. They are already theomorphic in the range of their power (as demonstrated by the scope of their building). They need not transform themselves into Gods; they are already showing the (almost omnipotent) power of Gods: "nothing will be lacking for them," says God, "which they set their minds to do" (11:6). In an earlier story, humans needed only to eat from the tree of life to become (in the words of Yahweh himself) "one of us" (3:22). To be sure, the blurring of divine and human is frowned upon in later Jewish literature (see esp. 1 En 12:4, 15:3–6). Yet the very fact that such stories *were* written and sacralized indicates that humans crossing over into the category of the divine was a real possibility inherent in Hebrew thought.

These stories are evidence of a way of thinking in Hebrew culture often neglected by exegetes who rigorously maintain a creator-creature binary across the entire Hebrew Bible. But this binary does not take into account the mediation of categories: i. e., the divine-human approximation (God in human form; humans in divine form) assumed by many texts in the Hebrew Bible. Yet even if we posit an inseparable barrier between creator and creatures, God the creator has still shared his form (or image) with human creatures (Gen 1:26). Their difference is never final.

The Meaning of Iconic Similarity

Let us follow the thread of humanity's iconic likeness to God in more depth. In Genesis, what the "image" (εἰκών) of God consists of may never (and may never have been *meant* to) be reduced to a single element. A range of characteristics and functions have been proposed in medieval and modern theology: sexuality, relationality, reason, etc.[28]

---

28 For a survey of Old Testament research on this topic, see Gunnlaugur A. Jónsson, *The Image of God: Genesis 1:26–28 in a Century of Old Testament Research,*

Initially, I am less interested in pinpointing the specific divine quality possessed by humans than in stating the basic fact: human beings, according to the first chapter of the Bible, are iconically like God. This fundamental likeness provides (as we see in Gen 3, 6, and 11) the basis for the further step: mixing with and potentially entering the class of divine beings.

Those who were part of the class of divine beings were, as we noted, called "the sons of God" (οἱ υἱοὶ τοῦ Θεοῦ) (Gen 6:2; Ps 28[29]:1; 88:7 [89:6]; 81[82]:6). Divine sonship links back to the divine image, as is indicated in Gen 5:3. Here Adam begets a son "in his likeness, according to his image" (כצלמו בדמותו; κατὰ τὴν ἰδέαν αὐτοῦ καὶ κατὰ τὴν εἰκόνα αὐτοῦ). The language in Gen 1:26 is similar, except for the prepositions, which appear to be interchangeable: "in our image, according to our likeness" (בצלמנו כדמותנו; κατ᾽ εἰκόνα ἡμετέραν καὶ καθ᾽ ὁμοίωσιν).[29] It seems, then, that even in Gen 1:26 Yahweh wants to draw humankind (אדם; ἄνθρωπος) into a kinship relation with himself. As an image of God, the human is a son of God. Accordingly, the author of the Gospel of Luke can write that Adam, created in God's image, is genealogically (and genetically?) speaking, "son of God" ([υἱός] τοῦ Θεοῦ) (3:38; cf. 17:28b). By making humankind in the image and likeness of himself and the other divine beings (note "Let us"), Yahweh makes humans his children and thus strikingly close to the "sons of God" who in Gen 6 and Ps 28(29):1 are part of the class of divine beings.

When we turn to the historical meaning of human iconicity, Hebrew Bible scholars have allowed us to see it at least in part as a *morphological* and thus *physical* similarity to Godself.[30] In the words of Benjamin Sommer, Genesis 1:26–27 "assert that human beings have the same form as God and other heavenly beings." The words צלם (εἰκών) and דמות (ὁμοίωσις) refer to the "physical contours of God."[31] To share

---

Vol. 26 (Stockholm: Almqvist & Wiksell, 1988), 253; Edward Mason Curtis, *Man as the Image of God in Genesis in the Light of Ancient Near Eastern Parallels* (Ph.D. Diss., University Of Pennsylvania, 1984), 40–50.

29   T. N. D. Mettinger, "Abbild oder Urbild?" *Zeitschrift für alttestamentliche Wissenschaft* 86 (1974): 406–407.

30   J. M. Miller, "In the "Image" and "Likeness" of God," *Journal of Biblical Literature* 91 (1972): 291–93.

31   Sommer, *The Bodies of God and the World of Ancient Israel* (Cambridge: Cambridge University Press, 2009), 69. Classical rabbinic texts often understand the צלם in Gen 1:26–27 to refer to the human body (Alon Goshen-Gottstein, "The Body as Image of God in Rabbinic Literature," *Harvard Theological Review*

God's image thus means to share God's corporeality. Although scholars of all stripes and times have downplayed the corporeality of God in the Jewish scriptures, the notion is unavoidable.

> In Genesis 2.7 God blows life-giving breath into the first human—an action that might suggest that God has a mouth or some organ with which to exhale. Less ambiguously, in Genesis 3.8, Adam hears the sound of God going for a stroll in the Garden of Eden at the breezy time of the day. A being who takes a walk is a being who has a body—more specifically, a body with something closely resembling legs. As we move forward in Genesis, we are told that God comes down from heaven to earth to take a close look at the tower the humans are building (Genesis 11.5) and that God walks to Abraham's tent, where He engages in conversation. (Genesis 18)[32]

Thus by making humankind iconically similar to himself, God apparently shares his bodily form.[33] Humans become the statues (εἰκόνες) of God ("statue" being a common meaning of εἰκών in Paul's day). This line of interpretation is confirmed in later Jewish literature. In *Vita Adae et Evae*, Adam's bodily face and likeness take on the image of God (13:3).[34] The patriarch Isaac affirms that not preserving the body profanes the image of God (TIsaac 6:33–7:1). R. Hillel goes to the bath to take care of the image of God (his body!) (*Lev. Rabb.* 34.3). Likewise, when Adam shares his image with Seth, he shares his bodily form (Gen 5:3). Just as Seth is embodied in a form akin to that of Adam, so Adam in Gen 1:26–27 is embodied in a form akin to that of God.

If Adam was truly the image of the divine body, he must have shared the glory (כבוד, δόξα) of that divine body. So later traditions see Adam as having a body of glory. In the "Words of the Luminaries" (4Q504), for instance, Adam is fashioned in the likeness (דמות) of God's glory (recalling the glory of Ezek 1:28). "All the glory of Adam" is sometimes mentioned in the Dead Sea Scrolls (e.g., CD-A 3.18–20), and is associated with eternal life ("plentiful days" in 1QHᵃ Col. IV

---

87 [1994]: 173–76). Importantly, Sommer points out that rabbinic texts also see the word דמות as interchangeable with כבוד (Greek δόξα), e.g., *Ex. Rabb.* 23:15; *Sifre Zuta* to Numbers 12:8. Also worth seeing on this subject is Eliot Wolfson, *Through a Speculum that Shines: Vision and Imagination in Medieval Jewish Mysticism* (Princeton: Princeton University Press, 1994), 47–49.

32   Sommer, *Bodies of God*, 2. See further 3–10.

33   *Ibid.*, 2.

34   J. R. Levison, *Portraits of Adam in Early Judaism: From Sirach to 2 Baruch* (Sheffield: JSOT Press, 1988), 178.

14–15). In one rabbinic tradition (*Gen. Rabb.* 8:10), the angels cannot even distinguish between the glory body of Adam, and the glory body of God. If the glory (or Glory) is God's body, or consubstantial with it,[35] then the God of glory and the glorious Adam are corporeally (i. e., iconically) related (and thus akin).[36] The corporeal sharing between humankind and God implies the sharing of identity. If the body is one the bases of identity, then by making himself corporeally akin to humanity, God partially shares his identity with human beings.

It is assumed by Paul, however, that humanity's corporeal participation in God has been diminished or wholly lost. Humankind after sin has lost the "glory" (δόξα), or brilliance of the divine body which Adam had (Rom 3:23). In the *Apocalypse of Moses*, Adam says to Eve: "I have been estranged from my glory (ἀπηλλοτριώθην τῆς δόξης μου) with which I was clothed" (20:2). This glory is later defined as "the great glory" (21:2) and "the glory of God" (21:6).[37] With the loss of glory, Adam, Eve—and all humanity—have lost their immortality which was conditioned upon obedience.[38]

In certain cases, however, that shining corporeality was proleptically regained. In the story of 2 Kings 2, for instance, the prophet Elijah ascends to heaven in a chariot of fire. "They [Elijah and his disciple Elisha] were walking and talking as they went. And lo, a chariot of fire (רכב־אש; ἅρμα πυρὸς) and horses of fire! And they distinguished between both men, and Elijah was taken up in a whirlwind into the sky (השמים; τὸν οὐρανόν)" (v. 11). Here God himself makes possible the

---

35 For כבוד as "body" or "substance" see Isa 17:4; Ps 16:9; Gen 49:6; Ps 7:6; Isa 10:3–4, 16; 22:18. For כבוד as the substance of God's body, see Sommer, *Bodies of God*, 70–72. God and כבוד are interchangeable for the priestly authors and for Ezekiel (*ibid.*, 72–74).

36 For further traditions about Adam's glorious body see Gary A. Anderson, *The Genesis of Perfection* (Louisville: Westminster John Knox Press, 2001), 124–34; James L. Kugel, *Traditions of the Bible: A Guide to the Bible As It Was at the Start of the Common Era* (Cambridge: Harvard University Press, 1998), 115–120.

37 For early rabbinic traditions of Adam's glory, see Scroggs, *The Last Adam: A Study in Pauline Anthropology* (Philadelphia: Fortress Press, 1966), 48–49.

38 Cf. Preston Sprinkle: "it seems that the predominant meaning conveyed in this loss of δόξα [in *Apoc. Mos.*] is that of immortality." See his reasoning in "The Afterlife in Romans: Understanding Paul's Glory Motif in Light of the Apocalypse of Moses and 2 Baruch" in *Lebendige Hoffnung—ewiger Tod?! Jenseitsvorstellungen im Hellenismus, Judentum und Christentum* (eds. Michael Labahn and Manfred Lang; Leipzig: Evangelische Verlagsanstalt, 2007), 206.

permanent ascent of his prophet to God's own abode.[39] Fire was associated with God's luminous body (Ex 19:18; 24:17; Deut 5:4). God himself was said to drive a chariot of fire in the midst of a whirlwind: "Lo, the Lord will come as fire (באש; ὡς πῦρ), and as a hurricane [are] his chariots (מרכבתיו; τὰ ἅρματα αὐτοῦ)" (Isa 66:15a; cf. Ps 104:3). Apparently Elijah would need to be something greater than human if he was not to be burned up in the heat of those divine flames.[40] Furthermore, by ascending in fire, the prophet never tastes death. It would be easy for a Hellenistic Jew to interpret Elijah's ascent as a form of immortalization and even deification. The Gospel writers, at any rate, thought it natural for Elijah to appear in glory on the Mount of Transfiguration (Mark 9:2–13; Matt 17:1–8; Luke 9:28–36). In his immortal and glorified guise, the prophet looks very much like a divine hero.

Another candidate for a Jewish form of deification is the patriarch Enoch.[41] After living 365 years, "Enoch pleased God, and was not found, for God transferred him" (Gen 5:24). This represents the Greek text. The Hebrew reads: "Enoch walked with God, and he was not." The Hebrew could, however, be translated: "Enoch traveled back and forth with the Gods (ויתהלך חנוך את־האלהים)."[42] The "Gods" were later understood to be angels. Thus the author of Jubilees declares "And he [Enoch] was therefore with the angels of God six jubilees of years" (4:21). Enoch's trek with angels takes up most of the Book of Watchers (1 En 17–36). In the appendix of The Book of Parables (ca. 40 B.C.E.–70 C.E.), Enoch may even have been transformed into a powerful angelic figure called the Son of Man (1 En 71:14). In 2 Enoch (late 1st cent. C.E.?), Enoch is extracted from his earthly clothing, anointed with shining and fragrant oil, and clothed in glorious garments. Suddenly Enoch recognizes himself as one of the "glorious ones" with "no observable difference" (22:8–10).[43] Such an angelification might

---

39 For the heavens as God's abode, note Ps 113:11 (ET 115:3): "Our God is in the heavens" (אלהינו בשמים; ὁ δὲ θεὸς ἡμῶν ἐν τῷ οὐρανῷ ἄνω).

40 Cf. Ezek 28:14 for the divine prince of Tyre walking on stones of fire.

41 Kaufmann grants that both Enoch and Elijah are rare examples of "biblical apotheosis" (Religion of Israel, 77).

42 Cf. the comments of James C. Vanderkam, Enoch: A Man for All Generations (Columbia: University of South Carolina Press, 1995), 12–14.

43 A much later Enochic text, Sefer Hekhalot or 3 Enoch (6th-7th c. C.E.), develops this idea even more. Here Enoch says of himself: "When the Holy One, blessed be he, took me to serve the throne of glory, the wheels of the chariot and all the

qualify as a form of deification. If in 1 Enoch, the patriarch truly is transformed into (or realizes himself as) the Son of Man (the text and interpretation are disputed), this would be an astounding development. In
the *Parables*, the Son of Man is a Prime Mediator figure with clearly divine attributes and functions (preexistence, 1 En 48:2–6; eschatological
rule and judgment, chs. 61–62). Assimilation or identification with
such a figure would, I think, qualify as a form of deification.

Even more than Enoch and Elijah, the Jews of Paul's time likened
Moses to the glory of the Gods (cf. Sir 45:2). The biblical text to focus
on here is Moses' descent from Mt. Sinai (Ex 34:29–35). There is still
dispute about the meaning of the mysterious phrase קָרַן עוֹר פָּנָיו
(NRSV, "the skin of his face shone"). Some scholars interpret the
phrase to mean that Moses sprouted horns. The LXX, however, clearly
envisions Moses as being bathed in God's light: "the appearance of the
skin of his face had been glorified" (δεδόξασται ἡ ὄψις τοῦ χρώματος
τοῦ προσώπου). Radiance, as noted previously, is characteristic of divinity. In Numbers 6:25, Yahweh's face shines. He is "wrapped in
light as with a garment" (Ps 103[104]:2). He appears in a pillar of fire
(e.g., Ex 13:21–22). The Psalmist asks the light of Yahweh's face to
shine on him (4:7 [ET 6]). The "horns" of light beaming from
Moses' face, furthermore, are reminiscent of lightning.[44] Lightning is
part of Yahweh's theophanic manifestation (Ps 76:19 [ET 77:18]). Ancient interpreters also noticed the fact that Moses' 40 day fast (not normally humanly possible) associated him with divine beings who do not
eat (Ex 34:28; Philo, *Mos.* 2.68–69).

---

needs of the Šekinah, at once my flesh turned to flame, my sinews to blazing
fire, my bones to juniper coals, my eyelashes to lightning flashes, my eyeballs
to fiery torches, the hairs of my head to hot flames, all my limbs to wings of
burning fire, and the substance of my body to blazing fire" (15:1). This text
is partially based on the verse, "He makes his angels winds, and his messengers
flames of fire" (Heb 1:7; Ps 104:4; cf. 2 En. 29:3 recension A). It describes a
form of deification.

44 Cf. Philo, who says that Moses' compatriots could not withstand the "assault of
sun-like splendor flashing like lightning" from Moses' face (*Mos.* 2.70).

The Glorified Moses in Philo

Our best way into the interpretive traditions surrounding the glorified
Moses is to examine the discussion of Paul's older contemporary,
Philo of Alexandria. According to Philo, Moses did not ascend Sinai
by virtue of his own will, excellence, or physical power. Rather he
was "called up," and conveyed up into the incorporeal realm by the "divine spirit" breathed into him from above (*Plant.* 23–27). The spirit
purged Moses to prepare for his priestly initiation on Sinai. For this initiation, Moses had to be clean in body and soul. That is, he had to cut
away all passion, and sanctify himself "from all the things that character-
ize mortal nature," including eating, drinking, and sexual intercourse
(*Mos.* 2.68). Moses, in other words, had to become like a divine
being. Philo is rather clear on this point. God's command to Moses,
"Come up to Me to the mountain and be there" (Ex 24:12) signifies
that Moses was "*divinized* by ascending not to the air or to the aether
or to heaven higher than all but to (a region) above the heavens"
(*QE* 2.40 on Ex. 24.12a, emphasis added).

This conclusion agrees with Philo's discussion elsewhere of Moses'
ascent. In *Questions on Exodus*, Philo calls Moses' upward call to Sinai "a
second birth better than the first." Moses' first birth, Philo says, was
"mixed with a body and had corruptible parents." Moses' second
birth was a coming into being "without a body."[45] In this respect,
Moses conformed to God's purely noetic nature, which was absolutely
one (*QE* 2.46 on Ex. 24.16b). As Philo says, Moses abandoned the
world of multiplicity, and was "resolved into the nature of unity." In
this way, Moses was "changed into the divine" (*QE* 2.29 on Ex. 24:2).

This temporary "change into the divine" foreshadowed the more
permanent change at the end of Moses' life. According to Philo,
Moses did not die like other people. In fact, he *could* not die like
them, because he was immutable. This is Philo's interpretation of the
fact that Moses could not be "added" to his people (a stock phrase
used to speak of the death of the patriarchs, e.g., Gen 25:8). Thus he
had to be willingly and consciously "translated," (μετανίστημι, cf.

---

45   The Armenian of this passage reads that Moses' coming into being was "from
     the aether and without a body." The Greek fragment, however, reads only ἄνευ
     σώματος. Cf. *Somn.* 1.36: Μωυσῆν ἀσώματον γενόμενον. Philo also finds Moses'
     bodilessness signified in Moses' pitching the Tent of Meeting "outside the
     camp" (Ex 33:7; *Gig.* 54; *Leg.*. 2.54–55; 3.46–48; *Det.* 160; *Ebr.* 100, 124).

Deut. 34:5–6) back to the divine realm (*Sac* 7–10; cf. *Leg Alleg.* 1.40; *Mut.* 19; *Migr.* 84; *Det.* 161).

Moses' translation was his final pilgrimage to the heavenly realm in which all the transformations he experienced at Sinai became permanent (*Mos.* 2.288).[46] His migration was thus an "exaltation," in which he "noticed that he was gradually being disengaged from the [bodily] elements with which he had been mixed" (*Virt.* 76). When Moses shed his mortal encasing, God resolved Moses' body and soul into a single unity, "transforming his whole being into mind, most like the sun (ὅλον δι' ὅλων μεθαρμοζόμενος εἰς νοῦν ἡλιοειδέστατον)" (*Mos* 2.288; cf. *Virt.* 53, 72–79).

It is important to notice the brilliant light imagery here, since it connects Moses to the divine glory traditions. In Exodus, Moses saw the divine glory, and participated in it. Philo appears to be translating these scriptural ideas into philosophical terms. So in Philo, Moses sees God's glorious Logos (or Mind) and is transformed into the brilliant substance of mind. Philosophically, Philo views mind (νοῦς) as a fiery substance. In *Flight and Finding* (133), he describes *mind* as a "hot and fiery pneuma" (ἔνθερμον καὶ πεπυρωμένον πνεῦμα), and in *On Dreams* (1.30–33), the mind itself is *pneuma*, bodiless and imperceptible.[47] This pneuma was widely considered to be a divine substance, which the Stoics called "creative fire" (πῦρ τεχνικόν). This, it appears, is what Moses was turned into. This is what it meant for Moses to be "changed into the divine." Philo calls this process "immortalization" (ἀπαθανατίζεσθαι) (*Mos.* 2.288).

Is it appropriate to view this immortalization and noetic transformation as a form of deification?[48] If Philo truly viewed immortalization as a

46 Meeks points out that the "striking thing about Philo's descriptions of Moses' translation is that they parallel exactly his descriptions of the ascent on Sinai." In both cases, Moses leaves the mortal, bodily realm to enter the "incorporeal and intelligible" (*Mos.* 2.288; *Virt.* 53, 76; *QG* 1.86), and comes by the "summons" of God (*Mos.* 2.288) (*The Prophet-King: Moses Traditions and the Johannine Christology* [Leiden: Brill, 1967], 124.

47 David Winston and John M. Dillon, *Two Treatise of Philo of Alexandria: A Commentary on De Gigantibus and Quod Deus Sit Immutabilis* (Chico, CA: Scholars Press, 1983), 202–03. Dillon notes that pneuma can be called a "bodiless" and "immaterial" substance insofar as it is free from mortal, changeable material.

48 Opinions on this issue vary. Crispin Fletcher-Louis somewhat precipitously states that "It is well known that in the second Temple period Philo deified Moses" ("4Q374: A Discourse on the Sinai Tradition: The Deification of Moses and Early Christology," *Dead Sea Discoveries* 3:3 [1996]: 242). Carl Hol-

transformation into divine substance, I think that we are justified in calling it a deification. Becoming divine reality, or mind, is also a sharing in the identity of the divine Logos. Thus transformation into mind is an assimilation to a divine being. Again, the Logos is God's mind (νοῦς—another meaning of λόγος). For Moses to be transformed into mind (μεθαρμοζόμενος εἰς νοῦν, *Mos.* 2.288) is thus an assimilation to the Divine Mind himself, or the Logos. But assimilation to the Logos is assimilation to a clearly divine being, Philo's "second God" (*QG* 2.62). Because Moses' transformation into divine substance is simultaneously an assimilation to a divine being, we are, I think, justified in calling the immortalization and noetification of Moses a form of "deification."

Lest Philo be accused of "over-Hellenizing," let me point out that the background of assimilation to God (or God's divine Image) is exe-

---

laday does not exclude a Philonic notion of deification, provided it is reserved for post-mortem existence (*Theios Aner in Hellenistic-Judaism: A Critique of the use of this Category in New Testament Christology* [Missoula: Scholars Press, 1977], 196–97). Donald Hagner allows only for a "nominal apotheosis" so as not to assert that Moses was fused with the Godhead" ("The Vision of God in Philo and John: A Comparative Study," *Journal of the Evangelical Theological Society* 14 (1971): 90). David Runia writes that the "logical outcome of Philo's adoption of Greek intellectualism is the affirmation of man's potential apotheosis, that the mind can gain a place in the noetic world on the level of the divine" (*Philo of Alexandria and the* Timaeus *of Plato* [Amsterdam: VU Boekhandel, 1983], 439). In a later study he denies Moses' deification, if it means that he had the same nature as the Existent. Moses' divinity is a "derived divinity" ("God and Man in Philo of Alexandria," 60, 69). Barry Blackburn thinks it "quite misleading" to speak of Moses' "apotheosis" since this same apotheosis will (according to Philo) "be experienced by the soul of every wise man" (*Theios Anēr and the Markan Miracle Traditions: A Critique of the Theios Anēr Concept as an Interpretive Background of the Miracle Traditions used by Mark* [Tübingen: Mohr Siebeck, 1991], 66). He again wants to emphasize that Moses is a creature who cannot belong to the ontological category of the Existent. (Such an ontological differentiation between God and deified persons is, however, compatible with deification as it was understood in the ancient world.) For John Lierman, Philo's Moses is "a divine figure" in the sense that he has been elevated to the "divine office" of "God" (one of the twin powers of the Existent; *Mut.* 19–22, 231). Moses is God because of his divine function, a criterion which Lierman thinks—following Charles Gieschen—makes a person divine. Thus Lierman accepts the deification of Moses, provided it is understood as "delegated" rather than "essential" divinity (*The New Testament Moses: Christian Perceptions of Moses and Israel in the Setting of Jewish Religion* [Tübingen: Mohr Siebeck, 2004], 231, 246).

getical. The Hebrew text of Genesis 1:26 can be translated "Let us make the human *as* our image" (בצלמנו) (taking the *bet* as a *bet essentiae*). The Jewish translators of Genesis at Alexandria did not understand the preposition this way. The LXX translates it by καϑ' εἰκόνα ἡμῶν, "*according to our image.*" Here, human beings ceased to *be* the image, and were reduced to being *according to the image* (or Image) of God. In this way of thinking, humans did not share the identity of the primal God in any direct sense. They shared it only with a mediate divine being called God's "Image." This raised the question about the identity of God's Image. Some Alexandrians apparently identified it with Wisdom (cf. Wisd 7:26). Philo identified it with the Logos (*Conf.* 146). Paul identified it with Christ (2 Cor 4:4), who is also the Wisdom of God (1 Cor 1:30). At any rate, human beings were created according to the likeness (καϑ' ὁμοίωσιν) of this divine being (Gen 1:26). It was only appropriate, then, for humans to undergo assimilation (ἐξομοίωσις) to this being as their redemptive goal. But assimilation to a specifically divine being is, I would argue, a form of deification.

Sharing God's Divine Sovereignty: The Divinity of Israelite Kings.[49]

Besides Moses, Enoch and Elijah, the other major biblical characters who seem to overlap with the divine identity are the Israelite kings. The Israelite king, it seems, is directly called a "God" in Ps 44:7 [ET 45:6; MT 45:7]), where a court poet addresses the king: "Your throne, O God (אלהים; ὁ ϑεός) endures forever and ever."[50] Similarly, the

---

49 For early research on the divinity of Israelite kings, see G. Widengren, *Sakrales Königtum im alten Testament und im Judentum* (Stuttgart: Kohlhammer, 1955); J. Morgenstern, "The King-God among the Western Semites and the Meaning of Epiphanes," *Vetus Testamentum* 10 (1960): 138–97; Aubrey Johnson, *Sacral Kingship in Ancient Israel* (Cardiff: University of Wales Press, 1967).

50 For recent discussion on this text, see Adela Yarbro and John Collins, *King and Messiah as Son of God: Divine, Human, and Angelic Messianic Figures in Biblical and Related Literature* (Grand Rapids, Eerdmans, 2008), 14, 56; Mark S. Smith, *Origins of Biblical Monotheism: Israel's Polytheistic Background and the Ugaritic Texts* (New York: Oxford University Press), 160–62. J. S. M. Mulder dates this psalm to the seventh-century B.C.E. (*Studies on Psalm 45* [Oss (the Netherlands): Offsetdrukkerij Witsiers, 1972], 158). He notes that the term אלהים in v. 7a, which refers to the king, has a good Egyptian parallel that occurs in the set phrase "the perfect (or beautiful) God." B. Couroyer uses this Egyptian expres-

prophet Isaiah bestows the name "Mighty God" (אל גבור) on a future
king (9:6).[51] Influential in the mid 20th century, Sigmund Mowinckel
translated "Mighty God (אל גבור)" as "Divine Hero,"[52] and commented:
"the heroic power which the child will possess is characterized as divine.
In form the name offers a precise parallel to the epithet applied to Aley-
an-Baal in the Ugaritic texts: 'ilu gaziru, 'the victorious or heroic god'"
(cf. also Deut 10:17; Jer 32:18; Neh 9:32; Ps 23[24]:8).[53] R. A. Carlson
prefers to relate the title "Mighty God" to the Assyrian royal title ilu qar-
rādu ("Strong God") which often appears.[54] Hans Wildberger, who
keeps the translation "mighty God," confirms that it is a divine epithet.[55]
אל גבור is directly applied to YHWH in Isa 10:21 (LXX θεὸς ἰσχύων)
and Jer 39[32]:18 (ὁ θεὸς ὁ μέγας καὶ ἰσχυρός). That the Israelite king
could be called "God" is less shocking in light of Ps 44:7 [ET 45:6].
Although this language is often explained (away) by Old Testament
scholars by the idea that the Israelite king merely represents Yahweh
on earth,[56] bearing the name "God" seems to indicate a closer relation
to Yahweh than representation.

---

sion as one of his arguments to demonstrate that אלהים is a vocative ("Dieu ou
Roi," *Revue Biblique* 78 [1971]: 234–39). For the king of Tyre as "God," note
Ezek 28:14. The Egyptian king is also addressed by his vassals as "my God" in
the El Amarna letters 157, 213, 215, 233, 241, 243, 270, 299, 301, 305, 306,
319, 363, 366) (as noted in Mark Smith, *God in Translation: Deities in Cross-cultural Discourse in the Biblical World* [Tübingen: Mohr Siebeck, 2008], 14).

51   This is one of four names given to an anticipated Israelite king. For a proposed
      fifth name, see H. Wildberger, "Die Thronnamen des Messias," *Theologische
      Literaturzeitung* 16 (1960): 329. The LXX translates the four names as "Angel
      of the Great Council" (Μεγάλης βουλῆς ἄγγελος). Some MSS, however, give
      the fuller reading: "Wonderful Counselor, Strong God (θεὸς ἰσχυρός), Author-
      itative Ruler of Peace, Father of the Coming World." See the apparatus in the
      Rahlf's edition of the Septuagint.
52   W. McClellan, ("El Gibbor," *Catholic Biblical Quarterly* 6 [1944]: 276–288)
      takes exception to the latter translation (since it can also be translated "Heroic
      God," or "a God of a Hero"). He agrees, however, that אל גבור is a divine
      name.
53   Sigmund Mowinckel, *He that Cometh: The Messiah Concept in the Old Testament
      and Later Judaism* (trans. G. W. Anderson Grand Rapids: Eerdmans, 2005), 105;
      cf. Wildberger, "Die Thronnamen," 317.
54   "The Anti-Assyrian Character of the Oracle in is IX:1–6," *Vetus Testamentum*
      24 (1974): 134.
55   *Isaiah: A Continental Commentary* (Minneapolis: Fortress Press, 1991), 403–404.
56   By way of example, Werner H. Schmidt, *The Faith of the Old Testament: A His-
      tory* (Oxford: Basil Blackwell, 1983), 182.

Furthermore, the name "Everlasting Father" (אֲבִיעַד), applied to the king in the same verse, most likely means "Father of Eternity" (cf. "Father of Years," used of El at Ugarit, and "Ancient of Days" in Dan 7:9). It indicates, said Mowinckel, "the one who produces, directs, and is lord of the ever-changing years … who thus produces and directs 'eternity', the entire fullness of events and reality. It is evident that such a name really belongs to a god, and not just any god, but *the* god, 'the high god', 'the supreme god', 'the father of the gods.'"[57] It is probably more accurate to conclude, however, that אֲבִיעַד is a hyperbolic way of granting the king immortality. Hugo Gressmann already noted as parallels the Egyptian royal titles "prince of eternity," and "lord of unendingness."[58] The additional implication of the king's immortality seems to have been understood by the psalmist who prays that the king may live as long as the sun endures (Ps 71[72]:5, LXX). Similarly in Psalm 20:5 [ET 21:4], the king asks for life and Yahweh gives it to him, "length of days forever and ever" (cf. Ps 60:7 [ET 61:6]).

Perhaps most famously, Yahweh declares to the king: "You are my son" (בְּנִי אַתָּה; Υἱός μου εἶ σύ) (Ps 2:6–7). Most students of the Bible are familiar with the "sons of God" as lesser divine beings. They appear in the divine council (Ps 81[82]:1); sing praises in the divine court (Ps 28 [29]:1), rule the nations (Deut 32:8 [LXX], Ps 81[82], esp. v.6), and impregnate human women (Gen 6:2). It seems slightly tendentious, then, to reduce the sonship of the Israelite king here to a mere metaphor.[59] At the very least, the king is depicted as entering into a kinship relation to God like humanity in Gen 1:26, (made according to) the image of God.

The realism of royal sonship language must be taken seriously. The king is actually "begotten" (יְלִדְתִּיךָ; γεγέννηκά σε) as son of God, not merely adopted (Ps 2:7).[60] Adela Yarbro and John Collins describe

---

57 *He that Cometh*, 106. Mowinckel cites for comparison Tob 13:6, 13; 14:7; Sir 36:22. Yet Mowinckel goes on to affirm that the "newborn king, who is described as a divine being with divine titles and faculties, who has appropriated the characteristics, achievements and name … of the sun god and supreme god, is nevertheless only an instrument in the hands of 'Yahweh,' 'God Almighty', who is the Author of all: he is a scion of David, a mere man … in the last resort the power and the glory belong to Yahweh" (107). It is true, at any rate, that the divinity or divine power of the Israelite king is not threatening to Yahweh.
58 Noted in Wildberger, *Commentary*, 404.
59 This is a move made by many. Kaufmann (*Religion of Israel*, 77), is a notable example.
60 Adela Yarbro and John Collins, *King and Messiah*, 19–22. The language of begetting is not part of an adoption formula.

this language as "mythical," non-ontological, and "metaphorical" (though they add that it is not "mere" metaphor).[61] This language, the caveats notwithstanding, is generally unhelpful because of its modern assumptions. What to us (speaking after the Enlightenment) is myth, was often simply the reality (indeed, physical reality) of the ancient author.[62] We need to be open to the idea, then, that what to us is myth and metaphor was to ancient Jews literal and real. The act of begetting probably occurred through investment with Yahweh's Spirit (an entity which we should not assume to be incorporeal). Every king was an "Anointed one" (מָשִׁיחַ; χριστός) (1 Sam 10:1; 24:6). The anointing of the king (Ps 2:2) meant more than that he had oil dripped on his head. It meant the inhabitation of the divine spirit—the closest thing the ancients had to divine DNA.[63]

This view of begetting is supported by the Collinses' reading of Ps 110:3b. They translate the last colon: "you [the Israelite king] have the dew wherewith I [God] have begotten you (יַלְדֻתֶיךָ)." The understanding of the last verb is in accordance with the Septuagint (ἐξεγέννησά σε), and is accepted by many commentators.[64] The Collinses rightly compare the phrase with the "dew" (possibly "fragrance") involved in the begetting of Hatshepsut the Egyptian Pharaoh. In an inscription, the mother of Hatshepsut addresses the God Amun, Lord of Thebes "'It is splendid to see thy front; thou has united my majesty with thy favors, thy dew is in all my limbs.' After this the majesty of the God did all he desired with her."[65] In this scene, the God Amun impregnated Hatshepsut's mother, possibly by means of the God's "dew" (apparently a sperm-like substance), so Hatshepsut was conceived. Back in Ps 110, the preceding colon in v. 3 indicates that the king has been begotten "In sacred splendor from the womb of the Dawn [or from the womb of Shachar] (מֵרֶחֶם מִשְׁחָר)." We know of Helel son of Shachar identified with the

---

61 Ibid., 204. It is readily granted that in Ps 2 we are reading poetry not philosophy, but is poetry not realistic? I fear that by denying any "ontological" value to divine begetting, they (unintentionally) rob it of its reality for the ancient audience.

62 For the realistic begetting of ancient Pharaohs, see ibid., 4–5.

63 This is not an argument for a "sexual" interpretation of divine begetting, only one along more physicalist lines.

64 E.g., Hans-Joachim Kraus, Psalms 60–150: A Commentary (Minneapolis: Fortress Press, 1993; 1989), 587; Matitiahu Tsevat, "God and the Gods in Assembly: An Interpretation of Ps 82," Hebrew Union College Annual (1969–70): 344.

65 Quoted in King and Messiah, 19. The full quote is on ibid., 5.

Babylonian king in Isaiah 14:12. Shachar the son of El was also a deity venerated at Ugarit. The Collinses prefer an Egyptian background, however, since that which comes forth from the Dawn is the sun, "the primary image for the deity in the Egyptian tradition."[66] At any rate, we have in Ps 110 a tradition about the realistic divine begetting of the Israelite king. A similarly realistic interpretation, then, should not be ruled out in Ps 2:7 with its "Today I have begotten you (σήμε-ρον γεγέννηκά σε)."[67]

The (hopefully less controversial!) point I wish to emphasize, how-ever, is that in both Ps 2 and Ps 110, the divine sonship of the king leads to a divine function—namely, rule:

Ask of me, and I will give the nations as your inheritance (κληρονομίαν), and the ends of the earth your possession.
You shall shepherd them with an iron rod (ἐν ῥάβδῳ σιδηρᾷ), and dash them in pieces like a potter's vessel. (Ps 2:8–9)
He [the king] will dominate from sea to sea; from the river to the ends of the inhabited world. (Ps 71[72]:8)

The Lord says to my lord,
'Sit at my right hand
Until I make your enemies a footstool for your feet.'
Yahweh sends out from Zion
your rod of power (ῥάβδον δυνάμεως),
and he dominates (κατακυρίευε) in the midst of your foes …
The Lord is at your right hand;
he shattered kings on the day of his wrath.
He will execute judgment among the nations,
filling them with corpses;
he will shatter heads
over the wide earth. (Ps 109[110]:1–2; 5–6)

I exalted an elect one over my people.
I found David my servant;

---

66 *Ibid.*, 18. For the association of Yahweh with the Sun, see the texts citied in *ibid.*, n. 92.
67 For further comments on the king's divine sonship, note N. Wyatt, *Myths of Power: A Study of Royal Myth and Ideology in Ugaritic and Biblical Tradition* (Muenster: Ugarit-Verlag, 1996), 283–91 (although this source is to be used with caution). We get a sense of how early Christians were reading Ps 2:7 from how they apply it to Jesus (Acts 13:33; Heb 1:5; 5:5). The language of sonship and of begetting was apparently taken very seriously. In these texts, I suggest, it was generally understood that Jesus did not become God's son only "metaphorically."

I anointed him with my holy oil.
For my hand will help him
and my arm will fully strengthen him ...
In my name his horn will be exalted.
I will set his hand on the sea, and his right hand on the rivers.[68]
He himself will invoke me:
'You are my Father!
My God and the helper of my salvation!'
I will make him my firstborn,
the most high over all those who reign on earth.
(Ps 88:20–22, 25–28 [Eng 89:19–21, 24–27])

  The Israelite king is God's viceregent on earth, and rules the world. It is
the supreme power of the king which helps him bridge the gap between
the human and the divine. Here again we are led back to Gen 1:26. For
here, whatever scholars suppose the image of God in this verse to be,
the consequence of being in the image is rule.[69] The idea of ruling is
mentioned twice in Gen 1:26–28, apparently for emphasis:

> "Let us make humankind in our image, according to our likeness; and let
> them rule (וירדו; ἀρχέτωσαν) over the fish of the sea, and over the birds of
> the air, and over the cattle, and over all the wild animals of the earth, and
> over every creeping thing that creeps upon the earth." ... God said to
> them, "Be fruitful and multiply, and fill the earth, dominate it, and rule
> (כבשה ורדו; κατακυριεύσατε αὐτῆς καὶ ἄρχετε) over the fish of the sea
> and over the birds of the air and over every living thing that moves
> upon the earth." (cf. Ps 8:7–9 [ET 6–8]; cf. Sir 17:4; Jub 2:13–14)

One has the impression here that the idea of the image-bearing ruler of
the earth has been taken from Israelite royal ideology and "democra-
tized" to apply to all human beings.[70] If so, the divine aura of Israelite
kings colored humankind in its original state. The king as God's son
was also God's image. It is no surprise that those who are said to be
(in) God's image are given a share of God's sovereignty.
  The sovereignty spoken of in Genesis is comprehensive over the
natural world: over fish, birds, cattle, wild animals—over the earth itself.
In the succinct paraphrase of the Qumran sectarians: "He [God] created
man to rule the world" (1QS 3.17; cf. Sib Or. 8.444–445). The sovereignty of the Israelite king is extended to the "nations" (ἔθνη) and "the

---

68 On this text, note Smith, *Origins of Biblical Monotheism*, 158–159.
69 The view that the divine image results in (or even consists in) power to rule is
    pervasive in Hebrew Bible scholarship (Jónsson, *Image of God*, 219–221).
70 Incidentally, the inbreathing of the spirit/breath of God in Gen 2:7 is reminis-
    cent of kings being endowed with the spirit through the process of anointing.

ends of the earth" (Ps 2:8)—"from the river to the ends of the inhabited
world" (Ps 71[72]:8). Psalm 8:7 (a royal Psalm) sums it up: "You have
set him up [humankind] over the works of your hands, everything
(πάντα) you have subjected underneath his feet." This is no ordinary
sovereignty. This is the universal divine sovereignty which over and
over again Yahweh claims for himself.

> His kingly rule dominates all things (καὶ ἡ βασιλεία αὐτοῦ πάντων
> δεσπόζει). (Ps 102[103]:19)

> All the ends of the earth (πάντα τὰ πέρατα τῆς γῆς) will remember and
> turn to the Lord, and all the ancestral nations (αἱ πατριαὶ τῶν ἐθνῶν)
> will worship before you. Rule is of the Lord; he himself dominates the na-
> tions (τῶν ἐθνῶν). (Ps 21:28–29 [ET 22:27–28])

> The Lord reigns, let the people be enraged. He sits on the cherubim, let the
> earth be shaken. The Lord is great and exalted in Zion, over all the peoples.
> (Ps 98[99]:1–2)

One is led to the conclusion that the king—and humanity in its original
state (Gen 1:26)—shared the universal sovereignty of God. It is Yahweh
who rules and judges the nations, and Yahweh donates that sovereignty
to the Israelite king—and by extension human beings in general. Yet if
the power of divine sovereignty is part of Yahweh's identity (as argued
in chapter 2), the king or human being who shares that sovereignty is
much more than Yahweh's representative. By virtue of his office,
such a one shares Yahweh's distinct role. It is no wonder that the
early church read the royal psalms as speaking of Christ whom they
knew shared the identity of God. He was the human being—and
king—who truly inherited God's universal rule; he was the Image of
God. *He was also widely considered to be divine.* Would exercising a divine
function have meant less for the ancient Israelite king?

Conclusion

The argument of this chapter has not been that Paul's Bible contains a
soteriology of deification. Rather, I argue that the LXX furnishes the
images and stories which—in a later time and culture—enabled Jews
to imagine a soteriology of deification. Humankind as God's corporeal
image and the Israelite king as his divine son were notions later transferred to the divine Christ. It is Christ, then, who for Paul opens the way

to attain the deification rooted in a more ancient theology. Although I fully admit the transcendence and unity of God present in the LXX, the Greek scriptures did not in fact impart a theology adverse to deification. To the contrary, the LXX presents a God willing to share his divine glory and universal sovereignty—two aspects of his divine identity. His fiery and brilliant corporeality is shared (at least for a short time) with Elijah and Moses. The sovereignty meant for Adam was given to Israelite kings, and expanded to include all nations. It is this same pattern of sharing in God's corporeal manifestation and in his divine sovereignty that, I will argue, appears in Paul. Yet Paul's interpretation of these themes takes them in a new direction. Paul reads Adam (the original human being) Christologically, as he does the promises made to ancient Israelite kings. For Paul, Christ took up the universal rule of the kings as well as "all the glory of Adam." Those who would share in those divine qualities must share them through Christ. For those who share in these qualities of Christ, the same participation in the divine identity becomes a genuine possibility. This argument will be fully developed in Part II of this study.

Part II
Sharing the Divine Identity

Chapter 4:
Divine Corporeality and the Pneumatic Body

> "He will transform the body of our
> humiliation so that it may be
> conformed to the body of his glory, by
> the power that also enables him to
> make all things subject to himself."
> (Phil 3:21)

Introduction

The following four chapters contain the heart of my argument for a Pauline form of deification. In the introduction, deification was defined as sharing in the qualities constitutive of the divine identity. These qualities were determined, in chapter 1, to be immortality and power. The results of chapter 2 indicated that sharing in divine power and immortality could be conceived of as an assimilation to a particular divinity. We will deal with Paul and the reception of power (or rule) in chapter 6, and moral assimilation to a particular God in chapter 7. In the following two chapters, our focus will be on sharing the divine quality of immortality.

The creation story of Genesis discussed in chapter 3 showed that humans, though made in (or as) the image of God, were kept from immortality. Paul's gospel, in turn, taught that humans could attain immortality through assimilation to the divine Christ (1 Cor 15:35–53). The Pauline mode of assimilation, I will argue, is corporeal. That is, believers assimilate to the glorious *body* of the divine Christ. In this way they receive an immortal body made up of a fine, ethereal stuff called "pneuma." In this chapter, I seek to establish this thesis by arguing three points: (1) that many Greco-Roman divinities (including Christ) are often thought to have non-fleshy (sometimes luminous) incorruptible bodies, (2) that Paul envisions believers as sharing in Christ's divine body, which he conceives of as pneumatic (1 Cor 15:44–45), and (3) that transformation into a pneumatic body constitutes a form of celestial immortality. In making these arguments, I will borrow heavily from ideas prevalent in Paul's time and culture, primarily from popular

(Stoic and Platonic) philosophy.[1] The following chapter will draw out the implications of Paul's notion of celestial immortality for a Pauline form of deification.

The Bodies of the Gods

That a God would have a body might seem strange to those accustomed to various Platonic theologies prevalent since Late Antiquity,[2] but this was a common idea in the first-century Mediterranean world. Some examples from representative poets and philosophers will establish this point. Aphrodite, it was said, was born from the "immortal flesh [or skin]" (ἀπ' ἀθανάτου χροὸς) of Ouranos (Hes., Theog. 191). In the *Iliad*, Diomedes wounded the flesh (again χρώς) of Aphrodite so that she bled ichor, or "immortal blood" (ἄμβροτον αἷμα) (5.339–40; cf. 382–400).[3] Although the Gods do not shed human tears, a tear-like "shining drop" (*lucida gutta*) falls from the eye of Demeter when she thinks of her daughter (Ovid, *Fasti* 4.521–22). A shining tear assumes a shining eye, placed on a face, part of a divine body. Such divine bodies were not omnipresent, but had to move from place to place by bounding from mountain to mountain or by flying on the winds or in a chariot (Hom., *Il.* 5.363–366; 8.41–52; 14.298–299). Votive inscriptions which depict the Gods receiving sacrifice typically depict them as bodies larger and more beautiful than the human worshippers. The large size of divine bodies is made patent in their epiphanies. So Aphrodite appears to the hero Anchises in a Homeric hymn:

> ... At last,
> Fully dressed, the queen among goddesses stood by the bed;
> Her head reached to the well-hewn crossbeams, and from her cheeks

---

1   For the relationship of Stoic and Platonic philosophy in this period, see Troels Engberg-Pedersen, "Setting the Scene: Stoicism and Platonism in the Transitional Period in Ancient Philosophy," in *Stoicism in Early Christianity* (eds. Tuomas Rasimus, Engberg-Pedersen, and Ismo Dunderberg; Grand Rapids: Baker Academic, 2010), 1–14. Engberg-Pedersen believes that Paul's worldview was basically Stoic (11), but that he (along with other philosophers of this period) was able to "absorb" elements from other philosophies (such as Platonism) while retaining his basic allegiance.

2   Platonic theology typically views the high God (sometimes conceived of as a Demiurge) as an ineffable, incorporeal, invisible being.

3   The wound of Aphrodite, I should add, was healed and her pain assuaged with a mere touch from the divine Dione (*Il.* 5.416–17).

Immortal beauty shone forth—that of bright-crowned Cytherea.
(*Hom. Hymn. Aphr.* 5.172–75; trans. Thelma Sargent)

In a similar way, Demeter reveals her true self to Metaneira:

So speaking, the goddess resumed her own stature and aspect,
Throwing aside her guise of old age. Beauty spread all around her,
And from her blue gown drifted the lovely odor of incense;
The light of the goddess's immortal presence shone far abroad,
And the wealth of her long golden hair lay over her shoulders,
And the thickly built room blazed with a brightness as if of lightning.
(*Hom. Hymn Dem.* 2.275–80)

Deities, as these texts indicate, were not bodiless. Rather they had (in the words of Jean Pierre Vernant) "super bodies" built from superior substances and endowed with a superior size, beauty, and power.

Philosophical sources maintain and develop the Greek understanding of divine corporeality. For most Greeks, a God is "a living immortal, which has both a soul and a body naturally united for all time" (*Phaedr.* 246c-d). The bodies and (lower) souls of Gods are, in addition, perfectly obedient to their minds (246a). In the philosophy of Aristotle, God is also a composite of soul and body (*Top.* 5. 1, 128b39–129a2; cf. *Cael.* 2. 3, 286a10–11 and *Pol.* 7.14, 1332b16–20). Yet Aristotle describes the Gods' "bodies and souls as greatly superior to entities bearing the same names found in human beings" (*Pol.* 7.14, 1332b18–20). The Gods, according to the Philosopher, have perfect bodies which do not disobey their minds or reduce the quality of their perfect (intellectual) life.[4] The superiority of divine bodies was traced back to the superiority of their substance. The bodies of the celestial Gods, Aristotle said, are made up of aether, which naturally moves in a circle.[5] In an aether-body, no mental energy is needed to propel the body to be moved in a particular direction.

In later philosophy, Epicureans insisted that the Gods had bodies—otherwise they would be deprived of sensation, practical wisdom, and pleasure (Cic., *Nat d.* 1.12.30). In *On the Nature of the Gods*, Cicero's Stoic representative declares in philosophical form what appears to be widely assumed in Greek culture. The Gods "are not held together by veins and nerves and bones; nor do they consume the sort of food and drink that would make their humors either too sharp or too dense; nor do they have the sorts of bodies that would lead them to

---

4   Bodéüs, *Aristotle and the Theology of the Living Immortals*, 131.
5   *Ibid.*, 71.

dread falls or blows or fear diseases produced by physical exhaustion" (*Nat d.* 2.59–60). The divine body envisioned by the Stoics is spherical, like the heavenly bodies. Nevertheless, Epicureans and most of the common folk in the ancient Mediterranean still envisioned divine bodies in human shape—though bigger, brighter, and more beautiful.

We have already witnessed the brightness of divine bodies in the Homeric *Hymn to Demeter* cited above. The brightness of divine bodies is also assumed in the story of Semele who asks to see the form of Zeus and is consequently torched by the flames surging from the God's body (Ovid, *Met.* 3.273–308). When Hannibal sees the Gods in the *Punica* of Silius Italicus, he beholds their "fiery limbs" (*flammea membra*) (12.727). Brilliant light is the rule for divine epiphanies (Virg., *Aen.* 2.590–91; 3.151; Ovid, *Fasti* 1.94).[6] According to Greek myth, Zeus had a wondrous body well described in an Orphic fragment as "full of light, immense, unshaken, undisturbed, strong-limbed, [and] immensely strong (περιφεγγές, ἀπείριτον, ἀστυφέλικτον, ἄτρομον, ὀβριμόγυιον, ὑπερμενές)" (Stob., *Anth.* 1.1.23).

Divine corporeality, according to these authors, was clearly different from human corporeality. Instead of having a dying, decaying body, the Gods had an immortal body unsusceptible to (at least serious) injury, and which embodies all the qualities which ancient Mediterranean peoples tended to value: light, strength, permanence, incorruption, etc.[7]

The next logical question to ask is whether the Jews of the Greco-Roman world also thought that (their) God had a bright and incorruptible "super body." A recent discussion by Benjamin Sommer helps to decide this question.[8] Sommer shows that in at least one stream of biblical tradition (the P source, deeply intertwined with Ezekiel), the Jewish God was conceived of corporeally.[9] These texts, it seems, proved influential for Paul's Christology, and so deserve closer examination.

Ezekiel's vision of God in the first chapter of his prophecy is justly famous and often cited. To the prophet appeared a chariot throne in the heavens drawn by cherubim. His description of the throne's occupant is as follows:

---

6   These texts are noted in Levene, "What is a God?" forthcoming.
7   The best treatment of divine corporeality is Jean Pierre Vernant, *Mortals and Immortals: Collected Essays* (Princeton: Princeton University Press, 1991), 27–49.
8   *The Bodies of God*, 334; cf. Mark Smith, *Origins of Biblical Monotheism*, 83–86.
9   Other biblical traditions also envision God as having a body (such as the classical "J source"), but not in the same way as P and Ezekiel, which I will focus on here.

... seated above the likeness of the throne was a likeness like the form of a human being from above. And I saw something like the appearance of electrum from the sight of his loins upward, and from the sight of his loins downward I saw something like an appearance of fire with its brilliance around it. Like the sight of a rainbow when it is in the cloud on a rainy day—thus was the array of the light around it. This was the sight of the likeness of the Glory of the Lord. I saw and I fell on my face; then I heard a voice speaking. (Ezek 1:26b-28, LXX)

Just as Isaiah "saw the Lord" (Isa 6:1), Ezekiel saw the Jewish God on his throne. Although the prophet's language is highly qualified, the picture of what he saw is relatively clear. He saw on the throne a massive human body, the torso and head like glowing metal, the legs like fire—all surrounded by a surreal, divine light. This is not an invisible, incorporeal God, but an anthropomorphic deity moving about in a super body. This super body is evidently made of intensely bright light and fire, or elements closely resembling these. It would not be off the mark to call this divine body a "body of glory." Ezekiel himself calls this entity the "Glory of the God of Israel" (כבוד אלהי ישראל; δόξα θεοῦ τοῦ Ισραηλ) in 9:3 and identifies this Glory with "Yahweh" or the "Lord" (יהוה; κύριος) in the following verse: "Now the Glory of the God of Israel had gone up from the cherubim on which he rested to the threshold of the house and called to the man in linen... and *Yahweh* said to him" (Ezek 9:3–4, emphasis added).[10] In Ezek 8:2–3, Yahweh is again his Glory, but here he has a hand and seems to be equivalent to "Spirit."[11]

According to Carey C. Newman, Glory in Ezek 1 is "equated with the divine, human form seated upon the throne. This remarkable development in the Glory tradition will have profound impact upon later visionary descriptions of God."[12] In the Parables of Enoch for instance, the "Son of Man" and "Elect One" is equated with the "Glory of the Lord." In Jewish apocalypses, the "sometimes anthropomorphically described כבוד יהוה became the sometimes anthropomorphically descri-

---

10 Only Codex Vaticanus omits the word κύριος ("the Lord") who speaks in v. 4 (merely reporting "he said"). All other MSS of the LXX have it. For discussion of these texts in Ezekiel with brief bibliography, see Jarl Fossum, "Glory" in *DDD*[2], 348–352.

11 Carey C. Newman, *Paul's Glory Christology: Tradition and Rhetoric* (Leiden: Brill, 1992), 93.

12 *Ibid.*, 74.

bed special angelic figure." "Glory thus denoted and connoted divine and semi-divine beings which populate the heavens."[13]

The text of Exodus presents a similar picture. Here, Yahweh's body consists of a sort of super-earthly, ever-burning fire, "stunningly bright, so that it had to be surrounded by dark clouds to protect anyone nearby."[14] This body was real enough to reach out and burn people (Lev 10:1–3; cf. 9:24), but it was no solid like flesh or any bulky material.[15] "In modern terms," says Sommer, "we might tentatively suggest that this body was made of energy rather than matter."[16] At any rate, Yahweh's body has no connection at all to the matter of this world. It is a higher, finer, more luminous stuff. It is what the priestly writers referred to as the *kabod* (Greek *doxa*), traditionally translated by "Glory."

In Exodus, however, the Glory is not necessarily anthropomorphic (it is said to fill the Tabernacle and burn on the summit of Sinai)—except in one place. In Moses' vision of God on Sinai in Ex 33, the prophet implores Yahweh, "Show me your *doxa*" (Ex 33:18). Yahweh takes this as a request to see his "person" or "face" (τὸ πρόσωπον) (33:20). Yahweh's "face" is apparently part of his body that will "pass by" Moses (v. 22; cf. Lev 9:4, 6, 23). We learn also from this passage that Yahweh has a "hand" and a "backside" (33:22–23). We gain the impression that Yahweh covered Moses as he walked (apparently on legs) past the prophet on the mount. In this vision, Yahweh quite literally prevented Moses from beholding his "face" (v. 23). What Moses saw (from the back) was apparently God's body of Glory characterized by intense light or brilliance. This is indicated by the fact that in Ex 34:29–35, Moses descends the mountain with his skin shining with the afterglow of God's Glory body.

It has sometimes been thought that the priestly "Glory" is not God's body, but only a divine attribute or an accompaniment to divine revelation. "This objection," notes Sommer, "does not stand up under scrutiny, because both the priestly authors and the prophet Ezekiel assert the identity of the *kabod* and God quite explicitly."[17] In Ezekiel 1, the author describes the super-human beings (later identified with cherubim)

---

13   *Ibid.*, 242. For fuller discussion, see 83–92. For the influence of Ezek 1 on these traditions, see 92–104.
14   Sommer, *Bodies of God*, 2.
15   *Ibid.*, 70–71.
16   *Ibid.*, 2.
17   *Ibid.*, 72.

underneath the *kabod* (mentioned in 1:28). In chapter 10, the author refers to one of these beings as the "living being I saw under the *God of Israel*" (v. 20, emphasis added). This interchange of referents shows that God and Glory were considered to be equivalent. Likewise in Exodus, when the *kabod* arrived at Mount Sinai (19:1–2, 24:15b), "the cloud covered the mountain, and then Yahweh's *kabod* dwelt on the mountain, and the cloud covered it for six days. On the seventh day, he [i.e., *Yahweh*] called to Moses from within the cloud" (24:15–16).[18] "The phrasing entails," says Sommer "the identity of the *kabod* and Yahweh, for these verses make clear that the *kabod* was located within the cloud, and it was from within the cloud that *God* spoke to Moses."[19] Sommer continues:

> In the last three verses of Exodus, the *kabod* enters the tent [of meeting], and in the immediately following verse (Lev 1:1 which continues the narrative without interruption), Yahweh calls to Moses from within the tent. Here again, the text makes the identity of the *kabod* and God clear, as it does in the verses that narrate how God accepted the first sacrifices one week later: "Yahweh's *kabod* manifested itself to the whole people, and a fire from where Yahweh was went out and consumed what was on the altar … ." (Lev 9:23)[20]

Whether or not one agrees that Yahweh *is* his Glory or is somehow coextensive with it, it is nonetheless evident that Glory can represent God's physical manifestation. Although theologians throughout the centuries have wanted to disassociate God's physical manifestation from his body (assuming that God is incorporeal), it seems best to disengage the Bible from technical Greek philosophy at this point. To the average Jew or Christian in the ancient world, I propose, it was not offensive to think of God's Glory as God's "body."[21] This Glory

---

18 The LXX runs: καὶ κατέβη ἡ δόξα τοῦ Θεοῦ ἐπὶ τὸ ὄρος τὸ Σινα, καὶ ἐκάλυψεν αὐτὸ ἡ νεφέλη ἓξ ἡμέρας, καὶ ἐκάλεσεν κύριος τὸν Μωυσῆν τῇ ἡμέρᾳ τῇ ἑβδόμῃ ἐκ μέσου τῆς νεφέλης (Ex 24:16, emphasis added).

19 *Bodies of God*, 73.

20 *Ibid.*, 73–74. For Yahweh as his Glory, consider also Ps 56:6 [ET 57:5] = 107:6 [ET 108:5]; 113:4; Isa 58:8; Jer 2:11; Ps 105[106]:20; 4 Ez 3:19; *L.A.B.* 17:1.

21 According to Newman, Glory is "the visible and mobile presence of Yahweh" (*Glory Christology*, 24). This definition rightly tries to encompass the wide semantic range of "Glory" in the Bible. Nevertheless, in the passages just discussed, Glory as divine "presence" is an insufficient description. In these texts, the mode of Yahweh's presence is specifically corporeal. God appears as a *body* of light.

body is clearly not a purely spiritual (i.e., immaterial) entity, but it is clearly not flesh either. It is, again, a higher, celestial substance, made up of ever-burning fire, bright enough to illumine the whole top of Mt. Sinai (Ex 24:17) or the whole camp of the Israelites at night (Ex 13:21; 40:38; Deut 1:33).

Turning to Paul, we note the close relation between Yahweh's glory body and the kind of body Paul attributes to Christ. According to Paul, Christ has a "body of Glory" (σῶμα τῆς δόξης) (Phil 3:21). The "Glory" here is probably a genitive of content or definition ("the body constituted by Glory"). This is the body which Christ gained in his resurrection, when he was raised by the "Glory" of the Father (Rom 6:4). Accordingly in 1 Corinthians, Christ is called the "Lord of Glory" (τὸν κύριον τῆς δόξης) (2:8).[22] When believers "behold the Glory of the Lord" (2 Cor 3:18), they appear to be beholding Christ himself, who is the image of God (2 Cor 4:4; cf. Col 1:15). If Moses could not see the face of God, Christians can see the Glory of God in the face (πρόσωπον) of Christ (2 Cor 4:6). This sort of language indicates that Paul understood the Glory language of Exodus and Ezekiel to refer to a visible, luminous and divine corporeality, and attributed this corporeality to Christ, who exists "in the form of God" (Phil 2:6).[23]

---

22 "As one of the many titles used to refer to an anthropomorphic depiction of God or his chief vizier, τὸν κύριον τῆς δόξης of 1 Corinthians 2:8 is best read against this grid of Jewish apocalypses where the special angelic figure seen in a throne vision is entitled 'the Lord of Glory' (1 Enoch 63:2)" (Newman, *Glory Christology*, 244).

23 According to Newman, Paul "came to identify Jesus as Glory" when he saw him as God's Glory in the Damascus Christophany (*Glory Christology*, 165). He fleshes out this argument exegetically on pages 184–240. He concludes that "Paul echoed the Glory tradition in his interpretation of the Christophany as a (i) theophany of δόξα, (ii) a Sinai-like revelation of כבוד יהוה, ... and (vi) as an apocalyptic throne vision in which he saw the principle agent of God, the manlike כבוד יהוה of Ezekiel 1:28" (*ibid.*, 246). For this position, see the sources cited in *ibid.*, 202, nn. 82 and 85. For the *image* of God as somatic in Paul, see the study of Stefanie Lorenzen, *Das paulinische Eikon-Konzept: Semantische Analysen zur Sapientia Salomonis, zu Philo und den Paulusbriefen* (WUNT 250; Tübingen: Mohr Siebeck, 2008), 139–256.

From the Glory Body to the Pneumatic Body

If Glory is a way of referring to Christ's divine corporeality, how is it related to Christ as the "life-making pneuma" (πνεῦμα ζῳοποιοῦν) (1 Cor 15:45; cf. 2 Cor 3:17)? Should we also conceive of the pneumatic Christ in corporeal terms? There is some reason to think that this "life-making pneuma" is a reference to Christ's physical constitution. This is because those conformed to the pneumatic Christ (v. 49) are said to inherit a "pneumatic *body*" (σῶμα πνευματικόν) (v. 44). It appears, then, that Christians become like Christ by conforming to his heavenly (ἐπου-ράνιος) body (v. 48–49). This is stated explicitly in Phil 3:21 ("He will transform the body of our humiliation that it may be conformed to his body of glory"). What we learn in 1 Cor 15:45 is that Christ's body is not only a body of glory, but also a body of pneuma.

In what follows, I would like to focus on the meaning of Paul's "pneumatic body" (1 Cor 15:44). Discourse about pneumatic bodies had a long pedigree in Stoic thought. In a recent book, Troels Engberg-Pedersen has fruitfully used Stoicism to disclose the meaning of Paul's pneumatic body.[24] Building on Engberg-Pedersen's argument, I

---

24 *Cosmology and Self in the Apostle Paul: The Material Spirit* (Oxford: Oxford University Press, 2010). The relation between Paul and Stoicism seems particularly close in the Corinthian correspondence. In 1910, Rudolf Bultmann's dissertation *Der Stil der paulinischen Predigt und die kynisch-stoische Diatribe* showed evidence of Cynic-Stoic diatribe in Paul's letters—drawing much data from the Corinthian epistles. More recently, David Balch argues that Paul in 1 Cor 7:32–35 uses Stoic technical terms in his discussion of marriage ("1 Cor 7:32–35 and Stoic Debates about Marriage, Anxiety, and Distraction," *Journal of Biblical Literature* 102 [1983]: 429–39). John T. Fitzgerald shows how much Paul's *peristasis* catalogues are indebted to Stoic rhetoric and ethics (*Cracks in an Earthen Vessel: An Examination of the Catalogues of Hardships in the Corinthian Correspondence* [Atlanta: Scholars Press, 1988]). (See in particular the material collected in his chapter 3: "The Hardships of the Sage" [47–116]). Engberg-Pedersen has already argued that both Paul and the Stoics share a fundamental structure of thought in their ethical and soteriological reflection (*Paul and the Stoics* [Louisville: Westminster John Knox, 2000]). (See also his essay, "Stoicism in the Apostle Paul: A Philosophical Reading" in *Stoicism: Traditions and Transformations* [eds. Stephen Strange and Jack Zupko; Cambridge: Cambridge University Press, 2004], 52–75). Recently, Jeffrey Asher has pointed out that Paul may have adopted the Stoic metaphor of sowing seeds to describe terrestrial generation in 1 Cor 15:42b–44a (*Polarity and Change in 1 Corinthians 15: A Study of Metaphysics, Rhetoric and Resurrection* [Tubingen: Mohr Siebeck, 2000]). Paul's use of "pneumatic body" (σῶμα πνευματικόν) in 1 Cor 15:44b

want to focus on its implications for a Pauline form of deification, which I understand as assimilation to the pneumatic body of a divine being (i. e., Christ) resulting in incorruptibility or eternal life (1 Cor 15:49–53). First, however, I will sketch the background of Paul's argument and terminology.

The Problem at Corinth

Current scholarship of 1 Cor 15 has generally moved away from the idea that the Corinthian problem was some notion of "(over-)realized eschatology." As Dale Martin has pointed out, it was not the futurity of the resurrection that was at issue, or even the resurrection itself, but the nature of the resurrection body.[25] In Martin's reconstruction, when the Corinthians heard Paul proclaim the "resurrection of the dead (νεκροί)," they understood this to mean the "resurrection of corpses [a meaning of νεκρός]."[26] The rotting bodies of human beings, according to the party of the "Strong," had no part in the kingdom of God.[27] This Corinthian disparagement of the body did not, however, mean that they were rigorously opposed to embodiment, eager to fly from this material realm of shadows. To the contrary, the Corinthians had no problem with the resurrection body being made up of "(corporeal) stuff," provided that it was not the dense, bulky, rotting matter (ὕλη) characteristic of life on earth. To enjoy life in the celestial sphere, the body had to be made up of a more subtle, purer substance than the

---

is a key instance of how Paul can (in the words of Jorunn Økland) "walk in and out of discourses" (in this case Stoic discourses) in an attempt to accommodate to the Corinthians' position. Økland points out that the fact that Paul "does not always appear as a Stoic philosopher does not prevent him from sometimes" supporting Stoic philosophical theories ("Genealogies of the Self" in *Metamorphoses: Resurrection, Body, and Transformative Practices in Early Christianity*, [eds. Turid Karlsen Seim and Økland; Berlin: W. de Gruyter, 2009], 91).

25 *The Corinthian Body* (New Haven: Yale University Press, 1995), 106–07.

26 Cf. Celsus' response to the resurrection in Origen's *Cels.* 5.14: "For what sort of human soul would have any further desire for a body that has rotted? … For what sort of body, after being entirely corrupted, could return to its original nature and that same condition which it had before it was dissolved?" (trans. Henry Chadwick).

27 *Corinthian Body,* 107–08. Philo remarks that a "corpse" (νεκρόν) cannot come into the sight of God (*Fug.* 10–11, 55–59).

dirt mentioned in Gen 2:7. Paul responds with a highly nuanced argument about the nature of the resurrection (or pneumatic) body.

The Nature of Paul's Pneumatic Body

In 1 Corinthians 15:39–53, Paul discusses the nature of the resurrection body in answer to the question "With what sort of body (ποίῳ δὲ σώματι) do they [those resurrected] come?" (15:35):

> Not all flesh is alike, but there is one flesh for human beings, another for animals, another for birds, and another for fish. There are both heavenly bodies and earthly bodies, but the glory (δόξα) of the heavenly is one thing, and that of the earthly is another. There is one glory of the sun, and another glory of the moon, and another glory of the stars; indeed, star differs from star in glory.
>
> So it is with the resurrection of the dead. What is sown is perishable, what is raised is imperishable. It is sown in dishonor, it is raised in glory (ἐν δόξῃ). It is sown in weakness, it is raised in power. It is sown a psychic body, it is raised a pneumatic body. If there is a psychic body, there is also a pneumatic body. Thus it is written, "The first man, Adam, became a living soul"; the last Adam became a life-giving pneuma. But it is not the pneumatic that is first, but the psychic, and then the pneumatic. The first man was from the earth, a man of dust; the second man is from heaven. As was the one of dust, so are those who are of the dust; and as is the one of heaven, so are those who are of heaven. Just as we have borne the image of the one of dust, we will also bear the image of the celestial one.
>
> What I am saying, brothers and sisters, is this: flesh and blood cannot inherit the kingdom of God, nor does the perishable inherit the imperishable. Listen, I will tell you a mystery! We will not all die, but we will all be changed, in a moment, in the twinkling of an eye, at the last trumpet. For the trumpet will sound, and the dead will be raised imperishable, and we will be changed. For this perishable body must put on imperishability, and this mortal body must put on immortality. (1 Cor 15:39–53, NRSV, modified)

Paul characterizes the pneumatic body by incorruptibility, glory, and power (1 Cor 15:42–43)—all divine qualities. It is also conformed to Christ, who is both a "life-making" (ζῳοποιοῦν) pneuma (v. 45) and "from heaven" (v. 47). The nature of the pneumatic body is "heavenly" (v. 48); it is not, Paul adds, made up of "flesh and blood," the constituents of present bodily life (v. 50). This latter remark is especially strik-

ing, and has troubled many a church father.[28] Most ancients admitted
that all bodily life on earth is constituted by flesh, by which is meant
not only skin, but bones, arteries, muscle, nerves and all the various tis-
sues and organs that make life possible on this planet. Flesh is the stuff of
terrestrial life. "Mortals are 'those who have blood in their veins,' and
this blood is conceived of as being produced by their eating of
grain."[29] To exist in a body without flesh is not to be human in the
way the ancients normally conceived of it. It was to be ἐπουράνιος—
heavenly, and not terrestrial; it was to exist in a corporeality existing
above the conditions of earthly life, without disease or decomposition.
It is to be "bloodless" (ἀναίμονες), a Homeric epithet of the Gods
(*Il.* 5.342).

Even though Paul defines the pneumatic body as a super-terrestrial
entity, we still have not discovered its constitution—what, that is to say,
it is *made of*. Here we cannot bypass the ongoing debate whether Paul's
σῶμα πνευματικόν (v. 44) refers to a body *controlled* by pneuma or a body
constituted by pneuma.[30] I do not hold these options to be mutually exclusive. Nonetheless I propose that Paul in 1 Cor 15:44 highlights the
nature (or composition) of the body for three reasons. First, the whole
context of 1 Cor 15:35–41 deals with what is best described as (ancient)
physics: the nature of corporeal entities that exist in earthly or super-
earthly environments. Paul makes frequent reference to bodily "stuff"
in his argument, namely "flesh" (vv. 39, 50), "dust" (vv. 47–49), and
perhaps even "glory" as the apparent substance of various bodies (v.

---

28 See, e.g., the comments of Irenaeus, *Haer.* 5.9–14; Tertullian, *Res.* 48–50.
    See further Outi Lehtipuu, "'Flesh and Blood Cannot Inherit the Kingdom
    of God': The Transformation of the Flesh in the Early Christian Debates Con-
    cerning Resurrection" in *Metamorphoses: Resurrection, Body, and Transformative
    Practices*, 147–68.
29 Jenny Strauss Clay, *The Wrath of Athena: Gods and Men in the Odyssey* (Lanham,
    Md.: Rowman & Littlefield, 1997), 144.
30 The debate has been going on at least since Augustine, who opposed the idea
    that the body was "changed into spirit" (*Civ.* 13.20). Conzelmann, following
    Schweitzer, sees "Hellenistic" terminology here: "Hellenism conceives of ef-
    fective supernatural power, 'Spirit,' in the form of substance" (*A Commentary
    on the First Epistle to the Corinthians* [trans. James Leitch Philadelphia: Fortress,
    1975], 283). Conzelmann himself thinks that the pneumatic body both consists
    of and is determined by pneuma.

41).[31] Thus the adjective "pneumatic" in v. 44 is best thought of along these physical lines, namely, as describing the "stuff" of the body.[32] Second, Paul is adamant that the new pneumatic body will not be composed of "flesh and blood" (v. 50). This insistence raises a question about the substance of the pneumatic body—if not of flesh and blood, then what? It is natural in this context to think that the substance is defined by the very adjective ("*pneumatic*")—the body is constituted by pneuma. Third, the pneumatic body, is, like Christ's body, "from heaven" (2 Cor 5:4) and "heavenly" (1 Cor 15:48). Merely to have a body controlled by pneuma (which is potentially attainable in this life [cf. Rom 8:9–10]) does not allow for actual existence in the heavenly sphere. The form of the body must be made suitable to celestial life, a dramatic change of "ecology" which involves a corresponding change in nature. Paul is therefore saying that the body can exist in heaven because it consists of a heavenly material, namely pneuma.[33]

The most recent objections to the physical understanding of pneuma have been laid out by Volker Rabens.[34] Since he has devoted an entire monograph to this subject, it is right to pause and examine his positive arguments. First of all, Rabens significantly changes the meaning of the Corinthian question of v. 35a ("How are the dead raised?") by paraphrasing it thus: "By what agency or power can this extraordinary thing happen?"[35] Rabens feels at liberty to change the terms of the question because Paul's harsh response in v. 36 assumes that the question in

---

31 Asher, *Polarity and Change*, 154, n. 17. Paul can view glory as a corporeal substance, given his reference to Christians gaining a "body of glory" (σῶμα τῆς δόξης) (Phil 3:21).

32 Cf. Tatian: "No demons possess a particle of flesh; their constitution is pneumatic, like [the constitution of] fire and air (πνευματικὴ δέ ἐστιν αὐτοῖς ἡ σύμπηξις ὡς πυρὸς καὶ ἀέρος)" (*Or.* 15.3).

33 *Pace* Gordon Fee who does not believe that πνευματικός signifies the stuff of the resurrection body (*The First Epistle to the Corinthians* [Grand Rapids: Eerdmans, 1987], 786). (His point about the pneumatic body belonging to the new age is, nevertheless, well taken.) He seems to wrongfully oppose an apocalyptic reading of this passage to a physicalist reading. (These are—as Engberg-Pedersen emphasizes—entirely compatible in ancient thought [*Cosmology and the Self*, 10–14, 17].) So when Fee says that the transformed body is a body "adapted to the eschatological existence" (*First Epistle*, 786), this new existence requires a change in nature for the new eschatological environment.

34 *The Holy Spirit and Ethics in Paul: Transformation and Empowering for Religious-Ethical Life* (Tübingen: Mohr Siebeck, 2010), 86–96.

35 *Ibid.*, 90.

v. 35a is not put "as a genuine inquiry." It seems strange, then, to see Rabens paraphrase the question to make it seem very much like a genuine inquiry (though a wholly different question). Is it not best to take the questions in v. 35 together, namely "*How* are the dead raised? With *what sort of body* do they come?" (emphasis added)? The questions, which interpret each other, appear to be about the nature (the "physics" if you will) of the resurrection body. Rabens admits this ("the Corinthians wanted to know what kind of embodiment believers would have at the resurrection"), but claims that their inquiry "does not specify an interest in the very physics of it [the body]."[36] I cannot help thinking that this is arbitrary given that one of the primary subject matters of physics (ancient and modern) is *bodies* and the *nature* of them. If Rabens means that Paul is not writing a philosophical treatise, that does not mean that he is not capable of assuming and creatively employing popular philosophical ideas about the physical nature of bodies.

Rabens quickly passes to an analysis of the "rhetoric and logic" of Paul's answer to the Corinthians to see if the Apostle is in fact interested in physical questions. Although Rabens criticizes Martin for tendentiously taking into account v. 40, which speaks of heavenly and earthly bodies as physical entities, Rabens himself devotes scant attention to these verses, as well as to vv. 51–55.[37] His focus is rather on vv. 42–50, because it is a "textual unit" (due in part to its putative chiastic structure), and (so Rabens) because it is on a different plane of thought than vv. 36–41.

Rabens argues that if the σῶμα πνευματικόν (v. 44) means a body made up of pneuma, then σῶμα ψυχικόν must mean a body made up of soul.[38] This is not entirely off the mark. In some way, the current physical body *is* made up of soul, if the soul is conceived of as the breath of life breathed into the earthly body in the creation account of Gen 2:7 (cited by Paul in 1 Cor 15:45). (The breath in Gen 2:7 does not appear to be an immaterial entity, but—like wind—something felt and physical.) Thus according to Genesis 2, humans in their current state are made up of two things: earth (thus Paul can call the first man "earthly" [χοϊκός]) and breath (the soul breathed into the earth by God). Put together, the earthly body inspired by soul (or breath) makes up the σῶμα ψυχικόν. Such a body is corruptible because the earthly substance, or

---

36   *Ibid.*, 90.
37   *Ibid.*, 91.
38   *Ibid.*, 95.

flesh, grows old and decays. In the current earthly state, Paul's converts have an initial dose of pneuma (a "life-giving breath") which renews their true or inner self even as the outer self (or flesh) continues to waste away (2 Cor 4:17). The flesh will no longer be a hindrance in the eschaton when the believer entirely becomes a pneumatic body not connected to earthly, corruptible flesh.[39] If the σῶμα ψυχικόν, then, can be conceived of as in some way made up of soul (or breath), there is no reason why the σῶμα πνευματικόν cannot be conceived of as being made up of pneuma. Rabens's objection thus does not stand.

Yet even if we admit Rabens's larger point that pneuma in Paul is not in any way material, this does not damage my argument for deification. Rabens wants to understand the pneumatic body as "supernatural."[40] Now it is not at all clear what this term means when removed from the framework of popular ancient physics. Does "supernatural" mean something immaterial and invisible like the Platonic concept of God? Or is "supernatural" a code-word for a theological entity which is wholly indeterminable because inaccessible to natural sensation and reason? At minimum, if by "supernatural" Rabens means transcending the human (Rabens pairs "natural" with the "merely human"[41]) and (in some fashion) like God, Rabens's logic does not contradict but rather supports my argument for deification. Whether the believer shares Christ's immortality by assimilation to a *material* or to an *im*material pneuma may in the end be left as a moot point. It is sufficient for my purposes that Rabens agree that the pneumatic body the believer receives is one "suited to heavenly immortality,"[42] and thus transcending our current human state. In the end, my argument for a Pauline form deification does not depend on Paul's usage of popular physics in 1 Cor 15:39–53, even if (as I believe and will proceed to argue) the physical interpretation of this text is the most illuminating and historical understanding of the passage.

To continue: if the pneumatic body is a body made up of pneuma, the question arises, "What, in the physics of Paul's day, was pneuma?" Scholars and exegetes are more and more coming to the conclusion that

---

39 As for Rabens' argument that adjectives ending in –ικός having "ethical or functional meanings," the writer's own context (which includes both ideas and words) always trumps appeals to grammar in the abstract (especially for so "pluriform a language as Koine Greek") (*ibid.*, 95).

40 *Ibid.*, 96.

41 *Ibid.*, 90.

42 *Ibid.*, 96, n. 71.

it did not mean immaterial "spirit." It is more suitably translated by "breath" or "wind." Among ancient philosophers and medical professionals, it was thought of as a corporeal substance, though not a solid, earthly substance like earth and water.[43] It was much more like air. Air, however, was thought to be naturally cold and misty, whereas pneuma was hot, fiery, fine, and subtle. Many Stoics described pneuma as a mixture of air and fire, and identified it with the substance of aether (αἰθήρ), or the fiery air that existed in the upper reaches of the universe.

Important for our purposes, the Stoics—who are, generally speaking, the philosophical vanguard in the first century C.E.—identified pneuma as the substance of the soul. Zeno, the founder of the Stoic school, called the soul "heated (ἔνθερμον) pneuma" (*SVF* 1.135; cf. 1.136–137; 2.715, 2.787). Other Stoic reports call the soul a "heated and fiery pneuma" (*SVF* 2.773), a "fiery and creative pneuma" (*SVF* 2.774), an "intelligent and hot pneuma" (*SVF* 2.779), or innate (σύμφυτον) pneuma (*SVF* 2.885). Many of these definitions come from Chrysippus, the architect of "orthodox" Stoicism. It is unlikely, however, that Paul had any direct contact with Chrysippus' thought. Paul would only have had direct contact with a "trickled down" version of Chrysippean pneumatic psychology widely diffused in Hellenistic philosophy.

Chronologically closer to Paul is the figure of Cicero, who (although by no means a Stoic) gives us the best digest of the sorts of teachings which would have been common coin in Paul's day.[44] Cicero had grown up with a Stoic philosopher in his home (the blind Stoic Diodotus),[45] and was deeply influenced by Panaetius and Posidonius.[46]

---

43   Cf. Origen: "It is a custom of holy scripture, when it wishes to point to something of an opposite nature to this dense and solid body, to call it pneuma" (*Princ.* 1.1.2; cf. his preface, §8). For Stoic proofs of the corporeal soul, see *SVF* 1.518; 2.790–800; Sen., *Ep.* 106.4–5. See further A. A. Long, "Soul and Body in Stoicism" in *Stoic Studies* (Cambridge: Cambridge University Press, 1996), 235.

44   Although he had respect for the Stoics (*Fin.* 4.1.2), Cicero seems to have viewed himself as a loyal Platonist, a member of the New Academy (*Acad.* 1.4.13). For Cicero's change from Old to New Academy beginning in 46 B.C.E., see John Glucker, "Cicero's Philosophical Affiliations" in *The Question of "Eclecticism": Studies in Later Greek Philosophy* (eds. John M. Dillon & A. A. Long; Berkeley: University of California, 1988), 34–69. See further David Sedley, "Philosophical Allegiance in the Greco-Roman World" in *Philosophia Togata: Essays on Philosophy and Roman Society* (eds. Miriam T. Griffin and Jonathan Barnes; Oxford: Clarendon, 1989), 118.

45   *Brut.* 308–309; *Acad.* 2.36.115.

Consequently he was well prepared to create characters (e. g., Cato the Younger in *Fin.* 3; Balbus in *Nat. d.* 2) who could faithfully relate the Stoic position on a particular topic. Moreover, Cicero himself could accept Stoic conclusions and propound arguments if he found them, according to his Academic criterion, probable (see, e. g., *Tusc.* 2.3.9, 4.4.7). By the same criterion of probability, however, Cicero could attack Stoic principles, or reformulate them and mix them with ideas from other schools. Sometimes Cicero's understanding of Stoicism is somewhat idiosyncratic. So I will endeavor to use his works with care.

The work I intend to focus on initially is the first discourse of Cicero's *Tusculan Disputations*, sometimes called "the Treatise on Death." Written in part as a self-consolation after the death of his daughter, the treatise lacks the Academic Skepticism characteristic of Cicero's other works of this period.[47] The ideas of the treatise, argues John Dillon, are rooted in the Middle Platonic tradition, specifically the Platonism of Antiochus of Ascalon. Alternatively, the teachings can be traced to the Stoic Posidonius.[48] A decision on this matter is not necessary, since Antiochus, who was "firmly wedded to Stoic physics,"[49] presented virtually the same physical doctrines.[50] Thus *Tusculan Disputations* 1 can be safely—though cautiously—mined for Stoic ideas.

In the treatise, Cicero agrees with Zeno and Panaetius that the soul is material, composed of fire or warm air (i. e., pneuma) (1.9.19; 1.18.42).[51] He calls this soul substance "more integral and pure" (*integriora ac puriora*) than flesh-and-blood bodies. Therefore, after severance from the flesh and blood body, the soul naturally rises far above the earth (*a terra longissime se efferant*), and finds rest in a region above the earth where the ethereal conditions resemble its own nature (1.41). There, in perfect equilibrium, it remains without want, since it is "nourished and maintained on the same food which maintains and

---

46 For Cicero, Panaetius was "almost the chief of the Stoics" (*princeps prope meo quidem iudicio Stoicorum*) (*Acad.* 2.33.107).

47 Glucker, "Cicero's Philosophical Affiliations," 67. "But for the consolations of religion … he reserved a corner which was not to be invaded by his skepticism," (*ibid.*, 69).

48 Dillon, *Middle Platonists*, 97–101.

49 *Ibid.*, 105.

50 "In matters of physics and theology he [Antiochus] seems to have differed from them [the Stoics] not at all" (*ibid*, 106).

51 Marcia L. Colish, *The Stoic Tradition from Antiquity to the Early Middle Ages* (2 vols.; Leiden: Brill, 1990), 1.142.

nourishes the stars" (*et sustentabitur iisdem rebus, quibus astra sustentantur et aluntur*) (1.43, cf. *Nat. d.* 2.46.118; cf. *SVF* 2.690). Heaven, in this model, is the soul's natural home (*domum*) (*Tusc.* 1.51).

The Stoic tenor of these notions is indicated by supportive material from Posidonius, who taught that[52]

> one cannot suppose that souls [after death] are carried downwards. For they are composed of fine particles and, not less fiery than pneumatic (πνευμα-τώδεις), souls are instead carried up by their lightness to the upper realms. There they abide by themselves ... So, when disembodied, they dwell in the region below the moon, and from there, due to the purity of the air, they receive more time for continuance. They partake of the vapors from the earth as a nourishment akin to their nature, like also the rest of the stars. And they do not have dissolution in those realms. Thus if the souls live on, they are the same as *daimones* [lesser deities]. (Sext. Emp., *Adv. Phys.* 1.72 [*SVF* 2.812], author's trans.; cf. *SVF* 2.809 and 810–22)

Such Stoic beliefs seemed to have found their way into first century Judaism. According to Essene belief, as it is reported by Josephus, souls emanate from the finest aether (ἐκ τοῦ λεπτοτάτου ... αἰθέρος). When released from the flesh, these aether-souls are thus naturally borne up (μετεώρους φέρεσθαι) (*B.J.* 2.154–55). When counseling his comrades at Jotapata, Josephus apparently reports his own view about souls. They are immortal, and can be called "a portion of God" (θεοῦ μοῖρα) dwelling in the body (*B.J.* 3.372). In a speech of Titus which likely presents Josephus' own views,[53] the historian asks: "For what brave man knows not that souls released from the flesh by the sword on the battlefield are hospitably welcomed by that purest of elements, the aether, and placed among the stars (ἄστροις ἐγκαθιδρύει), and that as good *daimones* (δαίμονες) and benignant heroes (ἥρωες) they manifest their presence to their posterity?" (*B.J.* 6.47, trans. H. St. J. Thackeray, LCL). It is unclear how widespread these views were among Jews. Yet if Josephus can be used as a barometer for his countrymen, these ideas were known and acceptable among Jews both in Palestine and the Diaspora.

---

52 In the following quote, Dillon believes that Sextus Empiricus uses Posidonius' commentary on the *Timaeus* (*Middle Platonists*, 111).

53 Tessa Rajak, *Josephus: The Historian and His Society* (London: Duckworth, 1983), 80–83.

Comparison of the Pauline Pneumatic Body
with the Stoic Soul

When we turn to compare this conception of the Stoic pneumatic soul with Paul's pneumatic body, we notice some basic similarities. Cicero's soul is "heavenly" (*caeleste*), which for Cicero means "eternal" (*aeterna*) (1.66). Paul's pneumatic body is also "heavenly" (ἐπουράνιος) (1 Cor 15:48–49), which means fitted for eternal life (cf. ἀθανασία, v. 53). The bodily substance of both Cicero's soul and Paul's pneumatic body is not "flesh and blood," but a finer, purer, subtler substance not subject to decay (*Tusc.* 1.65). Cicero leaves open whether this substance is air, fire, or a mixture of the two called αἰθήρ (*Tusc.* 1.65). At any rate, the supportive material from Posidonius indicates that the substance was viewed as pneumatic (πνευματώδης), like Paul's pneumatic body (1 Cor 15:44). Thus the two entities resemble each other in terms of their natural location, duration of life, and nature.

To sharpen our comparison, we turn to differences (apparent and real) between Pauline and Stoic eschatology as larger systems of thought.[54]

1. First to be noted is that Paul expressly rejects the idea that the spiritual body is "psychical" (literally "soulish" —ψυχικόν) (15:44)—thus unlike the Stoic soul (ψυχή). Paul's "soulish body," however, cannot so readily be identified with the Stoic soul. The soulish body appears, in fact, to be more or less our present, earthly body (the flesh animated and in part constituted by soul, characteristic of Adamic existence) which Paul seeks to transcend (15:45). Accordingly, the disagreement between Paul and the Stoics turns out to be at least partially verbal, since the Stoics affirm that the substance of the soul—*which they consider to be a type of body*—is pneuma. In both systems, then, we are dealing with the highest "part" of the human being (Paul's pneuma and the Stoic soul), which both parties conceive of as pneumatic. In addition, both parties view pneuma as the eschatological "stuff" of humanity after departure from earthly life.

2. A second difference between Pauline and Stoic eschatology deals with the Stoic emphasis on separation (in this case, the separation of body and soul). It seems that Paul would take issue with an analogous separation, namely the pneumatic body separating from the earthly

---

54 The use of "system" here merely refers to a network of ideas, which is often quite loose. No notion of "systematic" is implied.

body. Engberg-Pedersen explains: "Where the Stoics spoke of a separation of the soul *from* the body of flesh and blood, Paul's [sic] speaks of a
transformation *of* that same body."[55] Yet this difference too, it seems,
can sometimes be overdrawn. For even though Paul did not preach a
doctrine of the soul's separation from the body, he did preach a departure from *this* (earthly) body.[56] Though the eschatological "change"
from earthly to pneumatic body is envisioned as a clothing of the pneumatic body *on top of* the earthly body (1 Cor 15:52–54; 2 Cor 5:2–4),
it is also thought of as an *absence* from the earthly body: "… we would
rather be *away from the body* (ἐκδημῆσαι ἐκ τοῦ σώματος)," as Paul says,
"and at home with the Lord" (2 Cor 5:8, emphasis added; cf. Phil
1:20–24). Paul can also speak of the flesh being destroyed while the
pneuma is saved on the day of the Lord (1 Cor 5:5). Thus the separation
vs. transformation dichotomy may be too sharp. For Paul, the mortal is
apparently not shed but changed into the immortal. Yet even when put
in this way, Paul still advocates a form of separation—not from body itself, but from the *bulky, mortal, corruptible* body.[57] The present, earthly
body is mortal and corruptible *and will exist no more* come death or parousia. This earthly body is, in this view, not the "true self," as it were.
Only what is super-earthly, higher than mortal and corruptible life is
characteristic of the self—at least insofar as Christ (who is super-earthly)
defines the nature of the new celestial selfhood (1 Cor 15:49).

3. A third difference between Paul and the Stoics regards the actual
duration of the pneumatic substance. Paul says that the pneumatic body
will be characterized by incorruptibility and immortality (1 Cor 15:53).

---

55 "Stoic Understanding," 115–16.
56 That Paul's ἀπολύτρωσιν τοῦ σώματος (Rom 8:23) is a genitive of separation is
a real possibility and should be left open.
57 Cf. Engberg-Pedersen: "believers belong to the present evil world *were it not for*
God's loving intervention in sending his son *and* his pneuma to tear them out of
that world" (*Cosmology and Self*, 97, italics his, underlining mine); "[I]n believers, body and soul have received an infusion of divine, heavenly pneuma … this
may render both body and soul pneumatic through and through, thereby *remov-
ing them completely from the earthly sphere of sarx*" (ibid., 105, italics added). Engberg-Pedersen's idea of substantive change at the resurrection also assumes a full
departure from the earthly body. The pneumatic body is "an altogether different kind of body" even if it is continuous with the earthly body" ("Complete
and Incomplete Transformation in Paul—a Philosophical Reading of Paul on
Body and Spirit," in *Metamorphoses: Resurrection, Body and Transformative Practices
in Early Christianity* [eds. Turid Karlsen Seim and Jorunn Økland; Berlin & New
York: De Gruyter, 2009], 126, 128.

Although Cicero makes similar claims, other Stoic sources deny the immortality of the soul. For them, only the World Soul is strictly immortal (*SVF* 2.821). The human soul, in contrast, is destructible (Diog. Laert., *Vit. Philosoph.*, 7.156). The soul of the fool is destroyed immediately at death (*SVF* 2.809). The souls of the virtuous persist after death, but not after the conflagration (Diog. Laert., *Vit. Philosoph.* , 7.157; *SVF* 1.146; 2.810–11, 814, 817).[58] Cicero is aware of these teachings (*Tusc.* 1.77 = *SVF* 2.822). Thus the "eternity" of the Stoic soul seems to reflect Cicero's Platonic modification of Stoicism. (Platonists normally viewed the soul as immortal.) It is this Platonically modified Stoicism which more closely resembles Paul's view.

4. Another proposed difference between Pauline and Stoic eschatology is that, whereas the Stoics present a theory of celestial transformation (the soul becomes star-like), Paul seems to lack this idea. In his famous "Dream of Scipio," for instance, Cicero has Scipio Africanus say to his grandson that humans have "been given a soul out of those eternal fires which you call stars and planets (*ex illis sempiternis ignibus, quae sidera et stellas vocatis*), which are round and globular bodies animated by divine intelligences" (*Rep.* 6.15.15). In *Tusculan Disputations* 1.43, he writes that the pneuma-soul, when released from the body, pierces our atmosphere and flies upward until it "reaches to and recognizes a substance resembling its own (*regionem ... naturamque sui similem*)" and "stops among the fires which are formed of rarefied air and the tempered fire of the sun (*iunctis ex anima tenui et ex ardore solis temperato ignibus*)." There, as we saw, it is "nourished and maintained on the same food which maintains and nourishes the stars" (*Tusc.* 1.43). It is difficult not to think that the soul, as it makes its upward journey to the highest sphere, becomes star-like. Recall again that for Josephus, the soul released from the body is "settled among the stars (ἄστροις ἐγκαθιδρύει)" (*B.J.* 6.47). As πνεῦμα, it appears, the purified soul is actually the same or similar in substance as the stars, which are composed of aether (Cic., *Nat d.* 2.41; cf. Plut., *Def. Orac.* 10 [*Mor.* 415a-c]). Chrysippus, for instance, wrote that pneuma and aether "come under the same definition (εἰς κοινὸν λόγον)" (*SVF* 2.471).

---

58 For other texts and discussion on this topic, see René Hoven, *Stoïciens face au problem de l'au-delà* (Paris: Société d'Edition "Les Belles Lettres," 1971), 44–86.

Celestial Immortality

The idea that the pneumatic soul becomes star-like or settles among the heavenly bodies will here be called "celestial immortality." A brief sketch of celestial immortality in Greek and Roman thought will illumine this discussion, and show just how widely-diffused these ideas were in Paul's culture.

The kinship of soul and star was a theme, it seems, already in Pythagorean philosophy. Alexander Polyhistor tells us that in "Pythagorean" writings the soul is a portion torn off from aether (Diog. Laert., *Vit. Philosoph.*, 8.28; cf. Hipp., *Ref.* 6.25). From Varro we learn that Pythagoras said that the souls of brave men were changed into stars.[59]

In Ionian natural science, the idea that "the human soul has a very close relationship to the sky and the stars, and even that it comes from heaven and returns to it" is a "generally held belief."[60] Diogenes of Apollonia (fl. 425 B.C.E.) said that the soul was part of the air and thus a part of God (μόριον Θεοῦ) (DK 64 19 [§42]; cf. 20). Heraclitus called the soul a "spark of starry substance" (*scintilla stellaris essentiae*) (DK 22 A 15, *ap.* Macrobius, *Somn. Scip.* 14.19).

In the late fifth century B.C.E., Euripides introduced the following line on the Athenian stage: "Let the dead be covered by the earth, and, whence each part came to light, there let it return—pneuma to aether, the body to earth" (*Suppl.* 531–34, 1140; cf. *Hel.* 1013–16; *Orest.* 1683–1690). Here it appears that the souls are made of pneuma. They came from aether, and to aether they shall return. Near the end of Euripides' *Suppliant Women*, the chorus says of the dead children of Iphis that "the aether holds them now" (1140).[61] We cannot view this line, spoken to such a wide audience, as grasped only by the philosophers. The doctrine of the natural philosophers had trickled down even by the fifth century B.C.E., and had entered the sphere of mass consumption.

Euripides may have gotten his ideas about celestial transformation specifically from Anaxagoras (ca. 500–428 B.C.E.), whose views may be exposited in the following fragment:

---

59 See further Walter Burkert, *Lore and Science in Ancient Pythagoreanism* (trans. Edwin L. Minar; Cambridge: Harvard University Press, 1972), 363.

60 *Ibid.*, 362.

61 These texts are taken from M. R. Wright, *Cosmology in Antiquity* (London: Routledge, 1995), 122.

They return whence they came: the plants from earth, to earth; the sprouts from an ethereal parent (ἀπ' αἰθερίου γονῆς), returned to the heavenly vault (οὐράνιον … πόλον). Nothing dies of what comes to be; he showed that one is distinguished from another [solely] by a different form (μορφὴν ἑτέραν). (Eur. Nauck frag. 839,[62] cf. Anaxagoras DK 59 A 112, lines 8–14)

The relation of soul to heaven could even be taken to comic length. Aristophanes' *Pax* 832–34 (421 B.C.E.) refers to the soul of an astronomer becoming a star.

> *Slave*: So it's not true that when we die they make us stars?
> *Trygaios*: It's true
> *Slave*: Well, who's the latest star up there?
> *Trygaios*: Ion of Chios
> *Slave*: That puffball?
> *Trygaios*: There you are.
> *Slave*: And what are all the comets and shooting stars?
> *Trygaios*: After dinner, the rich stars go for a stroll, with fires in little pots to light the way. (trans. Kenneth McLeish)

The humor here seems to lie not in the ridiculousness of celestial transformation itself, but in the hyperbole. From the vague belief that the soul rises to the aether, Aristophanes lampoons the exaggerated conclusion that an individual man becomes an individual star.

A similar kinship between soul and stars appears in the Orphic gold tablets. About twenty tablets to date have been unearthed, variously inscribed from the fourth to the first centuries B.C.E., and found throughout Greece and southern Italy. In several of the tablets we find the line: "I am child of Earth and starry Sky (Γῆς παῖς εἰμι καὶ Οὐρανοῦ ἀστερόεντος)," sometimes with the additional line "but my race is heavenly (αὐτὰρ ἐμοὶ γένος οὐράνιον)"[63] or "My name is 'Starry'" (Ἀστέριος ὄνομα).[64] The phrase "child of Earth and starry Sky" is reminiscent of the line from Hesiod's *Theogony* that the Gods "were born from Earth and starry Sky" (106). Evidently a close relation between the Gods and the Orphic initiate is being suggested. In two other tablets we find the strange, possibly related, saying, "You have become a God instead of a mortal (θεὸς ἐγένου ἐξ ἀνθρώπου)."[65] In other texts the soul is told to boast to the Gods that it is a member of their "happy race"

---

62 A. Nauck, *Tragicorum Graecorum Fragmenta* (Leipzig: Teubner, 1889, rpt. 1964).
63 Text 2 from Petelia in the edition of Fritz Graf, *Ritual Texts for the Afterlife: Orpheus and the Bacchic Gold Tablets* (London: Routledge, 2007), 6–7.
64 Text 25 from Pharsalus (Thessaly) in *ibid.*, 34–35.
65 *Ibid.*, 8–9, 12–13.

(nos. 5, 6, 7). One tablet (no. 9) names an initiate, and says that she "has grown to be divine by law." Another tablet (no. 2) affirms that the initiate will "rule among the other heroes," who are considered demigods and children of Gods. The tablets suggest, at the very least, a close relation between the initiate, the stars, and the divine.[66]

A like relation is suggested in a magical papyrus (*PGM* 4.475–829) enabling an ascent to the heavens and immortalization. While in heaven, the magician declares to the Gods "I am a star (ἐγώ εἰμι ... ἀστήρ), wandering about with you, and shining forth out of the deep [unintelligible words follow]" (lines 573–575, trans. M. W. Meyer).

Walter Burkert notes that the "metamorphosis of the dead into a star is often mentioned in sepulchral verse."[67] Franz Cumont in the early twentieth century could point to two prominent gravestone inscriptions. The first, from the island of Amorgos, possibly dating from the first century C.E., reads "Mother, do not weep for me. What is the use? You ought rather to reverence me, for I have become a divine evening star" (ἀστήρ γὰρ γενόμην θεῖος ἀκρεσπέριος) (Peek[68] §1097). A second century C.E. inscription comes from Miletus where a child of eight is depicted as rising "every evening to the horn of the Great Goat [Capricorn]."[69] Today, however, we can point to far more inscriptions. As early as 432 B.C.E., a monument to the Athenian dead was raised after the battle of Potidaea. In it we read: "aether (αἰθέρ) received their souls, earth their bodies."[70] A third century (or later) inscription reads

---

66 For interpretation of these lines, see Sarah Iles Johnston, *ibid.*, 114, 124. For further background, see Miguel Herrero de Jáuregui, "Orphic Ideas of Immortality: Traditional Greek Images and a New Eschatological Thought," in *Lebendige Hoffnung—ewiger Tod?! Jenseitsvorstellungen im Hellenismus, Judentum und Christentum* (eds. Michael Labahn and Manfred Lang; Arbeiten zur Bible und ihrer Geschichte 24; Leipzig: Evangelische Verlagsanstalt, 2007), 289–314. For the Orphic tablets and "apotheosis," see Radcliffe G. Edmonds, *Myths of the Underworld Journey in Plato, Aristophanes, and the 'Orphic' Gold Tablets* (Cambridge: Cambridge University Press, 2004), 91–95.

67 *Lore and Science*, 360, n. 48.

68 Werner Peek, *Greek Verse Inscriptions; Epigrams on Funerary Stelae and Monuments = Griechische Vers-Inschriften: Grab-Epigramme* (Chicago: Ares Publishers, 1988).

69 Franz Cumont, *Afterlife in Roman Paganism* (New York: Dover, 1922), 105. Greek text in Peek §1829.

70 Richmond Alexander Lattimore, *Themes in Greek and Latin Epitaphs* (Urbana: University of Illinois Press, 1962), 31. Since the monument and inscription were funded and built by the state, it seems to have represented national sentiment.

that the soul of a thirteen year old girl is numbered among the stars (ἐνα-ρίθμιός ἐστιν ἄστροις) (Peek §1776). Richard Lattimore quotes an inscription from Sakkara: "He has gone to the circle of the sky (αἰθερίας ἀψίδος), the company of the blessed."[71] A second century inscription from Thasos reads: "The coffin may hold my glorious body, but the soul has gone hence into the aether (αἴ[θρη]ν)."[72] From Ostia (second century C.E.), we have an inscription on marble where it is said that, in exchange for a just life, the deceased receives a "heavenly place" (οὐράνιον χῶρον) where he "prominently beams forth light somewhere in the starry circle" (που ἐν ἀστερόεντι φα[εσφόρ]ος ἔξοχα κ[ύκλῳ]). The last line, though damaged, probably mentions his fellowship with the "blessed *daimones*" (μακάρου[ς] δαίμο[νας]) (Peek §648). It is said of a priest of Isis in the Roman period "As she approached the altar and was paying her vows, she went, respected by all, to the stars (ἄστρ' ἔβα). Thus without enduring sickness she joined the demigods (ἡμι-θέους)."[73] A Latin epitaph reads that "my divine and celestial soul will not pass beneath shadows. The universe and the stars took me up (*mundus me sumpsit et astra*)."[74] And another: "you go not to the *Manes* but to heaven and the stars (*caeli ad sidera pergis*)."[75] Again: "He returned his spirit (*spiritum*) to its own nature (*naturae suae*)"—the aether.[76] I do not claim that such epitaphs are representative of thoughts about the after-life in the Greco-Roman world.[77] They merely provide a sense of how widespread ideas of celestial immortality were.

---

71 *Ibid.*, 33.

72 *Ibid.*

73 *Ibid.*, 34.

74 *Ibid.*, 37.

75 *Ibid.*, 39.

76 *Ibid.* Angelos Chaniotis gives recent bibliography of this theme in epigraphy in "Megatheism: The Search for the Almighty God and the Competition of Cults," in *One God: Pagan Monotheism in the Roman Empire* (eds., Stephen Mitchell and Peter van Nuffelen; Cambridge: Cambridge University Press, 2010), 121, n. 40. Here he also cites a third century B.C.E. epitaph from Pherai: "I, Lykophron, the son of Philiskos, seem sprung from the root of great Zeus, but in truth am from the immortal fire; and I live among the heavenly stars, raised up by my father; but the body born of my mother occupies mother-earth." For further examples, see Imre Peres, *Griechische Grabinschriften und neu-testamentliche Eschatologie* (WUNT 157; Tübingen: Mohr Siebeck, 2003), 72–75, 81–105, 112–113, 117–120, 133–141, 196–246, and the index *s.v.* "Sterne."

77 Lattimore's *Themes* and the more recent work of Anne Le Bris (*La mort et les conceptions de l'au delà en Grèce ancienne à travers les épigrammes funéraires* [Paris:

Perhaps the most famous case of celestial immortality is that of Julius Caesar. There exist various accounts (see esp. Pliny, *Hist.* 2.93).[78] Perhaps the most vivid is found in Ovid's *Metamorphoses* (15. 843–51). As Caesar's assassins lunge toward the dictator, Zeus in heaven grants permission to Venus to rescue her son:

> Scarce had he [Zeus] spoken when fostering Venus took her place within the senate-house, unseen of all, caught up the passing soul of her Caesar from his body, and not suffering it to vanish into air, she bore it towards the stars of heaven. And as she bore it she felt it glow and burn, and released it from her bosom. Higher than the moon it mounted up and, leaving behind it a fiery train, gleamed as a star (*stella micat*). (trans. F. J. Miller, LCL)[79]

The idea is partially based on the fact that a comet appeared during Caesar's funeral games. Augustus (then Caesar Octavian) responded by placing a star on some of Caesar's statues, a symbol also found on Augustan coinage.[80] The "asterification" of Julius Caesar was understood as his postmortem deification. Julius was consecrated as the God *Divus Iulius*, and Augustus became *Divi filius* ("Son of God"). Ovid expects a similar deification for Augustus: "… may the aether desire you, so may you be late in going to the stars appointed for you" (*Trist.* 5.2.50–52). After Augustus' death, Ovid wrote that he had gone off to the "ethereal homes" (*aetherias … domos*) to reside "among the constellations in the dome of heaven (*convexa locatus sidera*) (*Ep. Pont.* 4, 13, 19–26;

L'Harmattan, 2001]) and Peres, *Griechische Grabinschriften* give a fuller picture. For a more general treatment of death and burial, see Jon Davies, *Death, Burial and Rebirth in the Religions of Antiquity* (London & New York: Routledge, 1999).

78 The primary witnesses are collected in J. T. Ramsey and A. Lewis Licht, *The Comet of 44 B.C. and Caesar's Funeral Games* (Atlanta: Scholars Press, 1997), 155–78. For the tradition of Caesar's apotheosis, see Dio Cass., *Rom. Hist.* 45.6.4–7.1; Serv. on *Aen.* 6.790, 8.681; Serv. on *Ecl.* 9.47; Suet. *Iul.* 88. Mary Frances Williams ("The Sidus Iulium, the Divinity of Men, and the Golden Age in Virgil's Aeneid," *Leeds International Classical Studies* 2:1 [2003]: 1–29) reviews the imagery in Virgil's Aeneid. See also Robert Gurval, "Caesar's Comet: The Politics and Poetics of an Augustan Myth," *Memoirs of the American Academy in Rome* 42 (1996): 39–71.

79 Cf. Horace *Odes* 1.12, lines 47–48: "The Julian star, like the moon among the smaller fires!" (*Iulium sidus velut inter ignis / Luna minores*). See further Dio Cass., *Rom. Hist.* 69.11.4.

80 For these coins, including those circulating in the east, see Kenneth Scott, "The Sidus Iulium and the Apotheosis of Caesar," *Classical Philology* 36 (1941): 261–64. For coins and art, see Stefan Weinstock, *Divus Julius* (Oxford: Clarendon, 1971), 370–84.

4.9.127–34). Similarly, Virgil mused on whether Augustus himself would be added "as a new constellation (*novum sidus*) to the lingering months, where, between the Virgin and the grasping Claws, a space is opening (lo! for you even now the blazing Scorpion draws in his arms, and has left more than a due portion of the heaven!)" (trans. H. Rushton Fairclough, LCL).[81]

The kinship between soul and stars seems to have found currency among scientists and medical professionals as well. Pliny the Elder lauds Hipparchus the astronomer (ca. 190–120 B.C.E.) for establishing "the relation between man and the stars," by clearly showing "that our souls are particles of divine fire" (*Nat.* 2.26.95). Galen wrote that the mind (νοῦς) "seems to have arrived from the celestial bodies (ἀφικνούμενος ἐκ τῶν ἄνω σωμάτων)"—the sun, moon, and stars—which are themselves characterized by an intelligence superior and more precise than that on earth (*De usu partium* 50.17.1= *SVF* 2.1151).

The idea of celestial transformation had a long history in Hellenistic philosophy as well. Plato repeatedly associated the souls of the righteous and wise with the stars (stars who are rightly called "Gods," *Tim.* 42b). The "most sovereign part of the soul" lifts up the human to "what is akin to us in heaven" (τὴν ἐν οὐρανῷ συγγένειαν) (*Tim.* 90a5). So in the *Phaedo*, a soul separated from its body flies "to a pure home that is above" (114b-c) in the "company of the Gods" (μετὰ θεῶν) (81a). In the *Timaeus*, each soul has a consort star to which the soul returns, provided it has been good (*Tim* 41–42). In the *Phaedrus*, the proper domain of the soul—depicted as a winged chariot—is the upper air in company with the Gods (247c).

The Platonist Heraclides Ponticus (c. 390-c. 310 B.C.E.) asserted that the soul was the purest type of fire, which ascends until it finds its home in the realm of the fixed stars (Tert., *De An.* 9) or the Milky Way. Varro quotes Epicharmus, who calls the human mind "fire taken from the sun (*istic est de sole sumptus ignis*)," and says that the sun is "all composed of mind" (*totus mentis est*) (*Ling. lat.* 5.59; cf. Philo, *Mos.* 2.288).[82]

The Latin poet Manilius (first century C.E.) speaks of all the "souls of heroes, outstanding men deemed worthy of heaven, freed from the

---

81 For further discussion on stars and emperors, see Clauss, *Kaiser und Gott*, 265–68.

82 Epicharmus himself was a Sicilian writer of comedy, flourishing in the early fifth century B.C.E. A body of philosophical and quasi-scientific writings bearing his name was available in the fourth century B.C.E. (*OCD³*, 532).

body and released from the globe of Earth" who dwell "in a heaven that is their own, live the infinite years of paradise and enjoy celestial bliss" (*Astronom.* 1.758−61, trans. G. P. Goold, LCL). After the heroes of mythology, he includes the sages Solon, Lycurgus, Plato, and Socrates. Among political heroes he mentions Themistocles, the kings of Rome (except the last), and a host of great Roman statesmen and conquerors capped by Julius Caesar and Augustus (762−801). As "similar" (*similes*) to the Gods in virtue, these men live closest to the Gods on the "belt of the Milky way" (1.802−804). Why wonder that men can comprehend heaven, when heaven exists in themselves (*quibus est et mundus in ipsis*) and each one is in a smaller likeness the image of God himself (*exemplumque dei quisque est in imagine parva*) (4.893−95)?

Contemporaneous with Paul, Seneca the Younger wrote in his treatise *To Marcia on Consolation* about her dead son "wholly departed from earth." Though he tarried for a little while in the lower heavens as he was purified, he soon "soared aloft and sped away to join the souls of the blessed." Above, he met the holy souls of "the Scipios and the Catos" and his own virtuous grandfather, who, in "the newfound light," instructs him in the movement of the stars. In their non-fleshy state, Marcia's son and father are "far loftier beings, dwelling in the highest heaven … Throughout the free and boundless spaces of eternity they wander; … their every way is level," and, being swift and unencumbered, they are "coextensive with the stars, and mixed together with them (*pervii sunt intermixtique sideribus*)" (25.1−3, trans. John Basore, LCL). Later Seneca speaks of the soul as "fiery matter (*flagrante materia*)" that will rejoin the essence of the stars (25.3; 26.6; cf. *Ep.* 102.28−30).[83]

We can conclude that the idea of celestial immortality was, if not widely believed, then at least widely known. It seems likely that Paul would have been aware of the idea, especially since the deified (and asterified) Julius Caesar was venerated as the founder of Corinth (a Roman colony).

---

83 For later evidence of celestial immortality, see Bert Selter, "*Eadem Spectamus Astra:* Astral Immortality as Common Ground between Pagan and Christian Monotheism," in *Monotheism Between Pagans and Christians in Late Antiquity*, (Stephen Mitchell & Peter van Nuffelen, eds.; Leuven: Peeters, 2010), 57−75.

Celestial Immortality in Jewish Sources

Regardless, Paul did not need to turn to Greece and Rome for knowledge of celestial immortality. Greece and Rome had already come to Judea and the Jewish Diaspora. Jewish writers used language of celestial transformation to illustrate postmortem immortality in a way similar to Greco-Roman authors. In 1 Enoch 104:2–4, 6 (the "Epistle of Enoch") the saints "are to shine as lights of the heaven; … they are to 'become companions of the host of heaven." In Daniel 12:2–3, the wise will shine "like the brightness of the firmament" and "like the stars forever and ever." In the *Parables* of Enoch, "the just shall be in the light of the sun" (58:2). The Gospel of Matthew says that the righteous "will shine out like the sun in the kingdom of their Father" (13:43; cf. 4 Ez 7:97). In Deborah's farewell speech in Ps. Philo, she speaks to the people of Israel: "But then [when you die] your likeness will be just as the stars of the heaven (*erit autem vestra similitudo tunc tamquam sidera celi*), which are now manifest among you" (*L.A.B.* 33:5). 2 Baruch 51:10 promises that the righteous will be "equal to the stars." In the book of Wisdom, the souls of the righteous will "shine" in the day of judgment (3:7). According to 2 Enoch, "They will be made to shine seven times brighter than the sun" (66:7). To the righteous in the *Testament of Moses*, it is promised that "God will raise you to the heights. Yes, he will fix you firmly in the heaven of the stars, in the place of their habitation" (10:9). We find a similar idea in 4 Maccabees—though in more florid language: "The moon in heaven, with the stars, does not stand so august as you [mother of the seven martyrs], who, after lighting the way of your star-like seven sons to piety, stand in honor before God and are firmly set in heaven with them" (17:5). Philo says that the reward of the righteous soul is "sharing the eternal life of the sun and moon and the whole universe" (*Opif.* 144; *Somn* 1.135–37, 138–145; *Gig.* 7; *QE* 2.114; *Mos.* 2.108). He claims that the human mind is "itself a star (ἀστὴρ οὖσα αὐτή), I dare say a copy and likeness of the heavenly company" (*Virt.* 12). In an earlier chapter, I noted that Philo envisioned Moses' translation as a transformation into "most sun-like mind" (*Mos.* 2.88). It is thus significant that he identifies the stars as "mind in its purest form (νοῦς … ἀκραιφνέστατος)" (*Gig.* 8). From such data, it is safe to say that celestial transformation would have been widely known to Jews of the first century C.E.

Paul and Celestial Immortality

The question is, did Paul posit a version of celestial immortality in 1 Corinthians 15? Paul's language is admittedly vague, but some tentative conclusions can be hazarded in light of the foregoing data. When Paul talked of the bodies of earthly beings, he used the term "flesh" (σάρξ). When he turned to heavenly bodies he used the term "glory" (δόξα; vv. 40–41). Though δόξα may simply mean "brightness" or "illumination," there is strong indication that in this context, δόξα is meant to contrast directly with σάρξ in v. 39. If σάρξ is the substance of earthly bodies, then δόξα is the brilliance of pneumatic bodies. A pneumatic body is a glory body. Pneuma, like the aether, shines. Just as Christ is pneuma (1 Cor 15:45), he has a body of glory (Phil 3:21). To receive a pneumatic body is to gain a body of glory like the divine Christ. These glory bodies can, to be sure, be on heaven or earth (1 Cor 15:40), but their chief location is heaven where the δόξα-bodies—sun, moon, stars—shine according to their purity or "weight of δόξα" (15:41; cf. 2 Cor 4:17). Engberg-Pedersen's comments are apropos here: "A 'psychic' body belongs *on earth* as exemplified by the 'earthly bodies' mentioned in [1 Cor] 15:39; a 'pneumatic' one belongs *in heaven* as exemplified by the 'heavenly bodies' mentioned in 15:41. Or to be even more precise: a 'pneumatic body' *is* a heavenly body like the sun, moon and stars."[84]

In other words, there is an implicit contrast between heavenly and earthly bodies underlying 1 Cor 15:39–49, and Paul associates the pneumatic body with the heavenly bodies. Specifically, the mention of the heavenly nature of Christ's body in 1 Cor 15:47 recalls the contrast between earthly and heavenly bodies in 15:40.[85] Paul seems, then, to be alluding to the fact that the pneumatic body of Christ and believers show the same brilliance (δόξα) as the heavenly bodies. In a word, they are "glorified." In a later letter, Paul promises believers a "glorification" (δοξάζω) of their bodies in conformity to the resurrected body of Jesus Christ (συμμόρφους τῆς εἰκόνος τοῦ υἱοῦ αὐτοῦ) (Rom 8:29–30).[86] This passage from Romans is similar to 1 Cor 15:49: "Just as we have borne the image of the one of dust, we will also bear the

---

84   "Stoic Understanding," 110.
85   *Ibid.*, 113.
86   On Pauline glorification, see Sprinkle, "The Afterlife in Romans," in *Lebendige Hoffnung—ewiger Tod?!* 201–234.

image (φορέσομεν καὶ τὴν εἰκόνα) of the celestial one" (cf. also Phil 3:21). In one passage, to be conformed to Christ's image is a glorification; in another, to bear Christ's image is to become heavenly (like the pneumatic Christ). Now if δόξα is the brilliance chiefly of heavenly bodies, then Paul's "glorification" is at least analogous to celestial immortality.[87] Engberg-Pedersen goes even so far as to say that the Christian souls become stars who *"will live on* in the upper regions of the cosmos."[88] He bases his comments partially on Paul's statement that the Philippians "shine like stars in the world (φωστῆρες ἐν κόσμῳ)" (2:14–15). Although in this passage, the Philippians are still on earth, Paul declares that their true city is in heaven—the realm of the stars (3:20). Engberg-Pedersen continues:

> Apparently, by acting here and now in conformity with Christ's resurrection into heaven, which has already taken place, and with a view to their own future salvation (cf. 2:12–13), the Philippians already proleptically appear *like* having the form that they will eventually have *in fact* when they have left this crooked and perverse generation behind … If the pneuma is already present now among the Philippians—as what is elsewhere called a 'down payment'—when they shine *like* stars, then we are very close to the idea we found in 1 Corinthians 15 to the effect that the pneuma will eventually turn those who are resurrected *into* 'stars in the world.' Then they will no longer shine *like* stars: they will *be* stars.[89]

Such language, if daring, properly sees Pauline soteriology in light of ancient cosmology—including ancient Christian cosmology. Origen, for instance, believed that bodily substance is "changed, in proportion to

---

87 Why does Paul not speak directly of glorification in 1 Cor 15? Although glorification and the "glory body" was a concept intelligible to a Jewish audience (or those familiar with the Jewish heritage), it would seem to be less intelligible to a Greek one. Paul's "pneumatic body" may then be an attempt to redescribe the concept of "glory" in terms intelligible to Greek physics. The closest physical concept to corporeal "glory" was the Stoic pneuma: an ethereal, fiery, fine, subtle substance, not subject to decay. Since it existed in the heavens, pneuma was envisioned as a bright or luminous body. Such was the substance of the Stoic soul—and, as it turns out, also the substance of the stars.

88 *Cosmology and Self*, 12, emphasis his.

89 *Ibid.*, 42–43, italics his. Cf. 103, where he remarks that the "souls [of the Philippian Christians] will live on as stars in heaven until the conflagration." Alan Segal also talks of the believer being "subsumed into the body of a heavenly savior" and becoming "a kind of star or celestial immortal" ("Paul and the Beginning of Jewish Mysticism" in *Death, Ecstasy, and Other Worldly Journeys* [eds. John J. Collins and Michael Fishbane; Albany: State University of New York Press, 1995], 104).

the quality or merits of those who wear it, into an ethereal condition ...
and will shine with light" (*Princ.* 2.3.7). He asserts that the differences in
the glory of the resurrection bodies are comparable to gradations of light
among the heavenly bodies, since "heavenly things are worthy of being
compared with the saints" (2.10.2). The pneumatic body, Origen believes, is eternal and meant to dwell in the heavens (2.10.3; cf. 2 Cor
5:1). After the resurrection, the saints will dwell in the air (1 Thess
4:17) for some time before ascending through the celestial spheres
(2.11.6). The ultimate destiny of the pneumatic body is to become
one pneuma (1 Cor 6:17) with God in the higher reaches of the universe (3.6.6). Most of these teachings Origen draws from Pauline
texts. Origen—closer to Paul's horizon of thought— is an early witness
of one who sees a version of celestial immortality in Paul. It is not at all
far-fetched to believe that the Apostle had such thoughts.

That Paul's version of celestial immortality is also a form of deification is indicated by the fact that celestial immortality means conformation to the "super body" of a divine being (Christ). Alan Segal's interpretation of Philippians 3:21 ("He will transform the body of our humiliation that it may be conformed to his body of glory") is elegant
for its simplicity: "The body of the believer eventually is to be transformed into the body of Christ."[90] It seems, at any rate, safe to conclude
that in Phil 3:21, Paul proposes that Christians will share in the "Glory
body," or brilliant corporeality of a divine being. The analogous passage
in 2 Cor 3:18 ("We all, beholding the glory of the Lord as in a mirror
are being metamorphosed into the same image from glory to glory [ἀπὸ
δόξης εἰς δόξαν]") indicates just how closely believers are conformed to
the Glory of the divine Christ, the image of God (2 Cor 4:4). Segal's
interpretation of 2 Cor 3:18 is worth quoting at length:

> Paul's term, "the glory of the Lord" must be taken both as a reference to
> Christ and as a technical term for the Kabod (כבוד), the human form of
> God appearing in biblical visions. In 2 Cor. 3:18, Paul says that Christians
> behold the Glory of the Lord as in a mirror and are transformed into his
> image. For Paul, as for the earliest Jewish mystics, to be privileged enough
> to see the Kabod or Glory of God is a prologue to transformation into His
> image.[91]

Here we have come full circle. Paul envisioned God's Glory as at least in
part the corporeal manifestation of the God Christ. The goal of salvation

---

90 *Ibid.*, 113.
91 *Ibid.*, 111.

is for Paul's converts to be conformed to this corporeal Glory. To be conformed to Christ's Glory body is evidently parallel to becoming "the same image" as a divine being (2 Cor 3:18). Thus this luminous corporeality of God known from the Hebrew Bible has been granted to Paul's converts through their participation in Christ. They are assimilated to the super body of the divine Christ. They share in the reality of Christ's divine body which guarantees their participation in Christ's attributes of incorruptibility and immortality. In the next chapter we will focus on the implications of these ideas for a Pauline form of deification.

Chapter 5:
Divine Corporeality and Deification

> "Just as a new snake blooms when
> it has laid down its old age with its skin,
> and glows with its fresh scales, so, when
> Hercules stripped off his mortal limbs,
> the better part of him was strong, and
> he began to look larger and become
> awe-inspiring with august dignity."
>
> —Ovid, *Met.* 9.265–70

Introduction

In the last chapter I argued that in 1 Cor 15:35–53, Paul presents a version of celestial immortality for his converts. What makes Paul's version of celestial immortality distinctive, however, is that he presents it as conformation to the luminous, pneumatic body of a particular divine being, namely Christ (1 Cor 15:49; cf. 2 Cor 3:18; Phil 3:21; Rom 8:29). This is the key that allows Paul's version of celestial immortality (or glorification) to be categorized as a form of deification. In this chapter, I will argue this point in depth, illuminating Paul by contemporaneous texts which indicate that in Paul's culture celestial immortality was widely viewed as a form of deification.

Celestial Immortality as Deification

Cicero makes much of deification in his "Dream of Scipio." There the soul/mind (*animus*) is made the true human essence, ruling the body like God rules the universe. As self-moving, the soul is eternal (*aeterna*) (6.28). The destiny of the soul is thus to live a life of beatitude in the sphere of the stars and the divine intelligences. Scipio Africanus (the main speaker) thus admonishes his grandson (and implicitly the reader): "Know, then, that you are a God (*deum te igitur scito esse*), if a God is that which lives, feels, remembers, and foresees, and which rules, governs, and moves the body over which it is set, just as the supreme God above rules this universe" (6.24.26; trans. C.W. Keyes, LCL).[1] The deity of the soul, for Cicero, is established in the case of Romulus, Liber Pater (Dionysus), the Tyndaridae (or the Dioscuri), and Hercules (Greek Heracles)—all of whom became heavenly Gods (*Tusc.* 1.28).

The case of Hercules seems to be especially paradigmatic. In Ovid's *Metamorphoses*, Hercules is said to have something "eternal" from Jupiter, "untouched and unharmed by death." When Hercules' divine essence "is quit of the earth, I [Jupiter] shall receive it into the celestial realm" (9.252–54). The transformation of Hercules from man to God is expressed in this way: "Just as a new snake blooms when it has laid down its old age with its skin, and glows with its fresh scales, so, when Hercules stripped off his mortal limbs, the better part of him was strong, and he began to look larger and become awe-inspiring with august dignity" (9.265–70). In this text, Hercules' inner divine and incorruptible self shines through his corruptible body as the fires of his funeral pyre eat away his flesh. It looks as though Ovid has taken the Hercules myth of deification and colored it with the popular philosophy of his day.[2] In the "Dream of Scipio," the "Jovian" part of every person would presumably be the mind/soul (*animus*). When the mind is virtuous—properly exercising dominion over the body—it secures for itself a divine destiny after death. Of course, the divinity of the essential self (the soul or mind) was not a specifically Stoic idea—it was widely held among Platonists as well, and finds popular expression in tomb inscriptions.[3]

A concrete example of deification in Cicero is the case of his daughter Tullia. Tullia had died in childbirth in February of 45 B.C.E. Her soul, according to Cicero, had joined the Gods and had become divine (Lactant., *Inst.* 1.15–16). In response to her death (or transformation), Cicero became, in his own language, crazy (τετύφεσθαι) about building her a temple (*fanum*) (*Ad Att.* 12.25.1; cf. 12.12.1; 12.18.1; 12.22.3;

---

1   Cf. *Tusc.* 1.66: "What then is divine? To be alive, to know, to discover, to remember. Therefore the soul, which I call divine, Euripides has dared to call 'God'"; and *Offic.* 3.44: "He [the upright man] should recall that he has a God as a witness—this is, as I judge, his own mind (*mens*), there being nothing which God gave more divine than this (*qua nihil homini dedit deus ipse divinius*)."

2   For deification in Ovid, see Godo Lieberg, "Apotheose und Unsterblichkeit in Ovids Metamorphosen" in *Silvae: Festschrift für Ernst Zinn* (eds. Michael von Albrecht und Eberhard Heck; Tübingen: Max Niemeyer, 1970), 125–35.

3   Colish, *Stoic Tradition*, 95.

12.36.1; 12.41.2).[4] Cicero's rationale (from his own work of self-consolation) is preserved in Lactantius: "If the offspring of Cadmus [Ino], or
Amphitryon [Hercules], or Tyndarus [Castor and Pollux], was worthy
of being extolled by fame to the heaven, the same honor ought undoubtedly to be appropriated to her [Tullia]. And this indeed I will
do; and with the approbation of the Gods, I will place you [Tullia],
the best and most learned of all women in their assembly, and will con-
secrate you to the estimation of all people" (*Inst.* 1.15). It seems evident
that Cicero's "Know, then, that you are a God" is not just a theoretical
statement with no practical weight. Those who proved by their virtuous
acts the divinity of their true self were assured of immortality.

    The logic of deification, given popular Stoic cosmology, follows
naturally from basic premises. If, according to Cicero, the heavens are
divine, and the same sort of divinity is assigned to the stars (Cic. *Nat.
d.* 2.39; cf. 2.42), then the star-like soul who rises to heaven is also divine. It will be helpful to turn to other texts to provide a context for this
idea.

The Divinity of the Heavens

The divinity of the celestial sphere has deep roots in Mediterranean culture. Walter Burkert writes that "The association of gods and sky is primeval and seems self-evident. Artistic representations from the archaic
period show the journey of the deified dead into the Beyond. A team
of winged horses may provide escort 'to Heaven.'"[5] Burkert adds that
"Greek catasterisms [transformations of people into stars or constella-
tions] go back to a very early period; this is attested at least for the
Bear and Orion, though these are exceptional cases."[6]

    The connection between the heavens and divinity flourished in po-
etry. Zeus "dwells in the aether," and received as his particular realm
"wide heaven amid the aether and clouds" (Hom., *Il.* 2.412, 15.192).
Olympus, the realm of the Gods, consists of "cloudless aether spread
wide" and is characterized by a shining white light where "the blessed
Gods are happy all their days" (*Od.* 6.42–46). For Hesiod, heaven was

---

4   Other references can be found in John Sullivan, "Consecratio in Cicero," *Classical Weekly* 37 (1944): 158.

5   *Lore and Science*, 359.

6   *Ibid.*, 360, n. 49. For Greek catasterisms, see Carolus Robert, *Eratosthenis catasterismorum reliquiae* (2d ed.; Berlin: Weidmann; 1963), 68, 134, 164.

established as "the eternally secure seat of the blessed Gods" (μακάρεσσι ϑεοῖς ἕδος ἀσφαλὲς αἰεί) (*Theog.* 128). According to Euripides, the "heavenly ones" (οὐρανίδαι) have their home in the aether (*Bacc.* 393–94). Euripides and Aeschylus identified Zeus himself with aether.[7]

> Do you this lofty, boundless aether (αἰϑέρα) see,
> Which holds the earth around in the embrace
> Of humid arms? This reckon Zeus,
> This regard as God (τοῦτον νόμιζε Ζῆνα, τόνδ' ἡγοῦ ϑεόν).
> (Nauck frg. 941, *ap.* Clem. Alex. *Strom.* 5.14.114.1)

This kinship between heaven and the divine was also recognized among philosophers. According to Pythagoras, "the uppermost air is ever-moved and pure and healthy, and all within it is immortal and consequently divine (ἀϑάνατα καὶ διὰ τοῦτο ϑεῖα)." Consequently he calls the sun, moon, and other stars "Gods" (ϑεοί) (Diog. Laert., *Vit. Philosoph.* 8.26–27). Alcmaeon of Croton (5th c. B.C.E.) "attributed divinity to the sun, moon, and other heavenly bodies, and also to the soul" (Cic., *Nat d.* 1.11.27).[8] Plato believed that the fixed stars were Gods "made mostly out of fire … brightest and fairest to the eye" (*Tim.* 40a). He later called them "divine living beings" (ζῷα ϑεῖα) (*Tim.* 40b5; cf. *Leg.* 821b). The *Epinomis*, traditionally attributed to Philip of Opus, viewed the stars as composed of aether. They make up the first type of Gods, "those that are visible, greatest, most honored, and most sharply seeing everywhere" (984c-d).[9]

Aristotle claimed that the ancients taught the divinity of the stars in mythic form (*Met.* 12.8, 1074b1). "Our forefathers," he reasons," assigned heaven (οὐρανόν), the upper region (τὸν ἄνω τόπον), to the Gods, in the belief that it alone was imperishable (ἀϑάνατον)" (*Cael.* 2.1, 284a12–14). It is a general rule, Aristotle himself says, that "the upper place (ὁ ἄνω τόπος) is more divine (ϑειότερος) than the lower" (*Cael.* 2.5, 288a5–6, cf. 1.3, 270b5–10). Again, he remarks that "[I]t is customary to give the name of *ouranos* [heaven] especially to the outermost and uppermost region, in which also we believe all divinity to have its seat" (ἐν ᾧ καὶ τὸ ϑεῖον πᾶν ἱδρῦσϑαι) (*Cael.* 1.9,

---

7 Wright, *Cosmology in Antiquity*, 111–112. The identification is also found in Servius's commentary on the Aeneid 10.18: *quia ipse [Zeus] est aether* (*SVF* 2.1061). He attributes this opinion to the *physici* (*SVF* 2.1066).

8 A similar belief is attributed to Xenophon, who said that "both the sun and the soul are God" (Cic., *Nat d.* 1.31).

9 The second type of Gods are the *daimones*, made up of air.

278b14–16; cf. *Cael.* 1.9, 279a25–28). He thus calls heaven a "divine body" (σῶμα Ͽεῖον) (*Cael.* 2.3, 286a11–12). For Aristotle, the aether was the fifth element defining superlunary substance in which the stars exist and of which they are composed (*Cael.* 270b12–17). This aether, he remarks, is "more divine (Ͽειοτέρα)" than the other elements (*Cael.* 1.2, 269a30).[10] Elsewhere he says that all souls are made up of a nature (φύσις) which is "more divine (Ͽειοτέρου)" than the other elements, "analogous to the element of the stars (ἀνάλογον οὖσα τῷ τῶν ἄστρων στοιχείῳ)" (*Gen. Animal.* 736b30–39).[11]

Aristotle's successor Theophrastus is able to call the stars "heavenly Gods (οὐρανίους Ͽεούς)" (*Piet.*, frag. 2.12–14).[12] Xenocrates, head of the Academy from 339 to 314 B.C.E., is reported to have taught in his book *On the Nature of the Gods* that Gods inhabit the planets, the sun, the moon, and that there is one "simple" deity whose members consist of the fixed stars (Cic., *Nat d.* 1.13.34).

Such high views of heaven are still propagated in the first century B.C.E. Augustine reports a tradition of Varro who divided the world into upper levels of aether and air, and lower levels of earth and water. "All these four parts, he [Varro] says, are full of souls; those which are in the aether and air being immortal, and those which are in the water and on the earth mortal. From the highest part of the heavens to the orbit of the moon there are souls, namely, the stars and planets; and these are not only understood to be Gods, but are seen to be such" (*Civ.* 7.6). For Ovid, the stars are "forms of the Gods (*formae deorum*)" (*Met.* 1.73). Everybody agrees that they are themselves Gods (*Fasti* 3.111–112). The stars dwell in the aether, and the human mind is made up from aetherial seeds (*Met.* 1.78–81). Thus Ovid can claim that "there is a God in us (*est deus in nobis*)." He identifies this God with pneuma (*spiritus*), which descends from the aetherial regions (*sedibus aetheriis*) (*Ars am.* 3.549–50; cf. *Fast.* 6.5–6; *Pont* 3.4.93–94).

In a similar vein, the Roman astronomer Manilius asks who can doubt, "that a link exists between heaven and the human (*hominem coniungere caelo*)?" Into human beings alone "has God come down and

---

10 Cf. the report in Cicero: "he [Aristotle] says that the celestial heat [*caeli ardorem* = aether] is God" (*Nat d.* 1.13.33).

11 This "more divine element" is said to be the pneuma in sperm; or alternatively the nature which exists "in" pneuma (*Gen. Animal.* 736b30–39).

12 The fragment can be found in W. Pötscher, *Theophrastus: Περὶ Εὐσεβείας* (Leiden: Brill, 1964). Cf. Cic., *Nat. d.* 1.35; Clem Al., *Protr.* 5.66.5.

dwells (*in unum descendit deus atque habitat*), and seeks himself in man's seeking of him" (*Astron.* 2.105, 107–08). Again, "Who could know heaven save by heaven's gift and discover God save one who is himself part of the Gods (*qui pars ipse deorum est*)?" (2.115–116). "Can one doubt," he asks, "that God dwells within our breasts (*habitare deum sub pectore nostro*) and that our souls return to the heaven whence they came (*in caelumque redire animas caeloque venire*)?" (4.886–87).

Similar views are proposed by Pliny the Elder: "The world (*mundum*) and this—whatever other name men have chosen to designate the sky whose vaulted roof encircles the universe, is fitly believed to be a deity (*numen*)" (*Nat.* 2.1.1). The heavenly bodies are also *numina* (2.9.54). Heaven (*caelum*) in general is characteristic of God (2.63.154). These views give us a sense of the spread of the dominant philosophical sentiments of the day, which later were integrated and reformulated by popular Stoicism.

The divinity of the heavens—and of the bodies in heaven—had a long pedigree in Stoic philosophy.[13] Their divinity derives from the fact that they are composed of a divine substance, namely aether (Cic., *Nat d.* 2.15.39; 2.15.42). A few representative quotes will illustrate this point. "Zeno declares that the aether is God (*aethera deum dicit*)" (Cic., *Nat d.* 1.14.36), and even "the supreme deity" (*Acad.* 2.41.126). Cleanthes called the stars "Gods" (θεοί) (*SVF* 1.510; cf. Cic., *Nat d.* 3.16.40), and aether a "most definite God (*certissimum deum*)" (*SVF* 1.530). Chrysippus wrote that the stars are "divine by nature (θεῖα τὴν φύσιν)" (*SVF* 2.527; cf. Philo, *Aet.* 47); and that the purest part of the aether is "the first God in a perceptible sense" (Diog. Laert., *Vit. Philosoph.*, 7.139; cf. Cic., *Nat. d.* 2.16.43; 2.21.54). According to Boethus of Sidon, "the sphere of the fixed stars is the substance of God" (Diog. Laert., *Vit. Philosoph.*, 7.148). Seneca also called the stars "Gods" (*di*) (*Ben.* 4.23.4). A general Stoic proposition was that "heaven is the outermost periphery in which everything divine is located" (Diog. Laert., *Vit. Philosoph.*, 7.138). Accordingly, Zeno, Chrysippus, and Posidonius all agreed that "the entire cosmos and the heaven are the substance of God" (*ibid.*, 7.148).

---

13   In his study *Origen and the Life of the Stars*, Scott writes that "it is a universal Stoic view that the stars are gods or are divine" (45).

The Human Pneuma as a Divine Reality

In popular Stoic thought, there was a fundamental kinship between the "divine" heaven (consisting of aether) and the human pneuma. Pneuma, as noted above, was a mixture of fire and air. The aether was viewed as a pure fire surrounding the cosmos. In practice, since pneuma and pure fire are described in similar ways, they came to be used synonymously.[14] Thus, although the fire of the soul (pneuma)[15] was not as pure as the fire of heaven (aether), it had a natural kinship with the pure fire in the upper reaches of the cosmos. Consequently, the divinity Stoics attributed to the aether was also secondarily attributed to pneuma. The substance of God (ἡ τοῦ θεοῦ οὐσία), according to Chrysippus, is an intelligent and fiery pneuma (πνεῦμα νοερὸν καὶ πυρῶδες) (SVF 2.1009). According to Alexander of Aphrodisias, the Stoic view of God is that he is a body which is "an intelligent and eternal pneuma" (Mixt. 224.32–225.4, SVF 2.310).

The result of all this is summed up by Herophilus who relates the Stoic view "that God is called an immortal, rational, excellent living being, so that every good soul is a God, even if it is contained in a human being." This is not a strict identification of the virtuous soul with God, since Herophilus makes clear that God, unlike the soul, is self-existent.[16] Nevertheless, God and the soul—or the soul's purest part—were apparently thought of as akin (even connatural), sharing an identity. In Ps. Plato's Axiochus, the soul has a pneuma dwelling within it (370c), yearns for its native aether (σύμφυλος αἰθήρ) (366a), and is akin (γεννητής) to the Gods (371d). The pneuma could even be called a God within, as Seneca writes: "God is near you, he is with you, he is within you (prope est a te deus, tecum est, intus est) ... a sacred pneuma dwells in us (sacer intra nos spiritus sedet)" (Ep. 41.1). For Cicero, the pneumatic nature of the soul amounts to the confession—sworn with an oath—that the soul is "divine" (divinum) (Tusc. 1.60; cf. Senect. 21.78; Leg. 2.11.28).[17] For when the mind

---

14   Ibid., 42. Again, Chrysippus wrote that pneuma and aether "come under the same definition (εἰς κοινὸν λόγον)" (SVF 2.471).

15   "For in fact our souls are fire (καὶ γὰρ αἱ ἡμέτεραι ψυχαὶ πῦρ εἰσιν)" (Cornutus, Nat. d. 2.4).

16   "Stoic Definitions" ap. Origen Selecta in Psalmos (PG 12.1053b).

17   In this heavenly, eternal, and divine state, Cicero leaves open whether humans will keep company with the Gods or be Gods themselves (which may in the end amount to the same thing, Tusc. 1.76). At any rate, that something was di-

gazes upon "the rising and setting of the stars and the diverse orbits of bodies precisely balanced with one another … it knows that these things pertain to itself. This is the "proof of its divinity (*argumentum divinitatis suae*)" (Sen., *Nat. Q. Pref.* §12).

These teachings are not off limits for Jews. Philo writes that "the soul is made of aether, a divine fragment (ἀπόσπασμα θεῖον)" (*Leg.* 3.161; cf. *Opif.* 77, 146, *Det.* 85–90; *Somn.* 1.34). Although Philo prefers the more Platonic notion of the human mind as the incorporeal image of God,[18] the Stoic notion of the mind as a divine fragment indicates that Philo was comfortable with positing a consubstantiality between the human soul and the divine Logos. In *Special Laws* 4.123, Philo calls the essence of the reasonable soul a "divine pneuma (πνεῦμα θεῖον)." Philo does not see this as Greek philosophy invading the heritage of Judaism. Rather, the soul as divine pneuma is "a truth vouched for by Moses especially, who in his story of the creation says that God breathed a breath of life (πνοὴ ζωῆς) upon the first man, the founder of our race, into the most dominant part of his body, the face, where the senses are stationed like bodyguards to the great king, the mind. And clearly what was thus breathed was an ethereal spirit (αἰθέριον πνεῦμα), or something if such there be better than ethereal spirit, even an effulgence (ἀπαύγασμα) of the blessed, thrice blessed nature of the Godhead" (*Spec.* 4.123). In this text Philo identifies the divine breath (πνοὴ ζωῆς) breathed into the human in Gen 2:7 with pneuma. Thomas Tobin notes that in "seven of the nine places where he quotes Gen 2:7, Philo also uses πνοή (*Op.* 134; *Leg.* 1.31, 42; *Plant.* 19; *Her.* 56; *Som.* 1.34; *Spec.* 4.123); twice he uses the term πνεῦμα (*Leg.* 3.161; *Det.* 80). … In the two cases where πνεῦμα is used, the interpretation (πνεῦμα) has been introduced into the quotation (πνοή). The interpretation of πνοή as πνεῦμα was an obvious one for anyone who wanted to interpret the passage by means of Stoic concepts."[19] The result of seeing the mind as a "divine fragment" was the notion that the mind itself was

---

vine in human beings is not a specifically Stoic view, but a view that Cicero attributes in general to the "wisest philosophers of old (*doctissimi illi veteres*)" (*Fin.* 2.114).

18 See esp. *Plant.* 18–20, and the comments of Thomas H. Tobin, *Creation of Man: Philo and the History of Interpretation* (Washington, D.C.: Catholic Biblical Association of America, 1983), 89–93.

19 *Ibid.*, 78, n. 62. See the Stoic texts he cites on 79–81. Tobin believes that the notion of the human mind as a "divine" or "ethereal fragment" is a Jewish interpretation of Gen 2:7 which predates Philo (81–87).

divine or participated in divinity. Philo makes this clear in another interpretation of Gen 2:7:

> he [God] breathed into him [Adam] from above his own Deity (τῆς ἰδίου θειότητος). The invisible Deity stamped on the invisible soul the impresses (τύπους) of Itself, to the end that not even the terrestrial region should be without a share in the image of God ... How then, was it likely that the mind of man, being so small, contained in such small bulks as a brain or a heart, should have room for all the vastness of sky and universe, had it not been an inseparable fragment (ἀπόσπασμα) of that divine and blessed soul? For no part of that which is divine cuts itself off and becomes separate, but does but extend itself. (*Det.* 86–87, 90)

In this text, the mind as a divine fragment is quite literally a part of the divine nature (specifically, the divine nature of the Logos). Philo clarifies this point by saying that a part of God has not been separated off. Rather, divinity—which is infinite—has simply extended itself into the human domain, and indeed into the deepest and truest part of the human self.

In popular philosophy, the divine soul is of a lesser degree of purity since its thoughts are held down by lower thoughts having to do with bodily urges and sensations (cf. Wisd 9:15). The divinity of the inner pneumatic self intensifies when, released from the body, it ascends into the aether, and attains greater levels of purity. The ascent is also a transition from the human to the divine sphere. Plutarch well illustrates this type of eschatology. In his *Life of Romulus*, he writes that the souls of virtuous human beings

> ascend from men to heroes, from heroes to demi-gods, and from demi-gods, after they have been made pure and holy, as in the final rites of initiation, and have freed themselves from mortality and sense, to Gods (εἰς θεούς), not by civic law, but in very truth and according to right reason [a Stoic slogan], thus achieving the fairest and most blessed consummation. (*Rom.* 28.6–8; cf. *Def. Orac.* 10 [*Mor.* 415a–c]; Sext. Emp., *Math.* 9.73–74)

If souls can be transformed into Gods (meaning, immortal, supersensuous beings), it appears that the celestial ascent of the soul (or the soul's highest part) constitutes a form of deification.[20] In the late first and early

---

20 One might ask at this point how a soul already divine can be deified. The ascent of the soul after death is a true deification (i. e., a *becoming* divine) insofar as the incipiently divine soul becomes more purely divine. As we have seen, the purity of the divine nature corresponds to the height of heaven the soul is able to reach.

second centuries (when Plutarch is writing), this form of deification is still generally thought to be reserved for great heroes and virtuous souls like that of Romulus.[21] Paul would open the gate of heaven to all his converts.

The understanding of the soul's heavenly ascent as a form of deification is colorfully depicted in Hellenistic myths of catasterism. A famous example is Callisto. In Ovid's version of the myth, Callisto is raped by Zeus, bears a son Arcas ("Bear"), and is then changed into a bear by Juno. When the grown-up Arcas unknowingly attempts to shoot his bear-mother in the forest, Zeus catches them up and transforms them both into constellations (*Met.* 2.401–507). That the catasterism of Callisto is viewed as a deification becomes clear with the response of Juno, who scoffs: "I forbid her to be a human being, and now she's been made a goddess (*facta est dea*)!" (2.521). Other examples of Ovid's "astero-deified" human beings include the Dioscuri (8.372), Hersilia (14.846–51), Ariadne (*Fasti* 3.459–461; 510–516); Jupiter's nurse (5.125–128); Chiron (5.413–14), Orion (5.541–44), and Io (5.619–20). (We have already reviewed the catasterisms of Julius Caesar and Augustus in the last chapter.) These texts also indicate that to the ancient mind celestial immortality constitutes a form of deification.

The cumulative weight of this evidence shows that there is a common tendency in popular philosophy (a mix of Stoicism with Platonic elements) to view the heavens as somehow divine, and to see the (pneumatic) soul which attains celestial immortality as divinized.

Deification in Paul

But can a like form of deification be found in Paul? To be sure, the idea that humans are naturally divine or connatural with God would be unacceptable to him. The idea of participating in divine reality (pneuma), however, is not at all far from Paul's logic in 1 Cor 15:37–53.[22] Eng-

---

21 We are, in other words, not yet at the stage in which the dead in general are said to be the recipients of apotheosis. For this conception, see Mark Waelkens, "Privatdeifikation in Kleinasien und in der griechisch-römischen Welt zu einer neuen Grabinschrift aus Phrygien" in *Archéologie et religions de l'anatolie ancienne: Mélanges en l'honneur du professeur Paul Naster* (eds. R. Donceel and R. Lebrun; Louvain: Centre d'histoire des Religions: 1983), 259–307.

22 The idea of sharing divine substance was not automatically unacceptable to a Jew. Philo posited that the soul is made of the same substance as the "divini-

berg-Pedersen has argued that Paul's logic of transformation in 1 Cor 15 fits the Aristotelian category of substantive change from earthly corporeality to pneumatic corporeality.[23] Christ's body is pneuma (he *is* "a life-making pneuma," 1 Cor 15:45), and believer's will share (or "wear," φορέω) his pneumatic body (v. 49). Insofar as they participate in Christ's pneumatic corporeality, believers participate in Christ's divine identity. The result is the human attainment of the clearest of all divine attributes: immortality (1 Cor 15:50–52). Paul's language of meeting the Lord "in the air" (εἰς ἀέρα) (1 Thess 4:17), of having a heavenly city (or citizenship) (Phil 3:20), and of bearing the image of the "Celestial Being" (ὁ ἐπουράνιος) (1 Cor 15:48–49) indicates that he envisioned an ascent to heaven or celestial sojourn after death (or the parousia) (cf. 2 Cor 12:1–4). When believers made this ascent, their pneumatic element was thought to wholly replace their mortal flesh. According to this logic, Paul was using the concepts, if not speaking the language of deification.

To further ground this argument in Paul's logic, however, we must attend carefully to his own language and horizon. When the Apostle speaks of pneuma he often speaks with reference to a divine figure (the frequently mentioned "holy pneuma"). This pneuma, received in baptism, Paul calls the pneuma Χριστοῦ, equivalent with the pneuma Θεοῦ in Rom 8:9. In other words, this "sacred pneuma" is an unmistakably divine entity. But is this divine pneuma integrated into the "self" of the redeemed, so as to become part of them? The pneuma "living in" (Rom 8:9; cf. 1 Cor 3:16; 6:19) the self of the believer at least indicates a high degree of integration of the divine and human selves. Paul's whole argument in Rom 6–8 is that when the pneuma indwells the believer, it changes the nature of the mind so that it can obey the promptings of God.[24] What we have in Rom 8, then, is the discussion of a new, pneumatic self. The pneuma of Christ, in the argument of Samuel Vollenweider, functions as the subject in Rom 8:9–11.[25] In other words,

---

ties," the heavenly bodies. This substance is "aether" (or perhaps a fine sort of fire) (*Mut.* 45–46, *Her.* 283).

23 *Cosmology and Self*, 37.

24 Cf. Seneca "a holy pneuma dwells in us (*sacer intra nos spiritus sedet*)" (*Ep.* 41.1; cf. 73.76); and Epictetus: "You are a portion of God, you have a small part of him in yourself ... You carry around a God with you" (*Diss.* 2.8.11–12).

25 "Der Geist Gottes als Selbst der Glaubenden" in *Horizonte neutestamentlicher Christologie: Studien zu Paulus und zur frühchristlichen Theologie* (WUNT 144; Tübingen: Mohr Siebeck, 2002), 172.

the divine pneuma *"acts not instead of the self, but as our self."*[26] The change can be described as a change of identity. The "old self" (παλαιὸς ἄνθρωπος), which Paul calls "the body of sin" (σῶμα τῆς ἁμαρτίας), dies (Rom 6:6). Paul's old "I" no longer lives, Christ (i. e., Christ's pneuma) lives in him (Gal 2:20). This is Paul's new pneumatic self, which is interwoven with a divine pneuma, Christ. In other words, something divine (Christ's pneuma) now partially makes up Paul's identity. Admittedly, the pneumatic self is the post-conversion self—and thus not a "natural" part of human beings—but the divine element has nonetheless been "naturalized" into the self of those "in Christ." Whether the divine element in humans is innate or introduced from the outside, the result is similar: the divine element dominates the mortal body and becomes the perceived true self. I do not think it is a mistake, then, to say that the redeemed are deified by a divine pneuma which defines their identity. The deification is not perfected, however, until Christ's pneuma totally takes over Paul present physical body (i. e., when his body becomes fully pneumatic, 1 Cor 15:44).

The strongest case for deification in 1 Cor 15, however, comes from v. 49. To simply posit that Paul's logic of becoming immortal and pneumatic is a form of deification remains unconvincing until Paul explicitly tells us that this transformation is a conformation to a divine being. In vs. 49, Paul characterizes transformation into the pneumatic body as "bearing" (or "wearing") "the image of the heavenly being," namely Christ.[27] The statement seems to parallel Paul's remark in Romans that Christians will be σύμμορφους ("isomorphic") to the image of God's Son (Rom 8:29), as well as the statement in Philippians that the transformed body of Christians will be σύμμορφον to Christ's Glory body (Phil 3:21). The destiny of Paul's converts, in other words, is to be assimilated to the pneumatic/glorified body of Christ—a divine being regularly worshiped in Paul's churches. To bear this divine image is to be isomorphic with a divine being. Such strong assimilation to a divine being (believers become "the *same* image" as the divine Christ, 2 Cor 3:18) can fairly be categorized as a form of deification.

---

26 *Ibid.*, 184, italics his.

27 "Being" is supplied here, since Paul writes only the adjective "heavenly" (ἐπου-ράνιος), leaving out the noun it modifies. Most interpreters assume that the noun is ἄνθρωπος, but this is not necessary.

There is some question, however, as to what Christ's image in 1 Cor
15:49 *is*—an image that, as is evident, defines the new self of Christians.
Important to note in the context of 1 Cor 15 is that Christ has already
been identified with pneuma (1 Cor 15:44; cf. 2 Cor 3:17). It may not
be off the mark, then, to think that Christ's image is itself Christ's pneumatic body.[28] In this reading, to bear Christ's image is precisely to have a
pneumatic body (1 Cor 15:44). This is nothing less than sharing in the
"super (i.e., immortal, incorruptible) body" of a divine being. To have
the pneumatic body is to be fully conformed to divine *pneuma* em-bod-
ied in Christ. As Paul says earlier in the chapter, Christ is the first fruits
of the resurrection (15:20, 23). The resurrection is the event in which
Christ was declared "Son of God" (Rom 1:3–4). Christ makes the transition, in other words, from an Adamic (psychic) human to a divine
being by becoming a "life-creating pneuma" (1 Cor 15:45). Those beings assimilated to Christ who gain pneumatic bodies share the same divine destiny and identity as Christ's "siblings" and "coheirs" (Rom
8:17, 29) who become corporeally akin to him.

It is might be objected, however, that when Christ is called upon as
a model of the resurrection, he is directly compared with Adam, the primal *human being* (v. 22, 45). Indeed, in 1 Cor 15:45, Christ himself is
called "the last Adam." Whatever Adam is in Paul's theology, he is
not a divine being. This raises serious doubts about whether Christ,
in his capacity as "last Adam," is here viewed as a divine being. Is he
not rather conceived of as the representative *human being* (cf. Rom
5:12–20)?[29]

My response is that Christ as the "last Adam" far outstrips the nature
of a human being and is in fact assumed to be divine in Paul's churches.
The resurrected Christ, in 1 Cor 15, has characteristics which would
have been recognized in Paul's context as clearly divine characteristics.
The most important is that Christ is "celestial" (ἐπουράνιος) (v.48).[30] I

---

28 Philo makes a similar move when he calls the pneuma of human beings (which
    he identifies with νοῦς or λόγος) the image (εἰκών) of God (*Det.* 83). Similarly,
    he says that the mind made after the image of God partakes of pneuma
    (*Leg.* 1.42). George H. van Kooten takes this to mean that pneuma is "virtually
    identical" with the image of God (*Paul's Anthropology in Context: The Image of
    God, Assimilation to God, and Tripartite Man in Ancient Judaism, Ancient Philosophy
    and Early Christianity* [WUNT 232; Tübingen: Mohr Siebeck, 2008], 65).
29 Robin Scroggs argued strongly along these lines in *The Last Adam*, 93–94.
30 In Greco-Roman culture, the *caelicolae* (heaven dwellers) were virtually synon-
    ymous with "Gods" (e.g., Eur., *Bacc.* 393–94; Virg., *Aen.* 6.786–787; Catul-

take this to be a statement about Christ's "ecology." Christ, the resurrected pneuma, exists in the highest reaches of the universe. Earlier it was shown that the heavens were widely associated with divinity in Paul's culture. We cannot so easily divorce Paul from that culture. The fact that Christ exists in a celestial, divine habitat requires a different form of existence—a form which is higher than human existence. There is, in other words, not just a locative gap between Christ's earthly life and his present existence: the locative gap implies a morphological or a "species" gap. To live in heaven, Christ must be a different sort of being than the earthlings who dwell below. Paul calls the resurrected Christ a πνεῦμα ζωοποιοῦν: life-creating "breath" or "pneuma"—in fact a fair definition of aether as it was commonly understood by Stoics. Ethereal living beings who are incorruptible and unborn are simply higher than human beings. According to popular Stoic conceptions, such beings do not differ from Gods. A quote from Sextus Empiricus illustrates this point:

> But if it is probable that living beings exist in the air, it is certainly reasonable that the nature of living beings should also exist in the aether, from which men too derive their share of intellectual power, having drawn it from there. And as ethereal living beings exist, and are deemed to be far superior to terrestrial living beings through being imperishable and unbegotten (ἄφθαρτα ... καὶ ἀγέννητα), it will be granted that Gods, which *do not different from these* (τούτων [i.e., θεῶν] μὴ διαφέροντας), exist as well. (*SVF* 2.1014 = Sext Emp. *Adv. Math.* [=*Adv Phys.*] 9.87, trans. R. G. Bury, LCL, modified, with emphasis added)[31]

Those who dwell in a celestial (i.e., ethereal and divine) environment are imperishable and unbegotten beings, which is to say, Gods. In Paul's mind Christ is such a being. Yet even apart from this general cultural assumption, it is evident that Paul and his converts worship Christ as a divine being because they have experienced his pneuma working in

---

lus 64.386; Apul., *De Deo Socr.* 146; Aug., *Civ.* 10.1). Note the contrast in Homer: "If you are a God, one of those who dwell in the broad heavens ... But if you are one of the mortal race, who dwell on earth" (*Od.*, 6.150, 153). We can also mention Ovid, who calls the divine Augustus *caeles* (heaven dweller) (*Ep. Pont.* 4.8.63–64).

31 Cf. Varro, *Antiq. rer. div.* Frg. 226 Cardauns, *ap.* Aug., *Civ.* 7.6: "the world is divided into two parts, heaven and earth; heaven into two, aether and air, and earth into water and soil; of these aether is highest, air second ... All four parts are full of souls, the immortal souls being in aether and air ... From the highest circuit of heaven to the circle of the moon, ethereal souls are the stars and planets, which are not only understood but seen to be heavenly Gods."

their communities. They baptize in the name of Christ and his pneuma. This pneuma lives in them and makes them into itself. Christ's pneuma is not a mere "spirit," but a divine reality. Pneuma is in fact the basis of Christ's immortality and divinity. Those conformed to the pneumatic Christ—who are made incorruptible, immortal, and pneumatic—share in Christ's divinity.

Connaturality

There is one last, persistent objection to deification in Paul which, though briefly touched on above, must be more fully confronted here. Although popular Stoic philosophy had little problem understanding the human mind (a modulation of pneuma) as connatural with the divine mind (concentrated where pneuma is most pure—in the aether), Paul, it seems, would strongly resist the idea that the pneumatic body was, is, or is made connatural with a divine being. I do not deny this point entirely. Paul was not a Stoic, and would probably have resisted Stoic ideas of connaturality had he known them to be specifically Stoic. Yet I do resist attempts based on this admission to show that there is *no* similarity between Paul and popular modes of thought in his culture. In fact, a fresh look at Paul's language leads one to think that Paul teaches a kind of "connaturality" with the divine Christ (even if not wholly understood in Stoic terms). In 1 Corinthians 6, Paul adds an intriguing statement about the close kinship of Christ and Christian: "all who cleave to the Lord [i.e., the divine Christ] are one pneuma (ἓν πνεῦμα) with him" (6:17).[32] This has sometimes been taken as a mystical or purely metaphorical saying—but these explanations seem too quickly to gloss over ancient modes of thought.[33] It is difficult to get around the observation that, given the context of the passage, Paul is suggesting a sexual metaphor for union (though

---

32 Interestingly, Clement of Alexandria connects this verse with 1 Cor 15:45: "'But he that is joined to the Lord is one pneuma'—a pneumatic body (πνευματικὸν σῶμα)—which is a different kind of union" (*Strom.* 7.14.88.3).

33 Origen cited 1 Cor 6:17 to illustrate how the soul of Jesus was united to the Logos by "supreme participation." The union is so close, he says, that a distinction between the Logos and the soul is not made: "the relation of the soul of Jesus to the firstborn of all creation, the divine Logos, is not that of two separate beings" (*Cels.* 6.47, trans. Henry Chadwick; cf. *Princ.* 2.6.3). Thus the soul of Jesus is deified (*Princ.* 2.6.6).

not fusion) with a divine being. Just as the man is "one body [or flesh]" with the prostitute (6:16), so the baptized human being and Christ are "one pneuma."[34] The individual has pneuma (1 Thess 5:23, cf. Rom 8:16) and Christ's pneuma lives within the individual (Rom 8:9); but the relationship between the two pneumata is sometimes so close that they are said to be "one." What does this mean for the identity of the believer and Christ? Is the essential self of the believer somehow mingled with Christ's divine self?

The best way to approach an answer to this question is to turn to the exposition of the late nineteenth and early twentieth century German theologian Otto Pfleiderer. Pfleiderer recognized that, according to Paul, the divine pneuma who takes up residence in the Christian self is something of a foreign body that stands in opposition to the impulses and passions of the old self.[35] Nonetheless, he also recognizes that in Paul the divine pneuma can be described as overlapping with the human pneuma in such a way that the two pneumata unite and form an entirely new being (or "new creation," 2 Cor 5:17), which is to say a new redeemed self. Thus Paul can even declare: "I have been crucified with Christ. I no longer live; Christ lives in me" (Gal 2:19–20). If the Lord Christ is pneuma (1 Cor 15:45), then Paul is saying that the pneuma of Christ lives in him (cf. Rom 8:9–10), and drives him to such an extent that his old self has been submerged ("*I* no longer live"). In its place, Paul has a new self, which he does not distinguish from the self of Christ ("*Christ* lives in me"). Pfleiderer comments:

> We have to consider statements of the Apostle which are of two different kinds; in the one, he implies that the Christian [divine] πνεῦμα and the natural human πνεῦμα co-exist and work upon one another; in the other, he makes no difference between them. Of the first kind, the most important are to be found in Rom. viii:16, αὐτὸ τὸ πνεῦμα συμμαρτυρεῖ τῷ πνεύματι ἡμῶν ὅτι ἐσμὲν τέκνα θεοῦ: and vers. 26, τί προσευξώμεθα καθὸ δεῖ οὐκ οἴδαμεν, ἀλλὰ αὐτὸ τὸ πνεῦμα ὑπερεντυγχάνει στεναγμοῖς ἀλαλήτοις: ix:1, συμμαρτυρούσης μοι τῆς συνειδήσεώς μου ἐν πνεύματι ἁγίῳ … But by the side of these passages there are also others to be found which do

---

34 Incidentally, this passage exemplifies how Paul thinks of pneuma in corporeal terms: to be one body (with a prostitute) is closely coordinated with being one pneuma (with Christ) (1 Cor 6:16–17).

35 *Primitive Christianity: Its Writings and Teachings in their Historical Connections* (ed. W. D. Morrison; trans. W. Montgomery; Clifton, NJ: Reference Book Publishers, 1965), 386.

not assume or even admit of any distinction between the divine and human πνεῦμα in the Christian.[36]

Pfleiderer cites Rom. 8:10, "the pneuma is life on account of righteousness." Since this statement is in contrast to "the body is dead due to sin" it seems right to see the pneuma as that of the Christian. But the Christian's pneuma can only "be" life in unity with the divine pneuma, as is indicated in Rom 8:9 and 11—verses which refer to the life-giving pneuma of God and Christ. In another passage, Paul easily glides from the human virtues of holiness, knowledge, patience, and goodness to the "holy pneuma" (πνεῦμα ἅγιον), a phrase which usually does not refer to his *own* pneuma, unless his own pneuma is being viewed as united with the divine pneuma within him (2 Cor 6:4–6). In these passages, Pfleiderer points out, we cannot separate the "objective" divine pneuma from the "subjective Christian spirit." Rather, "the divine πνεῦμα and the natural human πνεῦμα coalesce in the Christian into the unity of *a new subject*, a καινὸς or πνευματικὸς ἄνθρωπος (they unite therefore in substance, comp. 1 Cor vi.17)."[37] In a later treatment, Pfleiderer expounds the relation this way:

> the divine seems to have entered into the human, and so to have become one with him, ... they are related like form and content. In the 'spiritual man' the divine Spirit has become the proper energy and norm of his thought, feeling, and will ... The whole faith-life of the Christian is the manifestation under the conditions of human life of the divine Spirit which is given to him; he knows this Spirit—even if he occasionally sets him in contrast to himself as another subject—to be as a rule his own possession, his inwardly appropriated power, by which his ego is made capable of divine knowledge, volition, and action ... the apostle serves God in is spirit and in newness of the Spirit, and his conscience bears him witness in the Holy Spirit (Rom. i.9, vii.6, ix.1); his religious activity as well as his ethical self-estimate is therefore accomplished in the strength and according to the norm of the divine Spirit, who, however, has become his own new or divine-human spirit.[38]

Pfleiderer hastens to add that the union of human and divine pneuma is progressive, thus not fully complete. It also involves no fusion with di-

---

36 *Paulinism: A Contribution to the History of Primitive Christian Theology: Exposition of Paul's Doctrine* (trans. Peter Edwards; London: William and Norgate, 1877), 213–14; originally published as *Der Paulinismus: Ein Beitrag zur Geschichte der urchristlichen Theologie* (Leipzig: Hinrichs, 1873).

37 *Ibid.*, 215.

38 *Primitive Christianity*, 389.

vine reality such that the human reality (or personality) is annihilated. For Paul, identification with the divine in fact increases the life and freedom of the human subject. "It is this very process of the union of the divine and the human spirit, constantly advancing towards the unity of a personality in the image of God, which is ever becoming more complete." This union with the pneuma is not something automatic or compelled, but freely willed by the Christian and worked out in a process of increasing holiness.[39]

Returning to 1 Cor 6:17 (believers as one pneuma with Christ), we can categorize this statement as an expression of "union with Christ"—but this does not advance our understanding very much. Paul is talking about pneumatic union with a specifically divine being. I do not think it inappropriate to interpret the statement in physical terms (that is, in terms of ancient physics). Being physically "one pneuma" with Christ—thus "connatural"—was how Paul envisioned the union of the Christian self with a divine self (Christ). Pneuma is a form of body, thus to be one pneuma is to be one body with Christ (this is standard Pauline teaching, 1 Cor 12:12; Rom 12:5). But to share Christ's body (or bodily substance) is to share Christ's divine identity. Identification begins in baptism, when Christians receive a "dose" of the pneuma of Christ (1 Cor 12:13). A fuller identification comes at death or the parousia, when believers will receive bodies fully made up of the substance of this life-giving divinity. It is this kind of corporeal assimilation to and identification with the pneumatic Christ that leads to incorruptibility and immortality (basic divine qualities). It is this complex of ideas that I am calling a Pauline form of deification.

Conclusion

Paul, when speaking of the pneumatic body, does not propound conformity to "divinity" in general but to a specific divine being, namely Christ. Christ, already pneuma (1 Cor 15:45), models the glorious, celestial, and divine existence for human beings. Believers participate in Christ in the sense that they share Christ's nature (pneuma).[40] Those

---

39   *Paulinism*, 215–16.
40   This is the formulation of Stanley Stowers, "What is 'Pauline Participation in Christ'?" in *Redefining First-Century Jewish and Christian Identities* (ed. Fabian Udoh; Notre Dame: University of Notre Dame, 2008), 352–71.

who participate in Christ become the same nature as Christ (1 Cor 6:17). The nature that they share is pneuma.[41] Christians become more like the Christ-pneuma by becoming more pneumatic. These terms, I have argued, are to be understood not merely in a metaphorical or "spiritual" sense, but physically. The process of "pneumatification" is completed in the resurrection when believers fully relinquish the body of flesh to attain a fully pneumatic body, the substance of Christ's divine body. By sharing the bodily reality of Christ, those in Christ become divine (i. e., immortal, incorruptible) as Christ is divine.

Although undoubtedly different in some respects from the kind of deification proposed by the Stoics and in the ruler cult, I have argued for basic analogies.[42] In chapter 2, I developed the thesis that rulers could assimilate to specific Gods by participating in their divine qualities. In this chapter, I have focused on an analogy with popular (Stoic-Platonic) philosophy. Such philosophy posited that the soul was partially consubstantial with divine stuff (pneuma). At death, this divine stuff rose up to the aether attaining a purer and purer state until it settled among the celestial divinities. Paul, for his part, asserts that the redeemed are assimilated to a divine being, Christ (analogy one). Such assimilation means gaining a share in the divine Christ's identity (the pneumatic body) and eventually a full "pneumatification" at death or the parousia. The result is immortal and incorruptible life lived out in the celestial sphere (analogy two). The analogies are not perfect (no analogy ever is), nor are assimilation and pneumatification combined elsewhere as they are in Paul. Nonetheless, they do not need to be combined elsewhere because I am not arguing that Paul is borrowing from a pre-existing model of deification which lines up point by point with his own views. What the analogies show is that Paul was working with the logic, and sometimes the language of deification. Though fully admitting the differences, I think that the similarities are potent enough to redescribe this aspect of Paul's soteriology

---

41 According to Origen, "Everyone who shares in anything is undoubtedly of one substance and one nature with him who shares in the same thing (*sine dubio unius substantiae est uniusque naturae*)" (*Princ.* 4.9). He goes on to say that the human soul shares in the divine nature (which he calls "intellectual light") and is thus to some extent of one nature and substance as God. This results in human incorruptibility and immortality. In *Princ.* 4.10, he concludes that people "have a kind of blood-relationship (*consanguinitatem*) with God."

42 Analogy, I might add, never presumes genealogy. I am not interested in the origin of Paul's ideas, but a redescription of their content.

(namely, that involving assimilation to a divine being resulting in pneumatification and immortalization) as a form of deification.

My interpretation finds some confirmation from patristic interpreters (who were, again, much closer to Paul and Paul's horizon than ourselves). Origen, for instance, described God's act in the resurrection as a "lifting man up beyond human nature and making him change to a superior and more divine nature" (*Cels.* 5.23, trans. Henry Chadwick). This I take to be a concise paraphrase of Paul's teaching in 1 Cor 15:39–53. What modern interpreters see as a process of becoming more human (pneumatic conformation to the image of a heavenly being), Origen saw as a transcendence of human nature and a transformation into divine nature. In Paul, I have argued, this "divine nature" is pneumatic, and makes up the identity of the divine Christ. It is this identity—and thus immortality—which Paul's converts share. In the context of the ancient world, I do not think it inappropriate to call the eschatological transformation described in 1 Cor 15:39–53 a Pauline form of deification.

Chapter 6:
Deification and the Cosmic Rule of the Saints

"For he must reign until he has put
all his enemies under his feet (ὑπὸ τοὺς
πόδας αὐτοῦ). The last enemy to be
destroyed is Death. For God has put all
things (πάντα) in subjection
under his feet."
(1 Cor 15:25–27)

"All things (πάντα) are yours."
(1 Cor 3:16)

"The God of peace will shortly
crush Satan under your feet
(ὑπὸ τοὺς πόδας ὑμῶν)."
(Rom 16:20)

Introduction

In this chapter I continue to argue for a form of deification in Paul. Here, however, I turn from speaking about participating in Christ's immortality to participating in Christ's divine power, and particularly his power to rule. We switch gears, in other words, from realistic transformation into divine corporeality to Paul's language of fulfilling a specifically divine function: universal rule. Although not a participation in Christ's divine nature *per se*, power to rule is no less a trait constitutive of Christ's divine identity. Believers' reception of comprehensive power to rule is part of Paul's larger eschatological myth of divine forces fighting to achieve supremacy over the world. Although colored directly by Paul's Jewish background, this type of myth has been told and retold in a variety of different times and cultures. In this chapter, I will refer to this type of myth as "the battle of the Gods."

The Battle of the Gods: Cultural Antecedents

In the Syro-Palestinian city of Ugarit, the God Baal (the Lord) was said to battle Mot (Death) so that that the seasons could continue. Initially, Baal makes himself the servant of Mot (*CTA* 5.2.11–12, 19–20). Then, in a tragic defeat, he is swallowed by Mot and dies (5.6.8–10). He is then buried on the sacred mount (6.1.15–18), and mourned. In response, the Goddess Anat—driven by furious grief—(quite literally) sifts Death like wheat (6.2.30–37), and Baal is raised to life. The resurrected Baal then retakes his place as vice regent of El (chief deity in the Ugaritic pantheon), called "Father of Years" (5.6.2; 6.1.35–36). El himself proclaims after the resurrection: "For Mightiest Baal lives, the Prince, Lord of the Earth, is alive!" (6.3.20–21). In a future climactic combat, Baal then defeats Mot himself. "Then B[aa]l [is enthroned] on his royal throne, [On the resting place], the throne of his dominion" (6.5.5–6; 6.6.33–35).

In the natural world, Baal's victory is the victory of the autumn rains over the summer heat. But it is not only this. It is also the victory of the human farmers, or the human community who wins the struggle for survival. Baal "satis[fies] the multitudes of the earth" (4.7.49). When El mourns for the perished Baal, he cries out "Baal is dead—what (will happen) to the people / The son of Dagan—what (becomes) of the masses?" (5.6.23–25; 6.1.6–8). The furrows of the fields are dry and parched (6.4.1–3, 12–14). The natural world seems to perish. The signs of Baal's revival, in contrast, are the heavens raining oil and the wadis flowing with honey (6.3.6–7). The victory of Baal is the victory of the people; for he is their life.

In Daniel 7, four monstrous beasts appear out of the sea and receive temporary dominion.[1] The fourth beast is indescribably terrible and destructive. Nevertheless, by God's power this beast is killed and burned with fire, and the kingdoms of the three other beasts are removed (v. 11–12). In verse 13, a human-like being approaches the throne of the "Ancient of Days" to receive "dominion and glory and kingdom, that all peoples, nations and languages should serve him, his dominion is an everlasting dominion, which shall not pass away." Whoever this human-like one is, his victory is coordinated with the victory of God's people on earth. In Daniel 7:22, the Aramaic text reads: "until

---

1   For the Canaanite background to Daniel 7, see John J. Collins, *Daniel: A Commentary on the Book of Daniel* (Minneapolis: Fortress Press, 1993), 286–94.

the Ancient of Days came and judgment was given for the holy ones of the Most High." The LXX can be read to the effect that God gave judgment *to* the holy ones (τὴν κρίσιν ἔδωκε τοῖς ἁγίοις)."[2] The interpretation of the vision makes this reading plain: "The kingdom and the dominion and the greatness of the kingdoms under the whole heaven was given (ἐδόθη) to the people of the saints of the Most High. Their kingdom shall be an everlasting kingdom, and all dominions shall serve and obey them" (v. 27).

John Collins takes the view that the human-like one is the archangel Michael, the divine "prince" of Israel who represents the people of the holy ones, or righteous Israelites.[3] Just as Israel's angelic prince rules over the other angelic rulers of nations (Dan 12:1), so Israel rules (or will rule) over the nations themselves. As in heaven, so on earth. The victory of the mediating power in heaven ensures the victory and universal reign of the people of God on earth. Here again, Gods or supernatural forces battle with a practical effect on earth: humans share the victory of the God(s) who represent, support, and even embody them in heaven.

This type of myth was not foreign to a Greek or Roman audience. The battle of Actium in which Augustus (then Octavian) won full supremacy over the Mediterranean (31 B.C.E.) was adapted to the myth of Gods battling Gods. Ranged on one side was Augustus upheld by Neptune, Venus, Minerva and especially Apollo. On the other side were the theriomorphic Egyptian Gods of Cleopatra and Antony— "Monstrous Gods of every form," says Virgil, "and barking Anubis." The poet continues:

> In the middle of the fray storms Mavors [Mars], embossed in steel, with the grim Furies from on high, and in rent robe Discord strides exultant, while Bellona follows her with bloody scourge. Actian Apollo saw the sight, and

---

2   Theodotion removes most of the ambiguity: τὸ κρίμα ἔδωκεν ἁγίοις. For human figures being given power to judge, cf. John 5:22, 27; *Test. Abr.* Rec. A 13:4. See also Martin Hengel, "Sit at My Right Hand!" in *Studies in Early Christology* (Edinburgh: T & T Clark, 1995), 182–83.

3   *Commentary*, 310, 318–19. Martin Hengel thinks that if in Dan 7 the human-like one represents the holy ones of Israel (7:18, 22, 27), then the holy ones of Israel are actually the ones being enthroned and given power to act as judges over the nations ("Sit at My Right Hand!" 182). Along these same lines, Matthew Black claims that "Daniel was contemplating ... nothing less than the *apotheosis* of Israel in the end-time, a 'deification', as it were, of the 'saints of the Most High'" ("The Throne Theophany Prophetic Commission" in *Jews Greeks and Christians—Religious Cultures in Late Antiquity* [ed. Robert Hamerton-Kelly and Robin Scroggs; Leiden: Brill, 1976], 62).

from above was bending his bow; in terror at this all Egypt and India, all
Arabians, all Sabaeans turned to flee. (Virg., *Aen.* 8.698–706; trans. H.
Rushton Fairclough, LCL)

Propertius' poetic account of the battle is even more dramatic:

> The sea-god at last had curved the lines into two crescents, and the water
> quivered, reflecting the flashing of the weapons, when Apollo, leaving
> Delos, which stands firm under his protection … stood over Augustus'
> ship, and a sudden flame thrice flashed forth, bent into the zigzag of light-
> ning. He [Apollo] had not come with his locks streaming over his shoulders
> or brought the unwarlike melody of the tortoise lyre, but with aspect as
> when he looked upon Pelopean Agamemnon and emptied the Greek
> camp upon the insatiable pyre, or as when he put to rest throughout its
> winding coils the serpent Python, the terror of the peaceful Muses.
>   Anon he [Apollo] spoke: 'O savior of the world who are sprung from
> Alba Longa, Augustus, proved greater than your ancestors who fought with
> Hector, now conquer at sea: the land is already yours: my bow battles for
> you, and all this load of arrows on my shoulders is on your side. Free Rome
> from fear: relying on you as her champion, she now has freighted your ship
> with a nations' prayers.' (*Elegies* 4.6.25–42; trans. G. P. Goold, LCL)

When Cleopatra's ships are shattered, Augustus' father Julius Caesar
looks down "from the star of Venus" (*Idalio … ab astro*) and marvels
at the scene: "'I am a God (*sum deus*)," he says, and "this victory is
proof that you [Augustus] are of my blood (*nostri sanguinis*).' Triton
hails the outcome on his conch, and around the standards of liberty
all the Goddesses of the sea clap their hands (4.6.59–62).
    The result of the battle is Augustus' universal sovereignty.

> But Caesar, entering the walls of Rome in triple triumph, was dedicating to
> Italy's Gods his immortal votive gift—three hundred mighty shrines
> throughout the city. The streets were ringing with gladness and games
> and shouting, in all the temples was a band of matrons, in all were altars,
> and before the altars slain steers covered the ground. He [Augustus] himself,
> seated at the snowy threshold of shining Phoebus [Apollo] reviews the gifts
> of nations and hangs them on proud portals. The conquered peoples move
> in long array … . (Virg., *Aen.* 8.714–722)

Sitting at the threshold of Apollo's temple, Augustus' sovereignty is not
his alone. He has become vice-regent of the high God (Hor., *Odes*
1.12.51–52; cf. *Ep.* 1.19.43). Jupiter reigns over the world through

him.[4] This universal reign brings a new age of peace, justice, and culture.

> Your age, Caesar, has brought back rich harvests to the fields ... it has put a
> bridle on license which was straying beyond the proper limits, removed sin,
> and revived the ancient arts by which the name of Latium, the power of
> Italy, and the prestige and majesty of the Empire were extended from
> the sun's western bed to his rising. (Hor., *Odes* 4.15.4–16; trans. Niall
> Rudd, LCL; cf. 4.5)[5]

Paul's Myth of Battling Gods

Paul also has his myth of battling Gods.[6] For Paul, it is an apocalyptic
myth. Ranged on one side is the high God with his son and viceregent
Christ, surrounded and served by a host of angels. On the other side is
Satan, accompanied by the host of his minions, evil powers who lead
the world into corruption and sin. Here the forces of evil and the forces
of good are colored in black and white: order and goodness versus disorder and corruption; peace versus strife; the powers of life against the
powers of death. The present age is evil because Satan and his ministers
are in charge of the world (Gal 1:4; 2 Cor 4:4). They direct the vast and
diverse cults of Greco-Roman religion (1 Cor 10:20–21), and dwell in
the lower regions of the heavens (Eph 2:2; cf. Gal 4:3).

The apocalyptic war is also fought on the level of individual psychology. After the transgression of Adam, the demon-like entity Paul
calls "Sin" gained control over the mortal bodies of human beings, so
that they became instruments (or slaves) of Sin. The end result was
the reign of Death, whom Paul depicts as a king ruling from Adam
to Moses (Rom 5:14, 17, cf. v. 20). Paradoxically, the giving of the

---

4   For universal rule as a manifestation divinity in the Greco-Roman world, see
     Theoc., *Idyll.* 17, esp. lines 91–94; Plut. *Def. orac.* 29 [*Mor.* 426a]; and the
     Boeotian inscription to Nero as world ruler and singular deity in E. Mary
     Smallwood, *Documents Illustrating the Principates of Gaius Claudius and Nero*
     (Cambridge: Cambridge University Press, 1967), 35–37 §64.
5   For theomachy in other Latin authors, see François Ripoll, "Adaptations latines
     d'un thème homérique: la théomachie" *Phoenix* (2006): 236–258.
6   For a more thorough investigation of this myth, see Neil Forsyth, *The Old
     Enemy: Satan and the Combat Myth* (Princeton: Princeton University Press,
     1987), 260–284. See also the imaginative (but often uncritical) account of
     Peter W. Macky, *St. Paul's Cosmic War Myth: A Military Version of the Gospel*
     (New York: P. Lang, 1998).

Law provided no release from Death's reign. Evil deities hijacked the religion of Israel so that the Torah became an instrument of Sin (Rom 7:8, 13; cf. Gal 3:19b).[7] Sin deceived Paul himself through the commandment and "killed" him (Rom 7:11). Although Paul's mind approves the Law, the "law of sin" wins the battle within and takes Paul captive (7:22–23).

During his time on earth, the God Christ defeated Sin by dying "to" Sin (τῇ ἁμαρτίᾳ) (Rom 6:10). Believers have recapitulated this death through the ritual of baptism (6:2–4). Their minds are thus free from the slave master Sin (6:6–7, 20). Now the demon called Death only has claim over the external, physical bodies of humans (which Paul calls "the body of sin" [6:6] and "body of death" [7:24]). Within, however, believers have the freedom of the divine Spirit, a freedom which Paul depicts as slavery to God (6:22).

Even after Christ, however, the battle with Sin and Satan continues for believers. In theory, they have been freed from their slave master Sin, but Paul ever has to exhort them: "do not let Sin reign as king in your mortal body, so as to obey his lusts" (Rom 6:12). Paul must exhort his followers not to present their body parts as weapons (ὅπλα) to Sin, a distinctively military image (v. 13). Sin is still active as a kind of War-lord, who pays out military wages (ὀψώνια) in the coin of death (6:23). Even against believers, Satan is powerful as a tempter (1 Thess 3:5; 1 Cor 7:5) who uses deception to achieve his ends (2 Cor 11:3, 14; cf. Gal 1:8). He constantly seeks an opportunity to take advantage of God's elect to lead them into sin (2 Cor 2:11; 1 Cor 7:5). When Christians sin grievously, they fall into his power so that Satan can destroy their flesh (1 Cor 5:5). Believers will not attain full freedom until they are released from "the body of death," i.e., the body subject to death, or their outward flesh (Rom 7:24).

The salvation Paul speaks of is salvation from these divine powers. They have been conquered by Christ, the divine warrior king. Although Paul claims that the "Rulers" would not have crucified Christ

---

7   Commenting on 2 Cor 3:14–15 in light of 4:4, Sang Meyng Lee remarks: "The god of this age, Satan, has used the law, which should have revealed God to his people, as a means of blinding 'the minds of the unbelievers' in order that they were [*sic*] not able to recognize 'the light of the gospel of the glory of Christ,' the image of God. Satan will be soon defeated by not only Christ but also Christians" (*Paul's Cosmic Drama of Salvation: A Study of Paul's Undisputed Writings from Anthropological and Cosmological Perspectives* [WUNT 276; Tübingen: Mohr Siebeck, 2010], 154).

if they had known God's hidden wisdom (1 Cor 2:8), Paul does not expatiate on a battle of Christ versus his enemies on the cross (though see Col 2:15). Rather, Paul seems to locate the battle chiefly at "the end" (τὸ τέλος), when Christ "hands over the kingdom to God the Father, after he has destroyed every Ruler and every Authority and Power (ὅταν καταργήσῃ πᾶσαν ἀρχὴν καὶ πᾶσαν ἐξουσίαν καὶ δύναμιν)" (1 Cor 15:24). This is the closest indication we have of a battle scene at the parousia, although there are expanded accounts in the Deutero-Pauline literature:

> For it is indeed just of God to repay with affliction those who afflict you, and to give relief to the afflicted as well as to us, when the Lord Jesus is revealed from heaven with his mighty angels in flaming fire, inflicting vengeance on those who do not know God and on those who do not obey the gospel of our Lord Jesus. These will suffer the punishment of eternal destruction, separated from the presence of the Lord and from the glory of his might, when he comes to be glorified by his saints and to be marveled at on that day among all who have believed. (2 Thess 1:6–10; NRSV; cf. Rev 19:11–21)

This is the "coming wrath" from which Paul says that his converts are saved (1 Thess 1:10). It is a wrath of the Son of God "revealed from heaven against all ungodliness and wickedness" (Rom 1:18). It is a wrath against the enemies of believers, human and superhuman. The last enemy the God Christ will conquer is Death (1 Cor 15:26), envisioned as a personal entity, over whom Paul sings a victory hymn (v. 55). Death, along with beings called "Authorities," "Rulers," and "Powers" are widely viewed as demonic agents.[8] These enemies of God and his Messiah are conceived of as superhuman powers destined to be subjected under the feet of the divine Messiah (1 Cor 15:27–28), in fulfillment of Ps 8:7 [LXX] ("you have subjected everything [πάντα] under his feet,") which Paul apparently takes as a prophecy of Christ's future absolute rule.

When through his viceroy Christ the high God defeats the evil, lesser powers, a new world order emerges, free from the bondage of corruption (Rom 8:21–22). Those who are loyal to the high God—the members of Paul's churches—will appear at Christ's coming (1 Cor 15:23). They will stand before the Christ and receive incorruptible crowns (1 Thess 2:19; 1 Cor 9:25; cf. 2 Tim 4:8). They will be revealed as sons of God (Rom 8:18), co-heirs with the divine Christ

---

8   For recent discussion of this point, see Lee, *Cosmic Drama*, 155–61.

(8:17). As divine children and equal heirs, they will be given a share in Christ's divine sovereignty. It is Christ who has the right to sit at the judgment seat (2 Cor 5:10). But Christ gives this power to "the holy ones" (i. e., Pauline Christians) to judge the world and angels (1 Cor 6:2–3). Satan is now crushed beneath *their* [believers'] feet (Rom 16:25). Though the subjection of all things (including demonic powers) is given only to the Messiah, those "in Christ" rule with him in eternal life (ἐν ζωῇ βασιλεύσουσιν) (Rom 5:17; cf. 2 Tim 2:12). Christ's victory is their victory. Christ's divine sovereignty is their sovereignty. By assimilation to the divine Christ, the faithful take on Christ's divine function: universal rule. This is the basic pattern of deification that I seek to unpack in this chapter.

The Rule of the Saints in Pre-Christian Judaism

The idea that the saints share (or will share) God's rule is an old idea in Judaism, as a sampling of texts will show. As noted in chapter 3, humanity's share in divine sovereignty begins in Gen 1:26–28. There humans are given the task to rule the earth. This task is part of what makes them God's "icon" (εἰκών) or image.

In the Hebrew scriptures, the vision of royal humanity ruling the earth in Gen 1:26 anticipates the divine election of Israel to rule the human world. Royal humanity was reinterpreted to mean Israelite humanity. Adam's rule became paradigmatic for Israel's (or the Israelite king's) rule over the nations. Thus we find the promise in Deuteronomy that Israel will "be above all the nations (ὑπεράνω πάντων τῶν ἐθνῶν)." The Hebrew text can be read to mean that Yahweh makes Israel "as Elyon [the high God] over all the nations (עליון על כל־הגוים)" (26:19; cf. 15:6; Ex 7:1).

The theme of Israel's rule appears mainly in the prophets. In Isaiah, for instance, Israel's rule is part of the larger glorification of Jerusalem.

> Fearful, the sons of those who enslaved you will come to you, provoked to wrath before you, and the city will be called 'City of the Lord, Zion of the Holy One of Israel.' (Isa 60:14, LXX)

Earlier in this chapter we hear of the great wealth of the future Israel:

> Nations shall come to your light
> and kings to your brightness ... (v. 3)
> then you will see, fear, and be shocked in your heart, because the wealth of

the seas and nation and peoples will be transferred to you … (v. 5)
the islands shall wait for me,
the ships of Tarshish first …,
their silver and gold with them,
on account of the holy name of the Lord your God, and so that the Holy
One of Israel will be glorified
Foreigners shall build up your walls,
and their kings will stand ready before you … (vv. 9–10)
Your gates shall eternally be opened, night and day left unclosed, to bring
in to you the power of the nations and kings led in procession. For the nations and the kings who do not serve you as slaves will be destroyed, and
the nations will be wasted with barrenness … (vv. 11–12)
I will make an eternal joy, merriment for generations upon generations.
you shall suck the milk of nations and eat the riches of kings. (vv. 15–16)

The Israel of the future age is ruler not only of the territory of Palestine;
all the kings of the earth—even from the farthest corners—bring tribute
to her. In this scene, the Israelites are depicted as ruling "from the River
to the ends of the earth." But this is the same rule of the ideal (and coming) king, who will "dominate from sea to sea, from the river to the
ends of the inhabited world (κατακυριεύσει ἀπὸ θαλάσσης ἕως θαλάσσης
καὶ ἀπὸ ποταμοῦ ἕως περάτων τῆς οἰκουμένης)" (Ps 71[72]:8). He will
annihilate the war-like bow, the multitude and *pax* of the Gentiles.
He will rule over the waters as far as the sea, and the rivers as far as
the outlets of the earth" (Zech 10:10).

The idea of Israelite sovereignty was perpetuated in later Jewish literature, most often in an eschatological sense. Sometime during or
shortly after the Maccabean revolt, an "Animal Apocalypse" was written
in which the righteous were depicted as sheep (or lambs) and the
wicked nations as wild animals. In the final eschatological scenario,
the visionary sees "all the sheep that remained. And all the animals on
the earth and all the birds of heaven were falling down and worshiping
those sheep and making petition to them and obeying them in everything" (1 En 90:30, trans. G. W. E. Nickelsburg and J. C. Vanderkam).
Apparently, this author envisioned the nations as serving righteous Israelites in the eschaton. The bowing and "worshiping" is particularly
striking, since normally one would suppose these actions would be directed to God, depicted as "the Lord of the sheep" (vv. 29, 32).

Eschatological rule appears to be individualized in the *Testament of
the Twelve Patriarchs*. Here, the patriarch Dan promises that the person
who trusts in "the Holy One of Israel" will "reign in truth in the heavens" (TDan 5:13). Similarly, Benjamin exhorts his sons to be imitators

of "the good man [Joseph] … because of his compassion, in order that you may wear crowns of glory" (TBen 4:1).

A striking image of believers' eschatological reign comes from the *Testament of Job* (1ˢᵗ c. B.C.–Iˢᵗ c. C.E.). After Eliphas loudly bewails Job's fate, Job silences him with the cry: "Now I will show you my throne with the splendor of its majesty, which is among the holy ones:

> My throne is in the upper world,
> and its splendor and majesty come from the right hand of the Father
> The whole world shall pass away
> and its splendor fade. …
> But my throne is in the holy land,
> and its splendor is in the world of the changeless one.
> Rivers will dry up
> and the arrogance of their waves goes down into the depths of the abyss
> But the rivers of my land, where my throne is, do not dry up
> nor will they disappear
> but they will exist forever.
> These kings will pass away,
> and rulers come and go;
> but their splendor and boast shall be as in a mirror.
> But my kingdom is forever and ever, and its splendor and majesty are in the chariots of the Father.
> (33:2–9; trans. R.P. Spittler; cf. Job 36:7; TJob 40:3)

Although Job describes his throne in individual terms, we should not assume that eschatological sovereignty in "the upper world" was reserved solely for him. His destiny is meant to give hope to all the righteous.

The Qumran sectarians interpreted a phrase in Hab 1:12 ("you have appointed him to judge") to mean that "God is not to destroy his nation [Israel] at the hand of the peoples, but in the hand of his chosen ones [the Qumran community] God will place the judgment over all the peoples" (1QpHab 4:3–4). In a fragment from a Messianic apocalypse, the Lord "will honor the pious upon the throne of an eternal kingdom" (4Q521 fragment 2, col. 2:7). At the end of the War Scroll we hear this cry: "Rejoice, Zion, passionately! Exult, all the cites of Ju[dah! Open] [your gates continuously so that] the wealth of nations [can be brought to you!] Their kings shall wait on you, [al]l your [oppressors] lie prone before you, [the dust of your feet they shall lick]" (1QM 19:5–7; cf. 12:13–15).

In the "Epistle of Enoch" (1 En 92–105), the author promises the righteous that they will execute judgment on sinners (95:3; 96:1; cf. 1:9; 38:5). In 1 Enoch 108:12 (an appendix to 1 Enoch), it is said that God will bring out "into shining light" those who love his holy name, "and I [God] will set each one on the throne of his honor."

Forthright are the promises of the Wisdom of Solomon:

> The righteous, when they are visited, will shine forth
> and will run like sparks through the stubble.
> They will govern nations and rule over peoples,
> and the Lord will reign over them forever. (Wisd 3:7–8)
>   But the righteous live forever,
> and their reward is with the Lord;
> the Most High takes care for them.
> Therefore they will receive a glorious crown (τὸ βασίλειον τῆς εὐπρεπείας)
> and a beautiful diadem (τὸ διάδημα τοῦ κάλλους) from the hand of the Lord.
> (5:15–16)

At the turn of the era, a Jewish writer of a Sibylline Oracle wrote that in the time of the end "the faithful chosen Hebrews will rule over / exceedingly mighty men, having subjected them / as of old, since power will never fail" (2.174–76; trans. J. J. Collins).[9]

Here and elsewhere the victory and rule of the faithful community (whoever it may be) is a function of God's antecedent victory and rule. The faithful share in God's reign, because God opens it to them. This tradition is widely diffused in Jewish literature of both Palestine and the Diaspora. The pattern of Paul's soteriological thought is basically in tune with this pattern of Israel's final triumph and rule (transferred to Paul's communities).

Paul and the Promise of Eschatological Lordship

What makes Paul's promise of eschatological sovereignty distinctive, however, is that the rule he envisions is a rule believers receive *as siblings and co-heirs of a divine being* (Christ). It is by their assimilation to the divine Messiah—and specifically to his suffering—that those who endure obtain his rule (Rom 8:17). If Christ conquered death, the faithful will conquer death. They will obtain immortality, they will be invincible "super conquerors" (ὑπερνικάω) over the human and superhuman powers that threaten to separate them from the love of Christ (Rom 8:31, 37). Naturally, they will acquire this authority not of their own strength,

---

9   For the date of this oracle, see *OTP* 1:331.

but because they have been conformed to the image of the divine son (Rom 8:29).

With Christ, Paul makes his converts heirs of the world. When arguing against factionalism in Corinth, Paul told his converts that "all things are yours" (πάντα … ὑμῶν ἐστιν) (1 Cor 3:21).[10] This does not appear to be rhetorical hyperbole divorced from reality. In Paul's apocalyptic mindset, "all things" includes real superhuman entities: the powers called Death and Life (εἴτε ζωὴ εἴτε θάνατος), all present and future things (εἴτε ἐνεστῶτα εἴτε μέλλοντα), even the world itself (κόσμος) (1 Cor 3:22).[11] To have possession of these cosmic realities (cf. Rom 8:38)—and the cosmos itself—is at the very least to have some degree of power over them.[12] But to have power over Death is the prerogative of the Messiah who will defeat Death when the "end" comes (1 Cor 15:25–27). Christ is the one who really owns "all things." He is the "heir of all (κληρονόμον πάντων)" to borrow a phrase from Hebrews (1:2). Paul's proleptic transfer of cosmic ownership to his converts appears to be an implication of their being "in Christ." They are "coheirs" with Christ (Rom 8:17) to whom the whole world submits as the Lord of all (Phil 2:10–11). As participants in Christ, then, believers gain a share in the world. Therefore they should not be worried about mere human things (ἀνθρώποις) (1 Cor

---

10 What Paul promises the author of 4 Ezra still waits for: "If the world has indeed been created for us, why do we not possess our world as an inheritance?" (6:59).

11 The κόσμος is variously understood in this verse. Johannes Weiss, whose commentary is still unsurpassed in attention to religio-historical context and critical acumen, understood it as "the unlimited fullness of all living beings, human and angel (cf. 4:9)" (*Der erste Korintherbrief* [2d ed.; Göttingen: Vandenhoeck & Ruprecht, 1977], 89). Robertson and Plummer opted for "the physical universe" (*A Critical and Exegetical Commentary on the First Epistle of St. Paul to the Corinthians* [2nd ed., ICC Vol. 33 Edinburgh: T. & T. Clark, 1914], 73.). More recent commentators who want to limit "the world" to something smaller have trouble explaining why death, life, as well as all present and future things are included in it.

12 So Weiss: "all beings and fates cannot rule Christians, but are their (spiritual) possession and must serve them." Paul "views the Christians as those called in a proleptic way to future lordship as the ideal lords of the world." Again, paraphrasing Paul's logic, he says "since you belong to Christ, and through him you are free from the world, human beings, sin and death—and have become God's—all things lie at your feet and must serve you" (*Der erste Korintherbrief*, 89–90, 91).

3:21). Indeed, Paul implies that they are called to be something more than mere human beings (3:4).[13]

Commentators have rightly pointed out the Stoic background of the phrase "all things are yours" (Sen., *Ben.* 7.2.5–7.3.3; 7.10.6; Cic., *Fin.* 3.75; Diog. Laert., *Vit. Philosoph.* 7.125).[14] If this is a line borrowed from Stoic philosophy, it has been adapted to fit Paul's apocalyptic and mythic categories. A similar application by another Hellenistic Jew can perhaps give us a sense for how Paul understood the phrase. In his *Life of Moses*, Philo says that God gave Moses "the whole world (πάντα τὸν κόσμον) as a portion well fitted for his heir (κληρονόμος)." This gift gave Moses the power to perform miracles: to change the natural properties of elements: making the sea dry land and transforming water from rock. This ability to control the world and its elements, Philo says, is "no wonder."

> For if, as the proverb says, what belongs to friends is common [cf. Diog. Laert., *Vit. Philosoph.* 6.37], and the prophet is called the 'friend of God' [Ex 33:11], it would follow that he shares also God's creation (κτίσις), so far as it is serviceable. For God possesses all things (ὁ μὲν Θεὸς πάντα κεκτη-μένος), but needs nothing; while the good man, though he possesses noth-ing in the proper sense, not even himself, partakes of the precious things of God so far as he is capable [cf. 2 Cor 6:10] ... he has received no mere piece of land but the whole world as his portion (ὅλον τὸν κόσμον κλῆρον λαβών). (*Mos.* 1.156–57, trans. F. H. Colson, LCL, modified)

But not only does Moses as God's heir receive power over the elements. He also receives God's name. Philo continues: "Was not the joy of his partnership with the Father and Maker of all magnified also by the honor of being deemed worthy to bear the same title? For he was named God and king (Θεὸς καὶ βασιλεύς) of the whole nation [Ex 7:1]." To be sure, there are many interpretations of what receiving the name of "God" (Θεός) means for Moses. Suffice it to say, bearing the name of God was a function of Moses' lordship.[15] Moses already

---

13 "For when one says, "I belong to Paul," and another, "I belong to Apollos," are you not merely human (οὐκ ἄνθρωποί ἐστε)?" Origen comments on this no-tion: "the pneumatic is greater than 'human,' who is characterized either by soul or by body or by both, and not by the pneuma which is more divine than these. By very strong participation in the pneuma the pneumatic gains this name" (*Comm. Jo.* 2.21.138, my trans.).

14 Weiss, *Der erste Korintherbrief*, 90–91. Note also Herbert Braun, *Gesammelte Studien zum Neuen Testament und seiner Umwelt* (Tübingen: Mohr Siebeck 1962), 182–86.

15 Holladay, *Theios Aner in Hellenistic-Judaism*, 108–155.

had control over the physical elements. Now Philo calls him king (βασι-λεύς). In his capacity as king, lord of the elements, and "God," Moses became a model for the people who had followed him. Philo goes on with his account: "[H]e [Moses] … has set before us, like some well-wrought picture, a piece of work beautiful and godlike (θεοειδές), a model (παράδειγμα) for those who are willing to copy it [cf. 1 Cor 15:49; 2 Cor 3:18; Rom 8:29]. Happy are they who imprint, or strive to imprint, that image (τὸν τύπον) in their souls" (*Mos.* 1.158–59).

Philo's Moses, like Paul's Christ, lives out a model of sovereignty in which other human beings can participate. Moses rules the world along with every other friend and fellow heir of God. Similarly for Paul, Christ first gains a share in the name and sovereignty of God (see esp. (Phil 2:9–11), and then becomes a model (εἰκών) for those Christians who inherit (Rom 8:17; 1 Cor 3:21) and rule the world with him. Christians gain what Christ has as his fellow heirs. For Paul to say that his converts possess "all things," therefore, is clearly more than rhetorical flourish. For Paul, it means a ownership and kingship over the world with Christ in the eschaton.

That having "all things" involves a narrative of future rule seems to be implied also in 1 Cor 4:8. Here Paul chides the Corinthians: "Already you have all you want! Already you have become rich! Quite apart from us you have become kings (ἐβασιλεύσατε)!" That Paul was not merely mocking them, but affirming his own doctrine is indicated by his next remark (which does not seem altogether wry): "Indeed, I wish that you had become kings, so that we might be kings with you." Reigning as kings was evidently not the private fantasy of the Corinthians, or the doctrine of Paul's enemies.[16] It is, it appears, what Paul had told them of their eschatological destiny (cf. Philo *Prob.* 20; *Abr.* 261; *Post.* 128). As owners of all things and heirs with Christ, they will rule with Christ (βασιλεύσουσιν) (Rom 5:17; cf. 2 Tim

---

16 "In itself Paul would have greeted with joy the fact that in his community such a vivacious assurance of victory and salvation, such a conscious ownership and enjoyment of the 'power of the future world' was present. Indeed, he had been the very one who most of all had contributed to this—that the future, super-worldly, and salvific blessing of Christianity had been understood as already to be experienced in the present. It is all the more certain that this opinion as such was not offensive to him, only the way in which it was expressed" (Weiss, *Der erste Korintherbrief*, 107).

2:12).[17] We gather the gist of this teaching in a variety of other Pauline texts.

In Romans 8:32, we learn that attaining cosmic power was apparently part of Paul's gospel: "He who did not withhold his own Son, but gave him up for all of us, how can he not also grant us—with him—everything there is (τὰ πάντα)?" (my trans.).[18] Ownership of "everything" is a form of sovereignty, a universal sovereignty only Christ has claim to. To him God makes "all things" (πάντα) subject (1 Cor 15:27; Phil 3:21). Strictly speaking, sovereignty over "all things" is the sovereignty that only the Creator—or the one through whom all things were made (1 Cor 8:6)—can lay claim to. This is the sovereignty that makes up the divine identity of Christ, the Messiah, who is made Lord and heir of the world. Paul, it appears, envisions believers as sharing this universal sovereignty through their assimilation to Christ the divine son (Rom 8:29).

If believers in Christ will own and rule over the cosmos as co-heirs with Christ, they also will have the authority to judge it. In 1 Cor 6:2 (noted above), Paul asks his readers, "Do you not know that the saints [i.e., believers] will judge the cosmos (οἱ ἅγιοι τὸν κόσμον κρινοῦσιν)?" Included in the cosmos are both humans and angels (1 Cor 4:9). Accordingly, Paul asks, "Do you not know that we are to judge angels (ἀγγέλους κρινοῦμεν)?" (6:2–3). Paul's "Do you not know (οὐκ οἴδατε)" indicates that Christian judgment over angels was a well known teaching, most likely (as in his other uses of οὐκ οἴδατε) his own. The κόσμος may refer to those judged on Judgment day. More broadly, however, it could designate the creation in general. If this is correct, then the "judging" may not be viewed as a one-time event, but as a continuous action. In this sense, judging would imply authority over, and likely rule. A good case for the "ruling" sense of κρίνω can be made from LXX usage, where this is often the meaning of the term (e.g., Judges 4:4; 10:2–3; Ps 66:5 [MT 67:5]; Hos 13:9–10; cf.

---

17 The problem of the Corinthians is not that they speed up the time of their rule, (pace David H. Hay, Glory at the Right Hand: Psalm 110 in Early Christianity [Nashville: Abingdon Press, 1973], 62) but that they rule without Paul (χωρὶς ἡμῶν) (in an emphatic position, 1 Cor 4:8).

18 "All things" here probably refers to creation as a whole, the most common meaning in Paul (Rom 11:36; 1 Cor 8:6; 11:12; 15:27–28; Phil 3:21). In the words of James D. G. Dunn, "what seems to be envisaged is a sharing in Christ's lordship ... over 'the all'" (Romans 1–8 [WBC Vol. 38 Nashville: Thomas Nelson, 1988], 502).

Luke 22:30).[19] In Wisdom 3:8, likewise, those who "judge" (κρίνω) the nations are those who "rule" (κρατέω) the peoples. The NRSV thus rightly translates κρίνω in this verse by "govern" (cf. Luke 22:30).

Important to note is exactly who believers will judge. They will judge "angels," beings (whether good or evil) that are normally held to be superior to humanity.[20] In the eschaton, the tables are apparently turned, and humans gain authority over angels. This superiority is only natural for those who have been made into "the same image" as Christ, the image of God (2 Cor 3:18; 4:4; cf. *L.A.E.* 13–15). Properly speaking, however, only Christ has power over the angelic or superhuman world (1 Cor 15:24; Phil 2:10–11). His power to judge is what gives him the honor of the Father (cf. John 5:22–23). Humanity granted the power to judge angels is humanity sharing in Christ's divine prerogatives and honor.

In 1 Corinthians 15, Christ's role as the divine Messiah is "to destroy every Rule and Authority and Power" (v.24). James Tabor asserts that "this cosmic conquering role belongs not only to Jesus as Son of God, but to the 'many' sons to come as well. The very notion," he says, "of 'inheriting the kingdom of God' has to do with participating in a role of cosmic rule and judgment (1 Cor 15:50). Jesus only heads a group of transformed, immortal, glorified sons of God who have been given power over 'all things' to bring about God's final purposes in history."[21]

The logic of Tabor's reading is supported by Romans 16:20, where Paul promises Christians that Satan will soon be crushed beneath their feet. It is this enemy who may (if conflated with Death) be considered the "last" enemy (1 Cor 15:26). He is, at any rate, generally considered to be the greatest and most powerful enemy of God. He is, in Paul's lan-

---

19 Cf. also Judges 3:10, 30; 12:7–9, 11, 13–14; 15:20; 16:31). It also seems to be the sense in Ruth 1:1, 1 Sam 4:18; 2 Chron 26:21; Ps 2:10; 9:9; 71:2, 4; 95:10, 13; 97:9; 134:14; Prov 29:14; Mic 4:3; Isa 19:20; 51:22; Wisd 1:1; 3:8; 12:13–4, 18; Tob 3:2; 1 Macc 9:73; Pss Sol 17:29; Odes 3:10; Sir 4:15; 45:26. This sense of κρίνω does not seem to appear at all in the Pentateuch, although see Deut 32:36. Note also Scroggs, *Last Adam*, 67–68.

20 The identity of these "angels" has been disputed. Yet whether they are good, evil, or both good and evil, they are all generally considered to be superior to human beings.

21 "Paul's Notion of Many 'Sons of God' and its Hellenistic Contexts," 94. Importantly, Tabor notes that for "Jesus and the others, this conquering role is a temporary and functional one; when the *telos* comes, then all rule is returned to God (1 Cor. 15:28)" (*ibid.*).

guage, the "God of this world" (2 Cor 4:4). This is the enemy that Christians are said to stomp on. He will be subordinate to Pauline believers (their "footstool," as it were). Properly speaking, only Paul's divine Messiah has this powerful enemy under his feet (Ps 110:1; 1 Cor 15:27). Apparently, Satan under the feet of believers is part of a divine rule which Christ gives as a share to those "in Christ." They will enjoy the victory over the chief of evil powers. In this way, Christians fulfill what was later taken to be a solely Messianic promise that "he [the Messiah] will crush your [the serpent's] head" (Gen 3:15) (The serpent is taken to be the devil in 2 Cor 11:3.) Regardless of whether or not Paul knew this verse as a prophecy,[22] in Rom 16:20 he is asserting that Christians share a sovereignty distinctive to the divine Messiah.

The sovereignty that Christians gain in Christ is much greater and more divine than the sovereignty Adam had over beasts and birds in Gen 1:26 and 28. For it is a sovereignty not only over the world of animals and humans, but over powerful superhuman beings. It is a sovereignty of the Image of God, who is a divine being (2 Cor 4:4). It is a universal sovereignty insofar as it includes ownership of all things, and the judgment of the cosmos. This kind of rule is even more striking than the universal sovereignty given to the human-like one in Daniel 7 that is shared with the saints (v. 22).

Results: The Question of Deification

In more than one of his essays, Richard Bauckham has argued that "The one who functions as God shares the divine identity with God,"[23] and "it is the cosmic scope of Christ's sovereignty which places it in that unique [divine] category."[24] Although I would not claim that Pauline Christians achieve sovereignty in the same sense as Christ, Bauckham's logic when applied to the data presented above appears to work as well for Christians as it does for Christ himself. As in Daniel, the universal sovereignty Paul envisions for his converts could only be a divine sovereignty. It could only stem from the "Ancient of Days" as a part of his

---

22 The Septuagint reads: "you yourself will guard [or possibly "lie in wait for"] his head (αὐτός σου τηρήσει κεφαλήν)."
23 *Jesus and the God of Israel*, 138.
24 *Ibid.*, 176. Cf. 180: "Thus, it is because the Son exercises the uniquely divine sovereignty that he will and should be honoured just as the Father is."

identity which he shares with the divine Christ, and which Christ then shares with his siblings and co-heirs. Christ as divine Lord is more than the Second Adam. So the sovereignty he shares is more than the sovereignty of Adam. Christ's rule is a cosmic, and thus a divine rule. It is this divine rule which he shares with believers. If Christ is a prototype for believers, he is not just a human. (According to most Jews, no mere human has true claim to such vast cosmic power.) Christ is a divine prototype.

God made Christ an heir of the world (1 Cor 15:27).[25] He will own it and rule over it. According to Paul's gospel, believers are made "heirs of God and co-heirs with Christ" (Rom 8:17).[26] As co-heirs, they will have, it seems, an equal measure of Christ's divine ownership of the world and dominion over it. Christ has first priority to it, naturally, as the elder brother, but he willingly shares it with all those called his "siblings" and "sons of God" (Gal 3:26; Rom 8:17, 19, 29). They fulfill, or help Christ fulfill, a divine function.

Similarly, the authority to judge the world (both human and superhuman) is a widely recognized divine function.[27] According to Paul, it is God who judges the world (κρινεῖ ὁ Θεὸς τὸν κόσμον) (Rom 3:6; cf. Ps 95[96]:13), along with the divine Christ (2 Cor 5:10). Now if "[t]he one who functions as God shares the divine identity with God,"[28] the implications for deification are evident. For God (through Christ) to give humans ownership of "everything" (τὰ πάντα) and judgment over the "world" (which suggests a universal scope) is to give them a share of his divine sovereignty which constitutes (so Bauckham) his divine identity. This sharing in Christ's divine identity is what I am calling a Pauline version of deification.

---

25 Cf. the fuller Christological exegesis of Ps 8 in Heb 2:2–10

26 "The term 'heirs of God,'" notes C. E. B. Cranfield, "is not to be explained as meaning simply 'heirs of Abraham, who are to receive in due course the blessings which God promised to him and his seed." Christians will share "not just in various blessings God is able to bestow but in that which is peculiarly His own, the perfect and imperishable glory of His own life" (*A Critical and Exegetical Commentary on the Epistle to the Romans* [6th ed.; Edinburgh: Clark, 1975], 927).

27 See note 4 above. According to Paul M. Hoskins, "In Jewish thought the judge of angels is also a position that is held solely by God" ("The use of Biblical and Extrabiblical Parallels in the Interpretation of First Corinthians 6:2–3," *Catholic Biblical Quarterly* 63 [2001]: 292, citing 1 En 9–10; 90:20–27).

28 Bauckham, *Jesus and the God of Israel*, 138.

Conclusion

I close this chapter with another Jewish-Christian myth of future deification. This is a story from the *Testament of Adam*, an originally Jewish document with extensive Christian additions (3rd c. c.e.?). Immediately after Adam picked the death-dealing fruit, God spoke to him: "Adam, Adam, do not fear. You wanted to be a God; I will make you a God, not right now, but after a space of many years" (3:2; trans. S. E. Robinson). In this pseudepigraphon, Adam will receive this gift because he was created in God's image. In the present time, however, God consigns Adam and his descendents to death. Although the text does not use the language of a second Adam, it very quickly turns to Christ as the means and model of deification: "For your [Adam's] sake I will be born of the Virgin Mary. For your sake I will taste death and enter the house of the dead." Immediately the author turns to Christ's resurrection-exaltation: "And after three days, while I am in the tomb, I will raise up the body I received from you." But instead of being exalted to God's right hand, Christ sets Adam (or redeemed humanity) "at the right hand" of his divinity. In this way, the restored humanity in the person of the (new) Adam obtains the promise God had made earlier. The human who includes the human race, who has been given strength to rule everything (cf. Wisd 10:2) is "made a God" (3:2–4).[29]

The idea that humans might obtain divinity, and that this was, in fact, thought to be God's ancient design, was an idea, I think, not entirely foreign to Judaism.[30] The idea that rulers could become divine by participating in the powers of particular Gods was fairly widespread in the Greco-Roman world (chapter 2). A basic analogy exists in Paul, who envisions the faithful as sharing in the power of the divine Christ.

---

29 Cf. Theophilus of Antioch (*Autol.* 2.24): "When God set man ... in paradise to work it and guard it, he commanded him to eat of all the fruits, obviously including those of the tree of life; he commanded him not to taste of the tree of knowledge alone. God transferred him out of the earth from which he was made into paradise, giving him an opportunity for progress so that by growing and becoming mature, and furthermore having been declared a God (θεὸς ἀναδειχθείς), he might also ascend into heaven (for man was created in an intermediate state, neither entirely mortal nor entirely immortal, but capable of either state; similarly the place paradise—as regards beauty—was created intermediate between the world and heaven), possessing immortality" (trans. Robert M. Grant).

30 Note on this point Mettinger, *The Eden Narrative*, 130.

Pauline converts are not, however, only given super-human power (as a vague divine quality) but—through assimilation to the divine Christ—they are given cosmic rule. This is the specific divine function of a specific divine being. It is part of the divine Messiah's identity as Messiah and as divine. The idea that Paul envisioned humans obtaining divinity by sharing in the identity of the divine Christ is thus not beyond the pale of what was possible for the movement we now know as Pauline Christianity.[31]

The myth of the ruling, reigning, and lordship of the Christ-believer is part of another, larger Pauline myth which involves an assimilation to the God Christ. Christ sets the pattern of exercising divine power which his siblings assimilate to. Their divinity (expressed in ruling power) is the divinity of Christ. Just as Christ is subordinate to the Father (1 Cor 15:28), however, deified humans ever remain subordinate to their elder brother ("you belong to Christ," 1 Cor 3:23).

Christ's eternal superiority should always be duly acknowledged when treating this material. But it is often in the act of brilliantly highlighting Christ's superiority and lordship that theologians and biblical exegetes too quickly pass over (or simply ignore) elements of Paul's gospel that suggest a very high (indeed, divine) status for the redeemed. In response to this (under)emphasis, let me emphasize (once more) in sum-

---

31 It is not beyond the pale of the New Testament. Although I have deliberately ignored chronologically later texts in the interests of historical analysis, two texts must be briefly noted. The first is from the Pauline school, and asserts that God "raised us [Christians] up with him and seated us with him (συνεκάθι-σεν) [God, presumably] in the heavenly places in Christ Jesus" (Eph 2:6; cf. 2 Tim 2:12; Luke 22:30). What we have here is an ascension and enthronement of the believer (in Christ). The other text is Rev 3:21: "To the one who conquers I will give a place with me on my throne, just as I myself conquered and sat down with my Father on his throne" (cf. 5:10; 20:4, 6; 22:5). In both texts, believers appear to be σύνθρονος with a divine being. What may be envisioned here is a double throne, or *bisellium* where two deities can sit alongside each other. "The theological significance of this use of a *bisellium* in 3:21," David Aune comments, "is the equality that it presumes between those who share such a throne" (*Revelation 1–5* [WBC 52; Dallas: Word Books, 1997], 262). The verse is reminiscent of that daring declaration in one of the hymns of Qumran: "... for I have taken my seat ... in the heavens ... I shall be reckoned with Gods and established in the holy congregation" (4Q491c = 4Q491 frag. 11, lines 6–7). Bauckham's assertion that universal sovereignty "could not be seen as delegated to a being other than God" is in a sense correct (*Jesus and the God of Israel*, 197). Those humans who receive such a sovereignty in Christ are (like Christ) included in the class of Gods or divine beings.

mary fashion part of Paul's gospel which, it seems, has generally been given short shrift. The Apostle Paul taught a version of human dominion which—although it was in line with Jewish teachings about eschatological lordship—was nevertheless distinctive. For Paul taught that believers would become rulers in conformation to the universal rule of a divine being (Christ). Paul even made this divine being the brother and co-heir of the faithful. As co-heir, the destiny of Paul's converts is to own all things (1 Cor 3:21; Rom 8:32), judge superhuman powers (1 Cor 6:3), and rule the world (1 Cor 6:2; Rom 5:17) as siblings assimilated to the divine Christ (Rom 8:29). They will have victory over the "God of this world" (1 Cor 4:4), treading him underneath their feet (Rom 16:20), and "over-conquering" every enemy, "whether angels, or rulers, or things present, or things to come, or powers, or height, or depth, or anything else in all creation" (Rom 8:38–39). Exercising this superhuman and cosmic sovereignty is what it means, I have argued, to gain a share in Christ's divine identity. This is Paul's myth of the battle of the Gods. In this myth, believers share the victory of Christ as those who have themselves—having gained a share of his divine power and cosmic rule—become divine.

Chapter 7:
Paul and Moral Assimilation to God

> "Let us try to put the truth in this way. In God there is no sort of injustice whatsoever; he is supremely just, and the thing most like him is the person who has become as just as possible."
>
> —Plato, *Theaet.* 176b8-c3

Introduction

When in chapter 1 I asked the question "What is a God?" I laid down notions that were more or less common throughout the ancient Mediterranean basin: a God was an immortal being wielding some form of superhuman power. It was pointed out in that chapter that for Paul, these would not be the only two qualities constitutive of Godhood. In fact, for a first-century Jew, such a minimalist understanding of God would be seriously deficient because it lacked a moral component. For someone like Paul, it is just as likely that God would be defined in moral terms as a supremely good and just being. Such moral qualities would for Paul be just as much part of God's identity as immortality and power. A moral understanding of deity is, at any rate, closer to the "music" of the Hebrew scriptures that had so long played in Paul's ears. To quote just a few excerpts from the Psalms:

> Good and upright is the Lord (Ps 24[25]:8, LXX)
> Taste and see that the Lord is good (Ps 33:9 [ET 34:8])
> The Lord is just in all his ways, and holy in all his works (Ps 144[145]:17)

This fundamentally moral conception of God was not overly common in popular Greco-Roman theology. Hesiod's Zeus upholds justice, to be sure, but in the many popular folk tales about the Gods, their vast power and prestige often puts them in a category above human society and conventions. Thus they do not answer to human moral codes, or abide by them—as many early Jewish and Christian apologists delight to point out.

In the fourth century B.C.E., Plato responded to this popular Greek theology (represented chiefly by Homer) with what later moralists (Christian and non-Christian) thought was a devastating critique. Homer's Gods—at least by common human standards—were declared unjust. This critique was part of Plato's attempt to overhaul Greek theology in the *Republic* (see esp. books 2–3). To state it simply, Plato demanded that all Gods—if they were to be Gods—be just (or participate in Justice). This theology makes both Gods and humans equally subject to a higher moral code which can be accessed and perceived by both divine and human minds. This is a development distinctive to the philosophical tradition, and should not be taken as representative of how most Hellenized peoples (that is, non-philosophers) thought about the Gods in the ancient Mediterranean. Nevertheless, the idea of a fundamentally moral God proved to be influential in the popular philosophy which thrived in Paul's day.[1]

The basis of Plato's moral theology is a primal deity (or divine principle) who is Goodness and Justice, and therefore makes the entire world subject to this moral code. As Plato's Socrates argues:

> Now, God is really good, isn't he, and must be described as such?
> What else?
> And surely nothing good is harmful, is it?
> I suppose not.
> And can what isn't harmful do harm?
> Never.
> Or can what does no harm do anything bad?
> No.
> And can what does nothing bad be the cause of anything bad?
> How could it?
> Moreover, the good is beneficial?
> Yes.
> It is the cause of doing well?
> Yes.
> (*Resp.* 379b-c, trans. G.M.A. Grube)

Plato puts it more succinctly in *Timaeus* 29e: "He [the creator God] was good, and one who is good can never become jealous of anything. And so, being free of jealousy, he wanted everything to become as much like himself as possible."

---

1 Beginning in Paul's day, Platonism was making something of a come-back in philosophical circles, as evidenced by Philo. See further Engberg-Pedersen, "Setting the Scene: Stoicism and Platonism," 1–14.

Platonic Assimilation to God

God as good, just, and unjealous forms the philosophical basis for Plato's ethics of moral assimilation to God.[2] The classic text here is *Theaetetus* 176a-b:

> It is not possible, Theodorus, that evil should be destroyed—for there must always be something opposed to the good; nor is it possible that it should have its seat in heaven. But it must inevitably haunt this human life, and prowl about this earth. That is why one should make all haste to take flight from earth to heaven; and flight means assimilation to God as much as possible; and assimilation to God is to become just and holy with wisdom (ὁμοίωσις δὲ [Θεῷ] δίκαιον καὶ ὅσιον μετὰ φρονήσεως γενέσθαι).

Because God is morally good (sometimes thought of as *the* Good), assimilation to God is put in distinctly moral terms: it means to become just (or righteous), holy (i. e., just toward the Gods), with wisdom (not simply by habit or custom). These are classic Platonic virtues. In other passages as well, Plato defines assimilation to God as the practice of virtue (*Resp.* 613a7-b3; *Leg.* 716b-d; *Phaedr.* 246d; 248a; 249c; *Tim.* 47c, 89e-90d5; *Phaed.* 78b-84b; *Min.* 319a3–5). This was a truly revolutionary move in Greek theology. God is just, holy, and wise. To be just, holy, and wise thus became a way to participate in the very nature of God.

In the first century B.C.E., Plato's teaching about assimilation to God became the *telos* of Platonic ethics. This development has been attributed to Eudorus of Alexandria, who defined the end of human life to be ὁμοίωσις Θεῷ (*ap.* Stob., *Anth.* 2.7.3).[3] In later Middle Platonic thought, this formulation becomes standard. For Middle Platonists, assimilation to God meant living the life of virtue. The person who "practices virtue" (ἐπιτηδεύων ἀρετήν) is conformed to God (*Resp.* 613b). Eudorus develops the notion this way:

---

2   For recent research on assimilation to God in Plato, see Julia Annas, *Platonic Ethics, Old and New* (Ithaca: Cornell University Press, 1999), 52–71. J. M. Armstrong, "After the Ascent: Plato on Becoming Like God," *Oxford Studies in Ancient Philosophy* 26 (2004): 171–83; Timothy A. Mahoney, "Moral Virtue and Assimilation to God in Plato's *Timaeus*," *Oxford Studies in Ancient Philosophy* 28 (2005): 77–91; Daniel C. Russell, "Virtue as 'Likeness to God' in Plato and Seneca," *Journal of the History of Philosophy* 42 (2004): 241–60; Van Kooten, *Paul's Anthropology*, 129–35.

3   For Eudorus, see Dillon, *Middle Platonists*, 114–135, esp. 122–23, along with the passages cited in his general index, *s.v.* "Likeness to God," 455.

Socrates and Plato [say] the same things as Pythagoras: the [human] end is
assimilation to God. Yet Plato articulated it most clearly by adding, "according to what can" (*Theaet.* 176b), and it is by practical reason (φρόνησις)
alone that one can do this—and this was the life according to virtue. ...
Pythagoras says: 'Follow God!' It is clear that he did not mean the visible
and leading God, but the intelligible God, the one who keeps the cosmic
order in harmony. In Plato's *Timaeus* [90a-d], in the passage concerning the
three parts of philosophy, this is called the *natural* mode of assimilating to
God (I will add that it is the *Pythagorean* mode—and Plato ungrudgingly
indicates his [Pythagoras'] previous observation.) In the *Republic*, however,
we have the *ethical* mode of assimilating to God; whereas in the *Theaetetus*
[176d-e], we have the *rational* mode of assimilating to God. ... But Plato's
manifold way of speaking does not indicate manifold opinions. ... [I]t ends
in a single and harmonious teaching: the life according to virtue. It is, to
put it another way, the attainment and use of perfect virtue. (Stob.,
Anth. 2.7.3 §f; cf. Plut. *Sera* 5 [*Mor.* 550d-e])[4]

Virtue as the key to assimilation can be found also in the Jewish philos-
opher-exegete Philo (who fully quotes *Theaet.* 176a-c in *Fug.* 63, 82).
The anthropological basis of assimilation to God in Philo is Gen 1:26:
human beings made in the image and likeness of God—and specifically
the "second God" or Logos (*QG* 2.62; *Opif.* 144). Following, imitating,
or assimilating to this God (Philo does not draw a sharp distinction between these terms) involves a variety of virtues. For Philo, these virtues
include kindness and charity (*Spec. Leg.* 4.73; *Virt.* 163–68); beneficence and order (*Spec. Leg.* 4.188), contentment and frugality (*Virt.*
8–9), among several others.[5] Virtue, then, is what assimilates one to
God. This point is emphasized over and over again by Platonist philosophers.[6]

Virtue and Deification

Yet is assimilation to God by virtue a form of deification? In the *Nico-
machean Ethics*, Aristotle claims to be summing up a common belief
when he says that "Gods come to be from humans through surpassing

4   For a commentary on this passage, see Van Kooten, *Paul's Anthropology in Context*, 141–148.
5   See further Dillon, *Middle Platonists*, 148; David T. Runia, *Philo of Alexandria
and the Timaeus of Plato* (2 vols.; Amsterdam: VU Boekhandel, 1983), 297–
98; Wendy E. Helleman, "Philo of Alexandria on Deification and Assimilation
to God," *The Studia Philonica Annual* 2 (1990): 51–71.
6   See, e.g., Plot., *Enn.* 1.2.1 and the texts cited below.

virtue (ἐξ ἀνϑρώπων γίνονται ϑεοὶ δι' ἀρετῆς ὑπερβολήν)" (7.1.2, 1145a23). Aristotle is thinking of the great heroes of the past like Hector whose acts of virtue were in fact superhuman. A Homeric hero, says Aristotle, could be a "divine man" (ϑεῖον ἄνδρα). But after the age of heroes, such "divine people" were rare (1145a27).

Heracles is an even better example of an ancient hero deified by means of virtue. According to Diodorus of Sicily, the forefathers of Greece unanimously accorded Heracles immortality on "account of his surpassing virtue (διὰ τὴν ὑπερβολὴν τῆς ἀρετῆς)" (*Bibl.* 4.8.5.7). This is the very same phrase used by Aristotle to speak of deification above.[7] Cicero says something similar about Romulus, who mysteriously disappeared in a violent storm: "the story is that it was his virtue (*virtus*) that caused his translation to heaven (*in caelum dicitur sustulisse*)" (*Rep.* 1.25).[8] Livy writes that Romulus promoted the cult of Heracles as a supporter "of that immortality won by virtue (*virtute parta*) to which his own fates were leading him" (*Ab urbe cond.* 1.7.9; cf. 1.16). Four lines from Horace aptly sum up what appears to be a common Roman sentiment: "Virtue opens a way to heaven for those who deserve not to die (*virtus, recludens immeritis mori caelum*)" (*Odes* 3.2.21–22; trans. David West, cf. Virg., *Aen.* 6.130).

When discussing the deifying power of virtue (ἀρετή, *virtus*), however, one has to be clear on what virtue means. The virtue of the great heroes of old appears to be primarily a martial, not a moral virtue. But this does not mean that the deifying virtue of past heroes is unrelated to Platonic assimilation to God through virtue. In fact, Platonic assimilation to God appears to have been a way to philosophically redescribe—or if you will, *demythologize*—the old heroic ideal of deifying virtue. When Plato was still alive, Xenophon retold a famous myth of Prodicus about the adolescent Heracles (the model Greek hero). The young Heracles, according to the tale, was once approached by two women representing Virtue and Vice. Lady Virtue here clearly represents moral virtue, as is clear from her appearance: "For adornment

---

7   Cf. Plut., *Pelop.* 16; Isoc., *Phil.*, 132; Cic., *Leg.* 2.19; *Tusc* 1.28; *Nat d.* 2.62.
8   The deification of the ancient heroes through virtue became a model for deification in the Roman ruler cult. According to Valerius Maximus, Julius Caesar's virtues prepared for him the path to heaven (*virtutes aditum sibi in caelum struxerunt*) (*Factorum et dictorum memorabilium* 6.9.15). Ovid says the same: Caesar is the one whose virtue added him to the stars (*Caesar … quem virtus addidit astris*) (*Pont.* 4.8.63).

her body had purity, her eyes modesty, her bearing moderation" (Xen., *Mem.* 2.1.22). She exhorts Heracles in this way:

> If you wish the Gods to be gracious to you, you must serve the Gods; if you want to be cherished by your friends you must do good deeds for your friends; if you desire to be honored by some city, you must benefit the city; if you think you deserve to be admired by all Greece for your virtue you must attempt to be the cause of good for Greece. (*Mem.* 2.1.28, trans. Amy L. Bonnette, modified)

In this text, Heracles' virtue is no mere brute force. It is a moral force. The story of a moral Heracles is adapted by Dio Chrysostom (*Or.* 1.58–84), who brings us closer to Paul's day. Zeus, according to Dio, saw that Heracles "wished to be a ruler, not through desire for pleasure and personal gain, which leads most men to love power, but that he might be able to do the greatest good (εὖ ποιεῖν) to the greatest number" (65). To train and test his son, Zeus (through Hermes) leads Heracles to two women: Lady Royalty and Lady Tyranny. Lady Royalty is flanked by personifications of political virtues: Justice, Civic Order, Peace, and Law (or Right Reason). The companions of Lady Tyranny, in turn, are prominent political vices: Cruelty, Insolence, Lawlessness, Faction, and Flattery. When Heracles chooses to admire and love Lady Royalty as a true Goddess, Zeus entrusts Heracles with kingship over the human race. "This," Dio makes clear, "was what made him [Heracles] Deliverer of the earth and of the human race, not the fact that he defended them from the savage beasts—for how little damage could a lion or a wild bear inflict?" (84). Dio indicates that by the first century, Heraclean (i.e., heroic) virtue had been moralized. It was not brute force and battles that led Heracles to the stars, but—as we learn from a letter of Isocrates, it was "the qualities of the spirit, his devotion to humanity (φιλανθρωπίαν), and his good will (εὔνοιαν)" (*Phil.* 114).[9] Plutarch writes that it is not just power that makes up deity, but virtue (*Arist.* 6.2–4). Accordingly, it is "by his virtue" that a ruler "forms himself in the likeness of God (ἀλλ'αὐτὸς αὑτὸν εἰς ὁμοιότητα 9εῷ δι' ἀρε-

---

9   Cf. Seneca on the great Roman hero Scipio Africanus: "That his soul has indeed returned to heaven whence it came, I am convinced, not because he commanded mighty armies—for Cambyses also had mighty armies, and Cambyses was a madman who made successful use of his madness—but because he showed moderation (*moderationem*) and a sense of duty (*pietatem*) to a marvelous extent" (*Ep.* 86.1, trans. Richard Gummere, modified).

τῆς)" (*Princ. iner.* 3 [*Mor.* 780e-f]).[10] Likewise, in the speech of Maecenas to Augustus reported by Dio Cassius, it is a distinctly moral virtue
that "makes many equal to the Gods (ἀρετὴ μὲν γὰρ ἰσοθέους πολλοὺς
ποιεῖ)." "No one ever became a God by a vote," says Maecenas, "so
that for you [Augustus] who are good (ἀγαθός) and who rule well
the whole earth is a sanctuary, all cities are temples, and all human beings sacred statues" (*Rom. Hist.* 52.35.5; cf. Tac., *Ann.* 4.38.2).[11]

I conclude that virtue can indeed refer to a hero's astounding deeds
of power; but by the first century, the language of virtue had been moralized. Thus it is not so easy to distinguish virtue as miraculous power
from virtue as moral excellence. The astounding acts of a ruler or culture hero were often interpreted as acts of beneficence which are just as
much acts of moral and political virtue as they are of raw power. Deification by virtue thus accrued a distinctly moral component. The Jewish and Christian texts treated below, I believe, bear this judgment out.

Josephus, writing in the last quarter of the first century C.E., rewrote
the account of Moses' death for a Greek and Roman audience. At the
end of Moses' life, says Josephus, a "cloud of a sudden descended upon
him and he disappeared in a ravine" (*Ant.* 4.326). Moses, instead of
dying, mysteriously disappeared. The parallel to Romulus' miraculous
end and apotheosis is clear (Livy, *Ab urbe cond.*1:16; Cic., *Rep.* 2.10;
6.21; Plut., *Rom.* 27), but Josephus' account rather boldly contradicts
the biblical report that Moses died (Deut 34:5). The Jewish historian explains the contradiction by claiming that Moses had written in Deuteronomy an account of his own death for fear lest people say that
"by reason of his surpassing virtue (δι' ὑπερβολὴν τῆς περὶ αὐτὸν ἀρετῆς) he had gone back to the divine (πρὸς τὸ θεῖον αὐτὸν ἀναχωρῆσαι)"
(*Ant.* 4.326).[12] There are two points here: (1) the Jewish lawgiver's "virtue" is distinctly moral, and (2) his "return to the divine" appears to be a
Josephan euphemism for what Greeks called "deification." So Josephus
accomplishes two ends: (1) he backhandedly refers to Moses' death—
thus nodding to Deut 34—but since the account of his death was

---

10 Cf. Stob., *Anth.* 4.5.99: "The ruler is the image of God ordering all (ἄρχων δὲ
    εἰκὼν θεοῦ τοῦ πάντα κοσμοῦντος)."

11 Maecenas then advises Augustus, if he truly wants to be immortal, to worship
    the divine (τὸ θεῖον) according to ancestral laws (Dio Cass., *Rom.
    Hist.* 52.36.1).

12 For the phrase δι'ὑπερβολὴν ... ἀρετῆς, cf. Arist., *Nic. eth.* 7.1.2, 1145a23, and
    Diod., *Bibl.* 4.8.5.7 cited above.

only a "decoy" report, he (2) subtly implies that Moses' end was in reality no less grand than the other deified heroes of Greece and Rome.

Philo also seems open to the idea of deification through virtue. For the Jewish exegete, the soul is immortalized through the "greatest of the virtues" (τὴν μεγίστην τῶν ἀρετῶν)—namely godliness (θεοσέβειαν) (*Opif.* 154). Philonic immortalization, I have already argued, is a form of deification.[13] Immortalization is also related to the idea of Platonic assimilation to God. As David Sedley has shown, Aristotle's theory of human immortalization through contemplation (*Nic. eth.* 10.7.8, 1177b27–34) is in fact an Aristotelian interpretation of assimilation to God.[14]

The idea that virtue deifies persists into the third century c.e. when Origen declares that Jesus excelled all those deified by virtue—precisely by his surpassing (moral!) virtue. According to Origen, "Jesus is far, far superior to everyone who for his virtue (διὰ τὴν ἀρετήν) is called a son of God, since he is as it were the source and origin of such virtues" (*Cels.* 1.57). If I can crudely paraphrase, Origen states that his deified hero trumps other deified heroes by being the source of what was commonly thought to deify: virtue.[15]

The Mode of Deification through Moral Virtue

If I have established that it was a popular philosophical idea that (moral) virtue deifies, the question is *how*, exactly, does it do so? To answer this question we return to Plato. Plato, along with most later philosophers, conceives of virtue as a state of mind. Perhaps the chief virtue among Platonists is justice or righteousness (δικαιοσύνη). In the *Republic*, justice

---

13 See ch. 3, 106–109.

14 "'Becoming Like God' in the Timaeus and Aristotle" in *Interpreting the Timaeus – Critias: Proceedings of the IV Symposium Platonicum* (eds. T. Calvo and L. Brisson; Sankt Augustin: Academia, 1997), 336. If Aristotle denies that regular human beings can becomes Gods δι' ὑπερβολὴν ἀρετῆς, he affirms that human beings are immortalized (i. e., deified) by the rational virtue of contemplation (θεωρία). For assimilation to God as a form of deification in Plato, see Salvatore Lavecchia, "Die Ὁμοίωσις Θεῷ in Platons Philosophie," in *Perspektiven der Philosophie; Neues Jahrbuch* (eds. Wiebke Schrader, Georges Goedert and Martina Scherbel; Amsterdam & New York: Rodopi, 2005), 321–94.

15 Interestingly, Origen also claims that due to "their purity of character, surpassing human nature," judges in the Old Testament were called "Gods" by "traditional Jewish usage" (*Cels.* 4.31).

is a quality inherently other-directed (it provides the harmony of the ideal city). Yet justice is also depicted as an inward state, producing self-transcendence. In what follows, I will focus on justice as an inner state.

To explain justice in the ideal city, Plato displays it in the self. To do this, Plato engineers a "technology of the self" which essentially splits the self into two parts: the ruling part (the mind) and the subjugated part (the passions). In the *Timaeus*, the difference is expressed as a difference of motions within the soul. The reasoning part of the soul follows the uniform motion of the Same, whereas the non-rational part (subject to passions) follows the contrary and varied motion of Difference (35a–b; 41d–44c). Although in classical formulations of Plato's anthropology the soul is tripartite, a basic dividing line still appears between the higher and lower parts of the self. It is the mind (located in the head) which controls both the "spirited" and "desiring" parts (located in the chest and belly, respectively).[16] In the interpretation of the Middle Platonist Plutarch,

> The human soul, since it is a portion or a copy of the soul of the universe and is joined together on principles and in proportions corresponding to those which govern the universe, is not simple … but has as one part the intelligent and rational (τὸ νοερὸν καὶ λογιστικόν), whose natural duty it is to govern and rule the individual, and as another part the passionate and irrational (τὸ παθητικὸν καὶ ἄλογον), the variable and disorderly, which has need of a director. This second part is again subdivided into two parts, one of which, by nature ever willing to consort with the body and to serve the body, is called the desiring (ἐπιθυμητικόν); the other, which sometimes joins forces with this part and sometimes lends strength and vigor to reason, is called the spirited part (θυμοειδής). And Plato shows this difference chiefly by the opposition of the reasoning and intelligible part to the desiring and spirited part, since it is by the very fact that these last are different that they are frequently disobedient and quarrel with the better part. (*Virt. mor.* 3 [*Mor.* 441e–442a]; cf. Philo, *Leg.*1.69–70)[17]

---

16 *Tim.* 69c–71a, cf. Philo *Leg.* 3.114–115; *Spec. Leg.* 1.206 with the comments of Runia, *Philo and Timaeus*, 261–64, and esp. 388–89. This is not to deny that occasionally the mind can ally itself with the spirited part. It is merely to acknowledge that, in general, Plato and later Platonists conceive of the θυμοειδής as part of the lower soul (even animals have θύμος), vastly inferior to the divine mind.

17 Plutarch goes on to claim that Aristotle later "assigned the spirited to the desiring part, on the ground that anger is a sort of desire and appetency to requite pain" (*Mor.* 442b). Plutarch himself seems more or less sympathetic to this

Perhaps the most famous image of the tripartite soul functioning in a dualistic way is the image of the charioteer. In brief, the "spirited" and "desiring part" are depicted as two horses, and both are reined in by the charioteer or mind (*Phaedr.* 246a–254e; cf. Philo, *Leg.* 3.118, 127–28, 138). The spirited and desiring parts are essentially related to the needs and urges of the body, whereas the rational mind alone can transcend this mortal life, catching a glimpse of transcendent Beauty. So even though the parts are three, the deep structure of Platonic anthropology posits a basic dualism between (1) the parts of the self interwoven with the body and its desires, and (2) the mind which can (with practice and good breeding) transcend the lower (bodily) self. As Plato writes in the *Laws*:

> There are two elements that make up the whole of every person. One is strong and superior, and acts as master; the other, which is weaker and inferior, is a slave; and so a person must always respect the master in him in preference to the slave. (726a3–6; trans. Trevor J. Saunders, modified)

In the *Phaedo*, he says: "Look at it also this way: when the soul and the body are together, nature orders the one to be subject and to be ruled, and the other to rule and be master" (80a). It is natural for the mind to rule because it is superior and divine. When the mind does not rule, the soul is mastered by the passions: "anger, fear, pleasure, pain, envy, and desires." This is the state of internal injustice. Justice, on the other hand, comes about when the true self, the mind, begins to govern the lower, false self which is finally left behind at death (*Leg.* 863e–864a).

Justice, in this model, is that state in which the lower parts of the soul are ruled by the higher part. Like justice, the other virtues are qualities of mind which enable the state of self-mastery. This is how, for instance, Plato construed the three other cardinal virtues. Sound-thinking or temperance (σωφροσύνη) controls the desiring part in its urge for pleasure, while courage (ἀνδρεία) controls the irrational urge to fear. Wisdom (φρόνησις) means knowing the *rationale* for self-transcendence, which helps to promote it. (Some people, Plato notes, are simply virtuous by nature or habit. To be truly virtuous, however, one engages in self-mastery because one *understands* why it is right and true).

In the words of Daniel Russell (who expounds Plato's *Philebus*),

---

view. The point of the whole treatise (*On Moral Virtue*) from which these selections are taken is to prove (against the Stoics), that the soul is essentially twofold: one part ruling as mind, the other part (connected with body) fit to obey the mind.

the virtuous activity of a human being consists in bringing such order and limit into the inchoate materials of the self, such as one's desires, emotions, feelings, and pleasures. Thus humans have virtues insofar as they use wisdom and reason to bring order to unlimited matter that is, in the first instance, internal to themselves, such as one's passions and desires; and the virtues *are* this ordering of the aspects of oneself according to wisdom and reason. (see [Phileb] 64e)[18]

The overall goal of practicing virtue is not, however, simply self-mastery. It is self-transcendence. The ultimate goal, in other words, is to transcend the lower, false self. Justice is the chief virtue which produces self-transcendence, freeing the mind from slavery to the passions and lusts, and thus molding it for a higher divine life. The mind does not spend all its time controlling heart and belly. When the passions are tamed, the mind can soar above them. The roots of the mind are in heaven. That is, the mind (or soul) is thought of as having kinship with the divine. This idea is pervasive in Plato, and nicely illustrated in the following passage:

> It is necessary to think about the most sovereign form of our soul in this way, namely that God has given it as a *daimon* to each person. We say, first, that this [*daimon*] dwells in the top part of our bodies; and secondly that it lifts us up away from earth and toward our kinsfolk [or *kind*—συγ-γένεια] in heaven. We declare most rightly that we are a plant not earthly but celestial. (*Tim.* 90a)

In this text, the highest part of the human self is not even properly human, but daimonic. This is the part of the self that is directly connected to the divine by a kind of kinship (συγγένεια).[19]

The mind as akin to the divine becomes a fairly standard idea in first-century Stoic and Platonic philosophy.[20] Philo writes that "every person, in respect to the mind (διάνοια), is allied to the divine Reason [or the divine Logos—λόγῳ θείῳ], having come into being as a copy or fragment or effulgence of that blessed nature (τῆς μακαρίας φύσεως ἐκμάγειον ἢ ἀπόσπασμα ἢ ἀπαύγασμα)" (*Opif.* 146; cf. 135;

---

18 "Virtue as 'Likeness to God' in Plato and Seneca," 247–48. For a detailed discussion of the ruling function of mind in Plato, see George Klosko, "The 'Rule' of Reason in Plato's Psychology," *History of Philosophy Quarterly* 5 (1988): 341–56.

19 See further the comments of Runia, *Philo and Timaeus*, 286–89.

20 See Édouard des Places, *Syngeneia: La parenté de l'homme avec dieu d'homère a la patristique* (Paris: Librairie C. Klincksieck, 1964), 63–179. For συγγένεια in Philo, see Runia, *Philo and Timaeus*, 296–97.

Leg. 3.161).[21] Seneca says that the only difference between divine and human nature is that in humans the "better part" (*melior pars*) is mind (*animus*), whereas God *only has* "the better part." He is *all* mind (*totus est ratio*) (*Nat Q. Pref.* §14; cf. Epict., *Diatr.* 1.12.26; 1.14.11). Stoics conceived of God as pure, immanent mind or Reason. Platonists liked to distinguish the primal unknowable and transcendent God from a mediate divinity who is or expresses God's mind, such as the Logos (who often has demiurgic functions). Assimilation to God thus does not compromise (the high) God's transcendence, because it is conceived of as assimilation to the *mediate* God, or the Logos.[22]

For both Platonists and later Stoics, the goal of the virtuous life is the persistent approximation of this divine Mind. To quote Daniel Russell again: "human reason is continuous with divine reason," thus "our activity of bringing order to unlimited matter through reason is continuous with divine activity," and "it is with this aspect of ourselves that we are to identify."[23] Full assimilation to the divine Mind means actually becoming what one is: (wholly) mind. This idea we have already met in Philo, who says that Moses became "most sun-like mind" when he was translated out of this world (*Mos.* 2.288; cf. *Gig.* 60). This radical form of transcendence requires a release from this earthly, corruptible body (*Leg.* 1.108).

Detachment from the body and its lusts begins in this life through practicing the virtues. Since the body is impure, the virtues are often thought of as modes of purification. They are means by which the higher self becomes purer and keener until it best approximates the divine Mind. In a suggestive passage, Plato writes that with wisdom

> we have real courage and moderation and justice and, in a word, true virtue, with wisdom ... and wisdom itself is a kind of cleansing or purifica-

---

21 For human rationality as "divine" (θεῖος) in Philo, see *Leg.* 2.95; *Det.* 29; *Ebr.* 70; *Her.* 84; *Mut.* 184; *Somn.* 1.34. These passages are listed by Runia, *Philo and Timaeus*, 289–90. Runia emphasizes that compared with Plato, Philo's references to the divine mind of human beings is infrequent.

22 For the distinction, see Alcin., *Epit.*, 28.3, Stob., *Anth.* 2.7.3 §f, and the comments of Van Kooten, *Paul's Anthropology*, 158. This is a point central for Philo, as pointed out by Helleman, "Philo on Deification and Assimilation," *passim.* See further on this point Dillon, "The Transcendence of God in Philo: Some Possible Sources," in *Center for Hermeneutical Studies Protocol of the 16th Colloquy (April 1975)* (Vol. 16; Berkeley: Center for Hermeneutical Studies, 1975), 1–8.

23 "Virtue as 'Likeness to God' in Plato and Seneca," 248.

tion. It is likely that those who established the mystic [Eleusinian] rites for
us were not inferior persons but were speaking in riddles long ago when
they said that whoever arrives in the underworld uninitiated and unsancti-
fied will wallow in the mire, whereas he who arrives there purified and in-
itiated will dwell with the Gods. (*Phaedo* 69b-c, trans. Grube)

Much later, Plotinus develops the Platonic idea of purification by virtue:

> What then do we mean when we call these other [non-civic] virtues 'pu-
> rifications,' and how are we made really like by being purified? Since the
> soul is evil when it is thoroughly mixed with the body and shares its expe-
> riences and has all the same opinions, it will be good and possess virtue
> when it no longer has the same opinions but acts alone—this is intelligence
> and wisdom (νοεῖν τε καὶ φρονεῖν)—and does not share the body's experi-
> ences—this is self-control (σωφρονεῖν)—and is not afraid of departing
> from the body—this is courage (ἀνδρίζεσθαι)—and is ruled by reason
> and intellect without opposition—and this is justice (δικαιοσύνη). One
> would not be wrong in calling this state of the soul assimilation to God
> (ὁμοίωσιν ... πρὸς θεόν), in which its activity is intellectual, and it is free
> in this way from bodily affections. (*Enn.* 1.2.3, trans. A. H. Armstrong,
> LCL).[24]

Loyal to Plato, Plotinus describes the four cardinal virtues as ways of detachment from bodily affections and as a mode of self-transcendence.
The virtues of purification are higher than the civic virtues, which
merely control the passions. The ability to exercise purifying virtues already assumes that one has achieved the state of *apatheia*, and thus need
not subdue the lower self. At this stage, the task is not to control, but to
transcend the husk of one's non-noetic self. Since the body is associated
with impure affections, to transcend it by virtue is a form of purification.
The ultimate purification comes when the mind fully detaches from the
body at death. In this way, Plotinus helps to clarify Plato on the actual
goal of assimilation to God. Whereas Plato sees it as dwelling with the
Gods, Plotinus says that assimilation to God means "to be (a) God" (θεόν
εἶναι) (1.2.6).[25] It involves, in other words, a true transcendence of the
conditions of this earthly, human life. It involves deification.

---

24 This passage and others in the same tractate are helpfully commented on by Dil-
    lon, "Plotinus, Philo and Origen on the Grades of Virtue" in *Platonismus und
    Christentum: Festschrift für Heinrich Dörrie* (eds. H.-D. Blume and F. Mann; *Jahr-
    buch für Antike und Christentum, Ergänzungsband* 10; Münster: Aschendorffsche
    Verlagsbuchhandlung, 1983), 92–105; as well as by Van Kooten, *Paul's Anthro-
    pology*, 167–68.
25 See the comments of Van Kooten, *Paul's Anthropology*, 168–70.

In case I am charged with using too late a source to make this argument, I point out that this pattern of transcendence and deification is already laid out by Plutarch in the late first century. In a passage we have already seen before, but well worth emphasizing, Plutarch says that the souls of virtuous human beings

> ascend from men to heroes, from heroes to demi-gods, and from demi-gods, after they have been made pure and holy, as in the final rites of initiation, and have freed themselves from mortality and sense, to Gods (εἰς Ͽεούς), not by civic law, but in very truth and according to right reason, thus achieving the fairest and most blessed consummation. (*Rom.* 28.6–8; cf. *Def. Orac.* 10 [*Mor.* 415a–c])

Here we are clearly talking about post-mortem deification. Although self-transcendence through virtue belongs partly to this life, the "most blessed consummation" occurs when one has left the body behind. It occurs when the mind (or self) becomes so purified that it becomes (a) God.

Paul, Virtue, Self-Transcendence, and the Question of Deification

Do Paul's ethics at all resemble the ethics of deifying virtue in Stoic and Platonic philosophy?[26] On first blush, Paul does not present a theory of deifying virtue (or of virtue at all). That is, he does not present mind, the rational faculty, as naturally divine and thus the key to self-transcendence and deification. Upon further reflection, however, Paul does preach his own "technology of the self" enabling self-transcendence. In his version, however, the divine is not naturally within, but comes from outside and begins to control the passions of the lower self. "We have," says Paul, "the mind of Christ" (1 Cor 2:16). He means, if I can interpret the saying, that the pneuma of Christ has come into the self of believers and functions much as the naturally divine mind in the Platonic and Stoic systems of thought.[27] It functions, that is, as a

---

26 For Paul and virtue, see the excellent article by Engberg-Pedersen, "Paul, Virtues, and Vices," in *Paul in the Greco-Roman World* (ed., J. Paul Sampley: Harrisburg: Trinity Press, 2003), 608–34.

27 In 1 Cor 2:11–16, pneuma and mind are used interchangeably. "For what human being knows what is truly human except the human pneuma that is

higher self which controls and transcends the lower self. As in Plato, this ethic also has an anthropological basis, to which I briefly turn.

Paul's anthropology is frustratingly gapped and complex—but however one understands it in detail, it appears fundamentally dualistic.[28] Most are familiar with Paul's anthropological binaries: "inner human" vs. "outer human" (2 Cor 4:17), the "law of the mind" vs. one's "members [or limbs]" (Rom 7:23), and (most famously) "flesh" lusting against "pneuma" (Gal 5:16–26).[29] Whatever the "flesh" is in this passage, it appears to be the source of the disobedient urges of the false self. It leads to acts and expresses itself in urges which Greek moralists would identify with the passions—those primal, uncontrollable negative emotions which so deeply taint human life. In the vice list starting in Rom 1:29, Paul lists some of these passions: injustice (conspicuously heading the list), evil, greed, vice, jealousy, murder, strife, deceit, malignity, etc. The pneuma, on the other hand, functions as the true or higher self. It leads one not only to "crucify the flesh with its passions and desires" (Gal 5:24), but also to express virtues characteristic of the divine Christ: "love, joy, peace, patience, kindness, generosity, faithfulness, gentleness, and self-control" (Gal 5:22–23). "Self-control" (ἐγκράτεια) is duly emphasized at the end, and reveals Paul's basic point. The higher self has to control—and transcend—the lower self (or passions) to live virtuously.[30]

This basic dualism is reiterated and developed in Romans.[31] In chapter 7, Paul attempts to demonstrate the inability of the Gentiles to fol-

---

within? So also no one comprehends what is truly God's except the pneuma of God … But we have the mind (νοῦς) of Christ" (vv. 11, 16, NRSV).

28 For recent treatments of Pauline anthropology, see Udo Schnelle, *The Human Condition: Anthropology in the Teachings of Jesus, Paul, and John* (trans. O. C. Dean, Jr.; Edinburgh: T&T Clark, 1996); and Van Kooten, *Paul's Anthropology in Context*. Van Kooten sees a tripartite anthropology in Paul (*ibid.*, 269–312). Assuming he is right, a tripartite anthropology in Paul does not (as in Plato) undermine a more deep-structure dualism in Paul's anthropological thought.

29 For instructive comments on Gal 5:16–26, see Engberg-Pedersen, "Paul, Virtues, and Vices," 617–24 and Karl Olav Sandnes, *The Challenge of Homer: School, Pagan Poets and Early Christianity* (LNTS 400; London: T&T Clark, 2009), 261.

30 For a fuller treatment of self-mastery and control of the passions in Paul, see Stanley K. Stowers, *A Rereading of Romans: Justice, Jews, and Gentiles* (New Haven: Yale University Press, 1994), 42–82; *idem.*, "Paul and Self Mastery" in *Paul in the Greco-Roman World: A Handbook*, 524–550, esp. 534–40.

31 In what follows, I adhere closely to the interpretation of Stowers, *Rereading Romans*, 251–84.

low God's law due to their enslavement to the passions. He sees an inward split between mind (which yearns to do good), and "the law of sin" (or flesh) which leads well-meaning Gentiles into sin. By themselves, Gentiles cannot overcome this law of sin, even though their mind can approve of God's "holy, just, and good" law. Paul, whose "I" seems to represent the struggling Gentile, thus finds himself in a state of *akrasia*, or lack of self-control. In rhetorical agony and aporia, the victim of the passions revealingly cries out: "Who will deliver me from this body of death?" (Rom 7:24).

Paul's answer, unsurprisingly, is "Christ Jesus," and specifically the pneuma of Jesus who comes to inhabit believers and lead them to virtue and life. The presence of the divine pneuma of Christ makes Paul's body (or deeds of the body) dead, but his own pneuma alive (8:10, 13). He characterizes this state as being "driven" by the divine pneuma (8:14). The end of pneumatic possession is conformation to and co-glorification with the divine Christ (8:16, 29).

This is a highly simplified version of Paul's soteriology, but it is necessary to keep it simple to reveal the basic structure of his thought. What we have here is in substance a dualistic anthropology in which a higher, true self (the redeemed mind) tames and transcends a lower self (the passions or flesh). We can begin to see here a basic analogy between Paul's anthropology and the anthropology of popular Platonism and Stoicism in Paul's day. To be sure, the lower self is not identical with the body— but still the basic structure of the anthropology pits one part of the self against another.[32] Injustice and lack of inward harmony are expressions of the lower, false self, but these vices are controlled by the higher self led by the divine pneuma (the mind of Christ). Due to their passions, the Gentiles cannot live according to God's justice, but the one driven by God's pneuma cannot but be just and virtuous, fulfilling "the law of Christ" (Gal 6:2).

What this anthropology produces is an ethical vision of transformation and self-transcendence analogous to what we see in popular Platonism. Admittedly, Paul's version of self-transcendence is much more open to divine help—or rather divine possession. Paul teaches that

---

32 For Plato and Paul, "injustice" and "being in the flesh" are both states that are connected to the body. Although Paul has no animus against the body *per se*, he can be quite critical of the unredeemed, corruptible body and its lusts. Redemption, in my reading of Rom 8:23b, does require a separation from this corruptible body.

the divine pneuma enters the self and "drives" it in such a way so as to follow the law of God, and express the virtues of Christ. Still, Paul perceives the basic need to transcend his lower (fleshly) self and conform to the God within (Christ, or the pneuma). As part of his gospel, he constructs an anthropology that enables him to do just that.

This anthropology corresponds to an ethical vision that includes the notion of virtue. For Paul, it is adherence to Christ's virtues which enables self-transcendence. Even though Paul is not partial to the word "virtue" (ἀρετή)—using it only in Phil 4:8—he presents several virtue lists which could be described as qualities of the divine Christ.[33] For Paul, the virtues are "fruits of the pneuma" (Gal 5:22)—the pneuma which Christ is (1 Cor 15:45; 2 Cor 3:17). Being inhabited by the divine pneuma is analogous to being in the state of justice (or inward harmony). The divine pneuma of Christ develops virtue in the believer so that the believer's old self can be controlled and eventually transcended. The human being driven by the pneuma thus becomes a "son of God" (Rom 8:14, cf. 15–16, 19, 23; 1:4), a sonship fully realized when the believer is delivered from the present body (v. 23), glorified (vv. 17–18, 21, 30), and assimilated to the divine Christ (v. 29, cf. 17).

Deepening the Comparison

With this basic structural similarity between the Pauline and Platonic virtue systems in place,[34] we are prepared to look at the different nuances in both (Stoic-Platonic and Pauline) forms of ethical thinking. In Stoic ethics in particular, virtue is called the "perfection (or consummation) of reason."[35] The perfection of reason is the perfection of power—the power of the higher self to rule the lower self. Unlike the perfection

---

33 For a discussion of virtue in Phil 4:8, see Sandnes, *The Challenge of Homer*, 264–67.

34 For "virtue system," see Engberg-Pedersen, "Paul, Virtues, and Vices," 609–613.

35 For the expression, see Cic., *Fin.* 4.13.35. Seneca endows the Gods with perfect (*consummata*) virtue (*Ep.* 92.27). Early Stoics would describe virtues as modulations of reason, in the continued effort toward realizing self-mastery (*SVF* 1.202 = Plut., *Virt. mor.* 3 [*Mor.* 441b-c]). Note also Russell: "In Seneca, virtue is rationality, which is something transcendent and part of our divine nature, but it is also the essence of our humanity" ("Virtue as 'Likeness to God' in Plato and Seneca," 253).

of reason, one might argue, there is no perfection of pneuma in Paul—it is, as a divine entity, already perfect. And yet if we define the perfection of reason as that state in which the body perfectly follows reason, then there is an analogue in Paul's pneumatic ethics. As Paul knew, Christ-believers can have the divine pneuma, but not follow it perfectly. They could defile the pneuma within (cf. 1 Cor 6:15–16), or quench it (1 Thess 5:19; cf. Eph 4:30). In these cases, it is likely that the pneumatic Christ has not been "fully formed" in the Christian (following the language of Gal 4:19). Nevertheless, the inward pneuma can attain a sort of augmentation or perfection. At this point, the believer is prepared to fully follow or, as Paul prefers, "walk in" the pneuma (Gal 5:16).

Yet how is the divine pneuma "walked in"? Is pneuma a kind of thinking? Interestingly, the Stoics thought of the pneuma as a kind of fiery thought, a piece of the higher Mind. When Paul speaks of the renewal of the mind (Rom 12:2), this presumably occurs through the pneuma (a point he dwells on in Rom 8). If the pneuma is not the divine thought of the Christian, it is arguably what Pauline Christians constantly "think with" to instantiate right action in the world. "We have the mind of Christ" (1 Cor 2:16) is, I take it, a statement semantically parallel to "the pneuma of God dwells in you" (Rom 8:9).[36] The pneuma would in this reading have a noetic impact. It is the divine mind working within to guide the devotee of Christ into right thinking and consequently right action (again, Rom 12:2). Just as the human pneuma, a fragment of the divine Mind, thinks within the Stoic, so the pneuma is Christ's divine mind thinking (and at one point groaning) in the believer (Rom 8:26b).[37]

In popular Platonism and Stoicism, the mind is the divine part of the self ruling over the non-divine part. Stoics called the mind a "fragment of God" (Epict., *Diatr.* 1.14.6; 2.8.2), or the "God within" (Sen., *Ep.* 41.1). Philo is willing to maintain this terminology to express his Jewish understanding of humans in the image of God (e.g., *Opif.* 146; *Det.* 86–87, 90). My point, however, is *not* that the infused divine pneuma and the innate divine mind are the same thing in Pauline and popular Stoic ethics. Rather, I argue that they have a similar *func-*

---

36 As Van Kooten points out, those who have Christ's mind are the true *pneuma-tikoi* (*Paul's Anthropology in Context*, 306).

37 For a fuller exposition of the cognitive role of the pneuma, see Engberg-Pedersen, *Cosmology and the Self*, 75–87.

tion. Both Christ's divine pneuma and the naturally divine mind, that is, control and eventually transcend the lower self (the passions and desires). But if the mind is the divine part of the self in popular Stoic and Platonic thinking, is it right to speak of the pneuma as the divine part of the self in Paul?

Here again we run into a basic question of interpretation. It is agreed that the divine pneuma is not a "natural" part of Paul's redeemed self, but does the pneuma *become effectively integrated* into the redeemed self? Again, many interpreters have a strong initial impression that the divine pneuma is and always remains wholly external to the self of the redeemed. It is simply a divine agent working within the self not intrinsically connected to the inner operations of Paul's mind. But this judgment, as pointed out in chapter 5, seems not altogether true to Paul. "*We have the mind of Christ*" (1 Cor 2:16). Paul's converts have undergone a complete cognitive transformation. They are directed by a divine mind that transcends their old self. That divine mind is the pneumatic Christ. In 1 Cor 6:17, Paul presents the divine pneuma as becoming one with the pneuma of the redeemed. If in other passages he maintains a dialectic between his mind or pneuma and the divine pneuma, he is sometimes prepared to submerge his self in preference for the pneumatic Christ dwelling within: "*I no longer live*; Christ lives in me" (Gal 2:20, emphasis added). Is this mere hyperbole? I believe that something real is going on here not easy for us (who underestimate the power of spirit-possession) to grasp. The divine pneuma who comes to dwell in the believer comes to operate as the controlling mind of the self. Consequently, it is occasionally impossible to separate Paul's mind from Christ's. This is not to say that one cannot always intellectually distinguish Paul's pneuma (or mind) from Christ's mind. It is merely to confess that Christ's pneuma becomes so integrated into Paul's thinking and being that he can occasionally identify his true self with the pneumatic and divine Christ. This does not mean that Paul's self is obliterated; it does mean that that Paul's false self is transcended. Control by the divine mind is what makes Paul and his converts "not merely human" (οὐκ ἄνθρωποι) (1 Cor 3:4, NRSV).

Paul and Assimilation to God

For Paul, it is not only the pneumatic Christ within who leads him to transformation and self-transcendence, it is also the Christ without. As in Platonism, Paul's ethics presents a form of assimilation to God. In this case, it is the particular and peculiar God Christ.

The idea of imitating Christ is arguably basic to Paul's ethics.[38] In 1 Thess 1:6 he tells his converts: "you became imitators (μιμηταί) of us and of the Lord [Jesus]"—specifically in suffering religious persecution. In 1 Corinthians 11:1, Paul says, "Become imitators (μιμηταί) of me just as I am of Christ."[39] The question is how exactly do Christians imitate the divine Christ? My discussion will touch on three passages: Romans 15:1–8, 2 Corinthians 8:9, and Philippians 2:6–8—with no intent to present a full exegesis.[40] In each of these passages, Paul is engaged in ethical reflection. In each case he uses the model of Christ to morally shape the thoughts and dispositions of his listeners. As he says in that (difficult to translate) passage in Phil 2:5, "Ponder among yourselves what is also

---

38 Resistance to the idea of *imitatio Christi* in Paul was expressed by some scholars in the mid-twentieth century (such as Wilhelm Michaelis and Ernst Käsemann), but scholarship seems to have moved beyond this. For relevant treatments of the topic, see C. M. Proudfoot, "Imitation or Realistic Participation: A Study of Paul's Concept of 'Suffering with Christ'," *Interpretation* 17 (1963): 140–60; Richard A. Burridge, *Imitating Jesus: An Inclusive Approach to New Testament Ethics* (Grand Rapids: Eerdmans, 2007), 144–48. I realize that some scholars want to distinguish imitation from assimilation. In this chapter, however, both refer to the process of "becoming like" someone specifically in moral character. The imitation of Christ is moral assimilation to him.

39 The idea of imitating a deity through imitating the deity's messenger is also found in Philostratus' *Life of Apollonius*: "Let us go … Apollonius—you following God, and I you (ἴωμεν … Ἀπολλώνιε, σὺ μέν Θεῷ ἑπόμενος, ἐγὼ δὲ σοί)" (1.19).

40 For fuller exegetical treatments, see Michael Thompson, *Clothed with Christ: The Example and Teaching of Jesus in Romans 12.1–15.13* (JSNTSS 59; Sheffield: Sheffield Academic Press, 1991), 208–36; Linda L. Belleville, "'Imitate Me, Just as I Imitate Christ': Discipleship in the Corinthian Correspondence," in *Patterns of Discipleship in the New Testament* (ed. Richard N. Longenecker; Grand Rapids: Eerdmans, 1996), 120–42; Gerald F. Hawthorne, "The Imitation of Christ: Discipleship in Philippians," in *ibid.* 163–79; Stephen Fowl, "Christology and Ethics in Philippians 2:5–11," in *Where Christology Began: Essays on Philippians 2* (eds. R. P. Martin and B. J. Dodd; Louisville: Westminster John Knox, 1998), 140–53; Brian J. Dodd, "The Story of Christ and the Imitation of Paul in Philippians 2–3," in *ibid* 154–60; Van Kooten, *Paul's Anthropology*, 206–214; 357–92.

in Christ Jesus (τοῦτο φρονεῖτε ἐν ὑμῖν ὃ καὶ ἐν Χριστῷ Ἰησοῦ)." If I can interpret this remark, Paul wants his converts to cognitively assimilate Christ's example so that they can ethically conform to his divine character.

In Romans 14–15, Paul admonishes the faction of the "strong" to accommodate the desire of the "weak" Christians who wish to maintain stricter dietary practices.[41] In Romans 15, Paul points to Christ as the divine model of accommodation. "Christ did not please himself" (v. 3). Rather, he became a servant to the circumcised (i. e., the Jews) to bring about Gentile redemption (fulfilling the promise to the patriarchs) (vv. 5–9a). Christ, though a divine being, was born a Jewish peasant to fulfill God's design to bring in the Gentiles apart from Law (Rom 3:21). Paul thus urges "strong" Christians to imitate the accommodating Christ for the sake of communal harmony with "weak" believers.

In 2 Cor 8:9, Paul presents us with a version of his exchange formula: "For you know the generous act of our Lord Jesus Christ, that though he was rich, yet for your sakes he became poor, so that by his poverty you might become rich." In this chapter, Paul delicately attempts to persuade the (somewhat sensitive and suspicious) Corinthians to give to the church of Jerusalem. Paul considers the Corinthians to be rich, both monetarily and spiritually (1 Cor 1:4–7). In v. 9, he draws in Christ as a moral exemplar. It seems best to interpret Christ's act of self-impoverishment in terms of Christ's becoming human.[42] Christ, as a divine being, was immensely rich in power and glory. Yet to bestow a benefit on people, he became human—subjecting himself to weakness and bodily needs. This incarnational theology translates readily into monetary terms: the Corinthians who are rich should give to the Judean Christians who are (materially) poor. Giving money is thus made into ethical assimilation to the divine Christ.

The basic thought of 2 Cor 8:9 seems to be expanded in Phil 2:6–8. Here we learn that, in his preexistent state (following most interpreters), Christ was "in the form of God" and equal to God. In obedience to God, he was "born in human likeness." Taking on human form is characterized as a self-emptying act of conforming to a

---

41 For the (contested) identity of the "strong" and the "weak," see the discussion in Mark Reasoner, *The Strong and the Weak: Romans 14.1–15.13 in Context* (SNTSMS 103; Cambridge: Cambridge University Press, 1999).

42 Margaret Thrall, *The Second Epistle to the Corinthians* (2 vols.; ICC; Edinburgh: T&T Clark, 1994), 2.532–534.

"slave." Even in this slave form, Christ follows the command of his Father to further humiliation: death on a cross. All of this translates immediately into ethical exhortation: obedience to Paul (v. 12), the cessation of grumbling (v. 14), and mutual submission for the sake of unity (vv. 2–4). The point is that, at least in vv. 6–8, Christ is an ethical exemplar for the Philippians.[43] Just as he did not "think" (ἡγήσατο) equality with God was something to be exploited (v. 6), the Philippians should not "think" (ἡγούμενοι) themselves to be better than anyone else (v. 3). Christ's humility and self-subordination, even unto a shameful death, are exactly the kinds of virtues Paul wishes to foster among the Philippian Christians.

In all three passages, Christ's divine power is expressed through self-subjugating humility. This humility is chiefly expressed in his becoming human (Phil 2:6–8; 2 Cor 8:9), but it also includes Christ's acts while as a human (Rom 15:13), notably his dying on a cross (Phil 2:8). Thus assimilation to this particular God involves corresponding acts of humility and self-subordination. This is the peculiar character of the Christian God. As much as immortality and power are constitutive of Godhood in general, humility and self-subordination define Paul's conception of deity.[44]

It is no surprise, then, that when Paul speaks of imitating Christ he so often turns to the topic of suffering. Although suffering is not a Pauline virtue *per se*, fostering the basic Christic virtues of humility and self-subordination often lead to it. Suffering in this sense means quite literally to "bear under" (*sub-fero*) the burdens of hatred, abuse, and anger that arise as a result of practicing Christ's virtues. By assimilating to Christ's virtues, one assimilates to Christ. Paul, for instance, sees his suffering as a radical assimilation to the divine Christ. He bears the stigmata of Christ (Gal 6:17). He is always carrying around the death (or "dying," νέκρωσιν) of Jesus in his body, and being handed over to death for Jesus' sake (2 Cor 4:10–11). If this is a metaphor, it has a practical meaning. Assimilating to Paul's God involves the gradual death (through repeated suffering) of the physical body. Pauline ethics is a preparation for death.

---

43   Larry Hurtado, "Jesus as Lordly Example in Philippians 2:5–11," in *From Jesus to Paul: Studies in Honour of Francis Wright Beare* (eds. P. Richardson and J.C. Hurd; Waterloo, Ont.: Wilfred Laurier University Press, 1984), 113–26.
44   On this point, see Gorman, *Inhabiting*, 9–39; cf. 105–28.

Paul's Christic sufferings are, however, also acts of power. As is typical for Paul, divine power is expressed in weakness (cf. 2 Cor 13:4). In Philippians, Christ's self-subjugating humility results in the subjugation of the lesser powers to the rule of Christ (Phil 2:10–11; cf. Col 2:15). In 2 Cor 8:9, it results in the enrichment of the Gentiles. In Rom 15, it results in the confirmation of the promises to the patriarchs, that the nations would be included in God's salvation (15:13). It is through the acts of Christ's self-subjugation that the peculiar power of the Hebrew God known of old is manifested (1 Cor 1:24): a rescuing and right-making power (Rom 1:16–17). For Paul himself, participation in the death of Christ results in life. Carrying around Jesus' death results in a visible (indeed, corporeal) manifestation of life for Paul and his converts (2 Cor 4:10–12).[45]

Those who participate in the sufferings of Christ partake of the very power that makes Christ divine. The sufferings result, that is, in immortal life and superhuman power. The immortal life is the life of the pneuma who renews the true inward self while the body dies away (2 Cor 4:16–17). The superhuman power is the salvific effect Paul's suffering has on his communities. Paul abundantly shares the sufferings of Christ—and also what results: consolation (παράκλησις). This consolation is also a "salvation" (σωτηρία) which abundantly overflows to the Corinthian community (2 Cor 1:3–7). Paul affirms something similar in 2 Cor 4:12. He dies with Christ—i. e., he exercises Christ's self-subordinating virtue in his apostolic ministry—and this produces life for his community (i. e., health, safety).[46] The power of Paul's suffering is thus a Christic—which is to say *divine*—power. It is the kind of power, that is, which produces divine life in the community. The author of Colossians, though probably not Paul, has finely drawn out the logic of Paul's thought in the following saying: "I am now rejoicing in my sufferings for your sake, and in my flesh I am completing what is

---

45 For power in weakness in Paul, see R. Tannehill, *Dying and Rising with Christ* (Berlin: Alfred Töpelmann, 1967), 107, 112, 128; G.G. O'Collins, "Power Made Perfect in Weakness: 2 Cor 12–10" *CBQ* 33 (1971): 528–537; J. D. G. Dunn *Jesus and the Spirit: A Study of the Religious and Charismatic Experience of Jesus and the First Christians as Reflected in the New Testament* (London: SCM Press, 1975), 326–28.

46 For Paul as expressing Christ's self-subjugating humility, see Christian Wolff, "Humility and Self-Denial in Jesus' Life and Message and in the Apostolic Existence of Paul," in *Paul and Jesus: Collected Essays* (ed. A.J.M. Wedderburn; JSNTSS 37; Sheffield: Sheffield Academic Press, 1989), 145–160.

lacking in Christ's afflictions for the sake of (ὑπέρ) his body, that is, the church" (1:24). Paul's sufferings for the community are Christic sufferings that are nothing less than salvific. They are nothing less than manifestations of Christ's divine power to provide life and salvation for others.

I think it possible to call Paul's participation in Christ's power-through-weakness a "moral" form of assimilation to God since sharing Christ's life-giving power—which is manifest in humility and self-subjugating death—is a distinctly moral act. It involves subordinating the interests of the self for the benefit and salvation of others. Christ, like Yahweh, is a moral deity, a God whose divinity is expressed in a moral act of condescension for the benefit of others.[47] Christ's humility is a peculiar kind of divine trait; participation in his divinity results in a peculiar kind of deification.[48]

2 Corinthians 3:18 as Moral Assimilation to God

There is one final passage that cannot be passed over in a book on Paul and deification: 2 Corinthians 3:18.[49] This passage has been called the "most frankly theotic passage in Paul,"[50] and is of immediate relevance

---

47   Christ is not the only self-subordinating deity in the Greco-Roman world. Note the self-subordination of Polydeuces who "refused to become even a God by himself, but chose rather to become a demigod with his brother and to share his mortal portion upon the condition of yielding to Castor part of his own immortality" (Plut., *Frat. amor.* 12 [*Mor.* 484e]; cf. Philo, *Legat.* 84–85).

48   Assimilating to other types of Gods has a distinct color since other Gods, unsurprisingly, have different characters. In the *Phaedrus* 246e-253c, for instance, Plato writes of human beings assimilating to specific Gods (mythically characterized as Olympians) through specifically moral actions. For a discussion of this text in relation to Paul, see Van Kooten, *Paul's Anthropology*, 131–33. Cf. also Plut., *Sera* 5 (*Mor.* 550d-e). Some might claim that the (immoral) character of Greek Gods is different from the (moral) character of Christ. There is not a little Christian bias in this judgment. Nevertheless, if other Gods were not great moral exemplars, Plato's Gods (who can be nothing but good and just) certainly do not fall under this axe. (See further Van Kooten, *Paul's Anthropology*, 210).

49   Due to my other published treatments of this passage (Litwa, "2 Corinthians 3:18 and Theosis," and "Transformation through a Mirror: Moses in 2 Cor. 3.18" forthcoming in *JSNT*, spring 2012), my discussion will be abbreviated.

50   Finlan, "Can we Speak," 75.

(I argue) for the idea of moral assimilation to God. The text reads: "And all of us, with unveiled faces, seeing the glory of the Lord as though reflected in a mirror (κατοπτριζόμενοι), are being transformed (μεταμορφούμεθα) into the same image (τὴν αὐτὴν εἰκόνα) from one degree of glory to another (ἀπὸ δόξης εἰς δόξαν); for this comes from the Lord, the Spirit" (NRSV). Meister Eckhart minces no words when he paraphrases this verse: "We shall be completely transformed and changed into God!"[51] That this verse might sound like a form of deification may be granted, but a deification through moral assimilation to God? This seems unfounded. Nevertheless, moral assimilation to the God Christ is, I propose, basic to Paul's understanding of transformation in this verse.

The exegesis of 2 Cor 3:18 in its literary context is common in recent scholarship.[52] Since little new can be said, it seems best not to exhaust the reader by repeating the exercise. Instead, I will focus on 2 Cor 3:18 and its implications for deification. Specifically, my task will be to show how the verse supports a distinctly moral version of deification.

Perhaps the best way to present my moral reading of deification in 2 Cor 3:18 is to compare it with another recent interpretation that sees deification in this verse. In a stimulating book, April DeConick situates 2 Cor 3:18 in the context of ancient "vision mysticism," reconstructed from an assortment of Jewish, Hermetic, and Gnostic texts. She argues that Paul speaks in 2 Cor 3:18 of a "face-to-face encounter with oneself" because he employs the middle form of κατοπτρίζω, which, according to DeConick, designates self-vision. From this perspective, the vision in 3:18 is "a vision of one's divine self" into which one is transformed.[53] The larger framework of this interpretation she sketches as follows:

---

51 German sermon 6, translated by Edmund Colledge and Bernard McGinn in *Meister Eckhart: The Essential Sermons, Commentaries, Treatises, and Defense* (Mahwah, NJ: Paulist Press, 1981), 188.

52 Besides the commentaries, see Frances Back, *Verwandlung durch Offenbarung bei Paulus: Eine religionsgeschichtlich-exegetische Untersuchung zu 2 Kor 2,14–4,6* (WUNT 253; Tübingen: Mohr Siebeck, 2002), 77–159; Lorenzen, *Eikon*, 211–243; Paul B. Duff, "Transformed 'from Glory to Glory': Paul's Appeal to the Experience of His Readers in 2 Cor 3:18," *JBL* 127 (2008): 762–780; Blackwell, *Christosis*, 174–212.

53 DeConick, April D., *Voices of the Mystics, Early Christian Discourse in the Gospels of John and Thomas and Other Ancient Christian Literature* (JSNTSS 157; Sheffield: Sheffield Academic, 2001), 65–66.

within … visionary circles of early Jewish mysticism, it was believed that exceptionally righteous or worthy humans would be transformed into the divine upon gaining a vision of God. The paradigms for such transformations were the transformations of the heroes of the heavenly ascent narratives such as Moses, Ezekiel and Enoch as well as the Jewish tradition that the righteous would be transformed in the world to come.[54]

The mention of Moses is especially apropos to 2 Cor 3:18. Although Paul started in 3:6–13 to contrast himself with Moses—declaring himself a better minister of a better covenant who is not ashamed to reveal a greater glory of God—in 3:16–18, Moses has become an implicit model for Christian vision.[55] It was Moses who would go into the tabernacle, remove the veil, and behold the glory of the Lord in the ancient story (Ex 34:34; cf. 33:8–11). In the present time, however, Paul reserves this privilege for his converts (2 Cor 3:16). In the context of 2 Corinthians 3, Paul refers to the veil lying over the hearts of the Jews when they read the Torah (vv. 14–15). Then he draws his contrast: Christians (the "we all" in v. 18) see as in a mirror the "glory of the Lord"—a Lord whom Paul identifies with the pneuma (v. 17). This pneumatic Lord I take to be Christ.[56] The practice in which one sees

---

54 *Seek to See Him: Ascent and Vision Mysticism in the Gospel of Thomas* (Supplements to Vigiliae Christianae 33; Leiden: Brill, 1996), 31.

55 Cf. Duff, who sees Moses in 2 Cor 3:16–18 as "a type for all believers" ("From Glory to Glory," 767).

56 Several scholars have argued that the "Lord" in vv. 16–18 is a reference to Yahweh, not Christ (e. g., Murray Harris, *Second Epistle*, 314–15). Perhaps one can say that for Paul, the "Lord" is Yahweh *and* Christ because Paul, apostle of the new covenant, thinks of "Yahweh in Christ" (D. Greenwood, "The Lord is the Spirit: Some Considerations of 2 Corinthians 3.17," *Catholic Biblical Quarterly* 34 [1972]: 470). The identity of Yahweh had to a certain extent melded into the identity of Christ, such that they could share a name (Phil 2:10–11). But there are two indications that Paul thinks of the "Lord" in vv. 16 and 18 specifically as Christ. The first comes in v. 16 itself. There Paul says that for anyone who turns to the Lord, the veil is taken away. Turning back to v. 14, Paul says that the veil is (only) removed in Christ (ἐν Χριστῷ). This point suggests that Paul sees the "Lord" in v. 16 as Christ. Second, Paul indirectly clarifies who the "Lord" is in 4:5. Here the Apostle insists that "we do not preach ourselves, but Jesus Christ as Lord." *Jesus Christ as Lord*, according to Paul, is the basic content of his gospel, which is also the gospel "of the glory of *Christ*" (4:4; cf. "glory of the Lord" in 3:18). Although 4:5 is not a direct commentary on 3:16 and 18, it does at least show that Christ as "Lord" is at the forefront of Paul's mind as he speaks of the "Lord" in the same context.

the glorious, pneumatic Christ is transformative. It transforms the viewer, specifically, into "the same image" (τὴν αὐτὴν εἰκόνα) as Christ.[57]

The ambiguity here is whether Christians are transformed into Christ's image, or into the image of God *which Christ is*. Alan Segal evidently takes the latter view, using the language of "transformation into (the) Christ."[58] Christ, as Paul later clarifies, is the "image of God" (2

---

57   Some interpreters maintain an ecclesial reading of "the same image": "Christians are changed into the same image as each other" (N. T. Wright, "Reflected Glory: 2 Corinthians 3:18" in *The Glory of Christ in the New Testament* [eds. L. D. Hurst and N. T. Wright; Oxford: Clarendon Press, 1987], 147; cf. W. C. van Unnik, "'With Unveiled Face', an Exegesis of 2 Cor. iii 12–18" in *Sparsa Collecta: The Collected Essays of W. C. Van Unnik* [Leiden: Brill, 1973], 208–209; and Linda L. Belleville, *Reflections of Glory: Paul's Polemical Use of the Moses-Doxa Tradition in 2 Corinthians 3.1–18* [JSNTSS 52; Sheffield: JSOT Press, 1991], 290, 296). This interpretation is less likely, since Paul clearly says that Christians are, like Moses of old, looking at "the glory of the Lord" *not at the faces of each other*. Paul's whole image assumes that Christians are being transformed into what they are looking at—and they are not being transformed into each other. (Besides, what would it mean to be transformed into each other?)

58   *Life After Death: A History of the Afterlife in the Religions of the West* (New York: Doubleday, 2004), 416. Cf. Scroggs, who argues that in 2 Cor 3:18 believers are to be "transformed into that image in which Christ now exists." Scroggs calls this "a strict identity between Christ and the believer," and he draws on a number of texts to support the idea (*Last Adam*, 69–70, 83, 104). The language of transformation "into Christ" also appears in Jan Lambrecht, "Transformation in 2 Cor. 3,18" in *Studies on 2 Corinthians* (Leuven: Leuven University Press, 1994), 296, cf. 298, 306. J. A. Fitzmyer vehemently opposes this interpretation. "Paul never so expresses it," Fitzmyer underscores, "that the person is transformed *into* Christ himself, as the pagan myths might suggest." For Fitzmyer, the "same image" into which believers are being transformed is not the "same image" that Christ is, but a "likeness" of Christ ("Glory Reflected on the Face of Christ [2 Cor. 3.7–4.6] and a Palestinian Jewish Motif," *Theological Studies* 42 [1981]: 644). Thus the transformation, Fitzmyer affirms, does not turn one into Christ, but into a "Christian" (*ibid.*, 638). My sense is that Fitzmyer, in making this interpretation, desires to protect Paul from so-called "pagan" ideas in the larger culture. This is, I take it, an apologetic move. Yet it can also be opposed on exegetical grounds: if Paul thinks his converts are merely being changed into a likeness of Christ (which is something different than Christ), why did Paul use the adjective *"the same* image"? The adjective "the same" functions to underscore that the image is not other than the image which Christ himself is. Christians, in other words, are not being transformed into a lesser image than the true image. See further Lambrecht, "Transformation," 303–306.

Cor 4:4).[59] This implies more than that Christ is a perfect human being.[60] He is a divine being. Thus to be transformed into *the image that Christ is* (as I interpret it) is to be changed into the divine image. This amounts to, I argue, a participation in Christ's divinity.[61] The transformation is thus a deifying transformation.

How do we understand this deifying transformation? Eschatologically speaking, the transformation is a transformation into divine glory, and specifically a glorified/pneumatic body (see chapters 4–5). Unlike in similar passages, however (Rom 8:29; Phil 3:21; 1 Cor 15:49), Paul's focus in 2 Cor 3:18 does not appear to be eschatological. He uses a present tense verb: μεταμορφούμεθα—"we *are being* transformed." The only other place Paul uses the verb μεταμορφόω is in Rom 12:2, where he tells Gentile converts: "Do not be conformed to this world, but be transformed (μεταμορφοῦσθε) [again present tense] by the renewing of your minds, so that you may discern what is the will of God—what is good and acceptable and perfect." In this verse, Paul is clearly focused on ethical transformation. The repetition of the distinctive verb μεταμορφόω in Rom 12:2 (recall that Paul wrote Romans while in Corinth) indicates that it may be a development of his thought in 2 Cor 3:18. The metamorphosis in 3:18, in this reading, would be—at least in part—a moral metamorphosis.[62]

---

59 Back wrongfully attempts to divorce the image of God from the image of Christ (*Verwandlung*, 150).

60 *Pace* Scott Hafemann, *Paul, Moses, and the History of Israel* (Milton Keynes, UK: Paternoster, 2005), 407–34.

61 Litwa, "2 Cor 3:18 and Theosis," 118–128. That transformation in 2 Cor 3:18 is simultaneously a "divinization" Segal explicitly states, although he apparently makes the divinization equivalent to "angelification" (*Life After Death*, 419). Later, Segal writes that in "Paul's writing we have for the first time a record of the experience of mystic transformation of a limited human self into a transcendent divinity" (*ibid.*, 440).

62 Litwa, "2 Cor 3:18 and Theosis," 129–32. For the moral interpretation of transformation in 2 Cor 3:18, see also Harris, *Second Epistle*, 316. Perhaps the most vigorous advocate of the moral interpretation of 2 Cor 3:18 is Hafemann, *Paul, Moses, and the History of Israel*, 407–34. Although his interpretation is helpful in many respects, Hafemann errs in (1) opposing a moral and a material understanding of metamorphosis, and (2) in thinking that moral transformation means solely assimilation to the *human* Christ (or the "second Adam"). The virtues of Christ are just as much part of his divine identity as his human identity. No attempt to artificially separate them is convincing. Back disputes the moral interpretation of 2 Cor 3:18. "That Christians," he says, "are made capable through the reception of the Spirit for a new life in which the will of God

This means that going "from glory to glory" in 2 Cor 3:18 is a process that includes both a physical and a moral transformation.[63] Christians are being physically transformed as they are being morally transformed.[64] The moral transformation begins with a full cognitive transformation, and is accompanied by a gradual physical transformation.[65] The full cognitive transformation is the "renewal of the mind" (ἀνακαίνωσις τοῦ νοός) which leads to moral thinking and acting (Rom 12:2–21). This moral renewal appears to be parallel to the "renewal" of the inner self (ὁ ἔσω ἡμῶν ἀνακαινοῦται) mentioned in 2 Cor 4:16, which leads to "an eternal weight of glory" (v. 17).

Therefore, Pauline soteriology includes at least two levels of transformation: one moral, the other material. The moral transformation is the transformation of the mind to conform to the mind of Christ (cf. Phil 2:5; 1 Cor. 2:16). Naturally this leads to appropriate bodily action in the world. It is the mind which leads the body on the path of virtue. Material transformation is specifically the transformation of the body to conform to the resurrected and glorified body of Christ (Phil. 3.21). In the glorified and pneumatic body, there will be a perfect harmony between the body and the renewed mind. Moral and material transformation cannot be neatly partitioned off as present and eschatological. They both operate simultaneously until the full eschatological transformation occurs.

Let me return to the interpretation of DeConick to try to describe a distinctly Pauline understanding of deification in 2 Cor 3:18. First of all, I think that DeConick is fundamentally right that 2 Cor 3:18 in a Corinthian context should be read as implying a form of deification.[66] Fur-

---

can be fulfilled is indeed an important aspect of Pauline thought. It is not, however, the theme of 2 Cor 3" (*Verwandlung*, 154). Paul's concern to morally shape and reshape the lives and thought of the Corinthians is, I will argue, very much part of the logic of 2 Cor 3–4. Back's further contention that μεταμορφοῦσθαι in 2 Cor 3:18 and Rom 12:2 has an "entirely different meaning" is overstated (*ibid.*).

63 On ἀπὸ δόξης εἰς δόξαν, see Duff, "From Glory to Glory," 771–774. My sympathies remain with Thrall's interpretation, *Second Epistle*, 285–86.

64 Engberg-Pedersen, "Complete and Incomplete Transformation," 129–46.

65 *Ibid.*, 137–38.

66 In the old History of Religions School, scholars liked to compare the transformation in 2 Cor 3:18 with the deifying metamorphosis of initiates in the mystery cults (e. g., Apul., *Met.* 11.23). Given our increased knowledge of the mystery cults, this interpretation has long fallen out of favor. To conclude, however, that 2 Cor 3:18 is therefore not at all Hellenistic or has nothing to do with de-

thermore, the deifying transformation occurs through vision, which appears to be an element (as she says) of "Greek mysteriosophy."[67] To faithfully describe a *Pauline* form of deification, however, I think we need also to relate some Pauline distinctives in 2 Cor 3:18. This leads me to some slight disagreements and modifications of DeConick's position. First, Paul's vision in the mirror is not the vision of the divine self if that means that the self is *naturally* divine. The self, rather, sees Christ the Glory of God and becomes Christ—the divine Image—in a present process of metamorphosis. Second, the metamorphosis happens in community (the "we all" in 3:18), and is not just a process of individual mystical vision. Finally, Pauline present-tense metamorphosis is a *moral* metamorphosis. By seeing the glory of Christ, Paul's converts are prepared to live in conformation to Christ's divine character.

To sum up, Paul sees the same moral transformation going on in him as an apostle as that which (he hopes!) will affect his converts. Paul claims to be a more capable minister than Moses, with an unveiled face revealing the greater glory of God "in the face of Christ" (2 Cor 4:6). He claims that he and Christians are being transformed into the glory of Christ. Paul's focus in 3:18 is on the present, and his present character as a minister of Christ. As he says:

> We have renounced the shameful things that one hides; we refuse to practice cunning or to falsify God's word; but by the open statement of the truth we commend ourselves to the conscience of everyone in the sight of God. ... For we do not proclaim ourselves; we proclaim Jesus Christ as Lord and ourselves as your slaves for Jesus' sake. (2 Cor 4:2, 5)

Paul is a better minister because his conscience commends him as a candid slave of God and of others (cf. 2 Cor 1:12–14). Just as Christ, who took on the form of a slave (Phil 2:7), Paul has subordinated his self for

---

ification (as is concluded by Heinz-Dietrich Wendland, *Die Briefe an die Korinther* [Göttingen: Vandenhoeck & Ruprecht, 1980], 184–185, and more recently by Back, *Verwandlung*, 146–47) seems precipitous.

67   *Voices of the Mystics*, 66. The transformation of the soul by seeing an external object is vividly demonstrated in the *Phaedrus*. Here a stream of beauty coming in from the beloved causes the soul of the lover to, as Plato says, sprout wings. Growing wings is the beginning of a radical transformation which results in a form of deification. Seeing the image of Beauty through the beloved leads to an assimilation of the lover—not to Beauty itself—but to the character and customs of the patron God who enabled the vision of Beauty long ago (252d–253c). Here we have deifying vision specifically connected to moral transformation.

the sake of the Corinthian community. These are signs of the moral transformation Paul sees (or would like to see!) in his converts. To become "the same image" as the divine Christ is not, then, merely to become a shiny astral body in the eschatological sky. In this life, at least, it involves developing the self-subordinating virtues of Christ—assimilating to the Image of God—and thus to God himself.

Conclusion

We are now ready to draw together the threads of this chapter, giving some indication of how they form the complex tapestry of Pauline moral deification. In a recent book, George van Kooten brilliantly ties together Pauline ethics and the notion of assimilation to God.[68] He says, however, that the idea that assimilation to God implies deification is not fully drawn in Paul.[69] Becoming like God, if I can paraphrase, does not mean becoming divine. This judgment seems true enough in modern theology. Nevertheless, it raises some questions about whether ancient thinkers so firmly distinguished becoming *like* God from becoming divine.[70] Let me focus the discussion on Paul with some pointed questions. Does sharing in Christ's self-subordinating humility not mean sharing in Christ's divine identity? And does not Christ's divine humility *define* the nature of Paul's God? This is a theological judgment, for sure—but I am trying to reason it out historically (asking how far Paul himself thinks of divinity in moral terms). If, for Paul, Christ's virtue of self-subordinating love defines the identity of God, can one with the *same virtue* as Christ participate in Christ's divine identity?

Here I am reminded of that Pauline statement in 2 Cor 5:21: "For our sake he [the Father] made him [Christ] to be sin who knew no sin, so that in him we might become the righteousness (or justice—δικαιοσύνη) of God." Before we slide into a metaphorical explanation of this verse, I would like to remain open to the idea that humans participating in God's just nature, leads them to partially become what God is (Justice itself). I want to be open to this realistic interpretation (admittedly

---

68 *Paul's Anthropology in Context*, 92–219.
69 *Ibid.*, 180–81.
70 Note the comment of Sallustius: "We, when we are good, have union with the Gods because we are like them (δι᾽ ὁμοιότητα θεοῖς συναπτόμεθα)" (*Concerning the Gods and the Universe*, 14).

strange to our ears), because it might give us access to how many ancient people thought. At one point in the *Republic*, Plato speaks about the ideal of becoming Justice: "But if we discover what Justice is, will we not demand that the just man must differ from it in no respect, but that he be in every way the sort of thing which Justice is (ἀλλὰ πανταχῇ τοιοῦτον εἶναι οἷον δικαιοσύνη ἐστίν)?" (*Resp.* 472b6-c2). This is a bold formulation (the just person becomes what Justice is), yet Plato is equally satisfied with formulating the idea in this way: the just person "comes as close as possible" to Justice and "participates (μετέχῃ) in it far more than anyone else" (472c1–2). The two ideas shade into each other and seem basically equivalent: becoming Justice means participating in it and vice versa. The (near) equivalence is important, because justice is so central to Plato's concept of deity. To participate in Justice is to share the nature of God. It is, in some sense, to be what Plato's God is: "just and holy with wisdom." Similarly, in the great exchange formula of 2 Cor 5:21, humans are re-expressed as part of God's moral (i.e., just) identity. Christ is the Justice of God (1 Cor 1:30) not only because he represents justice, but because he is so integrated into God's just identity that he (at least for Christians) "is" Justice. Is it so amazing that similar thinking would apply to human beings conformed to Christ (i.e., assimilated to God)? Participating in justice is a participation in the nature of God. Participation in justice means sharing the divine identity. This is the import, I think, of Paul's statement that humans "become" divine Justice in 2 Cor 5:21.

Paul's notion of becoming divine Justice is analogous to the kind of moral assimilation to God we see in 2 Pet 1:4–7. Here, humans "flee" (ἀποφυγόντες) from the world with its lust of corruption (cf. φυγή in *Theaet.* 176b), and add to their faith "virtue" (ἀρετή)—which for Christians is the foundation of "knowledge," "self-control," "endurance," "godliness," "brotherly affection," and "love." This kind of moral assimilation to God is specifically what makes Christians "participants in God's *nature*" (θείας κοινωνοὶ φύσεως) (2 Pet 1:4, my emphasis). Based on the material discussed in this chapter, I do not think that these ideas are so distant from Paul. They are on a higher philosophical register, to be sure, but much of the logic is analogous. If we (moderns) cannot accept the ontology of such texts (and generally speaking we cannot), we should at least redescribe them in a way that is faithful to ancient conceptions.

Redescribing moral assimilation to Christ as participation in Christ's story—although true as far as it goes—is thus not a sufficient redescription of the Pauline idea. As I mentioned above, moral assimilation to Christ is to share in the very character that makes Christ divine. Christ, who re-expresses the nature of the Jewish God Yahweh, is a moral deity. Christ is a God whose divinity is expressed in moral acts of condescension for the benefit of others. For Paul, humility has become central to the meaning of God. Humility is the true power of Christ, because his divine power has always been the power to save. Thus self-subjugating humility is just as basic to the divine identity of Christ as is immortality. Christ reveals the identity of God. To share in Christ's humility, then, is to share in the identity of Paul's God. According to our definition proposed in the introduction (deification means sharing [a] God's identity), Paul's moral logic does indeed imply deification. Christ's humility is a peculiar trait distinctive to the identity of a peculiar Greco-Roman (and Christian) God; participation in this particular divine character results in a peculiar (Pauline) form of deification.

Part III:
Addressing the Challenges:
Monotheism and Divine Transcendence

Chapter 8:
Monotheism and Divine Multiplicity

> "Amid all these contests internal
> and external, amid all controversy, you
> will see throughout the world one
> uniform rule and doctrine, that there is
> one God, king and father of all things,
> and many Gods, sons of God and his
> coregents. The Greek says so, likewise
> the non-Greek."
> —Maximus of Tyre, *Or.* 11.5

> "… that is how most men
> apportion divinity; they hold that the
> control, the supreme sway, rests with
> one, the various functions (*officia*)
> among many."
> —Tertullian, *Apol.* 24.3

> "Behold, you [Yahweh] are the
> prince of Gods" (הנה אתה שר אלים).
> (1 QH[a] 18.8)

My argument for a Pauline form of deification has been made from concepts which I think were at work both in Paul's texts and in Paul's world. Nevertheless, I realize that many readers cannot accept my argument without raising major theological objections. Although some of these theological objections arise from our modern standpoint and assumptions, their roots are often traced to the ancient world, and so must be addressed here.

Perhaps the most common objection to the notion of deification in early Christian sources is the concept of "monotheism."[1] Monotheism

---

1   "[T]he Jewish monotheistic stance forbade apotheosis, the divinization of human figures, and thus clashed with a major theme in pagan religion of the time" (Hurtado, *Lord Jesus Christ*, 91). According to two proponents of deification in Christian sources: "Of course, Christian monotheism goes against any literal 'god making' of believers" (Finlan and Kharlamov, *Theosis*, 1). Cf. Mark Nispel: "In the case of worshiping the pagan gods or honoring deified rulers, the earliest Christian authors explicitly and vehemently reject the idea

has become something of a "hot topic" in ancient Near East studies, including Hebrew Bible.[2] Some New Testament scholars as well have become embroiled in the issue.[3] On the whole, however, the New Testament guild is not overly aware of just how flexible "monotheism" was in our period (the first century C.E.)—even up until the end of Late Antiquity. Many scholars still assume that monotheism was a doctrine which revolutionized the consciousness of all Jews after (though some claim before) the exile (sixth century B.C.E.), a doctrine which grew increasingly rigid and uniform in the centuries preceding the common era. To prove this thesis, many scholars are prepared simply to wave the wand of Second Isaiah (seen as something of an architect of exclusive monotheism), while side-stepping the issue of how far this prophet can be seen as representative of Second Temple Judaism as a whole. If Isaiah 40–55 forms the peak of monotheism (deliberately excluding the existence of other Gods), other evidence indicates that most post-exilic Jews were still on the plain (focusing worship on one God, while believing in a range of other divine powers).[4] The evidence for various forms of "inclusive monotheism" in the Hellenistic period (323–30 B.C.E.) is mounting; and there is little reason to suppose that the flexible forms of Jewish monotheism in this period became any less flexible in the early Roman empire (the first century C.E.). The idea of a rigorously exclusive monotheism in the first century now cannot be simply assumed.[5]

---

of any creature being considered a god as this was contrary to the church's monotheist confession" ("Christian Deification and the Early *Testimonia*," *VC* 53 [1999]: 291).

2 For recent research on monotheism, see Konrad Schmid, "The Quest for 'God': Monotheistic Arguments in the Priestly Texts of the Hebrew Bible" in *Reconsidering the Concept of Revolutionary Monotheism* (ed. Beate Pongratz-Leisten; Winona Lake: Eisenbrauns, 2011), 272–73, nn. 5–6.

3 To note just a few examples: Paul A. Rainbow, "Monotheism and Christology in 1 Corinthians 8:4–6" (D.Phil. thesis, Oxford, 1987); Larry Hurtado, "First-Century Jewish Monotheism" *JSNT* 71 (1998): 3–26; Carey Newman, James Davila and Gladys Lewis (eds.), *The Jewish Roots of Christological Monotheism: Papers from the St. Andrews Conference on the Historical Origins of the Worship of Jesus* (Leiden: Brill, 1999). For a discussion and critique of Hurtado's idea that worship is the "decisive criterion" for divinity in ancient Judaism, see the excursus at the end of chapter 9.

4 See Smith, *Origins of Biblical Monotheism*, 154–55; 179–94.

5 Rainbow provides a very full list of monotheistic statements in ancient Judaism ("Monotheism and Christology," 213–268), but argues that some ancient

This chapter is designed to problematize strict (or exclusivist) monotheism by indicating just how many "Gods" and divine figures ancient Jews up to and beyond the first century c.e. were willing to entertain. My goal, however, is not to deconstruct the category of "monotheism." Rather, I hope to present a theory which can make sense of ancient Jewish "monotheism" (a term I think we should retain) and multiple Gods. My ultimate intent is to show that first-century Jewish monotheism was open to the existence of multiple Gods—and thus deification— provided that the power and sovereignty of the high God remained totalizing and supreme.

Problematizing Exclusivist Monotheism

As many have pointed out in recent literature, the notion of monotheism contains a paradox. The reputed inventor of the term, Henry More[6]—a seventeenth century Cambridge Platonist—seems to have understood "monotheism" to mean the belief in numerically one God in contrast to "polytheism": belief in many Gods. Although this definition of monotheism accords with standard English dictionaries, it does not fit the ancient evidence. When we peruse the documents of the Jewish scriptures (whether Hebrew or Greek), it becomes evident that the great range of views represented there sometimes betray the belief in more than one God.[7] In fact, the very prohibition of the worship of other Gods (Ex 20:3; Deut 5:7) technically implies the existence of other Gods: "I am Yahweh your God; you shall have no other Gods

---

Jews—including Paul—clearly accepted the existence of superhuman powers who exercised divine functions and could (sometimes) be called "Gods" (36– 43). Rainbow shows that even texts that deny the existence of other Gods still speak of other superhuman powers as "Gods" (cf. esp. Deut 4:35, 39 with 3:24). He concludes that "ancient Jewish monotheists could speak of many gods as existing under the one God" (54–55; cf. 57).

6   It seems that More was the first to use "monotheism" in 1680, although Ralph Cudworth (the leader of the Cambridge Platonists) used the adjective "monotheist" in 1678 (Nathan MacDonald, *Deuteronomy and the Meaning of "Monotheism"* [Tübingen: Mohr Siebeck, 2003], 6 n. 4).

7   Even Yeḥezkel Kaufmann remarked that the "Bible nowhere denies the existence of the gods" (*Religion of Israel*, 20). For previous treatments of this issue, see John F. A. Sawyer, "Biblical Alternatives to Monotheism," *Theology* 87 (1984): 176–79; and Peter Hayman, "Monotheism—a Misused Word in Jewish Studies?" *JJS* 42 (1991): 1–15.

besides me (על־פני; LXX πλὴν ἐμοῦ; cf. Ex 22:19)."[8] Other statements directly assume that the reader believes in multiple "Gods." Exodus 22:27, for instance, reads: "You shall not speak evil of Gods (אלהים; LXX θεούς)." Particularly interesting are the statements of incomparability: "Who is like you, Yahweh, among the Gods (באלם; LXX ἐν θεοῖς)?" (Ex 15:11; cf. Ps 89:7).[9] To these statements we can add the host of other superhuman beings in the Hebrew Bible including dead ancestors (הים; LXX θεούς) (1 Sam 28:13), a host of angels (passim), starry sons of God (Job 38:7), six-winged beings called "seraphim" (Isa 6:1–3), and huge, quadruple-faced, griffin like entities called cherubim (Ezek 1:5–14; 10:1).[10] If we include later Jewish literature, we can swell the list with the "God" (אלהים) Melchizedek (11Q13), the archangels Michael (Dan 10:13, 21; 12:1; Rev 12:7), Raphael (Tob 5–12), Gabri-

---

8   In light of other uses of על־פני in the Hebrew Bible, MacDonald translates the phrase as "over and against me" (*Deuteronomy and the Meaning of "Monotheism,"* 77).

9   "The fact that Israel *did as a matter of fact compare its God with other gods* confirms that they took the existence of other gods seriously" (C. J. Labuschagne, *The Incomparability of Yahweh in the Old Testament* [Leiden: Brill, 1966], 144, emphasis his). Apparently, the "idea of incomparability did not [in itself] include any notion of exclusivism … supremacy was never reckoned at the expense of other gods" (53). Labuschagne discusses other incomparability texts such as Deut 33:26; 1 Sam 2:2; 2 Sam 7:22; 1 Kings 8:23; Jer 10:6, 7 (11–12). He notes that most of these texts are in prayers or hymns. Furthermore, statements of incomparability were not unique to Yahweh. Of Saul it is said "there is none like him (אין כמהו) among all the people" (1 Sam 10:24). Of Job, Yahweh said that "there is none like him (אין כמהו) on the earth" (1:8; 2:3). Even of Goliath's sword David says: "There is none like it (אין כמוה)" (1 Sam 21:10; cf. 26:15; 22:14). All of these statements appear to be rhetorical. David called the sword "incomparable" in part because it was the only one available to him (10). Statements of divine incomparability are also common in Mesopotamia. Of Marduk we hear that he is a "Mighty God, who has no equal among the great Gods." "Lord thou art exalted! Who equals thee? Marduk, among all the great Gods thou art exalted!" "Which God in heaven or on earth equals thee?" (quoted on 40). For the incomparability of Mesopotamian kings, see *ibid.*, 46–48.

10 On the cherubim, E. Theodore Mullen writes: "These creatures, though not portrayed in the literature as members of the [divine] court, obviously serve as helpers and messengers for the deity, and should be seen as members of the assembly like the seraphim" (*The Divine Council in Canaanite and Early Hebrew Literature* [Chico, Calif.: Scholars Press, 1980], 208, n. 164). See also Sang-Yol Cho, *Lesser Deities in the Ugaritic Texts and the Hebrew Bible: A Comparative Study of their Nature and Roles* (Piscataway, N.J.: Gorgias Press, 2007), 275–81.

el, and Phanuel (or Uriel) (1 En 40:9). The Jewish Sibyl calls God "the immortal Begetter of Gods and of all people" (γενετῆρα θεῶν πάντων τ' ἀνθρώπων), acknowledges the existence of Gods (θεούς), and even calls Rome's king ἰσόθεος (*Sib. Or.* 3.278; 3.429; 5.138–39).[11] Most interestingly, ancient Jewish documents also speak of a Prime Mediator figure, who appears at sundry times and in divers manners as the "angel of Yahweh" (Gen 16:7; 22:11; Ex 3:2, *passim*),[12] Wisdom (Prov 8; cf. Sir 24; Wisd 7),[13] "one like a son of man" (Dan 7; cf. 1 En 46–48, 53, 62), the Logos (ubiquitous in Philo), Yahoel (*Apoc. Abr.*), and later Metatron (3 En).[14]

What do we call these beings? They are certainly not human. They typically live in heaven. Most of them appear to be immortal. They have a measure of vertical "otherness" (or transcendence), and superhuman power. Traditionally, scholars (especially Jewish and Christian ones) have been uncomfortable with calling such beings "(subordinate) Gods," because ancient (and modern) Jews strongly maintained the language of "one God."

This "one God" language, it is worth noting, is often directed against a religious other—the polytheistic cults of Mesopotamia, Syria, Egypt, and later Greece and Rome. And surely, when later Jewish apologists like the authors of the *Sibylline Oracles* or the Jewish *Orphica* compare their doctrine of God with that of others, the Jewish God appears to be quite lonely. But when Jews look internally—refraining from apologetic or polemical comparison—one discovers that their understanding of God in fact allows for a host of other transcendent beings sometimes directly called "Gods."

Amidst the various numina mentioned by these ancient Jews, it is important to distinguish between two basic types. There are, first of

---

11 These texts from the *Sibylline Oracles* are noted by Rainbow, "Monotheism and Christology," 53. For a fuller survey of such divine figures, see John J. Collins, "Powers in Heaven: God, Gods, and Angels in the Dead Sea Scrolls" in *Religion in the Dead Sea Scrolls* (eds. John J. Collins and Robert A. Kugler; Grand Rapids: Eerdmans, 2000), 9–28.

12 See the recent discussion of the angel of Yahweh in Sommer, *Bodies of God and the World*, 38–44.

13 Bernhard Lang, *Wisdom and the Book of Proverbs: A Hebrew Goddess Redefined* (New York: Pilgrim Press, 1986), 192.

14 For a survey of Prime Mediator figures, see Hurtado, *One God, One Lord*, 41–92; and Daniel Boyarin, *Border Lines: The Partition of Judaeo-Christianity* (Philadelphia: University of Pennsylvania Press, 2004), 89–127.

all, the foreign and adversarial numina that are viewed (at least in terms of the final redaction of the Hebrew Bible) as dangerous and religiously unacceptable. These would include beings such as Baal, Chemosh, Bel, Nebo, Asherah, Tammuz, the Sun, etc. The LXX famously identifies these beings as "daimonia" (δαιμόνια) (Ps 95[96]:5)—lesser divine powers who later became "demons." The other type of numen includes beings who are clearly subordinate to Yahweh, and integrated into the celestial "bureaucracy," so to speak. There is no need for Yahweh to be jealous of these "sons of God" (בני אלים; LXX υἱοὶ θεοῦ)[15] who praise him in his heavenly court (Ps 28[29]:1), or the "Gods" (אלהים; LXX θεούς) who stand in his assembly (Ps 81[82]:1b), or the "mighty ones of the Gods" (גבורי אלים) who help him in the eschatological battle (1QM 15:13–15; 4Q400–407 *passim*; 4Q491 frag. 11).[16] These are beings in the divine entourage, whom Philo dubbed God's "lieutenants" (ὕπαρχοι) (e. g., *Somn.* 1.140). In the post-exilic redaction of biblical writings, it is clear that Yahweh has ultimate supremacy over these "Gods." He is, in the words of Daniel, the "God" of these "Gods" (אל אלים; OG ὁ θεὸς τῶν θεῶν) (11:36; cf. 2:47; Deut 10:17; Josh 22:22; Ps 50:1).

If we focused solely on the adversarial foreign deities, we could more readily construe biblical monotheism as "mathematical" monotheism (the doctrine of numerically one God). For monotheism—right-

---

15 It seems most appropriate to interpret the בני אלים (or בני אלהים) as "those in the category/class of Gods," on the analogy, e. g., of בני בליעל, "worthless fellows" (1 Sam 2:12; 10:27; 1 Kings 21:10; Deut 13:14; Judges 20:13, etc.), or the "people of light" (בני אור) (1QS 3.24–25). For this meaning, with further examples, see *BDB s.v.* בן §8.

16 For more references to angelic אלים and אלהים at Qumran, see Carol Newsom, *Songs of the Sabbath Sacrifice: A Critical Edition* (Atlanta: Scholars Press, 1985), 23–24. It is sometimes said or assumed that the אלים at Qumran are "merely" angels, and thus occasion no surprise. Though perhaps true, this view misses the point of what the designation means for the sectarian community. אלים, as most agree, means "Gods." If it is true that these "Gods" refer to angels, it seems just as true that these angels were nevertheless considered to be Gods. This is an important matter of native classification. The different classes of beings are nicely laid out in 1QM 17:6–8, where God "will raise up the kingdom of Michael in the midst of the Gods, and the realm of Israel in the midst of all flesh." Here we have two general classes: Gods and flesh, or (if I can paraphrase) the divine and the human. The angels, it seems evident, are in the divine class.

ly said to be the "negation of polytheism"[17]—is widely considered to come about when the existence of adversarial foreign Gods are denied (as they are, e.g., in Deut 4:35; Isa 45:5). Yet the situation becomes more complex when we acknowledge the presence of naturalized, "lieutenant" Gods interwoven into the warp and woof of Jewish thought and piety. Since these Gods never posed a threat, their existence was never (and never needed to be) denied (even by Second Isaiah). Indeed, such "Gods" and "sons of God" comfortably exist around Yahweh with little word of condemnation or caveat. How does the historian of religion reconcile this pervasive belief in other "Gods" (the ancient Jewish term) with strong (and later ritualized) statements of divine unity (Deut 6:4; cf. 32:39; Isa 45:5, etc.)?

At this juncture, it is often said by Jews and Christians that monotheism is less about number than about divine uniqueness.[18] For the Jewish insider, monotheism means that Yahweh is unique, not that he is alone (so-called "monism"). This theological assessment is helpful to a point. The problem is that "uniqueness," if it means (as it does etymologically) "one of a kind," simply is not an accurate description of ancient Jewish religion. The vocabulary of subordinate "Gods" indicates that Yahweh was not the only member of the Jewish class "God/divine being." Although undisputed in power and authority, he was not strictly speaking "unique" with respect to divinity. There is no doubt that due to Yahweh's role as creator and king, much of Jewish thought about God was focalized on the person of Yahweh. Nevertheless, the number of numina in the late Second Temple period indicate that Yahweh was simply not the *exclusive* focus of attention. Nor was his sovereignty *absolutely* unique. Rather, it was mediated through a host of other transcendent beings. The historian of religion must take seriously the presence of these other numina pervading biblical and parabiblical writings. The proof is in the texts, and it is evident that other beings subordinate

---

17 Raffaele Pettazzoni, "The Formation of Monotheism" in *Reader in Comparative Religion: An Anthropological Approach* (eds. William Armand Lessa and Evon Zartman Vogt; Evanston, Ill.: Row & Peterson, 1958), 46.

18 Cf. Richard Bauckham: "The essential element in what I have called Jewish monotheism, the element that makes it a kind of monotheism, is not the denial of the existence of other 'gods', but an understanding of the uniqueness of YHWH that puts him in a class of his own" (*Jesus and the God of Israel*, 86). See further Suzanne Nicholson, *Dynamic Oneness*, 245.

to Yahweh shared a measure of his sovereignty and immortality and thus could be called "Gods."[19]

One way of dealing with these Jewish "Gods" is to abandon the language of Jewish monotheism.[20] The assumption here is that plurality—any plurality—in the divine world is enough to question the legitimacy of monotheistic claims. The anthropologist E. B. Tylor recognized long ago that "Beings who in Christian or Moslem theology would be called angels, saints, [and] demons would under the same definition be called deities in polytheistic systems."[21] Herbert Spencer went further in declaring the "truth, obvious enough though habitually ignored, that the Hebrew religion, nominally monotheistic, retained a large infusion of polytheism." He believed that the "Archangels exercising powers in their respective spheres, and capable even of rebellion, were practically demigods; answering in fact, if not in name, to the inferior deities of other pantheons."[22] Similarly, Freud believed that ancient Israelites "found room for many deities of polytheism in an easily recognizable disguise, though in subordinate positions."[23]

The theory of Jewish "polytheism," though it strives to be honest with the data, is nevertheless somewhat repellant to sympathetic histor-

---

19 Thus I must respectfully disagree with Rainbow that the Jewish God Yahweh was divine "in a unique sense" ("Monotheism and Christology," 56). This amounts to the view that other Gods were Gods only in a nominal sense. It seems more accurate to think of these lieutenant Gods, rather, as Gods by *participation*. This means, to be sure, that they were considered to be Gods in a different sense than the primal God, but not in a *totally* different sense. The language of praise and theology in Jewish sources may suggest that God transcends the category of "God," but for the purposes of the history of religion, subordinate Gods should be categorized with God. In theology, God may be inherently unique, but in the history of religion, the Jewish God is still a token of the type "God."

20 For the rejection of Jewish monotheism, see Oswald Loretz, *Des Gottes Einzigkeit: Ein altorientalisches Argumentationsmodell zum "Schma Jisrael"* (Darmstadt: Wissenschaftliche Buchgesellschaft, 1997), 157–59; Barbara N. Porter, *One God Or Many? Concepts of Divinity in the Ancient World* (Chebeague, Me.: Casco Bay Assyriological Institute, 2000), 342. Cf. also Simon Price: "... the categories 'monotheism' and 'polytheism' do not promote historical understanding ... The terms 'polytheism' and 'monotheism' are best abandoned to the theologians" (*Religions of the Ancient Greeks* [Cambridge: Cambridge University Press, 1999], 11).

21 *Religion in Primitive Culture* (Gloucester, Mass.: P. Smith, 1970), 539.

22 *Principles of Sociology* (Hamden, Conn.: Archon Books, 1969), 598.

23 *Moses and Monotheism* (trans. Katherine Jones; New York: Vintage, 1939), 112.

iography. Such a theory says that if the ancient Jews believed in beings who functioned as Gods and who were called "Gods," they must have been polytheists. This theory, however logical, assumes a remarkable act of (witting or unwitting) misrecognition on the part of the Jews, who ritually confessed their God to be one (Deut 6:4). It is clear, at any rate, that *they* would not have agreed that they were polytheists. So anthropologists or historians of religion who so dub them are in danger of mowing down native conceptions. To avoid this, we should note the criterion once proposed by the Harvard comparativist Wilfred Cantwell Smith: "no statement about a religion is valid unless it can be acknowledged by that religion's believers."[24] Stated in this form, the criterion is somewhat rigid, and cannot be taken as universally valid. As a general guideline, however, it presents what seems to be a fair and healthy approach in religious studies. The historian simply does not have the authority to impose the category of "polytheism" on a people who would consider this type of religion (often associated with "idolatry") anathema (see, e.g., Philo, *Decal.* 65).

Our attempt to respect the views of the "insiders" involves us in a healthy engagement with theology. Biblical theologians are generally agreed that post-exilic Judaism maintained a belief in (at least "practical") monotheism.[25] Unfortunately, theologians have sometimes attempted to assert the uniqueness of Jewish monotheism by some rather artificial distinctions. Yeḥezkel Kaufmann, for instance, wrote that ancient Jewish monotheism was a "new religious category" involving the ideas of (1) "God above nature," (2) a supreme divine will not subject to fate, and (3) the absence of "myth and magic." These distinctions, Kaufmann affirmed, were what "paganism" never knew.[26] Yet here the great Israeli scholar, I think, was speaking from within the

---

24 "Comparative Religion: Whither and Why" in *The History of Religions: Essays in Methodology* (eds. Mircea Eliade and Joseph Mitsuo Kitagawa; Chicago: University of Chicago Press, 1959), 42.

25 Walther Eichrodt, *Theology of the Old Testament* (trans. J. A. Baker, 2 vols.; Philadelphia: Westminster Press, 1967), 1.220–27; Gerhard von Rad, *Theologie des Alten Testaments* (München: Kaiser Verlag, 1987), 224–25; Horst Dietrich Preuss, *Old Testament Theology* (2 vols. Louisville, Ky.: Westminster John Knox Press, 1995), 1.116–17. According to Ulrich Mauser, "The confession of the uniqueness and oneness of the God of Israel is the foundational confession (*Grundbekenntnis*) of the Old Testament" ("Heis Theos und Monos Theos in biblischer Theologie," *Jahrbuch für Biblische Theologie* 1 [1986]: 71–72).

26 Kaufmann, *Religion of Israel*, 226–27.

framework of his faith. A historian can acknowledge that the Bible contains Jewish myth (in the sense of a traditional, sacred tales)[27] and magical practices (note esp. 2 Kings 4:38–41; 6:1–7). In the Bible, Yahweh often appears as a storm and fertility God rather comfortably mixed with the world of nature (e. g., Ps 18:7–15; Hos 2:8; Jer 14:22). And, although to us the Bible may have little sense of "fate," this might not accord with ancient Jewish perceptions.[28] Even if problematic, however, Kaufmann's distinctions are helpful in that they illustrate how seriously religious people (Jews and Christians) view the differences between *their* "true" monotheism and *other* monotheisms—such as Greek philosophical monotheism, which seems to fulfill Kaufmann's criteria even better than the Jewish variety. Ancient Jews and Christians could not *but* be monotheistic and read their scriptures monotheistically. As insiders, their religious identity was (and is) at stake. So Rolf Rendtorff is (theologically) correct when he says that Israel *as Israel* never worshiped any other Gods than the one God. For without the confession of the one God, the community of Israel (which *confessed* one God) would not be Israel.

For insiders, monotheism is about identity. It is a boundary marker. The one God elects the one people for the one mission of glorifying God in the world.[29] Those who cannot confess this cannot be part of the Jewish (and later Christian) community. In the words of Mark Smith:

> Monotheistic statements [in the Hebrew Bible] do not herald a new age of religion but explain Yahwistic monolatry in absolute terms. As rhetoric, monotheism reinforced Israel's exclusive relationship with its deity. Monotheism is a kind of inner community discourse establishing a distance from outsiders; it uses the language of Yahweh's exceptional divine status beyond and in all reality ('there are no other deities but the Lord') to absolutize Yahweh's claim on Israel and to express Israel's ultimate fidelity to

---

27 See on this point John Van Seters, *Prologue to History: The Yahwist as Historian in Genesis* (Louisville: Westminster John Knox, 1992), 28–30.

28 Josephus appears to have seen fate in his Bible. See R. J. H. Schutt, "The Concept of God in the Works of Flavius Josephus," *JJS* 32 (1980): 183–84, 186. For fate in Qoheleth, see Penchansky, *Twilight of the Gods*, 18–22. The line in Philo the Epic Poet that Joseph "unraveled time's secrets in the flow of fate (πλημμυρίδι μοίρης)" seems also to be significant (frag. 3, line 10).

29 Note the rhetoric of Ephesians: "There is one body and one Spirit, just as you were called to the one hope of your calling, one Lord, one faith, one baptism, one God and Father of all" (4:4–6).

Yahweh. Monotheism is therefore not a new cultural step but expresses Israel's relationship with Yahweh.[30]

Or in the words of Jan Assmann: "Decisive is not the oneness of God, which is a philosophical idea, but the *difference* of God, which is a 'narrative truth' and the foundation of Israel's identity."[31]

In light of these observations, I have no desire to jettison monotheism as a term or concept basic to Jewish and Christian identity. Nevertheless, I think it is historically irresponsible to depict Jewish monotheism as perfectly "unique" because of dubious theological distinctions. The reality is, there are many different kinds of monotheisms (Egyptian, Greek, Christian, Muslim). The issue is that, in *this* (ancient Jewish) form of monotheism, we must squarely face the data set of *both* divine unity *and* multiple divinities.[32] In devising our theory, no part of that data set can be removed or submerged.

Towards a Theory of Ancient Jewish Monotheism

To find a mediating position between "Jewish polytheism" and "unique" monotheism, it is useful to attend, I think, to Eric Voegelin's model of "(political) summodeism."[33] In this model, Yahweh would be the imperial "high God," who shares his divine power with the hierarchically subordinate Gods below him.[34] Summodeism can be a form

---

30   *Origins of Biblical Monotheism*, 154.
31   *Of God and Gods: Egypt, Israel, and the Rise of Monotheism* (Madison, Wisc.: University of Wisconsin Press, 2008), 3–4.
32   There may be a "monotheizing tendency" in Scripture (James A. Sanders, *Canon and Community : A Guide to Canonical Criticism* [Philadelphia: Fortress Press, 1984], 17), but it is a tendency that never in fact undermines the basic plurality of God in the canon.
33   Eric Voegelin, *Israel and Revelation* (Columbia, Mo.: University of Missouri Press, 2001), 46–47, 267–68. The term "henotheism" is not preferred because it views one particular God as the sum or totality of divinity and not the summit of other deities who remain deities in their own right (Smith, *God in Translation*, 168; see also 169–74 for his discussion of summodeism).
34   In Syro-Palestinian theology, there were at least four tiers of divinity represented in the cosmic bureaucracy: (1) the high God (El), (2) the active or "patron" Gods (e.g., Baal), (3) the craftsmen Gods (e.g., Kothar-wa-Hasis), and (4) the messenger Gods (Lowell K. Handy, *Among the Host of Heaven: The Syro-Palestinian Pantheon as Bureaucracy* [Winona Lake: Eisenbrauns, 1994]). For the structure of the divine world in the Mediterranean (with a focus on Late Antiquity),

of monotheism, wherein all divine power is concentrated in the hands of a single God. Nevertheless, summodeism assumes a divine world with more than one grade and shade of divinity. The divine world is pictured as a loosely connected network or (in more structured systems) a hierarchy in which many lieutenant Gods fulfill the will of the one, supreme God.[35] (Standard scholarship on the "divine council" in the Hebrew Bible assumes this picture at least to some degree.) Unlike other hierarchies, however, the power differential between the high God and the subordinate Gods in summodeism is often very large—so that the supreme deity is never threatened.[36]

Summodeistic conceptions can be found in Ugarit, Babylon, Persia, Egypt, Greece, and Palestine. Given our focus on Paul's culture, however, it is best to illustrate the concept with Greek and Jewish varieties. I turn, first of all, to an important Neo-Pythagorean fragment ascribed to the philosopher Onatas (likely composed around the turn of the era):

> For God himself is the intellect, soul and ruler of the whole world. His powers, whose distributor he is, are perceptible, and so are those (powers) which go to and fro across the whole world. God himself, on the other hand, is neither visible nor perceptible, but may be contemplated by the mind and intellect alone, while his works and his deeds are manifest and perceptible for all men. It seems to me that God is not one (μὴ εἶς εἶμεν ὁ θεός), but the greatest and highest and ruler of all is one, while the numerous other (Gods) are different with regard to power; the one who is superior in power and greatness and virtue rules over them all.[37]

The basic summodeistic insight is that there is one chief God, and various divine powers. Although Philo, in contrast to Onatas, clearly argues for one God, one can see a summodeistic paradigm at work in his the-

---

see Ramsay MacMullen, *Paganism in the Roman Empire* (New Haven: Yale University Press, 1981), 73–94.

35 For the comparison of God with the great king of Persia, and served by divine beings analogous to "personal servants, bodyguards, attendants, and spies, subject-princes, generals and satraps" see Ps.-Arist., *Mund.* 6, 398a10–398b3.

36 Summodeism is thus different from polytheism where the divine powers are allowed to compete and conflict while being sovereign in their own sphere of power.

37 The text (taken from Stobaeus) can be found in Holger Thesleff, ed., *The Pythagorean Texts of the Hellenistic Period* (Åbo: Åbo Akademi, 1965), 139–40. The translation is taken from Henny Fiskå Hägg, *Clement of Alexandria and the Beginnings of Christian Apophaticism* (Oxford: Oxford University Press, 2006), 245. Cf. Maximus of Tyre, *Or.* 11.12; Apul., *Dogm. Plat.* 204–205; *De Deo Socr.* 132–150; Eus., *Praep. ev.* 4.5.1–3.

ology. For this Jewish philosopher, there is one invisible, unnamable creator God called the Existent (*Mut.* 11–15), along with another creator God, the Logos, whom Philo can call "the second God" (*QG* 2.62; *Leg.* 3.207–208; *Somn.* 1.229–230). Below the Logos are two Powers whom Philo calls "God" and "Lord" (*Abr.* 121–123). Next come the stars, which can be called "manifest and visible Gods" (*Opif.* 27; cf. *Spec.* 1.209, 2.165). Below these are the angels and disembodied souls, whom Philo views as equivalent to the Greek daimones (*Gig.* 6–16).[38] All these lesser divine beings are subordinate to the Existent.

Philo shows us that the Platonic picture of graded divinity could be adapted to Jewish philosophy. But a slave or businessman who knew nothing of philosophy would still assume a picture of graded divinity based on the common cultural narratives about the Gods. Every Greek knew that Zeus was king of the Gods, and that he presided in a council of twelve elite Gods called "Olympians." Below these great Gods were the host of astral deities and lesser Gods called "daimones." Greeks would also worship heroes or demigods who dwelt in localized places on or in the earth. Such a mix of deities can sometimes seem confusing, but in general a divine hierarchy emerges with reasonable clarity. There is a long way from Zeus Olympios to the daimonic Pan, but both beings clearly belong to the divine world. Graded divinity was part of Greek theology through and through.

Although more controversial, I would argue that graded divinity is also basic to Jewish mythology in Paul's time. For a clear window into this mythic world, we can turn to the apocalyptic visions of Daniel 7–12. In chapter 7, we find a primal deity, sovereign, eternal and enthroned (the "Ancient of Days"). Zooming in on a cloud to meet the enthroned God is a Prime Mediate divinity in anthropomorphic form (the "human-like one"). Below this divinity are archangelic princes who rule the various nations (Dan 10:13, 20). Below these are the ranks upon ranks of angels who attend court and worship the high God (Dan 7:10). Although this apocalyptic mythology is by no means the same as what is found in Greek sources, a similar pattern of gradations in the divine world emerges.

---

38 See also *QE* 2.68; David Winston, "Philo's Conception of the Divine Nature" in *Neoplatonism and Jewish Thought* (ed. Lenn E. Goodman, Albany: SUNY Press, 1992), 21–23; and Roberto Radice, "Philo's Theology and Theory of Creation," in *The Cambridge Companion to Philo* (ed., Adam Kamesar; Cambridge: Cambridge University Press, 2009), 128–29.

Paul's picture of the divine world, I would argue, is another variant of the graded divinity paradigm. He acknowledges a transcendent deity "from whom" everything exists and a mediate deity "through whom" everything exists (1 Cor 8:6). He envisions, in other words, a Prime Mediate demiurgic deity—Christ—and a primal God called "the Father." Below Christ is a whole range of angels and archangels (e. g., 1 Cor 6:3; 1 Thess 4:16). Thrown into the mix is a vast "evil empire" of "rulers," "authorities" and "powers" (Rom 8:38; 1 Cor 15:24) who are probably thought to dwell in the air with other angelic and daimonic princes (cf. Eph 2:2). Immortalized and pneumatified (i. e., deified) Christians are destined to enter the divine world at some point above these daimonic powers (1 Cor 6:2–3; Rom 16:20). Although I would not want to argue that Paul's Father and Son are rigorously ranked or that Paul's Father must necessarily be distant from the world (as in some Middle Platonist schemes), Paul still works with, it seems to me, a paradigm of graded divinity.

Perhaps one could argue that after the striking theological developments between the council of Nicea and Constantinople (325–381 C.E.), Christians did away with graded divinity.[39] In the theological revolution of the fourth century, divine "stuff" (οὐσία) was limited to three persons who came to be viewed as fundamentally coordinate, not subordinate. An "iron ceiling," so to speak, was thus constructed between the trinitarian Godhead and the various figures called "saints," "angels," and "daimones." These developments do not, it seems, hold true for earlier periods. Although Jews in the first century C.E. surely distinguished between the creator and creation, they worked with a picture of a graded divine world (summodeism) very common in the culture of their time.

The summodeistic model is helpful because it shows us that divinity is not a zero-sum game. In other words, other beings can share the deity of the primal God without *depleting* that deity. The primal God has all the power, and his subordinates wield a measure of that power in the world. The Most High does not need to compete with any lesser power for divinity. Thus calling certain beings "Gods" did not lessen the power and worship of the high God. If anything, it magnified God's power, since he gained more glory by the worship and submission of subordinate divine beings. In Pauline terms, all beings—includ-

---

39 See the comments of Lewis Ayres, *Nicaea and Its Legacy: An Approach to Fourth-Century Trinitarian Theology* (Oxford: Oxford University Press, 2004), 4, 14.

ing the celestial powers—worship the God Christ *to the greater glory of God* (Phil 2:10–11).

A potential problem with Voegelin's model is that it grants a degree of independence to the lesser deities which—although common in Mesopotamian, Greek, and Roman pantheons—does not accord well with Jewish thinking. At one time, perhaps lesser Gods in the Jewish mind had a measure of independent power. They could judge the world (Ps 81[82]:1–4), control their respective nations (4QDeut 32:8), mount a full-scale rebellion (Isa 14:12–14), fall from heaven, and impregnate human women (Gen 6:1–3). As Judaism developed, however, the deity and independence of Gods other than Yahweh were stripped away. The nations were no longer assigned to the sons of God, but to angels (Deut 32:8 LXX; cf. Dan 8–12). Helel ben Sha-char in Isa 14 became a rebellious angel (and later the devil). And Yah-weh was identified with El Elyon, who stood in the divine council to condemn all the other Gods to death (Ps 81[82]:6).[40]

The work of other anthropological and sociological theorists helps us to refine Voegelin's theory—helping us arrive at a more specifically Jewish variant. Tylor believed that it is not just the idea of a creator at the top of a divine hierarchy that makes summodeism a form of mon-otheism; it is the fact that the "distinctive attributes of deities" are as-signed to the all-powerful creator.[41] In other words, for summodeism to be monotheism, everything that makes the subordinate Gods divine must be fully possessed by the high God. In the words of Origen, "there is but one fount of deity" (*Princ.* 1.3.7), even though "we [Christians] do not hesitate to speak in one sense of two Gods" (*Dial.* 2.5–7). In more modern terms, one could say that Jewish summodeism is a true monotheism because Yahweh had usurped the entire sacred domain.[42] That is to say, everything which is divine is Yahweh's; there is no di-vinity outside Yahweh, even though there are other subordinate Gods. If there are to be other Gods, then these other Gods must all share the deity of the high God. They are not separate or independent divine powers. They function only to accomplish Yahweh's will and

---

40 See further Sommer, *Bodies of God*, 166–67, who generally follows Kaufmann.

41 Tylor, *Religion in Primitive Culture*, 539.

42 Norman K. Gottwald, *The Tribes of Yahweh: A Sociology of the Religion of Liber-ated Israel, 1250–1050 B.C.E.* (Maryknoll, N.Y.: Orbis, 1979), 680.

manifest his power.[43] Their deity functions only to "complete" or demonstrate the deity of the high God.[44]

In this refined understanding, Jewish monotheism would be a
"hard" version of summodeism, whereas the forms of summodeism
we see in the *Enuma Elish*, Homer, and Ovid would tend more toward
polytheism (the rule of independent powers). "Hard" summodeism can,
I think, be understood as a form of monotheism if we take monotheism
as less about number than about the religious conviction that "our God
has supreme power." Among the early Christian fathers, the term for
summodeism was "monarchy" (μοναρχία)—the single rule of the high
God who operated through various divine subordinates.[45] To again
quote the *Dialogue with Heraclides*, Origen asks his interlocutor: "Do
we profess two Gods?" (ὁμολογοῦμεν δύο θεούς;). Heraclides responds
"Yes, [but] the power is one" (ναί. ἡ δύναμις μία ἐστίν) (2.26–27).

Although my thesis about Jewish "summodeism" may sound odd
and new-fangled to many scholars, it is hardly original. In two important
introductory works, two widely-known Jewish scholars proposed essentially the same thesis a quarter century ago. Their insights are important
enough to summarize here.

In his classic study *Sinai and Zion*, Jon D. Levenson shows that
"monotheism" was not the great invention of Israel's creative genius,
but an expression of Israel's faith in a single benevolent sovereign despite contradictory experiences. On the experiential level, Jewish monotheism was in fact not so different from polytheism. Jews told myths of
their God changing his mind (such as in the myth of Noah's Flood), and
Mesopotamians who prayed to a deity sometimes acted and spoke as if
that deity was the only God. In the Bible (a post-exilic product), Yahweh is not considered to be the only God who exists. Rather, he is the
one who has the greatest power. Psalm 81[82] is "polytheistic" as it

---

43   For the high God ruling, working, and forming through his two "hands"—the
     Son and the Holy Spirit—see Iren., *Haer.* 4.14.1; 5.1.3; 5.6.1.
44   This conception of deity more closely resembles the Orphic view of Zeus—
     head, middle, and end of all things—from whom the other Gods come to
     be. See the comments of Miguel Herrero de Jáuregui, "Orphic God(s): Theog-
     onies and Hymns as Vehicles of Monotheism," in *Monotheism Between Pagans
     and Christians in Late Antiquity* (eds. Stephen Mitchell and Peter van Nuffelen;
     Leuven: Peeters, 2010), 79–90.
45   Hayman prefers the label "monarchistic" to "monotheistic" for Jews prior to
     the Middle Ages. This means that God is the sole object of worship, but not
     the only divine being ("Misused Word," 15).

clearly refers to other Gods besides Yahweh. But the psalm closes with monotheism in that Yahweh shows his supreme power by depriving the other Gods of their immortality. Unity is thus something that God has won by his triumph over other divine powers. Accordingly, ancient Jewish monotheism is not a philosophical doctrine, but a dynamic narrative of Yahweh's triumph over other deities. God's oneness means his sole rule. Other Gods in Mesopotamia and Egypt made similar claims to incomparability, oneness, and supremacy. Thus Israel's monotheism was not unique. What is distinctive in Israel are the prohibitions of worshiping other Gods. This means that Israel viewed her relation to God in more thoroughly covenantal ways. Worshiping other divine suzerains was viewed as a breach of covenant. Other divine rivals were thus rightfully scorned (and occasionally polemically identified with "idols").[46]

In Shaye Cohen's *From the Maccabees to the Mishnah*, we learn that Jews always affirmed the kingship of God. After the exile, God's kingship changed from more henotheistic expressions to monotheistic ones. Nevertheless, there always remained a tension in ancient Judaism between the "God of all" and the "God of Israel." Monotheism from the second century B.C.E. to the second century C.E. (the focus of Cohen's book) did not mean that other superhuman beings did not exist. Monotheism was a declaration of God's sovereignty over these lesser divine beings. What monotheism required was monolatry, and popular Judaism sometimes fell short of this rule.[47]

The Status of Other Numina

The summodeistic paradigm raises an important question about the status of other Jewish divinities. If monotheistic summodeism means that all the power is concentrated in God, and that other numina merely manifest that power—are the other numina still considered to be Gods? Although in Judaism all divinity was absorbed by the high God Yahweh, this does not (I think) necessarily mean that the numina below him were forced out of the class of "divine being." There was an attempt, for sure, to reclassify lesser numina as ambiguous intermediate

---

46 *Sinai and Zion: An Entry into the Jewish Bible* (New York: HarperCollins, 1985), 56–70.

47 *From the Maccabees to the Mishnah* (Philadelphia: Westminster, 1987), 81–84.

(often called "heavenly") beings.[48] If the intermediaries were good, it seems, they became angels. If bad, they became daimones (Ps 95 [96]:5). Although in some Jewish authors, angels and daimonic beings were not, it seems, viewed as divinities, I wonder if this is universally the case? Is there a compelling reason, for instance, to believe that when the Qumran sectarians called angelic beings "Gods" (אלים) they did not mean what they said? Paul calls Satan "the God of this world" (2 Cor 4:4). For sure, he did not think that *daimonia* deserved the name Gods (1 Cor 10:20)—but this is a typical polemical move from a religious insider. Much later, Augustine was willing to drop the polemics for the sake of honest debate. In the *City of God*, he writes:

> When the Platonists prefer to call daimones (or alternatively angels) 'Gods' rather than daimones and are prepared to count as Gods those who are created by the highest God ... let them express themselves in this way, as they wish, since there is no reason to have a dispute with them about words. In fact, when they call them [daimones/angels] 'immortal,' in the sense that they have at all events been created by the highest God, and 'blessed,' in the sense that they are blessed not in virtue of their own internal qualities but for the reason that they depend on their creator, then they are saying *the same thing as we are*, whatever terminology they use to express themselves. (*Civ.* 9.23, emphasis added)

This is a rare case in which an insider admits what I think a historian of religion must also confess—that Jews and Christians affirmed the unity of divinity in the context of a larger divine world (i.e., summodeism). Even in the fifth century C.E., Augustine was willing to allow, at least for the sake of argument, the existence of created "Gods" below the high God. Though the terminology differs, in essence the Platonists say the same thing as the Christians.

I conclude, then, that constructing an intermediate category between divine beings and human beings—the so-called "heavenly beings" such as angels and daimones—can sometimes obscure patterns

---

48 Thompson conceives of an intervening category between Gods and humans called "heavenly beings." These heavenly beings, she says, can be called "Gods." The humans who are called Gods, she claims, are really part of this non-divine class of heavenly beings (*God of the Gospel of John*, 43). This view does not accord with her general thesis that those who share in divine functions and prerogatives (such as Christ) ought to be viewed as sharing in the identity of God. Christ is not just a "heavenly being," he is (a) God. I fully recognize that he is not an independent God, but God only in relation to the one (i.e., Almighty high) God, the Father. The same understanding, I am arguing, applies to deified Christians.

of ancient thought. I am perfectly happy to admit that as Christians continue on through the centuries (especially after Nicea), angels and daimones are deprived of all divinity and put in an intermediate class of "heavenly beings." Nonetheless, I suggest that this is not so clear in the early period (the first century). Even in the fifth century, Augustine is willing to let daimones be lesser Gods (which seems to have been quite standard in the larger culture). So we cannot exclude the idea that Jews and Christians that preceded him were willing to class angels and daimones as "Gods." The evidence is ambiguous and deserves fuller research. Paul himself seems to waver between positions when he refers to the *daimonia* as "Gods and Lords," but polemically adds that they are only "so-called Gods" (1 Cor 8:5).

The real divinity of subordinate Gods becomes more clear when we come to terms with Prime Mediator figures. In the Judaism of Paul's time, Prime Mediator figures like Michael (Dan 7:11–12), Philo's Logos (the "second God," QG 2.62), Melchizedek (11Q Melch), and Christ ("in the form of God," Phil 2:6) seem to remain in the class of divine beings.

Some theologians might argue that Christ is much more than a Prime Mediator deity because of his close relationship with the Father ("I and the Father are one," John 10:30, etc.). I readily admit this—but I also point out that early Christians disagreed on this point. If some Christians emphasized the unity of Father and Son (sometimes verging into "modalistic monarchianism") other Christians underscored that Christ was definitely subordinate. Justin Martyr, for instance, calls the Logos (identified with Christ) a "second God" (*1 Apol.* 63.15; *Dial.* 56.4; cf. also Origen, *Cels.* 5.39), and early in his career, Eusebius of Caesarea was "happy to speak of the Son [Jesus] as 'a second God' in a clearly subordinationist sense."[49] The controversy was not really resolved (if it was ever completely "resolved"!) until the First Council of Constantinople (381 C.E.).

---

49 Ayres, *Nicaea and Its Legacy*, 59. In support of this point, we can cite Eus. *Praep. ev.* 7.12, 320c; *Dem. ev.* 5.4.9–14.

Paul and Summodeism

But we need to return to Paul in the first century. Did Paul uphold a
form of monotheistic summodeism? The Apostle—who repeatedly asserted that God was one (1 Cor 8:4; Gal 3:20; Rom 3:30)[50]—also
wrote that "there are many Gods and many Lords (θεοὶ πολλοὶ καὶ
κύριοι πολλοί)" (1 Cor 8:5; cf. Mic 4:5).[51] I believe that Paul (who
never ceased to be a Jew) affirmed divine plurality to be faithful—not
to the spirit of Hellenism—but to his Bible. As many have pointed
out, the Shema was clearly on Paul's mind as he dictated 1 Cor
8:4–6. In its LXX form, the Shema reads: "[the] Lord our God [the]
Lord is one (κύριος ὁ θεὸς ἡμῶν κύριος εἷς ἐστιν)" (Deut 6:4). Here
there are clearly two Lords (the "Lord our God" and the "Lord"),
and even though these two Lords do not add up to two Gods (note
the singular verb), they do add up to the theological statement that
God is plural (one yet two). Paul conceptualized this plurality in
terms of source and mediation. There is one primal God, Paul says,
from whom we exist, and one mediate—and arguably subordinate (1
Cor 15:24–28)—God (Christ), through whom we exist (1 Cor 8:6).[52]

---

50 See Charles H. Giblin, "Three Monotheistic Texts in Paul," *CBQ* 37 (1975):
527–547; and Nicholson, *Dynamic Oneness*.

51 When Paul says "Just as there are (εἰσίν) many Gods and many Lords" he uses
the indicative. Accordingly, this is not just a hypothetical proposition, or one
valid only to the religious "other" who worships these others Gods. In Paul's
system, there *are* many Gods and many Lords (see the discussion in Rainbow,
"Monotheism and Christology," 143–46); but *for us* (a relative statement) there
is one God and one Lord. The "for us" does not override the "there are"; it
only modifies it from the perspective of the community. Paul is thus in accord
with the Decalogue which says: "You shall have no other Gods before me" (Ex
20:3). The command presumes that there *are* other Gods, but "for us" (cf.
"Yahweh *our* God" in the Shema) there is only one God worthy of worship.
Paul prefers to call the Gods in competition with his God "so-called Gods"
(1 Cor 8:4–5) and δαιμόνια (in accordance with Ps 95[96]:5). In doing so,
he still acknowledges their power because he refuses to let his converts even
eat at their religious sanctuaries (1 Cor 10). Even visiting the domains of
these competitor Gods is enough to excite divine jealousy (10:22). If the δαιμόνια were not Gods in some sense, why would Paul's God be jealous?

52 The comments of Oskar Skarsaune, who reads 1 Cor 8:6 in the light of the
early Apologists, are especially illuminating ("Is Christianity Monotheistic? Patristic Perspectives on a Jewish/Christian Debate," in *Studia Patristica* 29 (1997):
356–363.

Paul's reading of the Shema gives us a sense for how ancient Jews could have understood divine plurality monotheistically while confessing God to be one. God encompasses all divinity, but this divinity (exhibited in his creative power) can also be shared by multiple entities (often by a Prime Mediator figure such as Michael, Yahoel, Metatron, etc.). In each case, however, the divinity shared by other beings is a "mediate" divinity, by which I mean a divinity inextricably connected to the one God that mediates between the primal God and the world. Some aspects of divinity cannot be shared (Christ the divine "Lord" does not fully overlap with the identity of God "the Father"), but other parts can (such as the power to rule or to live forever). It is the "*un*participated" side of divinity which, one could argue, made Yahweh's divinity distinctive (not unique!). Conversely, it was the idea of "participated divinity" which gave other beings who are *not* "God Most High" the power to be called "Gods" (Ps 81[82]:1, 6; John 10:34–36). Stated in more philosophical language, the Gods may be many in ancient Judaism, but divinity is one. Thus the unity of the God*head* was preserved for ancient Jews even if it is true that they believed in mediate divinities such as the various types of Prime Mediator figure.[53]

In accordance with this conclusion, I fully admit that the term "monotheism" has undergone much scholarly fine-tuning since it was coined by Henry More in the seventeenth century. More and those of his time, it seems, understood "mono-the-ism" in its full etymological sense: the doctrine of *one* God. The binary to monotheism was polytheism, the doctrine that there are "many Gods." Polytheism was often synonymous with "pagan" or illegitimate religion. Monolatry and henotheism, in turn, were often seen as intermediate steps toward the truly rational doctrine of one God. Thus monotheism as it was used by scholars since the Enlightenment has often simply meant "the one, true and reasonable religion."[54]

---

53 For Nero declared to be εἷς καὶ μόνος in a document which acknowledges other Gods, see Auffarth, "Herrscherkult und Christuskult," 294–306.

54 Variants of this theory were maintained by the positivist Auguste Comte, the anthropologist E. B. Tylor, and the famous Old Testament scholar Julius Wellhausen. It was Wellhausen who proposed the scheme from polytheism to henotheism to monotheism for the history of Israel. For brief surveys, see MacDonald, *Deuteronomy and the Meaning of "Monotheism,"* 6–51, and David L. Petersen, "Israel and Monotheism" in *Canon, Theology, and Old Testament Interpretation:*

It is no wonder that some theologians and students of the Bible (especially Christian and Jewish ones) sought (and seek) to defend biblical monotheism. Still today, it appears that some (perhaps most) take it as the religion most rational and true. For these scholars, one senses that there is a certain investment in seeing ancient Christian and Jewish texts—no matter how many numina appear in them—as still "monotheistic." To accommodate all the superhuman beings, several "broad" definitions of monotheism have been devised. These go under the name of "inclusive" monotheism (though the term is slightly oxymoronic). Inclusive monotheism includes form like "binitarian" and "trinitarian" monotheism. Such forms of monotheism essentially allow for more than one divine person to share a single Godhead.

Viewed from the outside, or "etically," inclusive monotheism must ever seem to involve a touch of theological acrobatics (God is one but many?).[55] There is, however, a real distinction here which has to do perhaps less with religious belief than it does with religious feeling and practice. Jews of Paul's time (including Paul himself), clearly felt that their God, who encompassed all divinity, is one.[56] This led, generally speaking, to a restriction of worship to the one God (following Ex 20:3). It is not then, the *number* of deities in the system, but the focus of *worship* (at least in principle) on the supreme deity that helps constitute "monotheism" in its ancient Jewish variety.[57] Jews worship Yahweh

---

Essays in Honor of Brevard S. Childs (eds. Gene M. Tucker et al.; Philadelphia: Fortress, 1988), 92–107.

55 So Jürgen Moltmann points out that if polytheism can be understood as a form of inclusive monotheism (as in Hinduism), what is the use of the term "monotheism"? ("Kein Monotheismus gleicht dem anderen: Destruktion eines untauglichen Begriffs," *Evangelische Theologie* 62 [2002]: 121–122).

56 Hurtado asserts that for "historical investigation," we "have no choice but to accept as monotheism the religion of those who profess to be monotheists" (*How on Earth did Jesus Become a God?*, 114. The approach is charitable and reasonable. Ironically, however, Hurtado's "historical" approach suffers under a rather obvious historical anachronism, since no ancient Jew ever professed to be a "monotheist," given that the word "monotheist" and "monotheism" had not yet been coined. All the same, Hurtado's point stands. Ancient Jews did confess—often and with conviction—that their God was one, and this must be taken seriously.

57 This is a point often repeated in the work of Hurtado. Note also Alfons Fürst, "Monotheism Between Cult and Politics: The Themes of the Ancient Debate Between Pagan and Christian Monotheism," in *One God: Pagan Monotheism*, 82–99.

alone because Yahweh is the God who saved (and saves) them. I would like to explore this issue further in the following section.

The Meaning of God's Oneness in Ancient Judaism

Yahweh is said to speak through the prophet Hosea: "You know no God but me, besides me there is no savior" (13:4). Here, the singularity of God is a statement not about number, but about power, and specifically power to save. The God who provides the ultimate benefaction (redemption) is perceived by his beneficiaries to be unique. This interpretation is evident in Second Isaiah's possible adaptation of the originally Hosean phrase: "I am God and there is no other" (45:22; 46:9; cf. 43:11). Even in Isaiah, however, this claim is not meant to underscore the mathematical oneness of Yahweh, but rather his power to save. The context makes this clear:

> But now thus says Yahweh,
> he who created you, O Jacob,
> he who formed you, O Israel:
> Do not fear, for I have redeemed you;
> I have called you by name, you are mine.
> When you pass through the waters, I will be with you;
> and through the rivers, they shall not overwhelm you;
> when you walk through fire you shall not be burned,
> and the flame shall not consume you.
> For I am Yahweh your God,
> the Holy One of Israel, your Savior. (Isa 43:1–3)[58]

When ancient Jews confessed God's unity, they confessed that Yahweh was their only Savior, and thus for them, their only God.

The first clause of Deut 6:4–6—part of the "Shema"— reads: "Hear O Israel: Yahweh our God, Yahweh is one (יהוה אחד; κύριος εἷς)."[59] In context, this is not primarily a statement about number. "Yah-

---

58 Cf. Isa 40:9–11; 41:10; 13–20; 42:14–16; 43:14–21; 43:25; 44:22, 24–28; 45:17; 46:4, 13; 48:20–21; 49:8–26; 51:3, 6, 10–11, etc.

59 Assmann points out that there are "hundreds of asservations such as 'Amun [Amun-Re, Re, Ptah, etc.] is one [unique]' in Egyptian texts, and the same applies to Mesopotamian, Anatolian, and Canaanite texts" (*Of God and Gods*, 107). Examples from Greco-Roman sources are also abundant. Take the fragment of Valerius Soranus preserved in Aug., *Civ.* 7.9: "Almighty Jupiter (*Iuppiter omnipotens*), king of nature and of Gods ... one God and all (*deus unus et*

weh is one" as a proposition implied that Yahweh was perceived to be unique.[60] Yahweh was not thought to be unique absolutely, but relatively, i. e.,—*for Israel.* "Yahweh is one," in other words, has an openly subjective side (note "Yahweh *our* God"). It expresses the exclusive commitment felt by Yahweh's worshippers. By confessing Yahweh's unity, Jews maintained their membership in the Jewish community.

The obligation trailing the declaration of Yahweh's oneness is love (6:5), a covenantal love that—as in a monogamous relationship—is by nature exclusive (cf. Song 2:16; 6:3).[61] "[O]nly as the God loved by Israel is Yahweh unique."[62] This love involved fearing Yahweh (6:2), which resulted in serving Yahweh and swearing only by his name (6:13). This fear prevented Israel—even while it enjoyed the bounty of the promised land—from paying cult to (lit. "walking after") other Gods (6:14). In other words, for Jews to declare Yahweh "one" was for them to declare their sole loyalty to Yahweh their king.

When the corresponding Ugaritic word *'aḥdy* ("one") is predicated of Baal, it is followed by Baal's statement: "I am the one who rules over Gods."[63] Similarly, I propose, Yahweh's oneness is about Yahweh's rule. In Deuteronomy 4:35, Israel is called to acknowledge that Yahweh is their God, and that he is one. His oneness is explained by his power: he removes them from Egypt by "trials, by signs and wonders, by war, by a mighty hand and an outstretched arm, and by terrifying displays of power" (Deut 4:34). It is power which strongly demonstrates to the beneficiaries the uniqueness of the Israelite God.

If we focus on the confession "God is one" in later sources, we continue to find that this statement is less about God's number than about God's power.[64] In the *Sibylline Oracles* fragment 1:7–8, God is declared

---

omnes)." According to Tertullian "one from eternity!" (εἷς or μόνος ἀπ᾽ αἰῶνιος) was the usual cheer for victors at games and contests (*Spect.* 25).

60 Mark Smith compares אֶחָד in Deut 6:4 to the Akkadian *išten*, meaning "one"—but applied to kings and deities with the sense of "unique, outstanding." "The phrase," Smith says, "is applied to the god who is the head or leader of a group of divinities" (*God in Translation*, 145).

61 Cf. MacDonald, *Deuteronomy and the Meaning of "Monotheism,"* 74.

62 Georg Braulik, "Das Deuteronomium und die Geburt des Monotheismus" in *Gott, der Einzige: Zur Entstehung des Monotheismus in Israel* (eds. Ernst Haag and Georg Braulik; Freiburg : Herder, 1985), 122.

63 Loretz, *Gottes Einzigkeit*, 57.

64 Erik Peterson's dissertation focuses on the "one God" phrase as an acclamation in response to a miracle (*Εἷς Θεός: Epigraphische, formgeschichtliche und religionsgeschichtliche Untersuchungen* [Göttingen: Hubert & Co, 1920], 39–40). My study

to be one (εἷς θεός).[65] God's oneness, emphasizes the Sibyl, means God's absolute sovereignty. God alone rules (μόνος ἄρχει). God is the omnipotent "monarch" (μόναρχος) and overseer of all (ὁρώμενος αὐτὸς ἅπαντα) (*Sib. Or.* 3:11, cf. frag. 1:15). The idea of there being one ruler collides with many divine rulers who would administer various parts of the cosmos (e. g., Demeter over grain, Dionysus over wine). The fact that there is "one God" means that God controls all heavenly and earthly phenomena (frag 1:32). Thus belief in one God is a statement about God's absolute and universal power.

In his work *On the Creation*, Philo of Alexandria approvingly quotes Philolaus, a Pythagorean philosopher of the fifth century B.C.E.: "There is a supreme Ruler of all things (ἡγεμὼν καὶ ἄρχων ἀπάντων), God, ever One (θεὸς εἷς ἀεὶ ὤν)" (§100). For Philo, God is the "great emperor" (μέγαλος βασίλευς) (*Decal.* 61) whom all divine powers serve as "lieutenants" (ὑπάρχους) (*Spec* 1:14) in the cosmic bureaucracy (*Conf.* 170–71; *Cher* 83; *Dec* 61; cf. Jos. *Ant* 1:155).[66] Popular Greek religion—a system in which the lower Gods are independently sovereign—approaches democracy, which Philo (the Alexandrian aristocrat) dubs "mob rule" (ὀχλοκρατία) (*Opif.* 171; *Dec.* 155). Likewise, the confession that "God is one," for Josephus, is a statement about "God's ruling power" (θεοκρατίαν). All ruling authority and power (ἀρχὴν καὶ τὸ κράτος) is invested in God (*C. Ap.* 2.167).

In the Gospel of Mark, when a scribe asks which is the preeminent commandment, Jesus responds with the Shema: "Hear, O Israel: the Lord our God, the Lord is one" (12:29–34). Joel Marcus notes that this declaration is linked with the idea of God's reign or kingdom.[67] When the scribe approves Jesus' emphasis on God's unity (v. 32), Jesus tells him: "You are not far from the kingdom of God (οὐ μακρὰν εἶ ἀπὸ τῆς βασιλείας τοῦ θεοῦ)." What appears to be in the background is the assumption that in the Shema the reign of God is (parti-

---

of εἷς θεός will focus on the doctrinal and confessional function of the phrase, which Peterson did not emphasize (see esp. his comments on 42).

65 John J. Collins dates frag. 1 of the *Sib. Or.* to "any time in the late Hellenistic or early Roman periods" (*OTP* 1.360).

66 Cf. Maximus of Tyre (2nd c. C.E.), who says that there is "one God the king and father of all" and there are "many Gods, Sons of God, co-rulers (συνάρχοντες) with God" (*Or.* 11.5).

67 "Authority to Forgive Sins upon the Earth: The Shema in the Gospel of Mark" in *The Gospels and the Scriptures of Israel* (eds. Craig A. Evans and W. Richard Stegner; Sheffield: Sheffield Academic Press, 1994), 197.

ally) realized in the human heart. The main thrust of Jesus' ministry is to announce the coming reign of God. Declaring Yahweh's unity was one way for him to do so.

The link between God's unity and God's rule is all the more clear in Rabbinic literature. By the early second century C.E., the Shema had become the ritualized recitation of three texts (Deut 6:4–9; 11:13–21; Num 15:38–41), girded with evening and morning blessings. In the Mishnah, R. Joshua b. Karḥa asked why the recitation of Deut 6:4–9 ("Hear O Israel...") preceded that of Deut 11:13–21 ("And it shall come to pass if you obey ..."). His answer was "so that a man may first take upon himself the yoke of the kingdom of heaven (עול מלכות שמים) and afterward take upon himself the yoke of the commandments" (m. *Ber.* 2.2, trans. Herbert Danby). Thus the paragraph of Deut 6:4–9, immediately highlighting God's unity, underscores the authority of God's kingship.[68] The purpose of the Shema was first to accept God's sovereignty. Therefore after the first line of the Shema ("Yahweh our God Yahweh is one"), there was introduced the formula: "Blessed be the name of His sovereign glory forever and ever" in order to declare allegiance to God's kingship.[69]

When the Rabbis were proclaiming God's unity, they were not thinking philosophically, but confessionally. The third evening blessing, which celebrates the redemption from Egypt, cries out that there is no God besides the Lord (ואין זולתו—a phrase recalling Deuteronomy and Deutero-Isaiah), and sings the famous rhetorical question in the Song of the Sea: "Who is like you among the Gods, O Lord? Who is like you?" God's act of power and benefaction at the Re(e)d Sea proved the singularity of his power. The third blessing was a way to confess that power.

Indeed, all the blessings surrounding the Shema emphasize the idea of God's exclusive sovereignty. The first morning and evening blessing highlight God's mastery over creation. The God who regularly brings

---

68 Reuven Kimmelman, "The Šĕma' and its Blessings: The Realization of God's Kingship" in *The Synagogue in Late Antiquity* (ed. Lee I. Levine; Philadelphia: The American Schools of Oriental Research, 1987), 74.

69 *Ibid.*, 77. Moshe Weinfeld thinks that this additional line was a response used in the Second Temple (citing t. *Pesaḥ* 3(2):19; y. *Pesaḥ* 4:9, 31b; b. *Pesaḥ* 56a) (*Deuteronomy 1–11: A New Translation with Introduction and Commentary* (AB 5; New York: Doubleday, 1991), 352.

the light and darkness is the undisputed master of the universe.[70] No other agent of creation is mentioned or needed. The second blessing emphasizes God's role in revelation. The third blessing, already noted above, "incorporates both a precedent and a model for realizing God's kingship": Israel's redemption at the Re(e)d Sea.[71] There Israel first accepted the yoke of God's kingship, crying out "This is my God!" and "The Lord shall reign forever and ever."[72] The saying "This is my God!" was taken to be a recognition of God's kingship (*Mekilta, Shirata* 3, Lauterbach 2.25–26).[73] By joining the opening of the Song of the Sea "This is my God!" (Ex 15:2) to the Song's culminating verse,[74] "The Lord shall reign forever and ever" (Ex 15:18), the whole song was viewed as a declaration of God's rule.[75]

Immediately after the Shema (indeed no pause is allowed to intervene, m. *Ber.* 2:2) came the "True and Firm" prayer. Moshe Weinfeld states that this prayer formally functioned as a loyalty oath sworn to an emperor or a king. In the oath, the vassal accepted the yoke of the kingdom by pledging fealty to the divine emperor. Part of the pledge was the declaration that the king was unique.[76] This was not strictly speaking an existential statement (i.e., "God alone exists"), but a relational and religious confession. The oneness of the king meant that all of one's energies were devoted to serving him. This is the oneness of covenantal love, not existence. It is not surprising, then, that m. *Ber.* 2:5 understands the entire Shema and its benedictions to be an acknowledgement of God's kingship.[77]

---

70 Kimmelman, "The Shema and its Rhetoric: The Case for the Shema being More than Creation, Revelation and Redemption," *Journal of Jewish Thought and Philosophy* 2 (1992): 118–21.
71 *Ibid.,* 129.
72 *Ibid.,* 132.
73 "No wonder," comments Kimmelman, "there are Genizah versions of the third blessing which instead of reading, 'This is my God,' read, 'The Lord is our King'" (*ibid.,* 133).
74 Cf. Targ. Ps.-Jon. and Neof. to Ex 15:18.
75 Kimmelman, "Shema and its Rhetoric," 130. The recitation, Kimmelman points out, is not descriptive, but performative. In the Shema, God *becomes* king for Israel (132).
76 Weinfeld, *Deuteronomy,* 353–54.
77 Thomas Lehnardt, "Der Gott der Welt ist unser König: Zur Vorstellung von der Königsherrschaft Gottes im Shema und seinen Benediktionen" in *Königsherrschaft Gottes und himmlischer Kult im Judentum, Urchristentum und in der hellen-*

The Shema itself as a loyalty oath is beautifully illustrated in a portion of haggadah from *Sifre Deuteronomy* 31. In one interpretation, the rabbis split up the two clauses in the first phrase: "The Lord, our God, over us (the children of Israel); the Lord is one, over all the creatures of the world." In this reading, both clauses of the opening phrase express God's rule. In the case of Israel, however, the rule is more intimate ("Yahweh *our* God"). God presently rules over the rest of creation, but in a general sense that is not currently acknowledged by the nations. A second interpretation presents a temporal reading of God's unity. Again the clauses of Deut 6:4 are atomized: "The Lord our God—in this world; the Lord is one—in the world to come, as it is said, the Lord shall be king over all the earth. In that day shall the Lord be one and his name one" (Zech 14:9). Again, both clauses of the first phrase signify Yahweh's sovereignty. Israel acknowledges this sovereignty in this world with the phrase "*our* God." The nations will acknowledge that sovereignty in the world to come: "The Lord shall be king *over all the earth*." The oneness signifies here the future universality of Yahweh's lordship.

Conclusion

In sum, for ancient Jews both before and after Paul, God's oneness (at least in part) designated God's universal sovereignty. The idea of oneness as sovereignty explains why the author of James says—in his memorable phrase—"You believe that God is one (εἷς ἐστιν ὁ θεός); you do well. Even the demons believe—and shudder" (2:19). The demons hardly tremble because God can be counted on one finger. They cringe because they realize that God's unity means his absolute and universal rule. Yahweh is "one" in a contrastive and elative sense. He is perceived as unique because all power and life is centralized in his person. As I argued in chapter 1, this ultimate power and life of God in fact constitutes his divinity. Yet even though all divinity is properly God's, divinity can be shared by other beings to whom God gives power and eternal life.

I conclude that first-century Judaism was indeed monotheistic, but not in a way that excludes the deification of human beings. First-century Jewish monotheism allows for mediate divinities to share the God-

---

istischen Welt (eds. Martin Hengel and Anna Maria Schwemer; Tübingen: Mohr Siebeck, 1991), 289.

head of the primal God. It also allows for human assimilation to a Prime Mediate divinity (such as Christ or the Son of Man in 1 En 70–71) with respect to distinctively divine characteristics (i. e., power and immortality). I am calling this form of assimilation "deification."

Deification becomes a possibility when humans assimilate to a specifically divine being. Paul made this kind of assimilation possible for all his converts. By assimilating to Christ in terms of power, immortality and virtue, Pauline Christians do not become mere intermediates between the divine and the human like angels or daimones. They become something higher than angels by their assimilation to a mediate God (Christ), who is already incorporated into the identity of "the Father"—God "Most High."

Chapter 9:
Creation and the Objection of Absolute Transcendence

> "Manhood and Godhood are not taken to be fixed natures infinitely far apart. Rather, manhood is an open, emerging nature, which transcends towards Godhood, in virtue of the image of God in which humanity was created."
>
> —Karl Rahner[1]

Introduction

Monotheism as discussed in the last chapter has often been paired with another (perhaps more grave) objection to deification—the doctrine of God's transcendence.[2] A strong doctrine of transcendence is often based on the idea of God creating the world (especially *ex nihilo*). *Creatio ex nihilo* implies that, since God created the world out of nothing, he "is utterly distinct from, and other than, the world."[3] A God who is so other than the world would seem to be a God who cannot share his identity (or identity-constituting qualities) with human beings. Creation, then, forever separates the identities of God and human beings. As creator, deity is "Wholly Other," completely foreign and alien to the created type of existence. A created being cannot be said to realistically participate in an uncreated being. God's identity is to create, and humans cannot participate in this "unique" divine identity.[4] Creation,

---

1   Quoted in Benjamin Drewery, "Deification," in *Christian Spirituality: Essays in Honour of Gordon Rupp* (London: SCM Press, 1975), 59–60.
2   For this doctrine, which Richard Bauckham calls "transcendent uniqueness," see his *Jesus and the God of Israel*, 86–87.
3   Kaufmann, *Religion of Israel*, 60.
4   Bauckham, *God Crucified*, 10–11. See further his essay, "The 'Most High God' and the Nature of Early Jewish Monotheism" in *Israel's God and Rebecca's Children: Christology and Community in Early Judaism and Christianity: Essays in Honor*

it is concluded, eliminates any notion of Christian deification. In the formulation of Yeḥezkel Kaufmann, "it is impossible, in the biblical view, to become god. There is no bridge between the created universe and God."[5]

Deification, however, is not disallowed by the biblical witness to creation. Scholars can naturally point to a biblical story of creation— representing even "the earliest period of Hebrew religion"—but this does not amount to a "profound gulf which separates the Creator from the created world."[6] The "glib assumption that the Bible's 'sharp distinction' between God and man precludes deification," writes Keith Norman, "is ill-conceived; in fact, this is an example of Greek philosophical metaphysics read into the text."[7] Norman's objection is worth considering. Although biblical authors (including Paul) obviously speak of creation, they do not normally conceive of God as "profoundly" separate and metaphysically alien from the world or human beings.[8] Such an idea, to my mind at least, is alien to the Christian Gospel which presents a God profoundly involved in humanity in an attempt to get humanity profoundly involved with God. For some of the great Jewish heroes of the past, as we saw in chapter 3, profound involvement with God amounted to deification.

Here I must address the objection of *creatio ex nihilo* head on. Blackwell appears to believe that Paul maintained a doctrine of *creatio ex nihilo*. Irenaeus, Cyril of Alexandria and Paul, Blackwell affirms, "all see creation as *ex nihilo*."[9] Blackwell states this even though he is familiar with

---

    of Larry W. Hurtado and Alan F. Segal (eds. David B. Capes, Larry W. Hurtado and Alan F. Segal; Waco, Tex.: Baylor University Press, 2007), 39–53. Here he has many ways of referring to God's "absolute" transcendence: "absolute difference in kind from all other reality" (40), "transcendent supremacy" (47), "absolute distinction of kind" (48), etc.

5   *Religion of Israel*, 77. Cf. James Starr, who affirms that God's "utter uniqueness and transcendence necessarily excludes … the apotheosis of human beings" (*Sharers in Divine Nature*, 74).

6   Russell, *Doctrine of Deification*, 53.

7   Keith Norman, "Deification: The Content of Athanasian Soteriology" (PhD diss., Duke University, 1980), 28.

8   Only after the doctrine of *creatio ex nihilo*, says Frances Young, was God "no longer conceived as ontologically intertwined with the world" ("'Creatio ex Nihilo': A Context for the Emergence of the Christian Doctrine of Creation," *SJT* 44 [1991]: 150).

9   *Christosis*, 259.

Frances Young,[10] who says that *creatio ex nihilo* only emerges in the late second century C.E. in the proto-orthodox conflict with "Gnosticism"—and that the doctrine only becomes *widespread* in the third century. In this judgment Young follows the monograph of Gerhard May.[11] May points out that *creatio ex nihilo* is a deeply philosophical doctrine. The problems which generated the need for this doctrine (passive matter as an eternal principle opposing God) would not have occurred to Paul, who was not beholden to technical metaphysics. For God to call "into existence the things that do not exist" (Rom 4:17, NRSV) is for God to create life out of death—not matter out of non-being. Thus to state that Paul believed in *creatio ex nihilo* is in my judgment anachronistic and misleading. We cannot assert that Paul believed in an absolute (metaphysical) separation between God and human beings based on this doctrine.[12]

Yet it seems to me that even later Christian theology (hardly metaphysically innocent), never posits an "absolute" gap between the Creator and human beings that the Creator himself has not already crossed. Starr readily points to "God's participation in human nature" and his "descent" into humanity (referring of course to Christ).[13] In *Sharers in Divine Nature*, he states that "God's transcendence in 2 Peter is absolute, broken only by the incarnation."[14] The direct statement, however, that humans (besides Christ) share in the divine nature (2 Pet 1:4) would seem to undermine Starr's notion of "absolute" transcendence. At any rate, Starr well represents the continued bias in Protestant scholarship that one human (Jesus) can be (a) God (realistically speaking), while

---

10 "Creatio ex Nihilo," 142.

11 *Creatio ex Nihilo: The Doctrine of 'Creation Out of Nothing' in Early Christian Thought* (London: T&T Clark International, 2004), 197. For a different view, see J.C. O'Neill "How Early is the Doctrine of *Creatio ex Nihilo?*" *JTS* 52 (2002): 449–65. O'Neill, in my view, wrongfully equates God's prior creation of matter out of nothing (before ordering it) with *creatio ex nihilo* (the creation of the *ordered* world out of nothing).

12 It has sometimes been thought that *creatio ex nihilo* was a way for Christianity to defeat the baneful influence of Platonism. Plato and later Platonists had always conceived of creation through pre-existent matter. From another perspective, however, the doctrine of *creatio ex nihilo* is Platonist to the core because it makes God absolutely transcendent—beyond the world and beyond creaturely "being" or existence. This is exactly where Plato would put the Form of the Good (*Resp.* 509b).

13 *Sharers in Divine Nature*, 76.

14 *Ibid.*, 154.

other humans cannot become God(s). Nonetheless, it seems fair to ask those scholars working with notions of "Wholly Other" transcendence (in the spirit of Athanasius): if God became human, why cannot humans become God? God may be "ontologically other than the world," in the words of C. Kavin Rowe,[15] but God in Christ has overcome that ontological gap.[16] The presumed "infinite qualitative distinction" between God and humans is technically nullified by the incarnation. This, I dare say, is the logic of Chalcedon: If Christ *really* became fully human, why cannot humans *really* become divine?

Although I am speaking in terms of later Christology, something of the logic of incarnation is at work already in Paul. Although Paul obviously has a doctrine of creation,[17] his notion of Christ throws into question every ontology which would interpose an absolute barrier between the Creator and the human world. Paul's Christology shows that one "in the form of God" (Phil 2:6) can be "born of woman" (Gal 4:4) and become "son of God" (Rom 1:4), "Lord" (Phil 2:9–11), and "life-making pneuma" (1 Cor 15:45). In the transfer from the human to the divine, therefore, believers in Pauline churches do not pass a boundary that Christ has not already crossed. The path has already been set by their elder brother, the image or model to which Paul's converts conform. Paul does not thematize a distinction between Christ's

---

15 "New Testament Iconography? Situating Paul in the Absence of Material Evidence" in *Picturing the New Testament: Studies in Ancient Visual Images* (eds. Annette Weissenrieder, Friederike Wendt and Petra von Gemünden; Tübingen: Mohr Siebeck, 2005), 293.

16 The doctrine of absolute transcendence can also be attacked on philosophical grounds. If God's transcendence were truly "absolute" he would be entirely unable to interact with the world. This may well describe the God of Maimonides, or Plotinus, but it hardly describes the biblical God, or the God known to Jews in the Second Temple period. Bauckham rightly believes that God is universally sovereign, but this does not make him "absolutely" transcendent. One would have to assume the philosophical doctrine of *creatio ex nihilo* to assert that God is "absolutely" different from the world. As I will argue later in this chapter, the Jewish doctrine of creation is less about putting God in a unique "Wholly Other" ontological category than it is about expressing a tremendous power differential. God as "maker" of the world is a way of speaking about God's comprehensive ownership and sovereignty.

17 The creator-creature distinction is directly set out in Rom 1:25. Significantly, Paul connects creation with resurrection (Rom 4:17) and calls transformed believers (part of) the "new creation" (2 Cor 5:17; Gal 6:15). See further Gottfried Nebe, "Creation in Paul's Theology" in *Creation in Jewish and Christian Tradition* (London: Sheffield Academic, 2002), 111–137.

sonship and believers' sonship as in later Christian theology. Nor does he set a limit to believers' conformation to Christ because Christ is viewed as a creator. Christians become "the same image" as the divine and human Christ (2 Cor 3:18). Christian theologians and exegetes must deal more squarely with the scandal of "the same."

Shareable and Unshareable Divinity

It is not enough, however, to point to the primitive incarnational theology in Paul's letters to undermine the argument from absolute (in essence, *philosophical*) transcendence. We must come to a deeper grasp of what in the ancient world it meant to participate in divinity. As a preface to this, I would like to affirm two basic agreements I have with those who deny deification on the grounds of creation: (1) Creation does indeed produce a gap between God and human beings, and (2) the power to create is characteristic of God's distinctive (not unique) divine identity. What I would like to emphasize, however, is that there are shareable and unshareable aspects of the divine identity. The power to create the physical world, it is safe to say, is an unshareable aspect of the Jewish God's identity. Those who argue for deification in Paul do not normally assert (to my knowledge) that deified humans share God's power to create the universe. Though perhaps some in the modern world would disagree, in biblical thought, at least, humans cannot create physical worlds. Deified humans, therefore, will never fully overlap with the divine identity. In this way, then, God's identity remains ever distinct. In this aspect (and many others) God remains transcendent.

The idea of transcendence, however, does not disallow a doctrine of deification. This is because deification involves participating only in those *shareable* aspects of the divine identity (e.g., immortality and ruling power) *not* the *unshareable* aspects (such as the power to create physical worlds). *Thus the objection of creation is really no objection at all to a Pauline form of deification as it is being presented here.* This is because deification requires not full, but only a partial overlap with the divine identity. Deification is about participation in, not a complete overlap or fusion with God's nature.

Mediate Divinity and Participation

Let me expand this thesis by developing a point about ancient concepts of divinity briefly touched on in the last chapter. For Paul, there is a difference between the divinity of God "the Father" and the divinity of Christ, which I have called the distinction between "primal" and "mediate" divinity. In making this distinction, however, I hardly want to push the idea that Paul's Christ is rigorously subordinate to the Father, or that the Father is somehow inaccessible to human beings—both of which are false. My point in making this distinction is ultimately one about participation. Generally speaking, mediate divinity is thought to be *shareable*, while primal divinity—though not "*Wholly* Other" as in Dialectical Theology—remains *unshareable*. In the words of a famous Platonist handbook, assimilating to God means assimilating to the God "*in* the heavens, not, of course, the God above the heavens, who does not possess virtue, being superior to this" (Alcin., *Epit.* 28.3).[18] The "first" or primal God (ὁ πρῶτος θεός), the text explains, is an "eternal," and "ineffable" "Father"; he has "neither genus, nor species, nor differentia, nor does he possess any attributes." He is not endowed with quality. Further, "he is not a part of anything, nor is he in the position of being a whole which has parts, nor is he the same as anything or different from anything" (10.3–4, trans. John Dillon, modified).[19] In the case of the *primal* God, then, it is right (for at least some ancient Mediterranean peoples) to speak of an unknowable divine essence which cannot be shared.

An unknowable unshareable divine essence also appears in Jewish texts. In *On the Creation of the World*, Philo approvingly quotes Philolaus (a fifth century B.C.E. Pythagorean): "There is a supreme Ruler of all things, God, ever One, abiding, without motion, Himself (alone) like unto Himself, different from all others (αὐτὸς αὐτῷ ὅμοιος, ἕτερος τῶν ἄλλων)" (§100). The primal God, who is clearly in mind here, is surely "other." Indeed, such a God can often be defined simply in terms of alterity. As in the famous Jewish oracle, "I am Yahweh, and there is no

---

18 Note the discussion of Van Kooten, *Paul's Anthropology*, 158.
19 Cf. Apuleius, *Deo Socr.*, 123–24: "But why should I now begin to speak of their Father [the Father of the Gods], who is the master and source of all things, freed from all bonds of being acted upon or acting, tied by no need for interchange in exercising any function ... this God alone—such is the amazing and ineffable excess of his majesty, cannot be comprehended" (see further *Apol.* 64.5–7).

other" (Isa 45:5)—greatness is defined as pure otherness. This "other," primal God of Jewish scripture corresponds to Philo's invisible, incomprehensible "Existent" who is pushed beyond attributes, qualities, names, predicates, and even being itself—"superior to the Good, purer than the One and more primal than the Monad" (*Contempl.* 2; cf. Plato, *Resp.* 509b9). With Philo we are well on the road to later Christian philosophy and apophatic theology.

But the full logic of Philo's position must be fleshed out to understand participation. On the one hand, nothing is similar to God (meaning the primal God, or the "Existent") (*Leg.* 2.1; *Somn.* 2.221).[20] On the other hand, Philo often talks about assimilating to God by doing various activities or developing certain virtues (e.g., *Abr.* 87; *Praem.* 126). As I pointed out in chapter 7, assimilation to God is a consistent teaching in Philo (e.g., *Virt.* 168).[21] But how can one assimilate to a God "more primal than the Monad"? I am hesitant to make Philo more consistent than he is, but it seems a fair interpretation that whenever Philo talks about assimilation to God, he has in mind the "second God," or the Logos. He says so directly in QG 2.62:

> For nothing mortal can be made in the likeness of the most high One and Father of the universe but (only) in that of the second God, who is His Logos. For it was right that the rational (part) of the human soul should be formed as an impression by the divine Logos, since the pre-Logos God [the most high One and Father] is superior to every rational nature. But He who is above the Logos (and) exists in the best and in a special form—what things that come into being can rightfully bear His likeness? Moreover, Scripture wishes also to show that God most justly avenges the virtuous and decent men because they have a certain kinship with His Logos, of which the human mind is a likeness and image. (trans. Ralph Marcus, LCL)[22]

Assimilation to the Logos, as we see in this text, already fits Philo's anthropology of the mind made in the image of the Logos (cf. *Opif.* 69; *Deus* 48; *Plant.* 18). Accordingly, rational actions and states like the virtues assimilate one to the second God (i.e., the Logos), not Philo's "most high One and Father." Again, although Philo's notion of participation is not totally consistent, its basic structure, it appears, is this: there is a primal, unknowable God whose essence cannot be shared, and there is a mediate God (the Logos), whose divine qualities *can* be

---

20   Van Kooten, *Paul's Anthropology*, 181–188

21   See Helleman, "Philo on Deification and Assimilation," 51–71.

22   For the Greek fragment and commentary, see Runia, *Philo and Timaeus*, 298.

shared. Humans are already in the image of the Logos, but require fuller assimilation to the Logos through virtue.

Although Paul is by no means as philosophically astute as Philo, a similar pattern of participation is implicit in his letters. That is, though Paul does not speak of the Father as the "Existent" "more primal than the Monad," his deep sense of the Father's alterity remains. At one point, he bursts out:

> O the depth of the riches and wisdom and knowledge of God! How un-
> searchable are his judgments and how inscrutable his ways!
> "For who has known the mind of the Lord?
> Or who has been his counselor?"
> "Or who has given a gift to him,
> to receive a gift in return?"
> For from him and through him and to him are all things. To him be the
> glory forever. Amen! (Rom 11:33–36, NRSV)

One can tell from the very "feel" of this passage that the divinity of the primal God (the "Father")—though not at all divorced from the world—is still too lofty to be shared in directly. Pauline religion, in other words, preserves a sense that the primal God's divinity is loftier than human conception and human participation. I do not want to push this point too far, since God and Christ are obviously closely inter-twined. (Paul is a true binitarian.) Nonetheless it is significant that Paul is hesitant to say that one can directly participate in or imitate God the Father.[23]

The pattern that emerges is this: if one cannot share in the essence of primal divinity, one can share the identity of Paul's Prime *Mediate* divin-ity. In other words: Paul's converts can participate in the divinity of the God Christ. He is the God whom Paul imitates (1 Cor 11:1). He is the God who lives in Paul (Gal 2:19–20). He is the God whom Paul fol-lows in the pattern of death and resurrection. When Paul talks of gaining immortality or of being an heir of the world, he seems to be thinking specifically of sharing in the attributes and prerogatives of the divine Christ. As I have emphasized in previous chapters, Pauline deification occurs through the mediate God, Christ.

---

23 Contrast the Deutero-Pauline affirmation of Eph 5:1: "Become imitators of God (μιμηταὶ τοῦ Θεοῦ) as beloved children."

Non-creating and Created Gods

It is sometimes thought that, though Christ can be included in the divine identity of the Father because of Christ's power to create (1 Cor 8:6), humans cannot be included in the divine identity because they are creatures who do not have any power to create (in the biblical sense). I want to address this objection here.

In chapter one, I set out two basic divine qualities which best defined divinity in the first-century Greco-Roman world: immortality and power. These are also, it seems to me, the basic divine qualities of the Jewish God Yahweh, as well as the God Christ. Christ in Pauline theology makes it possible for humans to share those divine qualities. Having these qualities, in the ancient mind, made one a God because a God *is* an immortal being with superhuman power. The power to create was not essential to Godhood in the ancient world. Having the power to create is thus not essential for deification.

Arguably, creation and Godhood are more closely associated in the Jewish conception of God. But here also I think we need to make a distinction. It seems to me that it is one thing to acknowledge that God created the world, and another to suppose that in first-century Christianity the power to create is somehow unique to the essence of divinity. To be sure, Isaiah makes Yahweh's power to create central to Yahweh's claim for deity (40:26; 41:20; 42:5; 45:7, 12, 18; 54:16). Yet here again I wonder if this prophet can be taken to be the rule and standard for all Jewish thought for all future time? There is some evidence, at least, that Jewish heroes and other numina who lacked the power to create continued to be thought of as "Gods" (Ex 15:11; 22:27; 1 Sam 28:13; Pss 49[50]:1; 136:2; 94[95]:3; 96[97]:9; 134[135]:5; 85[86]:8; 81[82]:1b, 6; 1QM 1:10–11; 17:7; 11QMelch; John 10:34–36). This kind of language cannot just be swept aside as a figure of speech. This is to excuse—in light of modern monotheistic categories—and not to explain. Our task is to redescribe this sort of language in a way that promotes understanding of divinity as it was conceived in the first century. First-century Jewish theology seems to have countenanced the idea of non-creating Gods.

Yet the plot thickens—for deification suggests not only that *non-creating* beings can be Gods, but that *created* beings can be Gods. To be sure, the idea of created Gods is paradoxical (perhaps even blasphemous) for those accustomed to modern conceptions of monotheism and *creatio ex nihilo*. In the ancient world, however, this was fairly staple theology. As

I said, for both Greeks and Jews in the first century, creative power was not an essential constituent of divinity. Accordingly, it cannot be admitted that *only* beings who created physical worlds were considered to be divine. None of the Olympian Gods were creators in this sense. In fact, most Gods in the ancient Mediterranean basin were not considered to be creators. Should it also surprise us that there are beings called "Gods" (אלהים; θεοί) in Jewish writings who had nothing to do with creation (note the texts cited in the previous paragraph). Are not these "Gods"—at least by Paul's day—considered to be created beings?[24] Up until the fourth century, Christians (such as Arius) asserted that Christ himself was both a God and a creature. They based this teaching in part on the Jewish text in Proverbs, where Wisdom (considered to be the divine Christ) says: "The Lord created me (ἔκτισέν με) the beginning of his ways" (Prov 8:22). The idea of created Gods, I suggest, was not foreign to ancient Judaism or Christianity. We are not dealing here with Apollo and Dionysus. We are dealing with genuinely Jewish and Christian Gods. What I am suggesting is that these other "Gods" were thought to participate in the *shareable* aspects of God's divinity (like immortality, virtue, and universal power), and that this allowed them legitimately (and realistically) to be called "Gods" while still remaining created beings.

The idea of created, or "generate" Gods was not, it seems, unusual before the fourth century C.E. Compare Alcinous, who gives us a digest of the kind of Platonism taught in the early empire:

> There are, furthermore, other divinities, the daimones, whom one could also term 'created Gods' (γενητοὺς θεούς), present in each of the elements, some of them visible, others invisible, in ether, and fire, and air, and water, so that no part of the world should be without a share in soul or in a living being superior to mortal nature. To their administration the whole sublunar and terrestrial sphere has been assigned. God is in fact himself the creator of the universe, and of the Gods and daimones … The rest is ruled over by his children (παῖδες), who do everything that they do in accordance with his command and in imitation of him. (*Epit.* 15.1–2; trans. John Dillon, modified)

Here the daimonic children of God share in God's divine rule by administering earth and the region below the moon. For Paul, however, these created Gods (or aerial daimones) are the very "Gods and

---

24 Admittedly, there is some ambiguity because in Genesis 1 angels and other superhuman beings are never said to be created.

Lords" he acknowledge in 1 Cor 8:5 (even if he polemically calls them "so-called Gods"). These are the beings who will one day submit to the human rule of the "sons of God" conformed to Christ (1 Cor 6:2–3; Rom 8:29). Pauline "sons of God" will be superior to the daimonic "Gods"—but *both are created beings.*

The "created Gods" of Alcinous are also related to the "offspring Gods" (ἔκγονοι θεοί) mentioned in the next chapter of his *Handbook* (16.1–2). These are apparently the super-lunary star Gods equivalent to the "children" (παῖδες) of God mentioned in the above quote. They are given charge of creating mortal winged, aquatic, and land animals (thus they are both creating and created Gods).[25] Philo and other Jews were well aware that Moses prohibited the *worship* of the stars (Deut 4:19). But—and I cannot emphasize this enough—this is something different from thinking that the stars are *divine*, as Philo clear does (*Opif.* 27; *Spec.* 1.19; *QG* 1.42).

Philo, to be sure, would seem to deny that created Gods are true Gods. The Jews, he says, rejected the "deceit concerning generate Gods (ἐπὶ τοῖς γενητοῖς θεοῖς). For no generate being (γενητός) is a God in truth, but only in opinion. This is because it lacks what is most necessary—eternity (ἀιδιότητα)" (*Virt.* 65). There are, however, certain other texts which would seem to mitigate the force of Philo's declaration here. Philo thinks that even plants can share in God's eternity (ἀιδιότης) (*Opif.* 44). He says elsewhere that the human mind that truly loves and sees God has roots that stretch "toward eternity" (πρὸς ἀιδιότητα) (*Cong.* 56). This agrees with the currently favored reading of Wisd 2:23 (according to the NRSV printing), which has humans called "the image of God's eternity" (εἰκόνα τῆς ἰδίας ἀιδιότητος). Eternity—by no means proper to human beings—is evidently something that they can share by participation in God.[26] Now if "eternity" in *Virt.* 65 means something like "unbegottenness," then certainly humans—and every other generated being—cannot share in that quality. Unbegottenness is an unshareable divine quality of the Existent. Nevertheless, Philo is willing to call other generated beings "Gods," such as the stars

---

25 It may have been the idea of multiple ἔκγονοι θεοί that made it necessary for the author of John's prologue to call Jesus μονογενής θεός (clarifying that God has only *one* divine offspring) (1:18).

26 See further Lorenzen, *Eikon,* 25–37.

(*Opif.* 27; *Spec.* 1.19; *QG* 42; cf. *Prov.* 2.50; *Opif.* 144).[27] The stars are in fact God's "heavenly offspring" (κατ᾽ οὐρανὸν ἔκγονοι) (*Opif.* 46, cf. Alcinous above!). Having admitted as much, Philo's strategy is to find some distinction in the grade of astral divinity. The stars are not Gods with absolute powers (θεοὺς αὐτοκράτορας), but divine lieutenants (ὑπάρχους) of the one true God (*Spec.* 1.13–14; cf. *Opif.* 46). The stars participate in the *shareable* aspects of divinity (immortality and power), but not in the *unshareable* aspects (such as eternity). Nonetheless, according to Philo's own consistent language, the stars are still "Gods."

How do we understand Philonic "Gods" besides the Existent? Although in some places Philo can be quite strict about what a God is "in truth," he seems also open to the idea that divinity can also be had by participation. In making this distinction, I propose that Philo distinguishes between at least two grades of divinity, what we might call "true God" and "participated God." Perhaps the most pivotal example is Moses, who (as we saw in an earlier chapter) Philo repeatedly calls "God" (cf. *Leg.* 1.40; *Sacr.* 9; *Migr.* 84; *Mut.* 128–29; *Somn.* 2.189; *Mos.* 1.158; *Prob.* 43). But Moses is only a "God" as a "participant" or "partner" (κοινωνός) in God's possessions (*Mos.* 1.155). He is not a God "in truth" (πρὸς ἀλήθειαν) (*Det.* 160–161). This is in accord with the general rule that "what comes to be" (τὸ γεγονός) is in all respects later and lesser (ὕστερον) than the maker (τοῦ πεποιηκότος)" (*Plant.* 132; cf. *Sac.* 92). Nonetheless, the inferiority of generate reality does not, apparently, exclude it from sharing in divinity. Again, I fear to make Philo more consistent than he is—but it appears that he is assuming a picture of graded divinity fairly common in his age. Philo may modify and restrict this idea of graded divinity (by declaring that the true God is the only God), yet he always slides back into what appears to have been the default philosophical and cultural presupposition: created beings can share divinity. Even for Philo, then, divinity was not a quality of ingenerate (i. e., primal) deity alone. It could be shared with generated beings.[28] This is precisely the logic of deification.

Later Christian interpreters, interestingly, still reflect the logic of created Gods. Famously, Origen spoke of Jesus the son of God as a cre-

---

27 Cf. Plato, *Apol.* 26d1–3: "Do I [Socrates] not believe that the sun and moon are Gods, just as other people?"

28 For an account of a scale of divine beings made of fire, aether, air and water all under the high God Uranus ("Heaven"), see the post-Platonic treatise *Epinomis* 981b-985c.

ated being (κτίσμα) (*Princ.* 4.4.1). Arnobius of Sicca leaves open the possibility for generate Gods begotten or otherwise brought forth by the high God: "[I]n addition to the King and Prince himself [God and Christ] there are other divine individuals (*alia numinum capita*) who when sorted out and counted, form, as it were, a sort of plebeian mass" (*Contra Gentes* 3.3; cf. 2.35; 7.35).[29] In his funeral oration for Basil the Great (mid-fourth century C.E.), Gregory of Nazianzus declared: "I am a creature of God and bidden to be a God (Θεοῦ τε κτίσμα τυγχάνων καὶ Θεὸς εἶναι κεκελευσμένος)" (*Or. Bas.* 48).[30]

God the Creator

In the first century C.E. at least, the deity of non-creating and created Gods never threatened the deity of the one God, because (among Jews and Christians) the divinity of God the Creator was assumed to be (1) infinite, and (2) indisputably distinctive.

With reference to (1), I pointed out in the last chapter that divinity was not a zero-sum game. God does not "lose" divinity when other beings share in it. Divinity, for ancient thinkers in general, is not a limited resource. In the words of one ancient writer: "it is the nature of the divine to penetrate to all things. The things of our earth receive their share of it, and the things above us according to their nearness to or distance from God receive more or less of divine benefit" (Ps.-Arist., *De Mundo* 6, 397b32–398a1). This is what makes God great: God can share his divinity and be no less God.

Second, in the Jewish scriptures—even if the divinity of other Gods is occasionally acknowledged, Yahweh's power to create undoubtedly proves the superiority of his divinity. He is higher than the other Gods (Isa 40:18–26; Jer 10:1–16; Ps 88:8–14 [ET 89:7–13]; 95 [96]:4–5; 134[135]:5–7; 135[136]:2–9), almighty (Job 26:5–14; Ps 134[135]:5–7), and (rhetorically speaking) incomparable (Isa 40:25–26; Job 38–39).

---

29 For more evidence of created Gods in patristic sources, see Michael Frede, "Monotheism and Pagan Philosophy in Later Antiquity" in *Pagan Monotheism in Late Antiquity*, 58–60.

30 Gregory will later say, in arguing that the Son and Father are consubstantial, that what is created cannot be God (*Or.* 29.4). This theological fine-tuning is not original with Gregory. It is indicative of larger doctrinal revolutions in the fourth century distinctive to Christian theologians.

It is worth dwelling on this point to get a better sense of what it means for God to be creator. God as creator is God as owner of the cosmos,[31] which indicates his power over it (see, e.g., Jer 10:12–13 = 51:15–16; Ps 28[29]; 103[104]; 134[135]:5–7). In the words of Herbert Niehr:

> Power is [the] dependence of everything created on its creator. Creation generates dependence, which is power. The primacy of one God over all the other Gods is grounded in creatorship (a theme in Second Isaiah), and the subordination of all the other gods under this one God is grounded in the dependency of the created on the creator. In other words, the primacy of the high God lies in the fact that he himself was not created.[32]

If a God created everything, he also rules everything. The idea of creation is thus a powerful theological way to express the kingly power of the primal God. This is what God's transcendence amounts to in biblical thought—not metaphysical otherness (as in later Christian philosophy)—but power. "Your hand fashioned and made me; and now you turn and destroy me" (Job 10:8). In this passage, God has absolute sovereignty over Job as the potter does over the clay (cf. Isa 29:15–16; 45:9–12; Jer 18:3–6, 11b). In the end, Job confesses "I know that you can do all things, and that no purpose of yours can be thwarted" (42:2). Paul himself uses the potter-clay metaphor to a similar effect (Rom 9:19–23). "But who indeed are you, a human being, to argue with God? Will what is molded say to the one who molds it, 'Why have you made me like this?'" (v. 20). In the words of Jan Assmann, "Creatorship is the legitimizing basis of sovereignty."[33]

Nevertheless, the power to create does not put God above the class of other divine beings. First of all, the Jewish God was not the only creator God known in the ancient world. One readily thinks of Plato's Demiurge, Marduk of Babylonian myth, Ahura Mazda in Zoroastrian-

---

31 For God as owner of the creation see Isa 43:1; Ps 8:4; 29:1–2; 74:16; 89:12; 95:5–7; 100:3; 115:15–16.
32 Herbert Niehr, "The Rise of YHWH in Judahite and Israelite Religion" in *The Triumph of Elohim: From Yahwisms to Judaisms* (ed. Diana Vikander Edelman; Grand Rapids: Eerdmans, 1996), 66–67.
33 Assmann, *Of God and Gods*, 61. Cf. Levenson, "We can capture the essence of the idea of creation in the Hebrew Bible with the word 'mastery'" (*Creation and the Persistence of Evil: The Jewish Drama of Divine Omnipotence* [San Francisco: Harper & Row, 1988], 3).

ism, and El at Ugarit.[34] All these Gods stood at the head of a bureaucracy of subordinate Gods. Historically speaking, the same can be said for Yahweh and the "Gods" around him in the divine assembly (Ps 81 [82]:1). Based on the very language of the Jewish scriptures, we cannot claim that the Jewish and Christian creator God was of a different species of divinity than other Gods (even if some Platonists—and later Jewish and Christian Platonists—wanted to put God "beyond being" [*Resp.* 509b]). The high God is, rather, the "royalty" of the same species—the apex of his class.[35]

There was, naturally, a difference in status between creating and created Gods. This is illustrated in the most popular Platonic dialogue of antiquity, the *Timaeus*. Here Plato envisions the creator God (or Demiurge) as organizing chaos into a harmony of earth, air, fire, and water—in short, a cosmos. Although the creator God creates the world soul and the soul of humans, he does not make the bodies of humans, or of any other mortal being. If he did, human bodies would be incorruptible, since whatever the creator God makes is unable to be dissolved. To fill out creation, then, the creator God generates the "young Gods" (νέοι θεοί) (*Tim.* 42d6). It is clear that these subordinate creators are Gods, even if they are of a lesser status than the chief creator God (*Tim.* 41a–42d).

Before one tosses aside this way of thinking as un-Jewish, I will note that Philo presents a similar picture of creation. Genesis 1:26 has the creator God famously declare, "Let *us* make human beings after *our* image and likeness." This statement, according to Philo, "plainly shows the taking with him of others as fellow workers (συνεργῶν)" (*Opif.* 75).[36]

---

34 For these Gods, see Norman Cohn, *Cosmos, Chaos, and the World to Come: The Ancient Roots of Apocalyptic Faith* (New Haven: Yale University Press, 1993), 5–9, 47, 81–83, 121.

35 For Paul, God the Father is not even the only creator God. The Father shares his creative power with Christ. Christ is God's Wisdom (1 Cor 1:30). If Wisdom of old was not an independent hypostasis, for Paul Christ the creator is certainly an independent being (1 Cor 8:4–6; cf. John 1:1–3). Christ as divine creator hardly threatens the divinity of the Father, although he shares more of the Father's divine identity.

36 For the interpretation of *Opif.* 72–75, I am dependent on David Runia, *Philo and Timaeus*, 207–212, idem., *Philo of Alexandria On the Creation of the Cosmos according to Moses* (Philo of Alexandria Commentary Series 1; Leiden: Brill, 2001), 236–44; and David Winston, "Theodicy and Creation of Man in Philo of Alexandria," in *Hellenica et Judaica: Hommage à Valentin Nikiprowetzky*

God requires these "fellow workers"—who are clearly creators—because human beings (unlike plants and stars) partake of both virtue and vice. God could create plants, because they are not capable of either virtue or vice; God could also create stars, because they (as superior to humans) are perfect minds and incapable of vice (*Opif.* 73–75). But to create humans—capable of vice and virtue—God needed the help of "subordinates" (ὑπήκοοι). Philo does not call these subordinates "Gods"—but he interestingly does not call them angels either. Based on *Conf.* 171–74, we might think of them as God's powers, the heavenly bodies, or the angels. In *Fug.*, 68–72, they are God's "powers." The important point is that these beings are creators who—if not Gods themselves—fulfill the same function as the young Gods who create in the *Timaeus* (41b–47e).[37] Philo calls his theory of human creation a "probable conjecture" (εἰκὸς στοχασμός) but as a "plausible and reasonable" (πιθανὴν καὶ εὔλογον) view it is likely his own (*Opif.* 73). At any rate, Philo assumes a clear status differential between the chief creator deity and his helpers. A similar status differential, one could argue, applies to Christ and deified Christians. Deified Christians are not creators (in the biblical sense), thus their divinity is subordinate to Christ.

The essential point is this: the fact that there were multiple Gods in the Jewish worldview never wiped out the high God's distinctiveness. For all the lieutenant "Gods" mentioned by Jews shared the power of the primal God, and manifested that power in the world. Their deity was totally dependent on the primal God. If the deity of these subordinate Gods in Judaism did not threaten the deity of the one (all-powerful) God, how much more the (even more subordinate!) divinity of deified human beings?

In fact, the only God who could possibly "threaten" the deity of the Father in Paul's thought is the deity called "Christ"—for this deity shares in God's creative power. He is the one "through whom" all things are made (1 Cor 8:6). Thus he shares in the deity of the primal God to a much greater degree than humans. But the Father's deity was not threatened by Christ, who remained in subordination (1 Cor 15:28). The creator God Christ shows that sharing divine identity does not create a situation of conflict, but adds "glory to God the Father" (Phil 2:11).

(eds. A. Caquot, M. Hadas-Lebel, and J. Riaud; Leuven-Paris: Peeters, 1986), 105–111. In general, I prefer the interpretation of Winston.

37 Cf. on this point Runia, *Philo and Timaeus*, 212.

The Question of Idolatry

To speak about created divinities, however, seems to invite the specter of idolatry. It is well known that for Paul the concept of idolatry is based on the fundamental distinction between the creator and the creation. Idolatry, as Paul defines it, means worshiping the creation instead of the creator (Rom 1:25). Perhaps above any other, this text would seem to undermine a notion of deification. For here Paul flatly condemns any worship of the creation, whether human, beast, or bird (1:23). Romans 1:23, with its language of "exchanging the glory of God for the simulation of the image (ἐν ὁμοιώματι εἰκόνος) of a human being" can in fact be read as a criticism of the ruler cult. This cult, pervasive throughout the empire, presented the image of a deified human being for worship—a practice which Paul condemned. Some scholars have concluded that the deification of a human being—even if it is by assimilation to Christ—would be the last thing to enter Paul's mind.

This objection fails, however, when we realize that though Paul forbids the *worship* of the creation, he *never claims that the creation cannot share in divinity*. (How else would the human Christ "born of woman" participate in the divinity of God?) Deification in Paul—if such there be—involves *no worship of the creation*. Rather, it is the assimilation of the human being to a mediate divinity (Christ) who has fully entered the creation. Pauline deification means a share in God's universal rule, virtue, and immortal corporeality. These are the shareable aspects of Christ's divine identity. These are what deified Christians share in. Fully overlapping with the divine identity (by becoming a creator deity) is neither possible nor required for deification. Humans never become lords *above* creation as Christ does—but they do become lords *of* creation *along with* Christ (see chapter 6). This is the basis of their divinity, a divinity which requires no formal cult (see the excursus below).

Conclusion

Thus in the Pauline understanding of deification, the threat of idolatry and the objection of absolute transcendence is simply bypassed. Humans do not share in the power to create. They *do* share in Christ's universal sovereignty, virtue, and immortality—aspects of Christ's divine identity which he openly shares with human beings. To say, then, that Paul's doctrine of creation disallows a vision of deification is to misunderstand what Pauline deification is. It was never asserted, to my knowledge, that Pauline deification means becoming a creator of physical worlds. It means becoming a "new creation" (2 Cor 5:17), after the model of Christ—a man who, when resurrected, showed his divine identity as Son of God (Rom 1:3–4), Lord (Phil 2:9–11), and life-making pneuma (1 Cor 15:45). Becoming a new creation does not mean becoming a creator, but a created being who can share in aspects of the divine identity which the divine Christ has made available to them as himself a human who was declared to be divine (Rom 1:3–4).

Excursus: Worship and Divinity

Scholars like Larry Hurtado argue strongly that to be a God in ancient Judaism required cult. "The evidence ... shows that it is in fact in the areas of worship that we find 'the decisive criterion' by which Jews maintained the uniqueness [i.e., the unique divinity] of God over against both idols and God's own deputies."[38] In this view, genuine deification would apparently require that deified Christians be worshiped. Although arguably we do see saint worship (commonly dubbed "veneration")[39] in post-Pauline Christianity, this practice does not appear in Paul. Consequently, in Hurtado's line of interpretation, Paul could not have taught the deification of the Christ believer.[40] To forestall this objection, I address it here.

The first point to note is that "worship" is a Jewish and Christian theological term not always precisely defined. Accordingly, Adela Yarbro and John Collins[41] have rightly critiqued Hurtado for not defining

---

38 Larry W. Hurtado, "First-Century Jewish Monotheism," *JSNT*, 71 (1998): 21–22.

39 See Peter Brown, *The Cult of the Saints: Its Rise and Function in Latin Christianity* (Chicago: University of Chicago Press, 1981).

40 According to Hurtado, "... the Jewish monotheistic stance forbade apotheosis, the divinization of human figures, and thus clashed with a major theme in pagan religion of the time" (*Lord Jesus Christ*, 91). Hurtado grants that the language used to describe the exaltation of Moses and Enoch "can be compared with divinization"; but since these figures had no regular cult, they were not genuine deifications (*ibid.*, 92). Hurtado's presupposition is that deification requires cult.

41 *King and Messiah as Son of God*, 212–13.

worship (and anyone who defines it as "honor due to [a] God" is merely running in circles).[42] It may be best to define worship in its most basic sense as the honor paid to a superior.[43] In this basic sense, all sorts of beings could receive worship. Humans could be worshiped by humans, Gods by Gods, and the whole range of Gods by the whole range of humans (Rom 13:7; 1 Pet 2:17). If Hurtado and others[44] claim that authentic worship requires blood sacrifice, they run into the embarrassing problem that Jesus (whom they consider to be [a Pauline] God) never received blood sacrifice.[45]

Before I talk about Judaism (arguably a type of Greco-Roman religion), it is important to note the larger currents of thought on cult in the Greco-Roman world. In ancient Mediterranean religions, one did not, it seems, have to receive cult to be a God. Greeks and Romans, it can be shown, commonly acknowledged Gods to whom they paid no cult at all. David Levene offers the example of Aurora, the Dawn goddess. "That she is a goddess is widely assumed in literary sources, and her most famous myth—the story of her love for Tithonus—is premised on her divinity and the gap between her and a mere human. But there is no evidence for any cult of Aurora anywhere in the Roman world."[46] The point is made by Ovid, who calls her temples *rarissima*, a superlative used euphemistically to mean "non-existent" (*Met.* 13.587–90). Earlier in the same century, Cicero employed the works of Carneades to implicitly question the distinction between Gods who are worshiped and Gods who are not (*Nat d.* 3.17.43–52). Achilles, says Carneades, was worshiped by the inhabitants of Astypalaea

42 Cf. Hurtado, who defines worship as "the sort of reverence that was reserved by ancient devout Jews for God alone" (*Lord Jesus Christ*, 31, n. 10), and the "specifically religious devotion of the sort given to a deity" (38, n. 36). These are patently circular definitions.
43 Gradel notes that "Roman thought did not include any clear distinction between 'honours' and 'worship' … Absolute and permanent power probably found expression throughout Roman history in divine honours bestowed on men as well as on gods" (*Emperor Worship*, 52–53; cf. 8, 29). The same, I think, could be said for Greek religion.
44 Note especially Loren Stuckenbruck, "'Angels' and 'God': Exploring the Limits of Early Jewish Monotheism" in *Early Jewish and Christian Monotheism* (eds. Stuckenbruck and Wendy E. Sproston North; London : T&T Clark International, 2004), 69.
45 See the discussion of J. Lionel North, "Jesus and Worship, God and Sacrifice" in *Early Jewish and Christian Monotheism*, 198–202.
46 "What is a God?", forthcoming.

because his mother was a God. By this logic, Orpheus and Rhesus—who both had divine mothers—ought to be Gods. This is logical despite the fact that the worship of Orpheus and Rhesus was not documented. Circe, descendent of the Sun was worshiped at the Roman colony of Circei. On this logic, Medea and Absyrtus—also descendents of the Sun—should also be considered deities. Again, this is true regardless of the fact that they lacked cult. But if the Sun and the Moon were Gods, Carneades continues, why not their cousins the Rainbow and the Clouds? Despite their lack of official cult, their claim to deity was the same. Clearly if Carneades' argument was going to work for the average Greco-Roman listener, the "decisive criterion" of divinity could not be worship.[47]

Later Christian apologists like Arnobius and Augustine delight to point out what might be called the Roman theology of micromanagement. I refer to all the Gods who—though true Gods—have carved out only the tiniest sphere of power: Lateranus, genius of hearths, Limentinus, protector of thresholds, Puta in charge of pruning, Nemestrinus the God of groves, and so forth.[48] Christian writers assume that such minor deities are widely considered to be Gods (otherwise their attempt to ridicule Roman theology would collapse). Yet it would be difficult to prove that such Gods received worship in the formal sense constructed by Hurtado. They may have periodically received a pinch of incense, or been invoked in an oath, but they were for the most part politely ignored. Worship was not a criterion for their divinity, let alone the "decisive" one. In the words of Arnobius, this is characteristic of the Gods: "they know of themselves what they are and they do not appraise themselves by adulations coming from elsewhere" (*Contra Gentes*, 7.15).

Were the rules different for ancient Jews? Did a Jewish God have to receive cult to be considered divine? It appears that Jews also believed that several beings were Gods although they paid them no cult. Philo calls the Logos the "Second God" (QG 2.62) but renders him no formal worship. He calls the stars "Gods" (*Opif.* 27; *Spec.* 1.19–20; QG 42), but rejects the worship of them (*Migr.* 178–181; *Her.* 96–99, 289;

---

47 We should also note the long list of deified abstraction that never received cult. Some of these include Aidos, Anaideia, Ara, Asebeia, Asphaleia, Athanasia, Bia, Boule, Charis, Demos, Eleos, Elpis, Eris, Eulabeia, Euphrosyne, Gelos, *among many more* (Pieter Willem van der Horst, "God (II)" in *DDD²*, 367).

48 For more examples, see Arnobius, *Contra Gentes* 4.7, 11, Aug., *Civ.* 4.8, 21; 6.9, and *passim*.

Congr. 48–49). The angels called "Gods" (אלים) at Qumran also do not appear to have received cult. The same could be said for the "the God" (אלהים) Melchizedek who appears in 11Q13.

Then again, there are beings not explicitly identified as Gods in Jewish texts who do appear to receive cult. The Jewish worship of angels appears to have been active during and beyond the first century C.E., as evidenced by repeated prohibitions of worshipping angels in rabbinic texts,[49] and a range of other Jewish and Christian sources.[50] For example, Ps.-Philo mentions that the Feast of Tabernacles is "an offering for your Watchers" who appear to be angelic figures (13:6). Levi, in the *Testament of Levi* wishes to learn the name of an angel so that he can call on the angel "in the day of tribulation" (5:5). The highest angels worship (*adorare*) Adam, as the image of God in the *Life of Adam and Eve* (14:1).[51] In the *Parables of Enoch* (1 En 37–71), "all those who dwell on the dry ground will [in the end time] fall down and worship" before the Son of Man (whose face is like the angels [1 En 46:1]) (48:5; cf. 62:6–9).[52] As we learn from the context, the worship of the Son

---

49 Stuckenbruck (*Angel Veneration and Christology: A Study in Early Judaism and in the Christology of the Apocalypse of John* [Tübingen: Mohr Siebeck, 1995]) surveys the material, starting with rabbinic texts (56–72), and turning to pre-Christian Jewish and later Christian texts (75–78; 80–103).

50 For a survey, see *ibid.*, 164–199. Stuckenbruck concludes that these texts show no evidence of an "angel cult" (a phrase he does not sufficiently define in this book), but that the texts do show that "angels could be made objects of veneration as beings aligned with and subordinate to God" (269). The worship of angels indicates that God's divinity was not threatened by the worship of lesser deities subordinate to him.

51 Bauckham's attempt to distinguish the worship given to Adam from "properly" divine worship is based on his theological concerns. "It was worship of God," he says, "where the context indicated that God's unique sovereignty was being acknowledged" (*Jesus and the God of Israel*, 204). This amounts to the view that honor bestowed (in this case, *proskynesis*) is worship only when it is given to God. This is circular (assuming that worship is simply what is given to God, and to no one else). Meaning, as Bauckham acknowledges, must be determined by context. It is evident that the angels in this text are truly called upon to worship Adam. As God's image—representing God's reality—the angels give to Adam what they normally give to God. For a more balanced presentation of *proskynesis* in Jewish literature, see *ibid.*, 131.

52 For discussion, see Crispin Fletcher-Louis, "The Worship of Divine Humanity as God's Image and the Worship of Jesus" in *The Jewish Roots of Christological Monotheism: Papers from the St. Andrews Conference on the Historical Origins of the Worship of Jesus* (eds. Carey C. Newman, James R. Davila and Gladys S. Lewis; Leiden: Brill, 1999), 113–14.

of Man is clearly integrated into the worship of the "Lord of Spirits," (i. e., God). The *Kerygma Petri* charges Jews with "worshipping angels and archangels, the months and the moon" (*NTA* 2.39 §2c; *ap.* Clem. Alex., *Strom.* 6.5.41.2). In what is to some a genuine Pauline epistle, Paul has to argue against "the worship of angels" (θρησκείᾳ τῶν ἀγγέλων) in one of his own congregations (Col 2:18).[53] In these texts it is not a question of failed "orthodoxy," but of actual practice in ancient Jewish communities. Whether or not it is "right" or "right-thinking," the cult of angels must be taken seriously as a historical reality.

It is evident, at any rate, that worship—like divinity—is not a zero-sum game: the primal God can be worshiped through an intermediary (sometimes called "God"). The same logic may be active in the "Son of God Text" from Qumran, where we learn that when war ceases on earth, all cities will pay homage to either the "Son of God" or to "the people of God."[54]

We can add to this evidence all the texts that show human beings reacting to angels as they would react to God. By way of example, we can cite the experience of Daniel. When he encountered an angel in Dan 10, he felt extreme weakness (vv. 8, 16), his face was forced to the ground (v.9), he was seized with terror (v. 12), he could not speak (v.15), shaking took hold of him (v.17), and he could not breathe

---

53 For additional texts on the worship of angels, see Stuckenbruck, "'Angels' and 'God': Exploring the Limits of Early Jewish Monotheism" in *Early Jewish and Christian Monotheism*, 55–66. Based on these texts, Stuckenbruck admits that "there is some evidence in early Jewish texts that allows for the 'cultic' worship of angels, if by this is meant reverence-honour-praise directed at angelic beings within the setting of the worshipping community. To the extent that the evidence adduced above reflects such veneration, it becomes misleading to conclude that 'cultic devotion' in the broad sense functioned as the decisive criterion that determined the boundaries of early non-Christian Jewish monotheistic belief" (*ibid.*, 68). In the same volume, North comes to a similar conclusion: "Jewish monotheism was not monolatry" ("Jesus and Worship, God and Sacrifice," 198).

54 John J. Collins, "Jewish Monotheism and Christian Theology" in *Aspects of Monotheism: How God is One* (eds. Hershel Shanks and Jack Meinhardt; Washington D. C.: Biblical Archaeology Society, 1997), 94. According to the Talmud, "There will come a time when 'Holy' will be said before the righteous as it is said before the Holy One, blessed be He [i.e., as in Isa 6:1–3]" (*b. B. Bat.* 75b). For the Jewish background on the cult of the saints, see William Horbury, *Messianism among Jews and Christians: Twelve Biblical and Historical Studies* (Edinburgh: T & T Clark, 2003), 351–80.

(v. 17) (cf. *Apoc. Zeph.* 6:5, 14). These are the same responses other seers and prophets have when facing God (Isa 6:5; 1 En 14:24).

Hurtado claims that Jews who worshiped angels were not part of "normative Judaism." It is difficult to know how Hurtado can make judgments about what kinds of Judaism were "normative" in the ancient world. Hurtado's focus on "normative" Jewish traditions leads him to too quickly pass over what goes under the name of Jewish "popular religion."[55] Far from being less representative of first-century Judaism, Jewish popular religion may even have been more representative and pervasive than what went on in the Diaspora synagogues and in the temple cult at Jerusalem.

At any rate, it appears that some Jews did worship angels even though Hurtado does not view such beings as divine. Admittedly, this worship may not have constituted regular or formal cult, and thus would not measure up to Hurtado's understanding of worship. Worship, for Hurtado, is "especially devotion offered in a specifically worship (liturgical) setting and expressive of the thanksgiving, praise, communion, and petition that directly represent, manifest, and reinforce the relationship of the worshipers with the deity."[56] This full and restrictive definition of worship, though it attempts to be historical, seems to owe something to the Christian experience of regular, liturgical worship.[57] At any rate, it seems advisable to say that whether they consist of one act or many, whether official or spontaneous, historians should not disqualify acts of worship because of restrictive definitions laid down in advance. This is in line with Hurtado's own plea to be inductive and not deductive in method. Thus one cannot exclude the worship of angels because it was not regular and in a liturgical setting. We honestly have little idea how regular and formal it may have been (the sources are full of gaps).

Based on this discussion, we should conclude, I think, that worship was not "the decisive criterion" for divinity—either in ancient Judaism or in the Greco-Roman world at large—and that there were in fact many beings without cult who could be and were considered divine.[58]

---

55 Helpful here is the material gathered by E. R. Goodenough in *Jewish Symbols in the Greco-Roman Period* (12 vols.; New York: Pantheon Books, 1953–68).

56 *Lord Jesus Christ*, 31, n. 10; cf. 38, n. 36.

57 Later he indicates that the worship he has in mind is "public, corporate cultic devotion" (*ibid.*, 34).

58 This would seem also to be the view of Thompson, who writes: "the word 'god' does not always carry within it an understanding of how that term applies

Lack of formal cult, therefore, is not and should not be an objection to a Pauline version of deification.

---

to the figure so designated. It certainly need not have implied a figure to be worshipped" (*God of the Gospel of John*, 22).

Conclusion

"I have become more and more
strongly convinced in the course of
these studies how much that is helpful
for the understanding of primitive
Christianity is to be learned from the
comparison with extra-biblical Jewish,
and heathen, religious history and how
indispensable, indeed, such comparison
is for the elucidation of some of the
most important questions. I am well
aware that, to many, my practice of
drawing parallels from the sphere of
heathen religion will appear
superfluous, while to some it will even
be offensive ... That, however, has
never made me waver in my conviction
... that Christianity as a historical
phenomenon is to be investigated by
the same methods as all other history,
and that, in particular, its origin is to be
understood by being studied as the
normal outcome of the manifold factors
in the religious and ethical life of the
time."

—Otto Pfleiderer[1]

The argument of this book has been that aspects of Pauline soteriology
fit the basic pattern of deification in the Greco-Roman world. I defined
this basic pattern as sharing in the divine qualities which are constitutive
of (a particular) divine identity. In chapter 1, I narrowed these qualities
down to two: immortality and power. In chapter 2, I tried to show that
(1) deification was a pervasive and multi-faceted idea in the Greco-
Roman world, and (2) that it sometimes featured human beings as assimilated to specific Gods. It was the burden of chapter 3 to show
that deification (so defined) was not an idea foreign to the Judaism of

---

1   Quote taken from Werner Georg Kümmel, *The New Testament: The History of
     the Investigation of its Problems* (Nashville: Abingdon Press, 1972), 210.

Paul's time. The Greek Bible already recognizes immortality as constitutive of deity (Gen 3:20; Ps 81[82]:6), and calls Israelite kings "God" (Ps 44[45]:7) and "son of God" (Ps 2:7) as vice-regents of God. At the center of Jewish thought, there was thus always an analogy between theomorphic human beings and an anthropomorphic deity (Gen 1:26; Ezek 1:26–28). In Paul, this analogy was centered on Christ, the divine Messiah and image of God (2 Cor 4:4) to whom believers assimilate to regain their theomorphic status. Nevertheless their "theomorphicity" went far beyond what was imagined for original humanity. It involved sharing in Christ's divine immortality and universal rule. These are the qualities, I argued, which constitute the divine identity of Christ. Sharing in Christ's immortality means sharing in the incorruptible corporeality of Christ's divine (pneumatic) body (chapters 4–5). Sharing in Christ's rule means taking part in the universal dominion specifically meant for the divine Messiah (God's begotten Son [Ps 2:7]) and creator of the cosmos [1 Cor 8:6]) (chapter 6). In chapter 7, I argued that sharing in Christ's divine identity also has a moral component. Pauline conformation to Christ is a form of assimilation to God. It is a process of gaining Christ's virtues, which are just as constitutive of his divine identity as immortality and power. Finally, in chapter 8, I proposed that the category of deification did not conflict with first-century Jewish monotheism, since summodeistic forms of monotheism allow other beings to share in divinity. The Creator's transcendent status (chapter 9) is also not an objection to deification because it was never asserted that Pauline Christians completely overlapped with God the Father's distinctive essence or shared his power to create physical worlds. The God who shares his divinity through Christ remains the "one" (i. e., all-powerful, sole-ruling) God who duly receives all worship and honor.

Limitations and Clarifications

In essence, this has been a comparative study. I have examined Pauline soteriology in light of a generic category prevalent in his own time and culture. In all comparisons there are both similarities and differences. If in this study I have emphasized the similarities between Greco-Roman deification and Pauline soteriology, it is because some scholars have (over)emphasized the differences. Indeed, I wonder if Russell's dubious claim that Christian writers generated "their own distinctive terminology for deification"[2] corresponds to the modern Christian desire to see Christian deification as essentially "other" from deification in the Greco-Roman world. Naturally, the patristic writers themselves would deny any real overlap between their form of deification and the forms which had preceded them in the larger culture. In modern scholarship, the denial of any real overlap continues as the dominant tradition of interpretation. A key early example is Otto Faller who argued that Christian deification is unique and thus essentially different from its "pagan" antecedent.[3] Today, the putative uniqueness of Christian deification is strongly reflected in the terminology used to describe it. Modern Christian advocates of deification throw scorn on (or simply avoid) the pejorative term "apotheosis" (even though it was used by Clement of Alexandria, Origen, Didymus the Blind, Ps.-Macarius and Maximus the Confessor) in preference for the (now) distinctively Christian terminology of "theosis."[4] In the words of Michael Gorman, "[T]heosis does not mean ... apotheosis, the unChristian notion of the post-mortem promotion of certain humans (heroes, emperors, etc.) to divinity."[5]

To be sure, there are distinctive elements of Christian deification. If nothing else, Christian deification is distinguished from its non-Christian counterparts by being focused on Christ. For the Christian, shareable divinity was centered on Christ; thus deification was usually thought of as a form of Christification, or "Christosis." Conformation to Christ, to be sure, distinguishes Christian deification in terms of its *content*. (Christ,

---

2   *Doctrine of Deification*, 344.

3   "Griechische Vergottung und christliche Vergöttlichung," 404–35. The assumed uniqueness of Christian deification has allowed theologically oriented researchers more or less to ignore Greco-Roman deification. This is indicated by the bibliography of deification compiled by Jeffery A. Witting in *Partakers of the Divine Nature*, 294–310. We have here virtually no engagement with studies of deification in the Greco-Roman world. It is as if Christian deification in the ancient world has been hermetically sealed off from discourses of deification in the larger culture.

4   Surprisingly, this practice most resembles the Neo-Platonists who also avoided deification terminology with the *apo*-prefix (Russell, *Doctrine of Deification*, 343–344).

5   *Inhabiting*, 4–5. Occasionally, "divinization" is preferred as a term for Christian deification, since it is (apparently) taken to mean sharing in the divine rather than explicitly becoming a God (which may in the end be a false distinction). The term "divinization" formed from the Latin *divinus*, means only to become "divine," which is a somewhat vague category. The terminology is reminiscent of the distinction employed in the western imperial cult between the emperor as *divus* ("divine") as opposed to *deus* ("God").

as it turns out, is a rather peculiar deity among ancient Mediterranean Gods.) In terms of the *form* or *structure* of deification, however, Pauline deification is not particularly exceptional.

There are, however, many attempts to distinguish between Christian and non-Christian forms of deification in a structural way. For example, it is said that in the Greco-Roman world, deification means actually becoming (a) God, whereas in Christian theology, it only means becoming *like* God. To put it structurally, Christian deification never envisions Christians as passing over into the category of "God." In modern theological parlance, it means nothing more than becoming truly human. Christian deification is thus not literal but metaphorical.[6]

These distinctions are somewhat problematic, however, because non-Christian sources too envision humans as becoming "like" Gods without an assumption that they become Gods. A study of Olga Tribulato on Greek compounds of the type ἰσόθεος ("equal to God" or "*like* (a) God") indicates that ἰσόθεος can only be attributed to individuals who are *not* Gods.[7] Christian theologians, for their part, often do not use "like" language, but simply speak of Christians as becoming "Gods." A favorite patristic proof-text for deification is Ps 81[82]:6: "I [God] have said, 'You [taken to be Christians] *are* Gods'"—not "like" Gods.[8] In accordance with this text, Clement of Alexandria writes that "The Logos of God became human so that you also might learn from a human in what way a human can become God (γένηται θεός)" (*Protrep.* 1.8.4). Clement also famously said that just as Plato makes philosophers and Aristotle men of science, so "he who obeys the Lord and follows the prophecy given through him, is fully perfected after the likeness of his teacher, and thus becomes a God while still moving about in the flesh (ἐν σαρκὶ περιπολῶν θεός)" (*Strom.* 7.16.101.4). Here likeness to God and Godhood are not distinguished. Origen presents the logic of such language:

> One more properly says that everything alongside the absolute God (αὐτόθεος) that is made God (θεοποιούμενον) by participation in his Godhead

6   "Of course, Christian monotheism goes against any literal 'god making' of believers" (Finlan and Kharlamov, *Theōsis*, 1).

7   "Greek Compounds of the Type ἰσόθεος 'Equal to a God', ἀξιόλογος 'Worthy of Note', ἀπειρομάχας 'Ignorant of War', etc.," *Mnemosyne* 60 (2007): 527–549. I owe this reference to Chaniotis, "Ithyphallic Hymn," 112, n. 104.

8   Carl Mosser has argued that for early patristic writers "Gods" in Ps 81[82]:6 simply means "sons of God"—but I wonder if "sons of God" does not also mean "Gods" ("The Earliest Patristic Interpretations of Psalm 82," 30–74)?

is not '*the* God' but 'God.' Of these Gods, the 'firstborn of all creation' [Christ], inasmuch as he is the first to be 'with *the* God' [John 1:1], having drawn Godhead to himself, is entirely more honored. He has administered the coming-to-be of these Gods, the other Gods alongside God [i.e., deified Christians], who have *the* God as God according to the scripture— 'God of Gods ...' [Ps 49:1, LXX]—by drawing from *the* God so as to make them Gods, unbegrudgingly sharing with them according to his own goodness ... God the Word is a minister of Godhead to all the rest of the Gods [Christians]." (*Comm. Jo.* 2.2–3, §§17, 19, my trans.; cf. Philo, *Somn.* 1.229–230; 1.61–67; *Leg.* 3.207–208; *Conf.* 146–147; Clem. Alex., *Strom.* 3.81.6)

Here we have a statement of graded divinity: there is one absolute God (ὁ θεός) and many deified Gods (θεοί). Christ is one of the deified Gods, along with Christians—although Christ is more honored. At any rate, there is little indication in this text that Christians are not Gods in a realistic sense.

Can these statements be swept aside as mere exaggeration and rhetoric? To say that for Clement or Origen (who are just as "monotheistic" as Paul), becoming a "God" only means becoming "*like* God" seems like hermeneutical imposition—an attempt, that is, to make all Christians throughout time fit a pre-defined "Christian" notion of deification (which must fit a pre-defined notion of monotheism). Clement and Origen, I will note, are not alone among patristic writers in using this language of "becoming (a) God." Stephen Finlan and Vladimir Kharlamov point out that the subject-verb sets θεὸς εἰμί ("to be God") and particularly θεὸς γίγνομαι ("to become God") were "extensively used" among the church fathers.[9] To avoid the danger of submerging ancient categories of perception and reality into our own, it seems best to affirm, at least tentatively, that these early Christian writers meant what they said and said what they meant: Christians can become God(s).

Another modern way for theologians to distinguish Christian from non-Christian deification (at least among Protestants) is to say that the latter form of deification is deification "by works" and the former "by (divine) grace." But this distinction also will not do, because many deifications in Greek mythology, as we saw in chapter 2, are purely due to the favor (even if erotic favor!) of the Gods. Furthermore, the way that Basil of Caesarea (to choose but one Christian example) speaks of deification certainly implies that some sort of human effort contributes to the process. Basil, like many others, speaks of deification by vir-

---

9   *Theōsis*, 6.

tue.[10] If deification is (at least partially) the outcome of virtue, how (we might ask) is virtue not at all related to human performance? Here in particular the absolute dichotomy between "works" and "grace" seems to be based on Christian (particularly Protestant) theology, not on historical analysis.[11]

To be sure, a comparativist must accept real differences between Christian and non-Christian forms of deification with open arms. No idea or complex of ideas is *exactly* the same as it is in another system of thought. Accordingly, let me be the first to acknowledge major differences in the mode and result of Pauline deification which distinguish it from some Greco-Roman counterparts. Paul's version of deification is not a self-deification by heroic victories and acts of benefaction, nor is it a deification that occurs fully in this life, nor does it allow those deified to claim cult. It is also a deification unusually open to divine help (though, again, excluding all human performance seems precipitous): "If we live by the pneuma, let us also walk by the pneuma" (Gal 5:25).

Such differences, however, do not wash away structural similarities. It seems to me that Paul maintained the basic premise of deification in the ancient Mediterranean world—i.e., that deification is a sharing in the identity-constituting qualities of deity or of a particular divine being (in Paul's case, Christ). In the case of Christian and non-Christian forms of deification, there is thus similarity *and* difference. The similarity is in the difference, and the difference is in the similarity. There is enough similarity, however, to recategorize elements of Paul's soteriology as a form of deification as it was recognizable in his culture.

Those who will continue to hunt for differences between Pauline soteriology and Greco-Roman forms of deification to disprove my thesis do not understand the nature of this project. In arguing for similarity, I have assumed that Paul was intelligent enough to adapt basic concepts of his culture to forms acceptable to his faith and Jewish heritage. I have never and will never make the argument that Paul consciously borrowed a system of deification, and then proceeded to teach it in an unmodified form. The analogies I have drawn in this book are not to be

---

10 Russell, *Doctrine of Deification*, 211–212. Eastern Christians are generally more comfortable with synergistic modes of attaining salvation (or deification).

11 According to Gavrilyuk, "Most patristic authors simply refused to construe 'works' as engaged in causal competition with grace. The soteriological primacy and necessity of grace are not undermined by the fact that human acceptance of divine help involves much struggle and ascetic effort" ("The Retrieval of Deification," 653).

construed as causal links. Neither genetic borrowing nor holistic correspondence are necessary for my argument. In the words of F. J. P.
Poole, "Comparison does not deal with phenomena *in toto* or in the
round, but only with an aspectual characteristic of them."[12] As wholes,
Pauline soteriology and Greco-Roman forms of deification do not
align. My argument is only that Paul was able to adapt and transform
certain *elements* of Greco-Roman forms of deification to his own soteriology. It is the adaptation of these basic elements that makes appropriate
the language of a distinctly *Pauline* form of deification.

Many, however, might still object that it is basically inappropriate to
call Pauline Christians—even if in their fully transformed, eschatological
state—"Gods" or even "divine." At best, we might call them intermediate beings—something like angels (an ambiguous sort of entity) as in
Luke 20:36. After all, Stoic teaching has the disembodied souls of the
just turning into daimones, not fully-fledged Gods (Sext. Emp.,
Math. 9.74), and Plato in the *Phaedrus* has the souls of the philosophers
riding as *companions* of the Gods in the upper reaches of the universe.
They follow in Zeus's *train*, live the life of the Gods, but are not explicitly said to be Gods themselves. Therefore why must the eschatologically transformed and glorified believers in Paul's churches be said to be
deified? Why not put them in an intermediary category like "heavenly
being"?

Here is my response. I recognize that many things in Paul are underdetermined, and that my reading of Paul most certainly involves many
inferences based on my comparison. In the end, I am open to leaving
the eschatological state of believers ambiguous as it stands in the text.
But to produce understanding of Paul's ideas, the scholar is called to *interpret* and draw legitimate inferences from the Pauline data. If Pauline
transformation merely involved an eschatological immortalization and
the reception of superhuman power to rule, perhaps we could leave it
as an "angelification" or something similar.

But Paul says more than this. Paul envisions transformation as a close
assimilation to the destiny and nature of a divine being (Christ). And
more: he envisions himself and his converts as sharing the divine identity of *this* being. It is not simply that Pauline Christians participate in
vague divine qualities. They participate in the very (physical and
moral) qualities which make *Christ* divine. They gain a share of *his* immortality and *his* ruling power and *his* virtue. There is no other divinity

---

12   Quoted in J. Z. Smith, *Drudgery Divine*, 53.

which they share but his. There is no other deity that Christians know. Christ's divinity is the same divinity as that of the Father. (For Paul, Christology is theology.) Thus by sharing Christ's identity, Christians participate in the very nature of the Christian God (cf. 2 Pet 1:4).

Now I am aware that there are many throughout history (especially before the Council of Nicea) who would put Christ in the category of an ambiguous intermediate being, and not view him as (a) God. To many early Christians, he may have been viewed as a sort of angel or archangel created at the beginning of time to mediate the making of this world and to maintain its harmony. But to someone living in the Greco-Roman world—and I do not exclude Jews and Christians from this world—such a being would usually be classified as divine (even if only in a vague sense). Such a being is immortal, endowed with super-human power, and should thus be called "(a) God." For the purposes of this book, however, it does not matter if Paul was a Christological "Arian" (Christ is a divine creature), or an "Athanasian" (Christ is fully equal to the Father). This question, it is fair to say, is underdetermined in Paul. But what is determined—whether from Pauline theology or from the worship practice of Pauline churches—is that Christ was a Pauline God; and the only way that this was possible was for Christ to share the identity of the primal God (the Father). Accordingly, those who in turn share the divine identity of Christ, can truly be said to be deified.

But do deified Christians become Gods or God? Although again this is an underdetermined issue in Paul, it would be irresponsible merely to skate past it. Let me use the analogy of Christ's own divinity (it is, after all, according to the *model* of Christ that Pauline Christians are deified). The divinity of Christ, as has been ably shown by Marianne Meye Thompson, is both functional and relational.[13] This means (1) that Christ's divinity is based on his exercise of divine functions and prerogatives, and (2) Christ's divinity is never independent of the divinity of the Father. Accordingly, Thompson writes: if "divinity" is "to be predicated of a figure [such as Christ], that predication will necessarily imply a relationship to the 'only true God.' [The Gospel of] John articulates this relationship primarily through the Father-Son dyad, through the emphasis on Jesus' carrying out divine functions and activities, and

---

13 *The God of the Gospel of John*, 232–233. Her conclusions concern the Gospel of John, but they apply much more broadly.

through categories that posit the closest possible unity between them."[14]
It is undoubtedly correct that in first-century Judaism and Christianity,
for a human to be called "God" does not imply that the human is an
independent "godling." Instead, it is a way of *relating* that deified
human to the *one* God. The same, I think, can be said for a Pauline
form of deification. It is both functional and relational. Deified Christians become divine by performing specifically divine functions and exercising specifically divine prerogatives that constitute the divine (specifically the *divine Christ's*) identity. By participating in Christ's life, power
and virtue, deified Christians manifest the divinity of Christ (just as
Christ manifests the divinity of the Father). In this way, deified Christians are always divine in relation to Christ, and through Christ, God.
This has been my assumption throughout the book. I have never and
never wish to claim that Christians become independent Gods. A purely
functional and relational mode of deification is a peculiarly Pauline
modification of deification as it was seen in the wider Greco-Roman
world. When Paul absorbed the thought structure of deification for
his soteriology, he modified it according to his Christian (and Jewish)
conceptions of God.

This study is not a full account of deification in Paul. In this book,
rather, I see myself as trying to isolate a certain set of mostly post-mortem (or post-parousia) features of a larger Pauline phenomenon in order
to shed as strong and precise a light as possible on particular features
(namely, assimilation to a divine being, sharing in divine power and immortality)—without aiming to exhaust every facet of this Pauline phenomenon. I have devoted only a single chapter to deification through
ethical transformation in this life. More could—and has—been said
on this topic.[15] Although other schemes of deification involve virtues,
the assimilation to specifically Christian virtues (i. e., virtues which belong to the divine Christ), makes Paul's vision of deification distinct.
Such assimilation to Christ also involves suffering (at least in this life)
and even death, since Christ is (distinctively) a "dying and rising
God." This kind of suffering and development of virtue is, furthermore,
necessarily a communal, not just an individual experience. Although I
have not discussed these points at length, others (such as Gorman)

---

14   *Ibid.*
15   Gorman's *Inhabiting* is generally ethical in its focus.

have.[16] I view such research (although worked out as theological exegesis rather than historical comparison) as in the end complementary to my own.

The mention of theological exegesis brings me to a necessary point. Throughout the book I have been intent on distinguishing my reading of Paul from a "theological reading." A theological reading (and here I mean a modern Christian theological reading) of Paul is very interested in the emic standpoint: how Paul himself would see his teachings. My approach, however, has been essentially etic. Viewing Paul from the outside, I have pinpointed some analogies between his eschatological ideas and other (chiefly Greco-Roman) ideas which involve deification. Based on similarities, I have then categorized an aspect of Paul's soteriology (that involving the reception of immortal corporeality, cosmic rule, and Christic virtues) as a form of deification. In essence, I have engaged in (1) the scholarly practice of defamiliarizing, recategorizing, and redescribing some of Paul's ideas, using (2) a category familiar in Paul's time and culture for (3) the purposes of increasing our understanding of the Apostle's thought. Although my redescription attempts to be historically faithful, it can be viewed as theologically problematic. For as William James points out,

> any object that is infinitely important to us and awakens our devotion feels to us as if it must be *sui generis* and unique. Probably a crab would be filled with a sense of personal outrage if it could hear us class it without ado or apology as a crustacean, and thus dispose of it. "I am no such thing," it would say; "I am MYSELF, MYSELF, alone."[17]

Likewise, I acknowledge that Paul, if he were given the chance to read this study might resist my classification of aspects of his thought as a form of "deification." This is, perhaps, little cause for wonder. To Paul, the ancient vocabulary of deification was something religiously "other" and unacceptable. (Many today, due in part to theological reasons, feel the same way.) Yet sometimes in the very place where religious insiders emphasize differences (to maintain their distinctive identity), there are (historically speaking) the most interesting similarities.

---

16 See Gorman's *Cruciformity: Paul's Narrative Spirituality of the Cross* (Grand Rapids: Eerdmans, 2001).

17 Quoted in J. Z. Smith, *Relating Religion: Essays in the Study of Religion* (Chicago: University of Chicago, 2004), 174. My language of "defamiliarizing," "redescribing," and the concern to "recategorize" stem from a reading of Smith's many essays in this book and elsewhere.

Pointing out these similarities is not an attempt to de-legitimate the insider's perspective, but to complement it.

To the scholar of religion, deification is not charged with implications of idolatry and false religion. It is a scholarly tool for comparing and categorizing different systems of transcending human existence in the ancient Mediterranean world. The historical search to understand Paul demands that the scholar have the right to translate Paul's thought into categories intelligible to Paul's own (and to our own) time. Ultimately I do not think that this procedure in any way undermines Paul's aim in composing his letters. At the very least, Paul *sought to be understood*. He did not want his ideas of moral assimilation to Christ, corporeal transformation, and universal rule to be eternal mysteries. (Even though, religiously speaking, they may be viewed as such.) To the scholar, these ideas *can* be understood and seen as fully coherent by examining them through the lens of an ancient category (reconstructed using modern scholarly tools)—namely, deification. If, to oppose himself to a religious other, Paul would reject the terminology of deification, he did not—historically speaking—reject the logic.

In saying this, I do not want to give the impression that a theological and/or emic reading of Paul must always be hostile to deification. In fact, the theological reading of Paul's soteriology as deification is an old and venerable tradition (far older than modern Pauline scholarship which grew out of the Reformation). Although in this book I have not been concerned to expound the patristic understanding of deification (which has already been done by Norman Russell and others), I want to emphasize, with Blackwell, the importance of patristic interpretation as a hermeneutical aid for reading Paul.[18] Deification is, arguably, one of the oldest ways of understanding Paul's soteriology among Christians. Some of the earliest and greatest theologians of the past—Irenaeus of Lyon, Clement of Alexandria, Augustine of Hippo (among many others)—saw deification in the Pauline literature within their own (deeply Christian) horizon. Admittedly they were reading Paul in a canon. But it was (interestingly) a chiefly Jewish canon—the majority of which was translated from Hebrew texts. (Thus there is not anything necessarily "un-Jewish" about deification in Paul.) The point is—in addition to historical readings—there are important theological reasons for taking Paul and deification with utmost seriousness. The objections of monotheism and transcendence mean little when thrown in the face

---

18 *Christosis*, 15–25.

of the Greek (and many Latin) fathers who believed in a fully transcendent, singular God and yet taught a vision of deification. To my mind, the considerable weight of the church fathers and mothers is enough of a motivation for modern theological readers to take seriously the historical reasons for seeing deification in Paul.

This remark brings me to some final evaluative comments about the study of Blackwell which focuses on patristic readings of Paul. It may seem odd to have two monographs on Paul and deification (a seemingly obscure topic) appear so closely in time. Lest one feel satisfied with just one approach, it seems worthwhile here to point out some key differences between Blackwell's interpretation and mine. This contrast, I hope, will get at the heart of what Pauline deification means.

First of all, Blackwell wants to oppose what he calls "attributive" and "essentialist" deification.[19] This is a way of drawing a distinction between those who share "ontologically in the essence of the divine" and those who "merely" participate in divine attributes such as power and immortality.[20] Those who participate "ontologically in the essence of the divine" are, according to Blackwell, the old enemies of orthodox Christianity, the "Gnostics" and (Neo-)Platonists.[21]

I would like to challenge this distinction between "attributive" and "essentialist" deification by posing some pointed questions. First, are power and immortality mere "attributes" of God divorced from the divine essence, or are they actually *part* of God's essence/nature? If power and immortality are not constitutive of God's essence/nature, in what sense are they "divine"? Can one participate in divine attributes and not in the divine nature/essence? What exactly is *deifying* about participating in divine attributes if they are not related to the divine essence? If there is nothing essentially divine about immortality, why is participation in this attribute called a form of "deification?" Blackwell does not want human beings to "become divine as God is divine."[22] But how else are they to become divine? Is it by sharing in a being who is not divine? (Blackwell indicates that Christ does not need to be divine

---

19 *Christosis*, 103–105.
20 *Ibid.*, 104.
21 *Ibid.*
22 *Ibid.*, 106.

for Paul to have a form of deification.[23]) *But how then is this a "deification"?*

Throughout this study, I have avoided the older theological language of divine "essence" in preference for the language of divine "identity." Power and immortality, I have claimed, partially make up God and Christ's divine identity, and therefore participation in Christ's divine power and immortality constitutes a form of deification. Would I be dubbed an "essentialist" in Blackwell's categories? It seems so.[24] Would this be a distortion of my position? Definitely, yes. Blackwell's categories, in my opinion, require revision. Let me say why—again, by asking more questions.

Is this distinction between "attributive" and "essentialist" deification not a brainchild of later Christian theology? Is it not a way to distinguish Pauline soteriology from undesirable "Gnostic" and philosophical ideas in the Greco-Roman world? Is this not the project of Irenaeus and Cyril?[25] Is this not a potential danger of reading Paul solely in light of Irenaeus (a heresiologist) and later post-Nicene theology? At bottom, is this not a way of reading Paul *against* his environment rather than *in* it? And what is the benefit? That the Pauline form of deification becomes orthodox, and therefore acceptable to modern Christian theologians and theological exegetes? That having become acceptable to modern (Western) theologians, deification can thus become a tool for (modern) ecumenical unity? Ultimately, however, this is not a historical proj-

---

23 On *ibid.*, 263, Blackwell asserts that "Since the patristic writers nor Paul argue for a sharing in the divine essence, as with essential deification, the explicit affirmation of [Christ's] deity is not necessary." This amounts to the rather unorthodox view that Christ has no relation to the divine essence (if believers share in *Christ*, but not the *divine essence*). If Christ does share the divine essence (as Nicea states), presumably Christians who share in Christ can also share the divine essence.

24 Blackwell has already categorized me as a proponent of "supernatural essential deification" (267). From my perspective, there could not be a terminology more misleading for the ideas I have presented in this book.

25 Blackwell writes, "The distinction between nature and grace that is fundamental to Cyril's theology is implicit in Irenaeus' as well ... With Cyril's interest in *refuting what he considers christological heresies*, he regularly discusses issues related to human and divine nature, with a clear distinction between each, and this metaphysical divide serves as the basis of all soteriological language" (106, emphasis mine). Blackwell, in my view, has read back the distinction between "nature and grace" and the "metaphysical divide" between humans and God into Paul. Paul was not familiar with these heresiological categories (cf. my "Introduction," 29 n. 110 above).

ect, but a theological one. This is where, I think, my own and Blackwell's study part ways. Blackwell admits that he is prompted "by modern ecumenical discussions about deification."[26] For the record, I have no quarrel with later theology or with ecumenical unity, but this is not my project here. I must confess that I truly am interested in hearing Paul's own voice in Paul's own time and culture. If Paul presented a form of deification, and if that form may in some way be analogous to Platonic—and even later Christian "Gnostic" thought—it matters not a whit to historical analysis, and should not be denied.

There is a second way that Blackwell's interpretation of Paul and deification diverges from my own. (And this seems to follow from his theological dichotomy of "attributive" vs. "essentialist" deification.) In the end, Blackwell seems to believe that for Paul deification never actually involves people transcending human nature. For instance, Blackwell describes deification as "the process of restoring the image and likeness of God."[27] The restoration of the image of God, he later says, is "the consummation of true humanity."[28] Somewhat later he speaks of deification as "the culmination of human flourishing in light of the divine-human encounter."[29] When he treats 1 Cor 15, moreover, he underscores that humans will be transformed into the image of Christ the heavenly *human*, which makes their manner of eschatological existence—although "heavenly"—merely human.[30]

Blackwell's purpose, it seems, is to protect the integrity of divine and human identity. Any sharing of identity, it seems, would constitute a form of fusion or "absorption."[31] Thus deification does not actually mean that the redeemed become God or Gods. God always remains pure God (except in the incarnation) and humans remain human. But is this latter point right—are deified humans merely human? I recognize Blackwell's concerns (and share them to a certain extent)—but I am led to ask: is this not another instance of a theological reading protecting Paul from his environment?

Let me again challenge Blackwell by asking some more pointed questions. How can there be a deification if, as Blackwell says, "believ-

---

26 *Christosis*, 251.
27 *Ibid.*, 253.
28 *Ibid.*, 256; cf. 248: "the eschatological state will include a transformed non-human creation which will be appropriate for human existence."
29 *Ibid.*, 263.
30 *Ibid.*, 218, cf. 247.
31 *Ibid.*, 253.

1 1 11 111111 1 1 11111

ers remain ontologically separate from the divine"?[32] And how does one remain ontologically separate from the divine if one participates in a distinctly divine quality (immortality)? To be sure, Blackwell says that believers are "ontologically changed" by their participation in what is clearly divine (immortality). How then do they remain "ontologically separate from the divine"? These are questions that I think Blackwell needs to answer to present a fully coherent and plausible reading of deification in Paul.

My concern here is not to overemphasize the differences between Blackwell's interpretation and mind. A history of interpretations reading ought, I believe, to be complimentary with a historical and comparative approach. I merely point out some areas where I think later theological and ecclesial concerns have deeply colored Blackwell's reading—a reading which I think he intends to have some real historical traction.[33]

Ultimately what I am trying to avoid is that old theological dichotomy called the "Judaism/Hellenism divide." It seems to me that a modern historical reading of Paul—given what we know about the spread of Greek culture before and after Alexander the Great—does not countenance a strong division between Jewish and Greek forms of thought. By the first century, many Jews as a cultural minority had made their own the "outlooks and criteria of acceptability of the majority [Greco-Roman] culture."[34] If Diaspora Jews were by no means universally assimilated in Greek culture, many were highly acculturated, and displayed significant accommodation to Hellenistic forms of thought.[35] This has been the basic assumption of this study.

---

32 Ibid., 267.

33 In the end, Blackwell provides a rather traditional Evangelical picture of Pauline soteriology. He works with a problem-solution model (ibid., 240–42). The problem is sin. Sin breaks the relationship between humans and God (240). In turn, "Christ, serving as the true image of God and a bridge between humanity and God, restored this relationship" (252). Blackwell wants to understand this restored relationship as descriptive of deification, and (from what I can gather) would be very cautious of believers actually sharing Christ's divine identity.

34 I borrow this phrase from Tobin, The Creation of Man, 36. For this insight, Tobin is himself dependent on V. Tcherikover, "Jewish Apologetic Literature Reconsidered," Eos 48 (1956):169–93.

35 For the meaning of "acculturation," "accommodation," and "assimilation," see John M. G. Barclay, "Paul Among Diaspora Jews: Anomaly or Apostate?" JSNT 60 (1995): 93–98. On the level of (soteriological) ideas, I see Paul as much more acculturated and accommodated than Barclay. Barclay also thinks that accommodation involves a loss of one's own "cultural uniqueness" (98).

I therefore have my radar up when I see attempts to seal off Pauline deification from Platonic (or broadly Greek) ideas of deification, and the old bugbear called "Gnosticism"[36]—especially when Blackwell has so little explored Platonic or "Gnostic" forms of deification. But Blackwell is not alone in this respect. It seems like many of the newer studies on the biblical roots or biblical forms of deification are still operating with the old *contra gentes* ("against the pagans") mentality. If any doctrine might seem quintessentially Greek, it would be deification. According to a common theological narrative (as pointed out above), the Greeks really did believe that humans could become Gods (i.e., immortal beings with superhuman power), whereas Hellenized Jews and (later) Christians in the Greco-Roman world could not have asserted this. To be sure, Christians used the *language* of deification, but all they meant was that humans become truly human.

Yet there seems to be some sort of confusion here. To Blackwell, apparently, Pauline deification means that believers are glorified, immortalized, and made incorruptible—but they never actually enter the class of Gods or divine beings. Nevertheless, it seems to me that to be immortal, incorruptible, and glorified is *exactly what it meant* in the ancient world to enter the class of divinity, and that the historian of religion who so classes them better represents ancient conceptions of the divine and human than the one who, for whatever reason, refuses to let human beings become anything more than human beings. The ancients, it seems to me, commonly supposed that to live forever, to have a body which never decays, and which is beaming with divine light is to be something more than human. This is what, in fact, deity is (even if it does not *exhaust* divinity as the ancients understood it). I have made the case that Paul, a Hellenized Jew of the first century, does not fundamentally disagree with this understanding of divinity. Ac-

---

I dispute this. First of all, interacting cultures are never perfectly unique. Second, accommodation does not threaten one's own minority cultural identity if that identity has already been formed and shaped by the larger culture. By Paul's day, "Hellenism" had long shaped Judaism in such a way that a "purely Jewish" idea could not be abstracted out and put in contrast with Greek thought. Greek elements in Paul's soteriology may have always been recognized by Paul as part of his own (Jewish) cultural heritage with no loss of identity.

36 This is important to me because I have made this mistake in the past (Litwa, "2 Cor. 3.18 and Its Implications for Theosis," 128–129). (Of course I still affirm that the divinity of Christ remains on a higher order than the divinity of Christians.)

cordingly, if Paul's converts truly participate (that is *take part*) in what
deity is (divine qualities constitutive of the divine identity), they can
be deities.[37] If they truly *participate* in deity, they can be *classed* with
deity. In other words, deified humans *transcend* corruptible, frail, mortal
human nature.

Admittedly, the realistic classification of human beings as Gods is
today a scandal of the Christian mind. Accordingly, every strategy imag-
inable has been devised to show that for Paul humans do not share the
identity (or essence or nature) of God, but only God's *energies* (or powers
or "attributes" non-essential to God's deity). When I speak of God's
"essence" and his "energies," I am using the later (medieval) language
of Gregory Palamas—but Blackwell's distinction between "essence"
and "attributes" seems to me to amount to much the same thing.[38] It
is a later theological distinction that protects Paul from his environment
and all the "pagan" ideas of what I would like to call a truly "realistic"
(non-metaphorical) version of deification.

Where, in the end, do we end up? In theological circles, deification
has been called a "mystery." In an attempt to translate this mystery, deification has become a doctrine of human perfectibility (what humanity
ought to be at "the culmination of human flourishing"[39]). But this understanding, in my view, represents neither the depth nor the strange-
ness (and thus real interest) of Pauline deification. Because this strange-
ness has appeared to be too "other" and "pagan" (i. e., Hellenistic) some
have, through whatever means of logic and exegesis, found some way to
avoid the scandal. To me, however, this is to live in a disenchanted
world, a world in which difference is hard to hear, a world in which

---

37 Although I have quoted Origen on this issue before (ch. 5, n. 41), it is worth
    reviewing. Origen says that "Everyone who shares in anything is undoubtedly
    of one substance and one nature with him who shares in the same thing (*sine
    dubio unius substantiae est uniusque naturae*)" (*Princ.* 4.9). He goes on to say that
    the human soul shares in the divine nature (which he calls "intellectual
    light") and is thus to some extent of one nature and substance as God. This re-
    sults in human incorruptibility and immortality. In *Princ.* 4.10, he concludes
    that people "have a kind of blood-relationship (*consanguinitatem*) with God."

38 Blackwell himself makes this connection: "Later Greek theologians reinforced
    the distinction inherent to attributive deification by speaking of participation in
    the divine energies rather than the divine essesnce [*sic*]. Accordingly, 'energetic
    deification' could be another way of speaking about 'attributive deification',
    and both stand in distinction to 'essential deification', which was roundly refut-
    ed [by patristic authors and apparently by Paul]" (*Christosis*, 105, n. 14).

39 *Ibid.*, 264.

the text cannot say but else than what has always and everywhere been believed.

Results

Although in the end many may not accept my argument for a Pauline version of deification, I want—in closing—to briefly relate what I think are its benefits. A generation ago, E. P. Sanders complained that we lack a category of perception for understanding Pauline soteriology. Against Bultmann's existential interpretation of Paul, Sanders asserted that (according to Paul) "Christians really are being changed from one stage of glory to another, the end really will come and those who are in Christ will really be transformed," and "those who believe belong to the Lord and become one with him."[40] How do we understand such language? It seems mythical, or (a term sometimes thought to be worse) "metaphysical." For Albert Schweitzer (and some others), "mysticism" was the category through which to understand these Pauline statements. Sanders, for his part, suggested the more felicitous term "participation." But this term was vague and unclear (how exactly does one "participate" in another person?), and scholars still had no system of ideas contemporary to Paul in which to fit the notion of participation. (Mystery religions, and contemporary Jewish literature provided little help.) Later scholars used the language of participating in Christ's "story," which seemed to make better sense to the modern mind. But the language of "narrative" brings us back to Sanders' original problem with Bultmann, since participating in Christ's story tends to downplay the physical realism of Paul's language, translating realistic terminology into rhetorical strategies and striking metaphors. Granted, Paul may participate in the story of becoming "one pneuma" with Christ (1 Cor 6:17), but he also (according to his physics) realistically *becomes* one pneuma with Christ. For Paul, in other words, it is not just a story. For "us" (moderns) it may have to be such. But for Paul it was more than this. Perhaps in this case scholars have too quickly elided the fact that in some respects we cannot "apply" Paul, but only (seek to) understand him. Yet for this we need a category to understand the realistic language of transformation and transcendence which Paul uses.

---

40 Sanders, *Paul and Palestinian Judaism*, 522–23.

I believe that deification provides us with such a category. It is first of all a native category. Anyone living in the Greco-Roman world would have been familiar with the basic logic of deification (even if it had many manifestations). Apart from its advantages as a historical explanation, deification also helps us conceptualize the logic of Paul's soteriology. For deification connects the ideas of transformation (attaining a superhuman state), divine reality (pneuma or Glory), and union with a divine being into a single complex of ideas. Paul's Greek converts, I think, could understand the "deifying" aspects of Paul's soteriology, because they understood the meaning of divinity, and the modes of participating in it. They understood, I believe, that participating in the identity-constituting qualities of a divine being resulted in a deification. (At the time, this was not generally considered to be radical or [meta-] physically impossible.)

The third benefit of deification is that, when used as a category, it helps us to see Paul's religion as part of a larger pattern of religion in the ancient Mediterranean basin. In short, Pauline soteriology is shaped by a larger "utopian" trend toward attaining transcendence in the ancient world. When put in these terms, the somatic realism of Paul's eschatology and his yearning for fellowship and even union with a divine being are seen as part of a larger, analogous trend in ancient Mediterranean religions.

If accepted today, deification would involve something of a paradigm shift in the academic study of Pauline soteriology. But this paradigm shift has already been long in the making. For some time, it has been recognized that juridical language is necessary but not sufficient for understanding Pauline soteriology. Atoning for individual transgression is not Paul's only concern. He is just as uneasy about a decaying body living in a hostile, corruptible, and daimon-possessed world. In response, he preached a form of physical (to us "metaphysical") transcendence which involved assimilation to the incorruptible body of a divine being and rule over the superhuman forces which he thought enslaved the people of his time. This, I have argued, is a form of deification. It is this concept, then, which I present as a tool for further investigation and deeper understanding of Pauline soteriology.

Bibliography

Primary Sources

Aelian. Translated by Nigel G. Wilson, et al. 5 vols. Loeb Classical Library. Cambridge, Mass.: Harvard University Press, 1949–1997.

Alcinous. *The Handbook of Platonism*. Translated by John Dillon. Oxford: Clarendon Press, 1993.

Alexander of Aphrodisias. *On Stoic Physics: A Study of the* De mixtione *with Preliminary Essays, Text, Translation and Commentary*. Translated by Robert B. Todd. Leiden: Brill, 1976.

Apollonius Rhodius. *Argonautica*. Translated by William H. Race. Loeb Classical Library. Cambridge, Mass.: Harvard University Press, 2009.

Apostolic Fathers. Translated by Bart D. Ehrman. 2 vols. Loeb Classical Library. Cambridge, Mass.: Harvard University Press, 2003.

Apuleius. *Rhetorical Works*. Translated by Stephen Harrison, John Hilton and Vincent Hunink. Oxford: Oxford University Press, 2001.

Aristophanes. Translated by Jeffrey Henderson. Loeb Classical Library. Cambridge, Mass.: Harvard University Press, 1936–2008.

Aristotle. Translated by H. Rackham, et al. 23 vols. Loeb Classical Library. Cambridge, Mass.: Harvard University Press, 1926–2011.

Arnobius of Sicca. *The Case Against the Pagans*. Translated by George E. McCracken. 2 vols. Ancient Christian Writers 7–8. Westminster, Md.: Newman Press, 1949.

Athenaeus. Translated by Douglas S. Olson. Loeb Classical Library. Cambridge, Mass.: Harvard University Press, 2007–2011.

Augustine. *The City of God*. Translated by Marcus Dods. New York: Modern Library, 1994.

Biblia Hebraica Stuttgartensia. Edited by K. Elliger and W. Rudolph. 5th ed. Stuttgart: Deutsche Bibelgesellschaft, 1977.

Callimachus. Translated by A. W. Mair, et al. 2 vols. Loeb Classical Library. Cambridge, Mass.: Harvard University Press, 1921–1973.

Cicero. Translated by L. H. G. Greenwood et. al. 28 vols. Loeb Classical Library. Cambridge, Mass.: Harvard University Press, 1913–2010.

Clement of Alexandria. *Les Stromates*. Translated by Marcel Caster. 7 vols. Sources chrétiennes 30, 38, 278–279, 428, 446. Paris, Éditions du Cerf, 1951–2001.

———. *Le Protreptique*. Translated by Claude Mondésert. 2d ed. Sources chrétiennes 2. Paris, Éditions du Cerf, 1961.

Dead Sea Scrolls Study Edition. Edited by Florentino García Martínez and Eibert J. C. Tigchelaar. 2 vols. Leiden: Brill, 1997–1998.

Dio Cassius. Translated by Earnest Cary and Herbert Baldwin Foster. 9 vols. Loeb Classical Library. London: Heinemann, 1914–1927.

Dio Chrysostom. Translated by J. W. Cohoon et al. 5 vols. Loeb Classical Library. Cambridge, Mass.: Harvard University Press, 1932–1951.

Diogenes Laertius. Translated by R. D. Hicks. 2 vols. Loeb Classical Library. Cambridge, Mass.: Harvard University Press, 1925.

Diodorus of Sicily. Translated by Charles Henry Oldfather. 12 vols. Loeb Classical Library. London: Heinemann, 1933–1967.

Dionysius of Halicarnassus. Translated by Earnest Cary, et al. 9 vols. Loeb Classical Library. Cambridge, Mass.: Harvard University Press, 1937–1985.

Epictetus. Translated by W. A. Oldfather. 2 vols. Loeb Classical Library. Cambridge, Mass.: Harvard University Press, 1925–1928.

Eratosthenis Catasterismorum reliquiae. Edited by Carolus Robert. 2d ed. Berlin: Weidmann, 1963.

Euripides. Translated by David Kovacs, et al. 8 vols. Loeb Classical Library. Cambridge, Mass.: Harvard University Press, 1994–2009.

Eusebius of Caesarea. *Preparation for the Gospel*. Translated by Edwin Hamilton Gifford. 2 vols. Grand Rapids, Mich.: Baker Book House, 1981.

Galen. *De usu partium libri xvii*. Edited by G. Helmreich. 2 vols. Leipzig: Teubner, 1907–1909.

Greek Alexander Romance. Translated by Richard Stoneman. London: Penguin Books, 1991.

Greek Magical Papyri in Translation, Including the Demotic Spells. Edited by Hans Dieter Betz. Chicago: Chicago University Press, 1986.

Gregory of Nazianzus. *Discours funèbres en l'honneur de son frère Césaire et de Basile de Césarée*. Edited by F. Boulenger. Paris: Picard, 1908.

Hermetica : The Greek Corpus Hermeticum and the Latin Asclepius in a New English Translation with Notes and Introduction. Translated by Brian P. Copenhaver. Cambridge: Cambridge University Press, 1992.

Herodian. Translated by C. R. Whittaker. 2 vols. Loeb Classical Library. Cambridge, Mass.: Harvard University Press, 1969–1970.

Herodotus. Translated by A. D. Godley. 4 vols. Loeb Classical Library. Cambridge, Mass.: Harvard University Press, 1920–1925.

Hesiod. Translated by Glenn W. Most. 2 vols. Loeb Classical Library. Cambridge, Mass.: Harvard University Press, 2007.

Hippolytus. *Refutatio omnium haeresium*. Edited by Miroslav Marcovich. Berlin and New York: Walter de Gruyter, 1986.

Homer. Translated by A. T. Murray. 4 vols. Loeb Classical Library. Cambridge, Mass.: Harvard University Press, 1919–1925.

The Homeric Hymns: A Verse Translation. Translated by Thelma Sargent. New York: W. W. Norton & Co., 1973.

Horace: Odes and Epodes. Translated by Niall Rudd. Loeb Classical Library. Cambridge, Mass.: Harvard University Press, 2004.

Inscriptiones Graecae: Inscriptiones Atticae Euclidis anno posteriores. Edited by Iohannes Kirchner. 2d edition. Minor Pars Prima; Preussische Akademie der Wissenschaften; Berlin: G. Reimer, 1916.

Irenaeus. *Contre les hérésies*. Edited and translated by Adelin Rousseau et Louis Doutreleau. 5 vols. Sources chrétiennes 100, 150, 152–153, 210–211. Paris: Éditions du Cerf, 1965–1982.

Isocrates. Translated by George Norlin et al. 3 vols. Loeb Classical Library. Cambridge, Mass.: Harvard University Press, 1928–1945.

Jacoby, Felix. *Die Fragmente der griechischen Historiker.* Leiden: Brill, 1923–1958.

Josephus. Translated by H. St J. Thackeray et al. 10 vols. Loeb Classical Library. Cambridge, Mass.: Harvard University Press, 1926–1965.

Justin Martyr. *Justin, Philosopher and Martyr, Apologies.* Edited by Denis Minns and Paul Parvis. Oxford: Oxford University Press, 2009.

Lactantius. *Divine Institutes.* Translated by Anthony Bowen and Peter Garnsey. Liverpool: Liverpool University Press, 2003.

Lauterbach, Jacob Z. *Mekilta de-Rabbi Ishmael.* 3 vols. Philadelphia: Jewish Publication Society of America, 1976.

Lettre d'Aristée a Philocrate. Edited by Pelletier, André. Sources chrétiennes 89. Paris: Éditions du Cerf, 1962.

Livy. Translated by B. O. Foster. 14 vols. Loeb Classical Library. Cambridge, Mass.: Harvard University Press, 1919–1959.

Longinus. Translated by Stephen Halliwell. Loeb Classical Library. Cambridge, Mass.: Harvard University Press, 1995.

Lucian. Translated by A. M. Harmon. 8 vols. Loeb Classical Library. Cambridge, Mass.: Harvard University Press, 1913–1967.

Macrobius. *Commentary on the Dream of Scipio.* Translated by William Harris Stahl. New York: Columbia University Press, 1990.

Manilius. Translated by G. P. Goold. Loeb Classical Library. Cambridge, Mass.: Harvard University Press, 1977.

Maximus of Tyre. *The Philosophical Orations.* Translated by Michael B. Trapp. Oxford: Clarendon, 1997.

Meister Eckhart: The Essential Sermons, Commentaries, Treatises, and Defense. Translated by Edmund Colledge and Bernard McGinn. Mahwah, NJ: Paulist Press, 1981.

Merkelbach, R. and M. L. West, *Fragmenta Hesiodea.* Oxford: Clarendon Press, 1967.

The Mishnah. Translated by Herbert Danby. Oxford: Clarendon, 1933.

Nauck, A, ed. *Tragicorum Graecorum fragmenta.* Leipzig: Teubner, 1889.

New Testament Apocrypha. Edited by Wilhelm Schneemelcher. Translated by R. McL. Wilson. 2 vols. 2d ed. Louisville: Westminster/John Knox Press, 1991.

Novum Testamentum Graece. Edited by Eberhard Nestle, Barbara Aland, Kurt Aland, et al. 27th ed. Stuttgart: Deutsche Bibelgesellschaft, 1996.

Numenius. *Fragments.* Edited by Édouard des Places. Paris: Société d'Édition "Les Belles Lettres," 1973.

Old Testament Pseudepigrapha. Translated by J. H. Charlesworth. 2 vols. Garden City, N.Y. : Doubleday, 1983.

Orientis Graeci Inscriptiones Selectae. Edited by Wilhelm Dittenberger. 2 vols. Lipsiae: S. Hirzel, 1903–1905.

Origen. *Contra Celsum.* Translated by Henry Chadwick. Cambridge: Cambridge University Press, 1953.

———. *On First Principles, Being Koetschau's Text of the De principiis.* Translated by G. W. Butterworth. Gloucester, Mass., P. Smith, 1973.

————. *Treatise on the Passover and Dialogue of Origen with Heraclides and his Fellow Bishops on the Father, the Son, and the Soul*. Translated by Robert J. Daly. Ancient Christian Writers 54. New York : Paulist Press, 1992

Ovid. Loeb Classical Library. Translated by Frank Justus Miller et al. 6 vols. Cambridge, Mass.: Harvard University Press: 1914–1936.

Pausanias. Translated by W. H. S. Jones, et al. 5 vols. Loeb Classical Library. Cambridge, Mass.: Harvard University Press, 1918–1935.

Peek, Werner, ed. *Greek Verse Inscriptions; Epigrams on Funerary Stelae and Monuments = Griechische Vers-Inschriften: Grab-Epigramme*. 1st American reprint ed. Chicago: Ares Publishers, 1988.

Philo. Translated by F. H. Colson, et al. 12 vols. Loeb Classical Library. Cambridge, Mass.: Harvard University Press, 1929–1962.

Philostratus. Translated by Christopher P. Jones. 6 vols. Loeb Classical Library. Cambridge, Mass.: Harvard University Press, 1921–2006.

Pindar. Translated by William H. Race. 2 vols. Loeb Classical Library. Cambridge, Mass.: Harvard University Press, 1997.

Plato: Complete Works. Edited by John M. Cooper. Indianapolis, Ind.: Hackett Pub., 1997.

Pliny. Translated by H. Rackham et al. 11 vols. Loeb Classical Library. Cambridge, Mass.: Harvard University Press, 1914–1963.

Plotinus. Translated by A. H. Armstrong. 7 vols. Loeb Classical Library. Cambridge, Mass.: Harvard University Press, 1966–1988.

Plutarch. Translated by Frank Cole Babbit et al. 28 vols. Loeb Classical Library. Cambridge, Mass.: Harvard University Press, 1914–2004.

Polybius. Translated by W. R. Paton 6 vols. Loeb Classical Library. Cambridge, Mass.: Harvard University Press, 1926–2011.

Propertius. Translated by G. P. Goold. Loeb Classical Library. Cambridge, Mass.: Harvard University Press, 1990.

Pseudo-Aristotle. *De Mundo*. Translated by E. S. Forster. Oxford: Clarendon Press, 1914.

Ritual Texts for the Afterlife: Orpheus and the Bacchic Gold Tablets. Edited by Fritz Graf and Sarah Iles Johnston. London: Routledge, 2007.

Sallustius. *Concerning the Gods and the Universe*. Translated by Arthur Darby Nock. Hildesheim: G. Olms, 1988.

Seneca. Translated by John W. Basore, et al. 13 vols. Loeb Classical Library. Cambridge, Mass.: Harvard University Press, 1913–2004.

Seneca the Elder. Translated by Michael Winterbottom. 2 vols. Loeb Classical Library. Cambridge, Mass.: Harvard University Press, 1974.

Septuaginta, id est Vetus Testamentum graece iuxta LXX interpretes. Edited by Alfred Rahlfs and Robert Hanhart. Rev. ed. Stuttgart: Deutsche Bibelgesellschaft, 2006.

Sextus Empiricus. Translated by Robert Gregg Bury. 4 vols. Loeb Classical Library. London: Heinemann, 1933–1949.

Sifre: A Tannaitic Commentary on the Book of Deuteronomy. Translated by Reuven Hammer. New Haven: Yale University Press, 1986.

Smallwood, E. Mary. *Documents Illustrating the Principates of Gaius, Claudius, and Nero*. Cambridge: Cambridge University Press, 1967.

Sophocles. Translated by Hugh Lloyd-Jones. 3 vols. Loeb Classical Library. Cambridge, Mass.: Harvard University Press, 1994–1996.

Stobaeus. *Ioannis Stobaei anthologium*. Edited by O. Hense and C. Wachsmuth. 5 vols. Berlin: Weidmann, 1958.

Strabo. Translated by Horace Jones. 8 vols. Loeb Classical Library. Cambridge, Mass.: Harvard University Press, 1917–1932.

Suetonius. Translated by J. C. Rolfe. 2 vols. Loeb Classical Library. Cambridge, Mass.: Harvard University Press, 1914.

Suidae Lexicon. Edited by Ada Adler. 5 vols. Stuttgart: Teubner, 1989–1994.

Supplementum Epigraphicum Graecum. Edited by J. J. E. Hondius et al. Amsterdam: J. C. Gieben 1923-

Tacitus. Translated by John Jackson, et al. 5 vols. Loeb Classical Library. Cambridge, Mass.: Harvard University Press, 1914–1937.

Tertullian. Translated by T. R. Glover, et al. Loeb Classical Library. Cambridge, Mass.: Harvard University Press, 1931.

———. *De Anima*. Translated by Jan Hendrik Waszink. Amsterdam: H. J. Paris, 1933.

Theocritus. *The Idylls of Theocritus*. Translated by Robert Wells. Manchester: Carcanet Press, 1988.

Theophilus of Antioch. *Ad Autolycum*. Translated by Robert M. Grant. Oxford: Clarendon, 1970.

———. *Antiquitates Rerum Divinarum*. Edited by Burkhart Cardauns. 2 vols. Abhandlungen der Geistes- und Sozialwissenschaftlichen Klasse: Einzelveröffentlichung. Mainz: Akademie der Wissenschaften und der Literatur, 1976.

Valerius Maximus. Translated by D.R. Shackleton Bailey. 2 vols. Loeb Classical Library. Cambridge, Mass.: Harvard University Press, 2000.

Varro. Translated by Roland G. Kent. 3 vols. Loeb Classical Library. Cambridge, Mass.: Harvard University Press, 1938.

Velleius Paterculus. Compendium of Roman History (Res gestae divi Augusti). Translated by Frederick W. Shipley. Loeb Classical Library. Cambridge, Mass.: Harvard University Press, 1992.

Virgil. Translated by H. Rushton Fairclough et al. 2 vols. Loeb Classical Library. Cambridge, Mass.: Harvard University Press, 1999.

Xenophon. *Memorabilia*. Translated by Amy L. Bonnette. Ithaca: Cornell University Press, 1994.

Secondary Sources

Anderson, Gary A. The Genesis of Perfection: Adam and Eve in Jewish and Christian Imagination. Louisville: Westminster John Knox Press, 2001.

Annas, Julia. Platonic Ethics, Old and New. Ithaca: Cornell University Press, 1999.

Armstrong, J. M. "After the Ascent: Plato on Becoming Like God." Oxford Studies in Ancient Philosophy 26 (2004): 171–83.

Asher, Jeffrey R. Polarity and Change in 1 Corinthians 15: A Study of Metaphysics, Rhetoric and Resurrection. Tübingen: Mohr Siebeck, 2000.

Assmann, Jan. Of God and Gods: Egypt, Israel, and the Rise of Monotheism. Madison: University of Wisconsin, 2008.

Athanassiadi, Polymnia and Michael Frede, eds. Pagan Monotheism in Late Antiquity. Oxford: Clarendon Press, 1999.

Auffarth, Christoph. "Herrscherkult und Christuskult." Pages 283–318 in Die Praxis der Herrscherverehrung in Rom und seinen Provinzen. Edited by Hubert Cancik and Konrad Hitzl. Tübingen: Mohr Siebeck, 2003.

Aune, David. Revelation 1–5. Word Biblical Commentary 52. Dallas: Word Books, 1997.

Ayres, Lewis. Nicaea and Its Legacy: An Approach to Fourth-Century Trinitarian Theology. Oxford: Oxford University Press, 2004.

Back, Frances. Verwandlung durch Offenbarung bei Paulus: Eine religionsgeschichtlich-exegetische Untersuchung zu 2 Kor 2,14–4,6. Wissenschaftliche Untersuchungen zum Neuen Testament 253. Tübingen: Mohr Siebeck, 2002.

Bacon, Helen H. "The Aeneid as a Drama of Election." Transactions of the American Philological Association 116 (1986): 305–334.

Badian, E. Protocol of the Colloquy of the Center for Hermeneutical Studies in Hellenistic and Modern Culture: The Deification of Alexander the Great. Berkeley: Center for Hermeneutical Studies, 1976.

———. "The Deification of Alexander the Great." Pages 27–71 in Ancient Macedonian Studies in Honor of Charles F. Edson, edited by Harry J. Dell. Thessaloniki: Institute for Balkan Studies, 1981.

Balch, David L. "1 Cor 7:32–35 and Stoic Debates about Marriage, Anxiety, and Distraction." Journal of Biblical Literature 102 (1983): 429–39.

Barclay, John M. G. "Paul Among Diaspora Jews: Anomaly or Apostate?" Journal for the Study of the New Testament 60 (1995): 89–120.

———. Jews in the Mediterranean Diaspora: From Alexander to Trajan (323 BCE-177CE). Edinburgh: T&T Clark, 1996.

Barr, James. The Garden of Eden and the Hope of Immortality. Minneapolis: Fortress, 1992.

Bauckham, Richard. God Crucified: Monotheism and Christology in the New Testament. Grand Rapids, Mich.: Eerdmans, 1999.

———. "The 'Most High God' and the Nature of Early Jewish Monotheism." Pages 39–53 in Israel's God and Rebecca's Children: Christology and Community in Early Judaism and Christianity: Essays in Honor of Larry W. Hurtado and Alan F. Segal. Edited by David B. Capes, Larry W. Hurtado and Alan F. Segal. Waco, Tex.: Baylor University Press, 2007.

———. Jesus and the God of Israel: God Crucified and Other Studies on the New Testament's Christology of Divine Identity. Grand Rapids: Eerdmans, 2008.

Beard, Mary, John North, and S. R. F. Price, eds. Religions of Rome. Cambridge: Cambridge University Press, 1998.

Belleville, Linda L. Reflections of Glory: *Paul's Polemical Use of the Moses-Doxa Tradition in 2 Corinthians 3.1–18*. Journal for the Study of the New Testament Supplement Series 52. Sheffield: JSOT Press, 1991.

———. "'Imitate Me, Just as I Imitate Christ': Discipleship in the Corinthian Correspondence," Pages 120–42 in Patterns of Discipleship in the New Testament. Edited by Richard N. Longenecker. Grand Rapids: Eerdmans, 1996.

Bianchi, Robert S. and Richard A. Fazzini. Cleopatra's Egypt: Age of the Ptolemies. Brooklyn, N.Y.: Brooklyn Museum, 1988.

Bilabel, Fr. "Fragmente aus der Heidelberger Papyrussammlung." Philologus, Zeitschrift für das klassische Alterum 80 (1925): 331–41.

Bilaniuk, Petro B. T. "The Mystery of Theosis or Divinization." Pages 337–59 in The Heritage of the Early Church: Essays in Honor of Georges Vasilievich Florovsky. Edited by David Neiman and Margaret Schatkin. Orientalia Christiana Analecta 195. Rome: Pontifical Institute of Oriental Studies, 1973.

Black, Matthew. "The Throne Theophany Prophetic Commission." Pages 57–73 in Jews Greeks and Christians—Religious Cultures in Late Antiquity. Edited by Robert Hamerton-Kelly and Robin Scroggs. Leiden: Brill, 1976.

Blackburn, Barry. Theios Anēr and the Markan Miracle Traditions: A Critique of the Theios Anēr Concept as an Interpretive Background of the Miracle Traditions used by Mark. Wissenschaftliche Untersuchungen zum Neuen Testament 40. Tübingen: Mohr Siebeck, 1991.

Blackwell, Ben C. Christosis: Pauline Soteriology in Light of Deification in Irenaeus and Cyril of Alexandria Tübingen: Mohr Siebeck, forthcoming.

Blank, Josef. "Gnosis und Agape: Zur christologischen Struktur paulinischer Mystik." Pages 1–13 in Grundfragen christlicher Mystik: *Wissenschaftliche Studientagung theologia mystica in Weingarten vom 7.–10. November 1985*. Edited by Margot Schmidt. Stuttgart-Bad Cannstatt: Friedrich Frommann, 1987.

Bodéüs, Richard. Aristotle and the Theology of the Living Immortals. Translated by Jan Edward Garrett. Albany: State University of New York, 2000.

Bousset, Wilhelm. Kyrios Christos: a History of the Belief in Christ from the Beginnings of Christianity to Irenaeus. Nashville: Abingdon Press, 1970.

Boyarin, Daniel. Border Lines: The Partition of Judaeo-Christianity. Philadelphia: University of Pennsylvania Press, 2004.

Braulik, Georg. "Das Deuteronomium und die Geburt des Monotheismus." 115–59 in Gott, der Einzige: Zur Entstehung des Monotheismus in Israel. Edited by Ernst Haag and Georg Braulik. Freiburg: Herder, 1985.

Braun, Herbert. Gesammelte Studien zum Neuen Testament und seiner Umwelt. Tübingen: Mohr Siebeck, 1962.

Bultmann, Rudolf Karl. Der Stil der paulinischen Predigt und die kynisch-stoische Diatribe. Göttingen: Vandenhoeck & Ruprecht, 1984.

Burkert, Walter. Lore and Science in Ancient Pythagoreanism. Translated by Edwin L. Minar. Cambridge, Mass.: Harvard University Press, 1972.

Burridge, Richard A. Imitating Jesus: An Inclusive Approach to New Testament Ethics. Grand Rapids: Eerdmans, 2007.

Calvin, John. Institutes of the Christian Religion. Edited by John T. McNeill. Translated by Ford Lewis Battles. 2 vols. Library of Christian Classics 20. Philadelphia: Westminster, 1960.

Capes, D. B. Old Testament Yahweh Texts in Paul's Christology. Wissenschaftliche Untersuchungen zum Neuen Testament 47. Tübingen: Mohr Siebeck, 1992.

Carlson, R. A. "The Anti-Assyrian Character of the Oracle in Isa IX:1–6." Vetus Testamentum 24 (1974): 130–35.

Chaniotis, Angelos. "The Divinity of Hellenistic Rulers." Pages 431–446 in A Companion to the Hellenistic World. Edited by Andrew Erskine. Malden: Blackwell, 2003.

———. "Megatheism: The Search for the Almighty God and the Competition of Cults." Pages 112–140 in One God: Pagan Monotheism in the Roman Empire. Edited by Stephen Mitchell and Peter van Nuffelen. Cambridge: Cambridge University Press, 2010.

———. "The Ithyphallic Hymn for Demetrios Poliorcetes and Hellenistic Religious Mentality." Pages 157–195 in More than Men, Less than Gods. Studies in Royal Cult and Imperial Worship. Proceedings of the International Colloquium Organized by the Belgian School at Athens (1–2 November 2007). Edited by P.P. Iossif, A.S. Chankowski, and C.C. Lorber. Leuven: Peeters, 2011.

Chesnut, Glenn F. "The Ruler and the Logos in Neopythagorean, Middle Platonic, and Late Stoic Political Philosoph." Aufstieg und Niedergang der Römischen Welt 16.2:1310–1332. Part 2, Principat 16.2. Edited by Wolfgang Hasse. Berlin: Walter de Gruyter, 1978.

Cho, Sang-Yol. Lesser Deities in the Ugaritic Texts and the Hebrew Bible: A Comparative Study of their Nature and Roles. Piscataway, N.J.: Gorgias Press, 2007.

Christensen, Michael J. and Jeffery A. Wittung, eds. Partakers of the Divine Nature: The History and Development of Deification in the Christian Traditions. Grand Rapids: Baker Academic, 2007.

Clauss, Manfred. "Deus Praesens: Der Römische Kaiser als Gott." Klio 78 (1996): 400–33.

———. Kaiser und Gott: Herrscherkult im römischen Reich. Stuttgart: Teubner, 1999.

Clay, Jenny Strauss. The Wrath of Athena: Gods and Men in the Odyssey. Lanham Md.: Rowman & Littlefield, 1997.

———. Hesiod's Cosmos. Cambridge: Cambridge University Press, 2003.

Cohen, Shaye. From the Maccabees to the Mishnah. Philadelphia: Westminster, 1987.

Cohn, Norman. Cosmos, Chaos, and the World to Come: The Ancient Roots of Apocalyptic Faith. New Haven: Yale University Press, 1993.

Colish, Marcia L. The Stoic Tradition from Antiquity to the Early Middle Ages. I. Stoicism in Classical Latin Literature. Leiden: Brill, 1990.

Collins, Adela Yarbro. "'How on Earth did Jesus Become a God?': A Reply."
    Pages 55–66 in Israel's God and Rebecca's Children: Christology and
    Community in Early Judaism and Christianity: Essays in Honor of Larry
    W. Hurtado and Alan F. Segal. Edited by David B. Capes, Larry W. Hur-
    tado and Alan F. Segal. Waco, Tex.: Baylor University Press, 2007.
Collins, Adela Yarbro and John J. Collins. King and Messiah as Son of God:
    Divine, Human, and Angelic Messianic Figures in Biblical and Related Lit-
    erature. Grand Rapids: Eerdmans, 2008.
Collins, John J. The Apocalyptic Vision of the Book of Daniel. Missoula:
    Scholars Press, 1977.
———. Daniel: A Commentary on the Book of Daniel. Hermeneia. Minne-
    apolis: Fortress Press, 1993.
———. "Jewish Monotheism and Christian Theology." Pages 81–105 in As-
    pects of Monotheism: How God is One. Edited by Hershel Shanks and
    Jack Meinhardt. Washington D. C.: Biblical Archaeology Society, 1997.
———. "Powers in Heaven: God, Gods, and Angels in the Dead Sea Scrolls."
    Pages 9–28 in Religion in the Dead Sea Scrolls. Edited by John J. Collins
    and Robert A. Kugler. Grand Rapids: Eerdmans, 2000.
———. "Life after Death in Pseudo-Phocylides." Pages 128–42 in Jewish Cult
    and Hellenistic Culture: Essays on the Jewish Encounter with Hellenism
    and Roman Rule. Leiden: Brill, 2005.
Collins, John J. and Gregory Sterling. Hellenism in the Land of Israel. Chris-
    tianity and Judaism in Antiquity. 13. Notre Dame: University of Notre
    Dame Press, 2001.
Collins, Paul M. Partaking in Divine Nature: Deification and Communion.
    London & New York: T&T Clark, 2010.
Colpe, Carsten. Die religionsgeschichtliche Schule: Darstellung und Kritik
    ihres Bildes vom gnostischen Erlösermythus. Göttingen: Vandenhoeck
    und Ruprecht, 1961.
Conzelmann, Hans. A Commentary on the First Epistle to the Corinthians.
    Edited by G. W. MacRae. Translated by James Leitch. Hermeneia. Phila-
    delphia: Fortress, 1975.
Couroyer, B. "Dieu ou roi." Revue Biblique 78 (1971): 234–39.
Cranfield, C. E. B. and W. Sanday. A Critical and Exegetical Commentary on
    the Epistle to the Romans. 2 vols. 6th ed. The International Critical Com-
    mentary 32. Edinburgh: Clark, 1975, 1979.
Cumont, Franz. Afterlife in Roman Paganism. New York: Dover, 1922.
Curtis, Edward Mason, Man as the Image of God in Genesis in the Light of
    Ancient Near Eastern Parallels. Ph.D. Diss., University Of Pennsylvania,
    1984.
Davies, Jon. Death, Burial and Rebirth in the Religions of Antiquity. London
    & New York: Routledge: 1999.
DeConick, April D. Seek to See Him: Ascent and Vision Mysticism in the
    Gospel of Thomas. Supplements to Vigiliae Christianae 33. Leiden:
    Brill, 1996.
———. Voices of the Mystics, Early Christian Discourse in the Gospels of
    John and Thomas and Other Ancient Christian Literature. Journal for

the Study of the New Testament Supplement Series 157. Sheffield: Sheffield Academic, 2001.
Deissmann, Adolf. Paul: A Study in Social and Religious History. Translated by
William Wilson. 2d ed. New York: George H. Doran Co., 1926.
de Jáuregui, Miguel Herrero. "Orphic Ideas of Immortality: Traditional Greek
Images and a New Eschatological Thought." Pages 289–314 in Lebendige
Hoffnung—ewiger Tod?! Jenseitsvorstellungen im Hellenismus, Judentum
und Christentum. Edited by Michael Labahn and Manfred Lang. Arbeiten
zur Bibel und ihrer Geschichte 24. Leipzig: Evangelische Verlagsanstalt,
2007.
———. "Orphic God(s): Theogonies and Hymns as Vehicles of Monotheism."
Pages 77–100 in Monotheism Between Pagans and Christians in Late Antiquity. Edited by Stephen Mitchell and Peter van Nuffelen. Leuven: Peeters, 2010.
des Places, Édouard. Syngeneia: La parenté de l'homme avec dieu d'homère a la
patristique. Paris: Librairie C. Klincksieck, 1964.
Dibelius, Martin, Botschaft und Geschichte: Gesammelte Aufsätze. Edited by
Günther Bornkamm. 2 vols. Tübingen: Mohr Siebeck, 1956.
Dillon, John M. "The Transcendence of God in Philo: Some Possible Sources." Pages 1–8 in Center for Hermeneutical Studies Protocol of the
16th Colloquy (April 1975). Vol. 16. Berkeley, 1975.
———. "Plotinus, Philo and Origen on the Grades of Virtue." Pages 92–105
in Platonismus und Christentum: Festschrift für Heinrich Dörrie. Edited
by H.-D. Blume and F. Mann. Jahrbuch für Antike und Christentum, Er-
gänzungsband 10. Münster: Aschendorffsche Verlagsbuchhandlung, 1983.
———. The Middle Platonists : A Study of Platonism, 80 B.C. to A.D. 220.
2d ed. London : Duckworth, 1996.
Dodd, Brian J. "The Story of Christ and the Imitation of Paul in Philippians
2–3." Pages 154–60 in Where Christology Began: Essays on Philippians
2. Edited by R. P. Martin and B. J. Dodd. Louisville: Westminster John
Knox, 1998.
Downing, F. Gerald. Cynics, Paul, and the Pauline Churches : Cynics and
Christian Origins II. London: Routledge, 1998.
Drewery, Benjamin. "Deification." Pages 33–62 in Christian Spirituality: Essays in Honour of Gordon Rupp. Edited by Peter Brooks. London: SCM
Press, 1975.
Duff, Paul B. "Transformed 'from Glory to Glory': Paul's Appeal to the Experience of His Readers in 2 Cor 3:18." Journal of Biblical Literature 127
(2008): 759–80.
Dunand, Francoise. "Les Associations dionysiaques au service du Pouvoir Lagide (III s. av. J.-C.)." Pages 85–104 in L'Association dionysiaque dans
les sociétés anciennes: Actes de la Table Rond organisée par l'École Française de Rome. Palais Farnèse: L'École française de Rome, 1986.
Dunn, James D. G. Jesus and the Spirit: A Study of the Religious and Charismatic Experience of Jesus and the First Christians as Reflected in the New
Testament. London: SCM Press, 1975.

————. Romans 1–8. Word Biblical Commentary 38. Nashville: Thomas Nelson, 1988.

————. Did the First Christians Worship Jesus? The New Testament Evidence. Louisville: Westminster John Knox, 2010.

Edelstein, Emma and Ludwig Edelstein. Asclepius: A Collection and Interpretation of the Testimonies. 2 vols. New York: Arno Press, 1975.

Edmonds, Radcliffe G. Myths of the Underworld Journey in Plato, Aristophanes, and the 'Orphic' Gold Tablets. Cambridge: Cambridge University Press, 2004.

Ehnmark, Erland. The Idea of God in Homer. Uppsala: Almquist Wiksells, 1935.

Eichrodt, Walther. Theology of the Old Testament. Translated by J. A. Baker. 2 vols. Philadelphia: Westminster Press, 1967.

Engberg-Pedersen, Troels. Paul and the Stoics. Louisville: Westminster John Knox, 2000.

————, ed. Paul Beyond the Judaism/Hellenism Divide. Louisville: Westminster/John Knox Press, 2001.

————. "Paul, Virtues, and Vices." Pages 608–34 in Paul in the Greco-Roman World. Edited by J. Paul Sampley. Harrisburg: Trinity Press, 2003.

————. "Stoicism in the Apostle Paul: A Philosophical Reading." Pages 52–75 in Stoicism: Traditions and Transformations. Edited by Stephen Strange and Jack Zupko. Cambridge: Cambridge University Press, 2004.

————. "Complete and Incomplete Transformation in Paul—a Philosophical Reading of Paul on Body and Spirit." Pages 123–46 in Metamorphoses: Resurrection, Body and Transformative Practices in Early Christianity. Edited by Turid Karlsen Seim and Jorunn Økland. Berlin & New York: De Gruyter, 2009.

————. "Setting the Scene: Stoicism and Platonism in the Transitional Period in Ancient Philosophy." Pages 1–14 in Stoicism in Early Christianity. Edited by Tuomas Rasimus, Troels Engberg-Pedersen, and Ismo Dunderberg. Grand Rapids: Baker Academic, 2010.

————. Cosmology and Self in the Apostle Paul: The Material Spirit. Oxford: Oxford University Press, 2010.

Fee, Gordon D. The First Epistle to the Corinthians. New International Commentary on the New Testament. Grand Rapids: Eerdmans, 1987.

————. Pauline Christology: An Exegetical-Theological Study. Peabody, Mass.: Hendrickson Publishers, 2007.

Faller, Otto. "Griechische Vergottung und christliche Vergöttlichung." Gregorianum 6 (1925): 404–35.

Finlan, Stephen. "Can we Speak of Theosis in Paul?" Pages 68–80 in Partakers of the Divine Nature: The History and Development of Deification in the Christian Traditions. Edited by Michael Christensen and Jeffery Wittung. Madison: Fairleigh Dickinson University Press, 2007.

Finlan, Stephen and Vladimir Kharlamov. Theōsis: Deification in Christian Theology. Eugene, Ore: Pickwick, 2006.

Fishwick, Duncan. The Imperial Cult in the Latin West: Studies in the Ruler Cult of the Western Provinces of the Roman Empire. Leiden: Brill, 1987.

Fitzgerald, John T. Cracks in an Earthen Vessel: An Examination of the Catalogues of Hardships in the Corinthian Correspondence. Atlanta: Scholars Press, 1988.

Fitzmyer, J. A. "Glory Reflected on the Face of Christ (2 Cor. 3.7–4.6) and a Palestinian Jewish Motif." Theological Studies 42 (1981) : 630–644

Fletcher-Louis, Crispin. "4Q374: A Discourse on the Sinai Tradition: The Deification of Moses and Early Christology." Dead Sea Discoveries 3 (1996): 236–52.

———. "The Worship of Divine Humanity as God's Image and the Worship of Jesus." Pages 112–28 in The Jewish Roots of Christological Monotheism: Papers from the St. Andrews Conference on the Historical Origins of the Worship of Jesus. Edited by Carey C. Newman, James R. Davila and Gladys S. Lewis. Leiden: Brill, 1999.

Fossum, Jarl. "Glory." Pages 348–352 in Dictionary of Deities and Demons in the Bible (DDD). Edited by K. van der Toorn, Bob Becking and Pieter Willem van der Horst. 2d edition. Leiden: Brill, 1999.

Fowl, Stephen. "Christology and Ethics in Philippians 2:5–11." Pages 140–53 in Where Christology Began: Essays on Philippians 2. Edited by R. P. Martin and B. J. Dodd. Louisville: Westminster/John Knox, 1998.

Fraser, PM. Ptolemaic Alexandria. 2 vols. Oxford: Clarendon, 1972.

Fredricksmeyer, E. A. "Divine Honors for Philip II." Transactions of the American Philological Association 109 (1979): 39–61.

———. "On the Background of the Ruler-Cult." Pages 145–56 in Ancient Macedonian Studies in Honor of Charles F. Edson. Edited by Harry J. Dell. Thessaloniki: Institute for Balkan Studies, 1981.

Freud, Sigmund. Moses and Monotheism. Translated by Katherine Jones. New York: Vintage, 1939.

Fürst, Alfons. "Monotheism Between Cult and Politics: The Themes of the Ancient Debate Between Pagan and Christian Monotheism." Pages 82–99 in One God: Pagan Monotheism in the Roman Empire. Edited by Stephen Mitchell and Peter van Nuffelen. Cambridge: Cambridge University Press, 2010.

Garr, W. Randall. In His Own Image and Likeness: Humanity, Divinity, and Monotheism. Leiden: Brill, 2003.

Gavrilyuk, Paul L. "The Retrieval of Deification: How a Once-despised Archaism Became an Ecumenical Desideratum." Modern Theology 25 (2009): 647–59.

George, Martin. "Vergöttlichung des Menschen. Von der platonischen Philosophie zur Soteriologie der griechischen Kirchenväter." Pages 115–56 in Die Weltlichkeit des Glaubens in der Alten Kirche: Festschrift für Ulrich Wickert zum siebzigsten Geburtstag. Edited by Dietmar Wyrwa. Berlin & New York: Walter de Gruyter, 1997.

Giblin, Charles H. "Three Monotheistic Texts in Paul." Catholic Biblical Quarterly 37 (1975): 527–547.

Gieschen, Charles. Angelomorphic Christology: Antecedents and Early Evidence. Leiden: Brill, 1998.

Glucker, John. "Cicero's Philosophical Affiliations." Pages 34–69 in The Question of "Eclecticism": Studies in Later Greek Philosophy. Edited by John M. Dillon & A. A. Long. Berkeley: University of California, 1988.

Goodenough, E. R. "The Political Philosophy of Hellenistic Kingship." Yale Classical Studies 1 (1928): 55–104.

———. Jewish Symbols in the Greco-Roman Period. 12 vols. New York: Pantheon Books, 1953–68.

Gorman, Michael. Cruciformity: Paul's Narrative Spirituality of the Cross. Grand Rapids: Eerdmans, 2001.

———. Inhabiting the Cruciform God: Kenosis, Justification, and Theosis in Paul's Narrative Soteriology. Grand Rapids: Eerdmans, 2009.

Goshen-Gottstein, Alon. "The Body as Image of God in Rabbinic Literature." Harvard Theological Review 87 (1994): 171–195.

Gottwald, Norman K. The Tribes of Yahweh : A Sociology of the Religion of Liberated Israel, 1250–1050 B.C.E. Maryknoll, N.Y.: Orbis Books, 1979.

Gradel, Ittai. Emperor Worship and Roman Religion. Oxford: Clarendon Press, 2002.

Graf, Fritz. "Les dieux des Grecs et le dieu des Romains: Plus ça change …" Archiv für Religionsgeschichte 5 (2003): 131–45.

Greenwood, David. "The Lord is the Spirit: Some Considerations of 2 Corinthians 3.17." Catholic Biblical Quarterly 34 (1972): 467–72.

Grimm, Günther. "Die Vergöttlichung Alexanders des Grossen in Ägypten und ihre Bedeutung für den ptolemäischen Königskult." Pages 103–112 in Das ptolemäische Ägypten: Akten des internationalen Symposions 27.–29. September 1976 in Berlin. Edited by Herwig Maehler and Volker Michael Strocka. Mainz: Philipp von Zabern, 1978.

Gross, Jules. La divinisation du chrétien d'après les pères grecs. Paris: J. Gabalda et Cie, 1938.

Gruen, Erich S. Heritage and Hellenism: The Reinvention of Jewish Tradition. Hellenistic Culture and Society 30. Berkeley: University of California Press, 1998.

Grundmann, Walter. Der Begriff der Kraft in der Neutestamentlichen Gedankenwelt. Stuttgart: Kohlhammer, 1932.

Gunnlaugur A. Jónsson. The Image of God: Genesis 1:26–28 in a Century of Old Testament Research. Coniectanea Biblica 26. Stockholm: Almqvist & Wiksell, 1988.

Gurval, Robert. "Caesar's Comet: The Politics and Poetics of an Augustan Myth." Memoirs of the American Academy in Rome 42 (1996): 39–71.

Guthrie, W. K. C. The Greeks and their Gods. London: Methuen, 1950.

Habicht, Christian. Gottmenschentum und griechische Städte. 2nd ed. München: C.H. Beck'sche Verlagsbuchhandlung, 1970.

———. Athens from Alexander to Antony. Cambridge, Mass.: Harvard University Press, 1997.

Hafemann, Scott. Paul, Moses, and the History of Israel. Milton Keynes, UK: Paternoster, 2005.

Hagner, Donald A. "The Vision of God in Philo and John: A Comparative Study." Journal of the Evangelical Theological Society 14 (1971): 81–93.

Hammond, N. G. L. "Heroic and Divine Honors in Macedonia before the Successors." Ancient World 30 (1999): 103–15.

Handy, Lowell K. Among the Host of Heaven: The Syro-Palestinian Pantheon as Bureaucracy. Winona Lake: Eisenbrauns, 1994.

Harnack, Adolf. Lehrbuch der Dogmengeschichte: Die Entstehung des kirchlichen Dogmas. 3 vols. 5th ed. Tübingen: Mohr Siebeck, 1931.

Harris, Murray J. The Second Epistle to the Corinthians: A Commentary on the Greek Text. The New International Greek Testament Commentary. Grand Rapids: Eerdmans, 2005.

Harrison, S. J. Apuleius: A Latin Sophist. Oxford: Oxford University Press, 2000.

Hauben, Hans. "Aspects du culte des souverains a l'epoque des Lagides." Pages 441–467 in Egitto e storia antica dall'Ellenismo all'eta Araba. Edited by Lucia Criscuolo and Giovanni Geraci. Bologna: Clueb, 1989.

Hawthorne, Gerald F. "The Imitation of Christ: Discipleship in Philippians." Pages 163–79 in Patterns of Discipleship in the New Testament. Edited by Richard N. Longenecker. Grand Rapids: Eerdmans, 1996.

Hay, David H. Glory at the Right Hand: Psalm 110 in Early Christianity. Society of Biblical Literature Monograph Series 18. Nashville: Abingdon Press, 1973.

Hayman, Peter. "Monotheism—a Misused Word in Jewish Studies?" Journal of Jewish Studies 42 (1991): 1–15.

Helleman, Wendy E. "Philo of Alexandria on Deification and Assimilation to God." The Studia Philonica Annual 2 (1990): 51–71.

Hengel, Martin. Judaism and Hellenism: Studies in their Encounter in Palestine during the Early Hellenistic Period. Philadelphia: Fortress Press, 1974.

———. The "Hellenization" of Judaea in the First Century After Christ. London: SCM Press, 1989.

———. "Sit at My Right Hand!" Pages 119–225 in Studies in Early Christology. Edinburgh: T & T Clark, 1995.

Hölbl, Gunther. A History of the Ptolemaic Empire. London: Routledge, 2001.

Holladay, Carl. Theios Aner in Hellenistic-Judaism: A Critique of the use of this Category in New Testament Christology. Missoula: Scholars Press, 1977.

Horbury, William. Jewish Messianism and the Cult of Christ. London: SCM Press, 1998.

———. Messianism among Jews and Christians: Twelve Biblical and Historical Studies. Edinburgh: T & T Clark, 2003.

Hornung, Erik. "The Pharaoh." Pages 283–314 in The Egyptians. Edited by Sergio Donadoni. Translated by Robert Bianchi et al. Chicago: University of Chicago, 1997.

Hoskins, Paul M. "The Use of Biblical and Extrabiblical Parallels in the Interpretation of First Corinthians 6:2–3." Catholic Biblical Quarterly 63 (2001): 287–297.

Hoven, René. Stoïciens face au problem de l'au-delà. Paris: Société d'Edition "Les Belles Lettres," 1971.

Hurtado, Larry W. "Jesus as Lordly Example in Philippians 2:5–11." Pages 113–26 in From Jesus to Paul: Studies in Honour of Francis Wright Beare. Edited by P. Richardson and J.C. Hurd. Waterloo, Ont.: Wilfred Laurier University Press, 1984.

———. "First-Century Jewish Monotheism." Journal for the Study of the New Testament 71 (1998): 3–26.

———. Lord Jesus Christ: Devotion to Jesus in Earliest Christianity. Grand Rapids: Eerdmans, 2003.

———. How on Earth did Jesus Become a God?: Historical Questions about Earliest Devotion to Jesus. Grand Rapids: Eerdmans, 2005.

Johnson, Aubrey. Sacral Kingship in Ancient Israel. Cardiff: University of Wales Press, 1967.

Johnson, Luke Timothy. Among the Gentiles: Greco-Roman Religion and Christianity. New Haven: Yale University Press, 2009.

Kangas, Ron. "Becoming God." Affirmation & Critique 7 (2002): 3–30.

Kaufmann, Yeḥezkel. History of the Religion of Israel: From the Babylonian Captivity to the End of Prophecy. New York: Ktav Pub. House, 1976.

Kennedy, H. A. A. St Paul and the Mystery-Religions. London: Hodder and Stoughton, 1913.

Kerényi, C. Asklepios: Archetypal Image of the Physician's Existence. Translated by Ralph Manheim. New York: Pantheon, 1959.

Kimmelman, Reuven. "The Šĕma' and its Blessings : The Realization of God's Kingship." Pages 73–86 in The Synagogue in Late Antiquity. Edited by Lee I. Levine,. Philadelphia: The American Schools of Oriental Research, 1987.

———. "The Shema and its Rhetoric: The Case for the Shema being More than Creation, Revelation and Redemption." Journal of Jewish Thought and Philosophy 2 (1992): 111–56.

King, Charles. "The Organization of Roman Religious Beliefs." Classical Antiquity 22 (2003): 275–312.

Klosko, George. "The 'Rule' of Reason in Plato's Psychology." History of Philosophy Quarterly 5 (1988): 341–56.

Kraus, Hans-Joachim. Psalms 60–150 : A Commentary. Minneapolis: Fortress Press, 1993.

Kugel, James L. Traditions of the Bible: A Guide to the Bible As It Was at the Start of the Common Era. Cambridge, Mass.: Harvard University Press, 1998.

Kümmel, Werner Georg. The New Testament: The History of the Investigation of its Problems. Nashville: Abingdon Press, 1972.

Labuschagne, C. J. The Incomparability of Yahweh in the Old Testament. Leiden: Brill, 1966.

Lambrecht, Jan. "Transformation in 2 Cor. 3,18." Pages 295–307 in Studies on 2 Corinthians. Edited by Lambrecht and Reimund Bieringer. Leuven: Leuven University Press, 1994.

Lane Fox, Robin. Pagans and Christians. London: Viking, 1986.

Lang, Bernhard. Wisdom and the Book of Proverbs: A Hebrew Goddess Redefined. New York: Pilgrim Press, 1986.

Lattey, Cuthbert. "The Deification of Man in Clement of Alexandria: Some Further Notes." Journal of Theological Studies 17 (1916): 257–62.

Lattimore, Richmond Alexander. Themes in Greek and Latin Epitaphs. Urbana: University of Illinois Press, 1962.

Lavecchia, Salvatore, "Die Ὁμοίωσις Θεῷ in Platons Philosophie." Pages 321–94 in Perspektiven der Philosophie; Neues Jahrbuch. Edited by Wiebke Schrader, Georges Goedert and Martina Scherbel. Amsterdam & New York: Rodopi, 2005.

Le Bris, Anne. La mort et les conceptions de l'au delà en Grèce ancienne à travers les épigrammes funéraires. Paris: L'Harmattan, 2001.

Lee, Sang Meyng. Paul's Cosmic Drama of Salvation: A Study of Paul's Undisputed Writings from Anthropological and Cosmological Perspectives. Wissenschaftliche Untersuchungen zum Neuen Testament 276. Tübingen: Mohr Siebeck, 2010.

Lehnardt, Thomas. "Der Gott der Welt ist unser König: Zur Vorstellung von der Königsherrschaft Gottes im Shema und seinen Benediktionen." Pages 285–308 in Königsherrschaft Gottes und himmlischer Kult im Judentum, Urchristentum und in der hellenistischen Welt. Edited by Martin Hengel and Anna Maria Schwemer. Tübingen: Mohr Siebeck, 1991.

Lehtipuu, Outi. "'Flesh and Blood Cannot Inherit the Kingdom of God': The Transformation of the Flesh in the Early Christian Debates Concerning Resurrection." Pages 147–68 in Metamorphoses: Resurrection, Body, and Transformative Practices in Early Christianity. Edited by Turid Karlsen Seim and Jorunn Økland. Berlin: Walter de Gruyter, 2009.

Levenson, Jon Douglas. Sinai and Zion: An Entry into the Jewish Bible. Minneapolis: Winston Press, 1985.

———. Creation and the Persistence of Evil : The Jewish Drama of Divine Omnipotence. San Francisco: Harper & Row, 1988.

Levison, J. R. Portraits of Adam in Early Judaism: From Sirach to 2 Baruch. Journal for the Study of the Pseudepigrapha Supplement Series 1. Sheffield: JSOT Press, 1988.

Lieberg, Godo. "Apotheose und Unsterblichkeit in Ovids Metamorphosen." Pages 125–35 in Silvae: Festschrift für Ernst Zinn. Edited by Michael von Albrecht und Eberhard Heck. Tübingen: Max Niemeyer, 1970.

Lierman, John. The New Testament Moses: Christian Perceptions of Moses and Israel in the Setting of Jewish Religion. Tubingen: Mohr Siebeck, 2004.

Linder, M. and John Scheid. "Quand croire c'est faire. Le problème de la croyance dans la Rome ancienne." Archives de Sciences Sociales des Religions 38 (1993): 47–61.

Litwa, M. David. "2 Corinthians 3:18 and its Implications for Theosis." Journal of Theological Interpretation 2 (2008): 117–133.

Long, A. A. Stoic Studies. Cambridge: Cambridge University Press, 1996.

Lorenzen, Stefanie. Das paulinische Eikon-Konzept: Semantische Analysen zur Sapientia Salomonis, zu Philo und den Paulusbriefen. Wissenschaftliche Untersuchungen zum Neuen Testament 250. Tübingen: Mohr Siebeck, 2008.

Loretz, Oswald. Des Gottes Einzigkeit: Ein altorientalisches Argumentationsmodell zum "Schma Jisrael." Darmstadt: Wissenschaftliche Buchgesellschaft, 1997.

MacDonald, Nathan. Deuteronomy and the Meaning of "Monotheism. " Tübingen: Mohr Siebeck, 2003.

Macky, Peter W. St. Paul's Cosmic War Myth: A Military Version of the Gospel. Westminster College Library of Biblical Symbolism 2. New York: P. Lang, 1998.

MacMullen, Ramsay. Paganism in the Roman Empire. New Haven: Yale University Press, 1981.

Mahoney, Timothy A. "Moral Virtue and Assimilation to God in Plato's Timaeus." Oxford Studies in Ancient Philosophy 28 (2005): 77–91.

Maloney, George A. The Undreamed has Happened: God Lives Within Us. Scranton: University of Scranton Press, 2003.

Marcus, Joel. "Authority to Forgive Sins upon the Earth: The Shema in the Gospel of Mark." Pages 196–211 in The Gospels and the Scriptures of Israel. Edited by Craig A. Evans and W. Richard Stegner. Sheffield: Sheffield Academic Press, 1994.

Marguerat, Daniel. "La mystique de l'Apôtre Paul." Pages 307–329 in Paul De Tarse: Congrès de l'ACFEB. Edited by Jacques Schlosser. Paris: Les Éditions du Cerf, 1996.

Martin, Dale B. The Corinthian Body. New Haven: Yale University Press, 1995.

Mauser, Ulrich. "Heis Theos und Monos Theos in Biblischer Theologie." Jahrbuch für biblische Theologie 1 (1986): 71–87.

May, Gerhard. Creatio ex Nihilo: The Doctrine of 'Creation Out of Nothing' in Early Christian Thought. London: T&T Clark International, 2004.

McClellan, W. "El Gibbor." Catholic Biblical Quarterly 6 (1944): 276–288.

Meeks, Wayne. The Prophet-King: Moses Traditions and the Johannine Christology. Leiden: Brill, 1967.

Mettinger, T. N. D. "Abbild oder Urbild?" Zeitschrift für Alttestamentliche Wissenschaft 86 (1974): 403–24.

———. The Eden Narrative: A Literary and Religio-historical Study of Genesis 2–3. Winona Lake: Eisenbrauns, 2007.

Mikalson, Jon D. Religion in Hellenistic Athens. Berkeley: University of California Press, 1998.

Miller, J. M. "In the "Image" and "Likeness" of God." Journal of Biblical Literature 91 (1972): 289–304.

Moltmann, Jürgen. "Kein Monotheismus gleicht dem anderen: Destruktion eines untauglichen Begriffs." Evangelische Theologie 62 (2002): 112–122.

Morgenstern, J. "The King-God among the Western Semites and the Meaning of Epiphanes." Vetus Testamentum 10 (1960): 138–97.

Mosser Carl, "The Earliest Patristic Interpretations of Psalm 82, Jewish Antecedents, and the Origin of Christian Deification." Journal of Theological Studies 56 (2005): 30–74.

Mowinckel, Sigmund. He that Cometh: The Messiah Concept in the Old Testament and Later Judaism. Translated by G. W. Anderson. Grand Rapids: Eerdmans, 2005.

Mulder, J. S. M. Studies on Psalm 45. Oss (the Netherlands): Offsetdrukkerij Witsiers, 1972.

Mullen, E. Theodore. The Divine Council in Canaanite and Early Hebrew Literature. Chico, Calif.: Scholars Press, 1980.

Myers, K. Sara, ed. Ovid Metamorphoses Book XIV. Cambridge Greek and Latin Classics. Cambridge: Cambridge University Press, 2009.

Nebe, Gottfried. "Creation in Paul's Theology." Pages 111–137 in Creation in Jewish and Christian Tradition. London: Sheffield Academic, 2002.

Newsom, Carol. Songs of the Sabbath Sacrifice: A Critical Edition. Atlanta: Scholars Press, 1985.

Nicholson, Suzanne. Dynamic Oneness: The Significance and Flexibility of Paul's One-God Language. Eugene, Oreg: Pickwick, 2010.

Niehr, Herbert. "The Rise of YHWH in Judahite and Israelite Religion." Pages 45–72 in The Triumph of Elohim: From Yahwisms to Judaisms. Edited by Diana Vikander Edelman. Grand Rapids: Eerdmans, 1996.

Nispel, Mark D., "Christian Deification and the Early Testimonia." Vigiliae Christianae 53 (1999): 289–304.

Nock, Arthur Darby. "Deification and Julian." Pages 833–46 in Essays on Religion and the Ancient World. 2 vols. Vol. 2. Cambridge, Mass.: Harvard University Press, 1972.

Norris, Frederick W. "Deification: Consensual and Cogent." Scottish Journal of Theology 49 (1996): 411–28.

North, J. Lionel. "Jesus and Worship, God and Sacrifice." Pages 186–202 in Early Jewish and Christian Monotheism. Edited by Loren T. Stuckenbruck and Wendy E. Sproston North. London: T&T Clark International, 2004.

Nussbaum, Martha. Love's Knowledge: Essays on Philosophy and Literature. New York: Oxford University Press, 1990.

O'Collins, G.G. "Power Made Perfect in Weakness: 2 Cor 12–10." Catholic Biblical Quarterly 33 (1971): 528–537.

Økland, Jorunn. "Genealogies of the Self." Pages 83–107 in Metamorphoses: Resurrection, Body, and Transformative Practices in Early Christianity. Edited by Turid Karlsen Seim and Jorunn Økland. Berlin: Walter de Gruyter, 2009.

Olson, Roger E. "Deification in Contemporary Theology." Theology Today 64 (2007): 186–200.

O'Neill, J.C. "How Early is the Doctrine of Creatio ex Nihilo?" Journal of Theological Studies 52 (2002): 449–65.

Otto, Rudolf. The Idea of the Holy. Translated by John W. Harvey. London: Oxford: University Press, 1950.

Penchansky, David. Twilight of the Gods: Polytheism in the Hebrew Bible. Louisville: Westminster John Knox, 2005.

Peres, Imre. Griechische Grabinschriften und neutestamentliche Eschatologie. Wissenschaftliche Untersuchungen zum Neuen Testament 157. Tübingen: Mohr Siebeck, 2003.

Petersen, David L. "Israel and Monotheism." Pages 92–107 in Canon, Theology, and Old Testament Interpretation : Essays in Honor of Brevard S. Childs. Edited by Gene M. Tucker, David L. Petersen, Robert R. Wilson and Brevard S. Childs. Philadelphia: Fortress Press, 1988.

Peterson, Erik. Εἷς Θεός: Epigraphische, formgeschichtliche und religionsgeschichtliche Untersuchungen. Göttingen: Hubert & Co, 1920.

Pettazzoni, Raffaele. "The Formation of Monotheism." Pages 40–47 in Reader in Comparative Religion: an Anthropological Approach. Edited by William Armand Lessa and Evon Zartman Vogt. Evanston, Ill.: Row & Peterson, 1958.

Pfleiderer, Otto. Paulinism: A Contribution to the History of Primitive Christian Theology: Exposition of Paul's Doctrine. Translated by Peter Edwards. London: William and Norgate, 1877.

———. Primitive Christianity: Its Writings and Teachings in their Historical Connections. Edited by W. D. Morrison. Translated by W. Montgomery. Clifton, NJ: Reference Book Publishers, 1965.

Pollini, J. "Man Or God: Divine Assimilation and Imitation in the Late Republic and Early Principate." Pages 334–63 in Between Republic and Empire: Interpretations of Augustus and His Principate. Edited by Kurt A. Raaflaub, Mark Toher and G. W. Bowersock. Berkeley: University of California Press, 1990.

Porter, Barbara N. One God Or Many? Concepts of Divinity in the Ancient World. Transactions of the Casco Bay Assyriological Institute 1. Chebeague, Maine.: Casco Bay Assyriological Institute, 2000.

Pötscher, Walter. "ΘΕΟΣ: Studien zur älteren griechischen Gottesvorstellung." Diss. Wien, 1953.

———. Theophrastus: Περὶ Εὐσεβείας. Leiden: Brill, 1964.

Pouilloux, Jean. Recherches sur l'histoire et les cultes de Thasos: De la fondation de la cité à 196 avant J.-C. Paris: E. de Boccard, 1954.

Preuss, Horst Dietrich. Old Testament Theology. Old Testament Library. Louisville, Ky.: Westminster John Knox Press, 1995.

Price, S. R. F. "Gods and Emperors: The Greek Language of the Roman Imperial Cult." Journal of Hellenic Studies 54 (1984): 79–95.

———. Rituals and Power: The Roman Imperial Cult in Asia Minor. Cambridge: Cambridge University Press, 1984.

———. Religions of the Ancient Greeks. Key Themes in Ancient History. Cambridge: Cambridge University Press, 1999.

Proudfoot, C. M. "Imitation or Realistic Participation: A Study of Paul's Concept of 'Suffering with Christ.'" Interpretation 17 (1963): 140–60.

Rad, Gerhard von. Theologie des Alten Testaments. München: Kaiser Verlag, 1987.

Radice, Roberto. "Philo's Theology and Theory of Creation." Pages 124–45 in The Cambridge Companion to Philo. Edited by Adam Kamesar. Cambridge: Cambridge University Press, 2009.

Rajak, Tessa. Josephus, the Historian and His Society. London: Duckworth, 1983.

Ramsey, J. T. and A. Lewis Licht. The Comet of 44 B.C. and Caesar's Funeral Games. Edited by A. Lewis Licht. Atlanta: Scholars Press, 1997.

Reasoner, Mark. The Strong and the Weak: Romans 14.1–15.13 in Context. Society for New Testament Studies Monograph Series 103. Cambridge: Cambridge University Press, 1999.

Reitzenstein, Richard. Hellenistic Mystery-Religions: Their Basic Ideas and Significance. Translated by John E. Steely. Pittsburgh: Pickwick Press, 1978.

Rice, E. E. The Grand Procession of Ptolemy Philadelphus. Oxford Classical and Philosophical Monographs. London & New York: Oxford University Press, 1983.

Riewald, Paulus. "De Imperatorum Romanorum Cum Certis Dis et Comparatione et Aequatione." Diss. Halle, 1912.

Ripoll, François. "Adaptations latines d'un thème homérique: la théomachie." Phoenix: The Journal of the Classics Association of Canada 60 (2006): 236–258.

Robertson, Archibald and Alfred Plummer. A Critical and Exegetical Commentary on the First Epistle of St. Paul to the Corinthians. The International Critical Commentary 33. 2d ed. Edinburgh: T&T. Clark, 1914.

Roloff, Dietrich. Gottähnlichkeit, Vergöttlichung und Erhöhung zu seligem Leben: Untersuchungen zur Herkunft der platonischen Angleichung an Gott. Untersuchungen zur Antiken Literatur und Geschichte 4. Berlin: Walter de Gruyter, 1970.

Rowe, C. Kavin. "New Testament Iconography? Situating Paul in the Absence of Material Evidence." Pages 289–312 in Picturing the New Testament: Studies in Ancient Visual Images. Edited by Annette Weissenrieder, Friederike Wendt and Petra von Gemünden. Tübingen: Mohr Siebeck, 2005.

Rowe, William. "Adolf von Harnack and the Concept of Hellenization." Pages 69–98 in Hellenization Revisited: Shaping a Christian Response within the Greco-Roman World. Edited by Wendy E. Helleman. Lanham: University Press of America, 1994.

Ruffatto, K. J. "Polemics with Enochic Traditions in the Exagoge of Ezekiel the Tragedian." Journal for the Study of Pseudepigrapha 15 (2006): 195–210.

Runia, David T. Philo of Alexandria and the Timaeus of Plato. 2 vols. Amsterdam: VU Boekhandel, 1983.

———. "God and Man in Philo of Alexandria." Journal of Theological Studies 39 (1988): 48–75.

———. Philo of Alexandria: On the Creation of the Cosmos according to Moses. Philo of Alexandria Commentary Series 1. Leiden: Brill, 2001.

Russell, Daniel C. "Virtue as 'Likeness to God' in Plato and Seneca." Journal of the History of Philosophy 42 (2004): 241–60.

Russell, Norman. The Doctrine of Deification in the Greek Patristic Tradition. Oxford: Oxford University Press, 2004.

———. Fellow Workers with God: Orthodox Thinking on Theosis. Crestwood, N.Y.: St. Vladimir's Seminary Press, 2009.

Sanders, E. P. Paul and Palestinian Judaism: A Comparison of Patterns of Religion. Philadelphia: Fortress Press, 1977.

Sanders, James A. Canon and Community: A Guide to Canonical Criticism. Guides to Biblical Scholarship. Philadelphia: Fortress Press, 1984.

Sanders, Lionel J. "Dionysius I of Syracuse and the Origins of the Ruler Cult." Historia 40 (1991): 275–87.

Sandnes, Karl Olav. The Challenge of Homer: School, Pagan Poets and Early Christianity. Library of New Testament Studies 400. London: T&T Clark, 2009.

Sawyer, John F. A. "Biblical Alternatives to Monotheism." Theology 87 (1984): 172–80.

Schmid, Konrad. "The Quest for 'God': Monotheistic Arguments in the Priestly Texts of the Hebrew Bible." Pages 271–289 in Reconsidering the Concept of Revolutionary Monotheism. Edited by Beate Pongratz-Leisten. Winona Lake: Eisenbrauns, 2011.

Schmidt, Werner H. The Faith of the Old Testament: A History. Oxford: Basil Blackwell, 1983.

Schutt, R. J. H. "The Concept of God in the Works of Flavius Josephus." Journal of Jewish Studies 32 (1980): 171–87.

Schweitzer, Albert. Paul and His Interpreters: A Critical History. London: Adam and Charles Black, 1912.

———. Die Mystik des Apostels Paulus. Tübingen: Mohr Siebeck, 1930.

Scott, Kenneth. "The Deification of Demetrius Poliorcetes: Part II." American Journal of Philology 49 (1928): 217–39.

———. "The Sidus Iulium and the Apotheosis of Caesar." Classical Philology 36 (1941): 257–72.

Scroggs, Robin. The Last Adam: A Study in Pauline Anthropology. Philadelphia: Fortress Press, 1966.

Sedley, David. "Philosophical Allegiance in the Greco-Roman World." Pages 97–119 in Philosophia Togata: Essays on Philosophy and Roman Society. Edited by Miriam T. Griffin and Jonathan Barnes. Oxford : Clarendon Press, 1989.

———. "Becoming Like God" in the Timaeus and Aristotle." Pages 327–339 in Interpreting the Timaeus – Critias: Proceedings of the IV Symposium Platonicum. Edited T. Calvo and L. Brisson. Sankt Augustin: Academia, 1997.

Segal, Alan F. "Paul and the Beginning of Jewish Mysticism." Pages 93–120 in Death, Ecstasy, and Other Worldly Journeys. Edited by John J. Collins and Michael Fishbane. Albany: State University of New York Press, 1995.

———. Life After Death: A History of the Afterlife in the Religions of the West. New York: Doubleday, 2004.

Selter, Bert. "Eadem Spectamus Astra: Astral Immortality as Common Ground between Pagan and Christian Monotheism. Pages 57–75 in Monotheism Between Pagans and Christians in Late Antiquity. Edited by Stephen Mitchell and Peter van Nuffelen. Leuven: Peeters, 2010.

Skarsaune Oskar. "Is Christianity Monotheistic? Patristic Perspectives on a Jewish/Christian Debate." Pages 340–363 in Studia Patristica. Vol. 29. Edited by Elizabeth A. Livingstone. Leuven: Peeters, 1997.

Smelik, Willem. "On Mystical Transformation of the Righteous into Light in Judaism." Journal for the Study of Judaism 26 (1995): 122–44.

Smith, Jonathan Z. "Native Cults in the Hellenistic Period." History of Religions 11 (1971): 236–49.

———. Map is Not Territory: Studies in the History of Religion. Chicago: University of Chicago Press, 1978.

———. Imagining Religion: From Babylon to Jonestown. Chicago: University of Chicago Press, 1988.

———. Drudgery Divine. Chicago: University of Chicago Press, 1990.

———. Relating Religion: Essays in the Study of Religion. Chicago: University of Chicago Press, 2004.

Smith, Mark S. The Origins of Biblical Monotheism: Israel's Polytheistic Background and the Ugaritic Texts. New York: Oxford University Press, 2001.

———. The Memoirs of God: History, Memory, and the Experience of the Divine in Ancient Israel. Minneapolis: Fortress Press, 2004.

———. God in Translation: Deities in Cross-Cultural Discourse: Deities in Cross-Cultural Discourse in the Biblical World. Tübingen: Mohr Siebeck, 2008.

Smith, Wilfred Cantwell. "Comparative Religion: Whither and Why." Pages 31–58 in The History of Religions: Essays in Methodology. Edited by Mircea Eliade and Joseph Mitsuo Kitagawa. Chicago: University of Chicago Press, 1959.

Solmsen, Friedrich, Reinhold Merkelbach, and M. L. West, eds. Hesiodi Theogonia, Opera et Dies, Scutum. 3d ed. Oxford: Clarendon, 1990.

Sommer, Benjamin D. The Bodies of God and the World of Ancient Israel. Cambridge: Cambridge University Press, 2009.

Spencer, Herbert. Principles of Sociology. Abridged ed. Hamden, Conn.: Archon Books, 1969.

Sprinkle, Preston. "The Afterlife in Romans: Understanding Paul's Glory Motif in Light of the Apocalypse of Moses and 2 Baruch." Pages 201–234 in Lebendige Hoffnung—ewiger Tod?! Jenseitsvorstellungen im Hellenismus, Judentum und Christentum. Edited by Michael Labahn and Manfred Lang. Leipzig: Evangelische Verlagsanstalt, 2007.

Starr, James M. Sharers in Divine Nature: 2 Peter 1:4 in its Hellenistic Context. Stockholm: Almquist & Wiksell, 2000.

Stewart, Z., ed. Arthur Darby Nock: Essays on Religion in the Ancient World. 2 vols. Oxford: Clarendon Press, 1972.

Stowers, Stanley K. A Rereading of Romans: Justice, Jews, and Gentiles. New Haven: Yale University Press, 1994.

———. "Paul and Self Mastery." Pages 524–550 in Paul in the Greco-Roman World: A Handbook. Edited by J. Paul Sampley. Harrisburg: Trinity Press, 2003.

————. "What is 'Pauline Participation in Christ'?" Pages 352–71 in Redefining First-Century Jewish and Christian Identities. Edited by Fabian Udoh. Notre Dame: University of Notre Dame, 2008.

Stuckenbruck, Loren T. Angel Veneration and Christology: A Study in Early Judaism and in the Christology of the Apocalypse of John. Tübingen: Mohr Siebeck, 1995.

————. "'Angels' and 'God': Exploring the Limits of Early Jewish Monotheism." Pages 45–70 in Early Jewish and Christian Monotheism. Edited by Loren T. Stuckenbruck and Wendy E. Sproston North. London: T&T Clark International, 2004.

Sullivan, John. "Consecratio in Cicero." Classical Weekly 37 (1944): 157–59.

Tabor, James. "Paul's Notion of Many 'Sons of God' and its Hellenistic Contexts." Helios 13 (1986): 87–97.

————. Things Unutterable: Paul's Ascent to Paradise in its Greco-Roman, Judaic, and Early Christian Contexts. Lanham: University Press of America, 1986.

Tannehill, R. Dying and Rising with Christ. Berlin: Alfred Töpelmann, 1967.

Thesleff, H. ed. The Pythagorean Texts of the Hellenistic Period. Åbo: Åbo Akademi, 1965.

Thompson, Marianne Meye. The God of the Gospel of John. Grand Rapids: Eerdmans, 2001.

Thompson, Michael. Clothed with Christ: The Example and Teaching of Jesus in Romans 12.1–15.13. Journal for the Study of the New Testament Supplement Series 59. Sheffield: Sheffield Academic Press, 1991.

Thrall, Margaret. The Second Epistle to the Corinthians. 2 vols. International Critical Commentary. Edinburgh: T&T Clark, 1994.

Tobin, Thomas H. The Creation of Man: Philo and the History of Interpretation. Catholic Biblical Quarterly Monograph Series 14. Washington, D.C.: Catholic Biblical Association, 1983.

Tondriau, J. "Rois Lagides comparés ou identifés à des divinités." Chronique d'Égypte 45–46 (1948): 127–46.

————. "La dynastie Ptolemaique et la religion Dionysiaque." Chronique d'Égypte 49–50 (1950): 283–316.

Tsevat, Matitiahu. "God and the Gods in Assembly: An Interpretation of Ps 82." Hebrew Union College Annual (1969–70): 123–37.

Turner, Eric. "Ptolemaic Egypt." Pages 118–174 in Cambridge Ancient History. 14 vols. Vol. 7.1. 2d ed. Cambridge: Cambridge University Press, 1984.

Tylor, Edward B. Religion in Primitive Culture. Gloucester, Mass.: P. Smith, 1958.

Underhill, Evelyn. Mysticism: A Study in the Nature and Development of Man's Spiritual Consciousness. 12th ed. New York: Meridian, 1955.

Unnik, W. C., van "'With Unveiled Face', an Exegesis of 2 Cor. iii 12–18." Pages 194–210 in Sparsa Collecta: The Collected Essays of W. C. van Unnik (Leiden: Brill, 1973).

Van der Horst, Pieter Willem. "God (II)." Pages 365–369 in Dictionary of Deities and Demons in the Bible (DDD). Edited by K. van der Toorn, Bob Becking and Pieter Willem van der Horst. 2d ed. Leiden: Brill, 1999.

Vanderkam, James C. Enoch: A Man for All Generations. Columbia: University of South Carolina Press, 1995.

Van Kooten, George H. Paul's Anthropology in Context: The Image of God, Assimilation to God, and Tripartite Man in Ancient Judaism, Ancient Philosophy and Early Christianity. Wissenschaftliche Untersuchungen zum Neuen Testament 232. Tübingen: Mohr Siebeck, 2008.

Van Seters, John. Prologue to History: The Yahwist as Historian in Genesis. Louisville: Westminster John Knox, 1992.

Vernant, Jean Pierre. Mortals and Immortals: Collected Essays. Edited by Froma I. Zeitlin. Princeton, N.J.: Princeton University Press, 1991.

Versnel, H. S. "Thrice One: Three Greek Experiments in Oneness." Pages 79–164 in One God Or Many? Concepts of Divinity in the Ancient World. Edited by Barbara Nevling Porter. Casco Bay: Casco Bay Assyriological Institute, 2000.

Voegelin, Eric. Israel and Revelation. The Collected Works of Eric Voegelin: Order and History. Vol. 14.1. Columbia, Mo.: University of Missouri Press, 2001.

Vollenweider, Samuel. "Der Geist Gottes als Selbst der Glaubenden." Pages 163–180 in Horizonte neutestamentlicher Christologie: Studien zu Paulus und zur frühchristlichen Theologie. Tübingen: Mohr Siebeck, 2002.

Waelkens, Mark. "Privatdeifikation in Kleinasien und in der griechisch-römischen Welt zu einer neuen Grabinschrift aus Phrygien." Pages 259–307 in Archéologie et religions de l'anatolie ancienne: Mélanges en l'honneur du professeur Paul Naster. Edited by R. Donceel and R. Lebrun. Louvain: Centre d'histoire des Religions: 1983.

Walbank, F. W. "Monarchies and Monarchic Ideas." Pages 62–100 in Cambridge Ancient History. 14 vols. Vol. 7.1. 2d ed. Cambridge: Cambridge University Press, 1984.

Weinfeld, Moshe. Deuteronomy 1–11: A New Translation with Introduction and Commentary. Anchor Bible 5. New York: Doubleday, 1991.

Weinstock, Stefan. Divus Julius. Oxford: Clarendon, 1971.

Weiss, Johannes. Der erste Korintherbrief. 2d ed. Göttingen: Vandenhoeck & Ruprecht, 1910.

Wendland, Heinz-Dietrich. Die Briefe an die Korinther. Göttingen: Vandenhoeck & Ruprecht, 1980.

West, M. L. Hesiod: Works & Days. Oxford: Clarendon, 1978.

White, L. Michael and John T. Fitzgerald. "Quod est Comparandum: The Problem of Parallels." Pages 13–40 in Early Christianity and Classical Culture: Comparative Studies in Honor of Abraham J. Malherbe. Edited by L. Michael White, John T. Fitzgerald and Thomas H. Olbricht. Leiden: Brill, 2003.

Whitman, Cedric Hubbell and Charles Segal. The Heroic Paradox: Essays on Homer, Sophocles, and Aristophanes. Ithaca: Cornell University Press, 1982.

Widengren, G. Sakrales Königtum im alten Testament und im Judentum. Stuttgart: Kohlhammer, 1955.
Wildberger, Hans. "Die Thronnamen des Messias." Theologische Literaturzeitung 16 (1960): 314–32.
———. Isaiah : A Continental Commentary. Minneapolis : Fortress Press, 1991.
Wildung, Dietrich, and Günter Grimm. Götter und Pharaonen: Römer- und Pelizaeus-Museum, Hildesheim, 29. Mai-16. September, 1979. Mainz/Rhein: P. von Zabern, 1979.
Williams, Mary Frances. "The Sidus Iulium, the Divinity of Men, and the Golden Age in Virgil's Aeneid." Leeds International Classical Studies 2 (2003): 1–29.
Windisch, Hans. Paulus und Christus. Leipzig: J.C. Hinrichs'sche, 1934.
Winston, David and John M. Dillon. Two Treatises of Philo of Alexandria: A Commentary on De Gigantibus and Quod Deus Sit Immutabilis. Brown Judaic Studies 32. Chico, CA: Scholars Press, 1983.
———. "Theodicy and Creation of Man in Philo of Alexandria." Pages 105–111 in Hellenica et Judaica: Hommage à Valentin Nikiprowetzky. Edited by A. Caquot, M. Hadas-Lebel and J. Riaud. Leuven-Paris: Peeters, 1986.
———. "Philo's Conception of the Divine Nature." Pages 21–42 in Neoplatonism and Jewish Thought. Edited by Lenn E. Goodman. Studies in Neoplatonism: Ancient and Modern 7. Albany: SUNY Press, 1992.
Wolff, Christian. "Humility and Self-Denial in Jesus' Life and Message and in the Apostolic Existence of Paul." Pages 145–160 in Paul and Jesus: Collected Essays. Edited by A.J.M. Wedderburn. Journal for the Study of the New Testament Supplement Series 37. Sheffield: Sheffield Academic Press, 1989.
Wolfson, Eliot. Through a Speculum that Shines: Vision and Imagination in Medieval Jewish Mysticism. Princeton: Princeton University Press, 1994.
Wright, M. R. Cosmology in Antiquity. London: Routledge, 1995.
Wright, N. T. "Reflected Glory: 2 Corinthians 3:18." Pages 139–50 in The Glory of Christ in the New Testament. Edited by L. D. Hurst and N. T. Wright. Oxford: Clarendon Press, 1987.
Wyatt, N. Myths of Power: A Study of Royal Myth and Ideology in Ugaritic and Biblical Tradition. Muenster: Ugarit-Verlag, 1996.
Young, Frances. "'Creatio ex Nihilo': A Context for the Emergence of the Christian Doctrine of Creation." Scottish Journal of Theology 44 (1991): 139–51.

Subject Index

CPSIA information can be obtained
at www.ICGtesting.com
Printed in the USA
JSHW010546140723
44205JS00001B/153